ORIENTAL AND LINGUISTIC STUDIES

ORIENTAL
AND
LINGUISTIC STUDIES

THE EAST AND WEST; RELIGION AND MYTHOLOGY; ORTHOGRAPHY AND PHONOLOGY; HINDU ASTRONOMY.

BY

WILLIAM DWIGHT WHITNEY,

PROFESSOR OF SANSKRIT AND COMPARATIVE PHILOLOGY IN YALK COLLEGE

GYAN

Published by

Gyan Publishing House
5, Ansari Road
Daryaganj, New Delhi-110002
Phone: 011-47034999, 9811692060
E-mail: books@gyanbooks.com

Distribution Network
gyanbooks.com
India, USA, Canada, UK, Australia, France

ISBN : 978-81-212-2392-8 (PB)
First Published, 1874

2nd Impression 2021

Printed at: Gyan Press, Delhi.

Oriental and Linguistic Studies
Author: William Dwight Whitney

ORIENTAL AND LINGUISTIC STUDIES.

SECOND SERIES.

THE EAST AND WEST; RELIGION AND MYTHOLOGY; ORTHOGRAPHY AND PHONOLOGY; HINDU ASTRONOMY.

BY

WILLIAM DWIGHT WHITNEY,

PROFESSOR OF SANSKRIT AND COMPARATIVE PHILOLOGY IN YALE COLLEGE.

NEW YORK:
SCRIBNER, ARMSTRONG, AND COMPANY,
1874.

To

PROFESSORS RUDOLF ROTH AND ALBRECHT WEBER,

MY EARLY TEACHERS AND LIFELONG FRIENDS,

THIS VOLUME

IS AFFECTIONATELY DEDICATED.

PREFACE.

I PUT forth this second volume of essays on subjects connected with language and with the Orient, in compliance with a conditional promise given two years ago, at the end of the Preface to the first volume. The condition, "if the reception accorded to its predecessor were sufficiently encouraging," has been at least measurably fulfilled; I have no right to complain of the way in which the somewhat doubtful venture has been met, both by the general public and by the narrower and more critical community of scholars. The intrinsic and widely felt interest of the themes treated has been enough to insure a welcome to even such imperfect attempts at their earnest discussion. I hope that the same fortune may attend this continuation of the series.

It is also in strict adherence to the terms of my promise, that the essays here published are throughout on other classes of subjects than those before treated. I have even excluded any further discussions of the foundation and methods of linguistic study — the matter which I had most at heart in the making up of the former volume. I might have felt called upon to do differently in this regard, if there had appeared in the interval anything which demanded notice as placing the subject in a new light; or, especially, any serious attempt to controvert my views and the reasonings by which they were sustained. But that is not the case; though the essays have provoked in one or two quarters a certain amount of vituperation, they have not been met on their own ground, of fact and argument; and I believe that I am not mistaken in claiming that their general theory of language and of the method of its study has been and is steadily gaining ground among scholars.

Most of the articles composing the volume are reproduced here nearly as when first issued,[1] with only a careful revisal. To the first, however, I have made an addition, obviously called for; and to the fourth (on Müller's "Chips") I have appended a brief notice of other later works of the same author, chiefly made up from criticisms furnished at the time to the columns of the "Nation" (New York). But the eighth, ninth, eleventh, and twelfth articles are entirely rewritten, though including more or less matter already published. The eighth is almost wholly new, except as many of its views and descriptions are nearly identical with those given in two articles on the Standard Alphabet of Professor Lepsius, in the seventh and eighth volumes of the Journal of the American Oriental Society. The ninth is founded in good measure on an appendix to the latter of the articles just mentioned.[2] The eleventh in like manner has for its basis a paper

[1] A statement of the times and places of original publication will be found as before, at the end of the volume.

[2] The concluding subject of the eighth, and the main argument of the ninth were communicated to the Am. Philol. Association in July last, and abstract are published in the Proceedings of the Association at that meeting.

in the Transactions of the American Philological Association for 1870, and it contains elements from other articles quoted or referred to in its notes. The subjects compendiously discussed, finally, in the twelfth have been for the most part treated in greater detail in the notes to the Sûrya-Siddhânta, in two articles in the eighth volume of the Journal of the American Oriental Society, in another in the first volume (new series) of the Journal of the Royal Asiatic Society (London), and in a note to Cowell's new edition of Colebrooke's Essays (vol. i., p. 126 *seq.*). The added illustrative chart is from the Sûrya-Siddhânta.

NEW HAVEN, Conn., *October*, 1874.

CONTENTS.

I.

THE BRITISH IN INDIA.

A GREAT misfortune, or a signal judgment, has befallen the British dominion in India.[1] For many years past indistinctly foreseen — perhaps rather, dimly augured and dreaded — the storm has burst forth at last with a suddenness and a fury which have taken by surprise its victims, England, and the world. The great native army, so long the sword and shield of English authority in her Eastern possessions, the pride of her policy, the reliance of her governors, has dissolved and deserted her; nay, much worse than that, has turned upon her with the ferocity of a wild beast long thought tamed, but which has only suppressed its brutal instincts in order to sate them more horribly when its keeper is thrown off his guard. Throughout a region more extensive than England itself, the English, a few months ago the rulers and masters, are now mangled and dishonored corpses, or hunted fugitives, or fighting for their own and one another's lives. Even this is not the worst; those who administer the affairs of a conquered people, we know, must carry their lives as in their hand, exposed to sudden outbursts of the subjected; but here the hand of vengeance has not struck only at the instruments of alien dominion; their innocent families have been butchered under circumstances the most horrible; gentle women and tender children have been done

[1] This was written early in 1858, when the work of crushing the mutiny was well advanced toward completion.

to death with a refinement of hideous cruelty of which only North American Indians, or South Sea cannibals, would have been thought capable. All England is mourning her dead. All England is roused to take vengeance on the murderers, to vindicate her sullied honor, to re-establish her profaned authority; and, what is much better, the public opinion of England, long too little regardful of her Eastern empire, has been cruelly but effectually awakened to its relations to her, to her duties toward it; she is asking what she has done to draw upon herself this calamity, what she has to do to render impossible its recurrence. Meanwhile the whole world looks on with intense interest, to see what the result will be, for England and for India, its sympathies strongly pronounced in favor of the one side or the other, or balancing between the two combatants, uncertain with whom lies the greater share of wrong.

The parties engaged in the struggle, its scene, the stake depending on it, lend it a surpassing significance. England, on the one hand, is the great representative of the progressive tendencies of modern culture, the foremost civilizing and Christianizing power, which is doing more than any other to bind together the nations of the earth in one bond of brotherhood by community of interests and institutions. India, on the other hand, constituting by reason of its immensity, its natural resources, and its isolation from the rest of Asia, a continent by itself, always sustaining a population more numerous than that of Africa and both the Americas taken together, and rich in productions sought of all the world, has been, since the beginning of intercourse among men, a mark for ever increasing attention. From the time when Solomon's navies visited its Ophir,[1] and dim rumors of the "Ethiopians of the sunrise" reached the ears of

[1] Lassen's identification of Ophir with the western coast of India is not, to be sure, beyond question.

Homer, when Alexander was forced by his mutinous army back from its frontier, when Greek and barbarian kings contended for the possession of its western provinces, when the cravings of Roman luxury were supplied from its marts, when its wealth and helplessness made it the prey of Mohammedan rapacity, till at last European nations strove for its possession, and it became the dependency of a little islet in the far-off western ocean, how rich in varying phases and wide-reaching relations is the history of India! Within the present century, too, a new interest has been added to it. Fifty years ago the world hardly knew that India was the seat of a civilization older than that of Greece and Rome, the cradle of institutions which had spread themselves over two thirds of Asia, the birthplace of a literature not less extensive and varied than the classical; and that the race which had made the country their home, and wrought these works there, was of near kindred with our own, that its earliest recorded conditions were those of our own ancestors, that its ancient language was the key to all the languages of Europe, the key to all linguistic study. The knowledge of these facts has made the concerns of India nearer and dearer to every enlightened mind, has placed her under the more especial protection of the whole civilized world, and has made it the duty of all to watch that she be not treated with calculating selfishness, or with greedy rapacity, as a prey in the hand of the spoiler, but with the consideration, and the true regard to her welfare and progress, which such a history commands. We ourselves, as Americans, have those especial responsibilities in this matter which flow from our especial relations to England, as nearest akin with her in language, institutions, and interests, and as exercising by our public opinion an appreciable influence on hers. It is important, then, that we fully understand and rightly judge all the questions involved in the relations subsisting between England and India; particularly at such a time as this, when in every one's mind are starting the inquiries: by what tenure do the British hold India? what is their right there, and what the position they occupy toward the natives of the land? what is the character of this revolt, and what does it indicate? what will be the issue of the struggle, and what its after results?

Nothing, in our view, can shed so much light on all these points of inquiry, as a brief general sketch of the history of India, and of the different incursions and conquests of which it has been the arena. The British are not the first race of foreigners who have forced their way into the country and wrenched its possession from the hands of its older occupants; and we cannot rightly understand the character of their dominion, if we know not by what it was preceded, from whom it was won, and over whom extended; we cannot appreciate the value of the changes it introduced, if we know not the conditions in the midst of which it was founded.

Who were the absolute aborigines of India it is not now possible to tell. In the belt of land which stretches across the country almost under the Tropic of Cancer, a region of rugged mountains and impenetrable forests, infested with wild beasts and haunted by yet more dangerous diseases, is found a chain of wild tribes, of dark color, but not of Ethiopian features, and of the humblest endowments and capacities of culture. Too little is yet known of their languages to indicate with certainty whether they are the scanty remains of an earliest Indian population, or offshoots of the race next to be mentioned, debased by thousands of years of savage life. Nearly all the southern half of India, the elevated plateau of the Dekhan, as it is called, with its bordering mountain ranges and its low narrow coasts, is occupied by a family of people closely akin with one another in physical characteristics and in speech, and known as the

Dravidian or the Tamulic family. Whence and when they came we know not at present; whether they poured into India over its western frontier, or crept through the passes of the Himalaya from the great plateau of Central Asia; whether, again, they hunted the black tribes, their predecessors, into the mountains, or entered along with them, their own kith and kin: all this remains still to be learned, if the evidences be not too uncertain to be trusted, from the comparative study of their languages. We do know with certainty that, probably about two thousand years before the Christian era, this race, or these two races, were in full possession of the whole territory of India. They were not, however, to remain longer undisturbed. To the northwest, just beyond the mountains which beset the entrance to the Cabul valley, the passage through which many nations have since trodden on their way to the conquest of Hindustan, lay a branch of the great Indo-European family, the most highly gifted of all the children of men, although not destined till more than a thousand years later to assume and assert their rightful place at the head of the race. By degrees their tribes threaded the mountain passes, descended into the rich valley, itself like a paradise to comers from the north, and, tempted ever onward by the increasing beauty and fertility which opened before them, advanced and took possession of the Penjab, the vestibule of India.

Thus was begun the first invasion and conquest of India by a people of foreign extraction of which history gives us any distinct account. It is the most important fact in all the annals of the country, for this intruding people became the founders of everything which we are accustomed to call Indian. The Aryan tribes — for that is the name they gave themselves, both in their old and new homes — brought with them institutions of a simplicity almost primitive, the germs only of the culture which they were afterwards to develop so magnificently; they brought the oldest and least altered reflex of that condition and mode of life which were once common to Persian, Greek, Roman, German, Slave, and Celt, a religion of which the myths and the divinities bear a strange resemblance to those of earliest pagan Europe, a language of which the wonderfully preserved elements and transparent structure explain, to a degree elsewhere unknown, the history and relations of European languages, the history of all language. Hardly, too, had they entered the country which was to be henceforth the theatre of their action, when they made an imperishable record of both language and institutions, in the hymns of the Veda, that venerable document, the oldest, the most authentic, the fullest of all that are left to illustrate the pre-historic history of our branch of the human race.[1]

The Aryan conquest bore the character common to all conquests in the olden time. The new race felt its immense superiority, in natural capacity and culture, to that with which it came in contact; it regarded the latter as barbarous and unclean, as fit only to be exterminated or enslaved. When the torrent of invasion burst forth from the Penjab, and poured through the fertile valley of Hindustan, it almost swept from existence the former owners of the soil. A part saved themselves in the mountains on either hand, whither it was useless to follow them; a part were reduced to servitude. As the institutions of the intruders developed themselves, and they became sundered into three great classes or castes, the priestly, the military, and the agricultural, or the Brahman, the Kshatriya, and the Vaiçya, such of the aborigines as yet remained were formed into a fourth class, the Çudra, a class which had no rights, but only duties, whose highest virtue was to serve humbly and faithfully the other three, cut off from all the privileges of educa-

[1] See the preceding volume, first article.

tion and religion which they enjoyed, without hope except that of being born again after death into one of the higher castes, as the reward of devoted service to them. It was only in the northern half of India, however, that the Aryan occupation was thus complete; the expansive force of the race mainly exhausted itself in the territory of the Ganges and its tributaries; to the south, beyond the Narmadâ (Nerbudda), the dividing line between Hindustan and the Dekhan, the old population still maintained itself and perpetuated its language. It could not, indeed, resist the shaping and transforming influence of the superior race: by hostile expeditions and conquests, by peaceable colonization and intercourse, the Dravidian tribes were brought to know and accept the Aryan civilization; they adopted the Brahmanic religion and polity; their languages became thickly sown with Sanskrit words, and were written in characters derived from the Sanskrit alphabet; their literature was but a repetition or an echo of the Sanskrit literature.

Thus all India was brought under the sway, physical or intellectual and moral, of the alien race; it was thoroughly Aryanized; it became, as far as is possible for a country so vast, in customs, beliefs, and institutions, a unit, an exponent of one and the same culture. It is not a part of our present purpose to follow in any detail the history of Aryan India, to exhibit to view the religions, the philosophies, the civil institutions, the arts, the sciences which the land was made to bring forth under its new masters, or to describe the literature in which all these are recorded. We have to deal with India chiefly as affected from without; and, thanks to the mountains, the deserts, and the oceans which make its borders, for near three thousand years after the invasion we have described it was left undisturbed, to develop its own character and work out its own destiny. The alarms of war did, indeed, resound from time to time along its northwestern frontier, but even the echo of them hardly penetrated into the heart of the country. The first Darius might send his generals on an expedition of conquest down the Indus, and write the name of India on the list of his subject provinces; Alexander might penetrate into the Penjab, and find there no obstacle which could quite stay the victorious progress of his veteran army: but Indian history soon forgot the insults. During centuries, even, that followed, Greco-Bactrian, Indo-Greek, Parthian, Indo-Scythic dynasties might dispute the possession of the valleys of the Cabul and Indus, but into the great interior neither their arms nor their influence could penetrate. Down to a thousand years after Christ, India stood aloof from the commotions which were convulsing Europe, and central and western Asia. Meantime all nations visited her marts to buy her rich productions; her silk, cotton, indigo, spices, and precious stones supplied the wants and ministered to the luxury of the East and the West. The natural development of her internal resources and her foreign commerce had combined to give her enormous wealth. At the same time, she had become greatly weakened in respect to power to repel the spoiler. The Indian race and its civilization had reached the period of decline. The effect of the sultry climate and of the profusion of nature's gifts which distinguish India could not fail to be highly unfavorable upon any race which came in from the north, and the Aryans had begun to deteriorate, in some respects at least, from almost the first moment when they became exposed to the peculiar influences of the country. The stout arms were weakened, and the pure hearts corrupted; the primitive freedom of manners and customs was brought under the rigorous servitude of caste; the old simple worship of the powers of nature grew into a strange compound of mystical philosophy and debasing superstition. Quietism became the prevailing character of the people; they asked only to live in peace, to maintain in strictness the purity of caste, to perform the inherited ceremonies of a formal worship, and to do in all things as their fathers had done. It was not, however, until after a long and violent struggle that India was thus forced into the iron framework of the Brahmanic polity. About five centuries before Christ had arisen the great Indian protestant reformer, Buddha: he strove to break down the supremacy of the priestly caste; he taught the equality of all conditions of men, the worthlessness of ceremonies and sacrifices, the efficacy of faith, knowledge, and good works for the attainment of salvation: and although the philosophical basis of his doctrine was atheistic, and although the beatitude which it held up as the object to be striven after was annihilation, yet its generous humanity and its pure morality gave it immense power, and for a long time it disputed with Brahmanism the dominion of India. It did not confine itself to the land of its birth: while Brahmanism was as exclusive as Judaism, Buddhism was as expansive and universal in its spirit as Christianity; its peaceful missionaries carried its doctrines from country to country, till Ceylon, Farther India, and the isles of the Indian Ocean, till Tartary, Tibet, and China had accepted the religion of the Indian teacher. Meantime, in India itself its power was slowly undermined; the Brahmans had too strong a hold upon the mind of the people to be shaken off; the ancient tradition proved mightier than the new doctrine; and about eight centuries after Christ, Buddhism and its votaries were utterly extirpated or driven out, and the Brahmans reigned supreme. But they were not left long to enjoy in peace the fruits of their victory, for already the Moslem was at the gate.

India had need of regeneration, but she received only retribution. It was a hard and cruel fate that brought upon her the wild hordes of her Mohammedan conquerors, for they could not, in the nature of things, do aught but add to the misery of her condition. The Arab conquest was almost nowhere a permanently regenerative one. The power for good which lay in the one half of its fundamental dogma, "There is no god but God," was neutralized by the other half, "Mohammed is the prophet of God." The Koran had not borrowed enough from the Bible to make it long a safe guide to the human mind, and the furious zeal which it inspired was much more destructive than constructive. It is true that here and there the fusion of an ancient civilization with the youthful energy of the Arab tribes, themselves sprung of a noble stock, quickened by the consciousness of a glorious career of conquest, and enriched with the spoils of empires overthrown, kindled for a time a bright fire of intellect, and the Moslem capitals became the brilliant spots of the earth, and the Moslem civilization an important link between the culture of the ancient and that of the modern world; but the flame soon burned out; the standard of Mohammed dropped from the weakened hands of its Arab bearers, and was taken up by one tribe after another of fierce barbarians from Central Asia, who made it the signal only of plunder and desolation. Thus, in Persia, Islam had the power to dissolve and penetrate the old institutions with a new spirit, and to bring out a fresh product; after passing through a frightful process, after suffering the destruction of its nationality, the overthrow of its ancient customs, the annihilation of its religion, the profanation of its monuments, Persia came forth rejuvenated, and entered upon a new career of intellectual activity, which is perhaps the proudest in its whole history. But it could not be thus in India. Islam was too weak to effect anything there save by brute force, and India was too vast and populous to be utterly crushed and made over in the Mohammedan mill. Between the Hindu and the Mohammedan there could be neither compromise nor fusion; peace and prosperity were impossible in the land of which they disputed the possession.

It was the resurrection of Persian nationality which led directly to the overthrow of Indian. As the weakness of the central authority of the Caliphs at Bagdad began to be felt, the eastern provinces of Persia shook off its yoke, and under the successive dynasties of the Taherites, the Soffarides, the Samanides, all the country from the Caspian to the confines of India was independent, the Persian language prevailed even as that of state and of religion, and the new Persian literature sprang into being. Yet the springs of action there were not wholly Persian; as enemies on the frontier, as mercenaries, as slaves even, the Turkish tribes were beginning to exercise a powerful influence on the progress of events. About the year 967, Sebektagin, originally a Turkish slave of a Samanid general, was established in Ghazna, as governor of that province of the Samanid empire. He soon rendered himself virtually independent, and upon his death his son Mahmud openly renounced his allegiance, assumed the title of "Sultan," till then unknown, and made Ghazna the capital of a new realm, which ere long included a great part of the possessions of his former masters. Ghazna lies in one of the elevated valleys of the Soliman mountains, the range which forms the eastern boundary of Persia, and at the base of which is stretched the valley of the Indus; and its site is but little to the southwest of the city of Cabul, to which it commands easy access. Thus had the vulture built its eyrie upon the heights that overlook the goodly land of India, and was ready to swoop upon its prey.

Now began the age of blood in India's history; the heart recoils from the picture of the miseries which Mohammedan rapacity and bigotry were to inflict upon the unhappy country. The very position of Mahmud's capital was a constant threat to India, sufficiently indicating which way ambition and the lust of plunder would carry him: he is said to have taken a solemn vow that he would make every year a holy raid into the unbelievers' country, for the glory of the Prophet, and he faithfully kept it. In the year 1001 the first Mohammedan army crossed the Indus, and within twenty-three years the Sultan had made twelve great expeditions into the interior of the country, besides many lesser ones. They were rather devastating forays than campaigns of conquest; fire and sword were carried through the land, and an immeasurable booty brought back to the capital in the mountains, which with the spoils of India was built up into the most magnificent city of the Moslem world; but though the Hindu sovereigns as far eastward as to the confluence of the Ganges and Jumna, and southward to the peninsula of Guzerat, quailed at the name of the destroyer, and acknowledged his supremacy, he founded no enduring dominion in the country.

The glories of the house of Ghazna were soon obscured. Mahmud's son was stripped of most of his Persian possessions by the rising dynasty of Seljuk, and his grandson lost all of India save the Penjab. In the next century the wild Afghan tribes began to descend from their mountains northward of Cabul, to take their part in the struggle for empire. Yet the Ghaznevids maintained themselves near two hundred years, with varying fortunes; their capital itself was more than once lost and won again; their provinces in Hindustan were conquered anew, and recovered their independence; but in the year 1184 the last weakling descendant of Mahmud was thrust from the throne by the Afghan chief Mohammed Ghori. Herein lay the hopelessness of the fate of India; no sooner was one race and generation of spoilers sated with murder and booty, and weakened by excess, than another pressed forward to take its place, with a fresh appetite, and with the full vigor of the northern savage. The new Afghan dynasty carried its arms far beyond the limits of Mahmud's conquests; in 1193 the holy city of Benares was taken, and the Moslem soldiers reveled in the devastation of that chief sanctuary of the infidel; in 1227 Ujjayinî (Ojein), the capital of the fertile plateau of Malwa, and the chief seat of Indian literature and science, met the same fate; in 1235 Altumsh reigned from the Indus to the mouth of the Ganges, from the Himalaya to the Nerbudda.

At this period the Mongols were in the midst of their career of conquest in Asia: Genghis Khan had founded there the most extensive empire which the world has ever seen, reaching from the Chinese seas to the frontiers of Germany: and in or about the year 1241, they for the first time entered India. They were beaten back, but only for a season; they retired with plunder enough to be encouraged to return again; and from this time forward the country was never long free from their ravages, although three centuries were still to elapse before a Mogul dynasty should sit upon the throne of Delhi.

A new Afghan family, called the Khilji, overthrew in 1288 the Ghori. And as every change of dynasty was fraught with fresh evils to India, so there followed now, under Ala-ed-din, the second Khilji, a new era of devastation. Hitherto the Dekhan had escaped; the deep valley of the Nerbudda had been the limit of Moslem ravages; the land beyond was an undiscovered territory. About 1295, however, the bloodhounds snuffed the scent of prey in the south, and passed the barrier. A booty beyond their wildest dreams was the reward of their enterprise, and now the Dekhan was penetrated in every direction; expedition after expedition brought back from thence such treasures as the pen of the Mohammedan historians had scarcely the power to describe. Here, in 1306, we meet with the first mention of the Mahrattas, as a tribe subdued by Ala's generals. The dynasty soon sank under the load of wealth and the corruption it brought, and, about 1321, Ghazi Beg Toghluk founded a new line of monarchs. The devastation of the Dekhan still went on. Under Ghazi's successor, Mohammed, the condition of all India reached a climax of misery; anarchy, oppression, and utter desolation reigned from one end of the land to the other. Then followed a gentle sovereign, who showed during a reign of thirty years some solicitude for the welfare of his subjects, a thing so rare in the history of Mohammedan India that it deserves to be noted; but after his death the old condition of affairs returned again.

Now broke over India the hurricane of the last great Mogul invasion, under Tamerlane, the scourge of mankind. In 1397 this ferocious monarch crossed the Indus, and after a campaign in the Penjab, attended with even more than the usual horrors of a Mogul campaign, he marched upon Delhi. As he neared the city, and the battle-field where the fate of the empire was to be decided, he conceived suspicions of the slaves whom his army was dragging along with it, as part of the fruits of the expedition, and gave orders that every one should immediately be put to death. He was obeyed, and in one hour a hundred thousand souls were massacred in cold blood. In the contest that followed he won an easy victory: he entered Delhi, and for fifteen days the city was given over to the tender mercies of his soldiers. When it was thoroughly stripped of all that could be carried away, the inhabitants were driven to the gates, and the army allowed to indemnify itself for its sacrifice before the battle; even common soldiers, we are told, took to themselves from fifty to five hundred slaves. Then the conqueror marched slowly back, as one must march when so laden, skirting the base of the Himalaya, and wreaking Mohammedan zeal and piety on the numerous communities of fire-worshipers, fugitives from Persia, who had found refuge there: wherever he went, he left behind him a wilderness, with smoking ruins and pools of blood. He returned to his capital, and never troubled India again: his work was done: he had put to death hundreds of thousands of human beings, had dragged into slavery tens of thousands more, had brought away untold treasure, had turned a blooming country into a desert; what more could he desire? To such an expedition do the rights of the recent Emperor of Delhi to rule over India date back.

During a century and a quarter, however, the claims of the house of Timur remained in abeyance. Two dynasties occupied in the mean time the throne of Delhi. The first, the Sadat, lifted its head as soon as aught in India dared to look up after the storm had passed over, and commenced with calling itself a deputy of the Mogul conqueror: it maintained itself for less than thirty-five years, and was succeeded by a last Afghan dynasty, called the Lodi. It is unnecessary to follow the history of this period more closely: it is distinguished by nothing; it is one weary succession of confusion, oppression, and intestine war; a progress from misery to misery.

Next follows for the unhappy country a time of comparative peace, good government, and prosperity, the golden age of the Mohammedan period of Indian history. Baber, a descendant of Tamerlane and of Genghis Khan, was at this time Sultan of a part of the country between the Oxus and Jaxartes; he was a man of remarkable enterprise and ability, both as warrior and as statesman; yet he was unable to maintain himself in the possession of his paternal kingdom against the hordes of adventurers that came swarming in from the north upon him. Driven southward, he possessed himself of Cabul and its dependencies, and from thence was tempted to undertake the conquest of India, which he regarded as rightfully belonging to him, the representative of its former Mogul conqueror. After first establishing his authority over the Penjab, he set out thence, in 1525, with only fifteen thousand veteran warriors at his back, vanquished the Indian army on the fateful field of Panniput, and seated himself upon the throne of Indian empire at Delhi. So much easier was it to conquer India than to keep an insignificant province in Tartary! Baber was no mere plunderer, like his predecessors; his ambition was to found a great empire in India, and his capacity was equal to the undertaking. He died, however, in 1530, before the work was half accomplished. The Memoirs which he left are more worthy than anything else the Orient has produced to be placed by the side of Cæsar's Commentaries. His son and successor, Humayûn, inherited no small share of his father's abilities; yet, after ten years of valiant struggle against the rebellious Afghan chieftains and his traitor brothers, he was driven out of the country. Fifteen years he remained in exile, and then, returning with Persian auxiliaries, favored by happy circumstances, good counsels, and valor, he placed himself once more upon the throne. The next year, 1556, he died, and his young son, Akbar, born upon the Indus during his flight, his companion and aid in all his adventures since, reigned in his stead.

To Akbar India and the world have given the title of Great, and no monarch, perhaps, ever better deserved it. He possessed every virtue that can adorn a ruler; energy, prudence, justice, mercy, were conspicuous in all his conduct; he lived for the best good of his subjects, Hindu not less than Moslem; he established entire toleration throughout his dominions, and even indulged in visionary plans for the establishment of a new religion, which, founded on simple love to God and good will to men, should comprehend and unite Moslem, Hindu, and Christian. He governed the natives of the country through their own countrymen and by their own customs; he promoted Indian literature and science; he encouraged agriculture by great public works, and by the introduction of new products and methods from the west; he secured the northwestern frontier against farther inroads. His long reign of fifty years was the climax of India's prosperity. The famous Ayîn Akbarî, 'Institutes of Akbar,' composed under his direction by his great minister, Abul Fazl, gives a most instructive picture of his polity, and of the condition of the country under his management. His son and grandson successively followed him; the one, known as Jehangîr, reigning from 1605 to 1627, the other, Shah Jehan, from 1627 to 1656. Little need be said of these princes; they were given to luxurious and dishonorable pleasures, careless of the highest interests of the empire, and faithless and unscrupulous in their policy. The blood of the race of Baber, which had given to India three generations of rulers of so eminent qualities, was beginning to degenerate; but its virtue was sooner exhausted than its ability; the reins of government were still grasped with a strong hand, and general tranquillity maintained; and the institutions of Akbar still subsisted to secure the peace and happiness of the people. Shah Jehan, on his accession to the throne, had put to death every other male descendant of Baber, that he might have no rivals to fear; in the year 1655 he himself fell sick, and the flames of civil war were at once lighted up all over the realm by his four sons, fighting for empire and for life. He recovered, but too late; Aurengzîb, the youngest but one of the four, had triumphed over his brothers by dint of superior craft and ability, and had no mind to sink to the condition of a subject again; Shah Jehan was dethroned, and lived long enough to see meted out to his own descendants the fate to which he had doomed his father's. Aurengzîb was a despot and an oppressor of his people, a bigoted Mohammedan, jealous and suspicious in the extreme, of profound dissimulation and inexorable cruelty. His terrible energy and executive capacity, and his unscrupulous use of all the arts of treachery and craft, kept India quiet under his sceptre; but it was a deceitful quiet; the old hatred between Hindu and Moslem was revived in all its intensity, the bonds which bound the empire together were dissolved, its strength was exhausted by intestine and foreign warfare, and it was ready to fall to pieces as soon as the grasp of a strong central authority should be removed.

We have now for some time taken no notice of the state of affairs in the Dekhan. Its history had been from the middle of the fourteenth century almost entirely severed from that of Hindustan. For a time, under the weak and wicked Mohammed Khilji, it had been nearly cleared of its Mohammedan invaders; then an army of mutinous mercenaries, Afghans and Turks, had established there, under a dynasty called the Bahmanî, an independent realm, which, after subsisting for near two centuries, had broken up, about the time of Baber's invasion, into several separate kingdoms. No sooner was the great Akbar firmly fixed upon his throne than he turned his arms southward, to recover the provinces formerly subject to the throne of Delhi; but, after a vigorous beginning, he had to leave the contest as a legacy to his posterity. A fatal legacy it proved. Jehangîr, indeed, was content with maintaining what his father had won; but the whole reign of Shah Jehan was occupied with wasting and harassing warfare against the sovereigns of the south, which exhausted the resources of both the combatants. It was in the Dekhan that Aurengzîb had laid the foundations of the power which he used to dethrone his father; it was in the Dekhan that he wore out his strength in desperate struggles with a foe at first deemed insignificant, but which finally rose upon the ruins of his empire. This foe was the nation of the Mahrattas, a name henceforth prominent among the first in Indian history.

The Mahrattas were a people of Hindu origin, originally occupying the fastnesses of the mountains which overhang the western shore of India, to the north and south of Bombay. We have noted the first mention of them, in 1306. During the three centuries which had since elapsed, they had continued a simple tribe of mountaineers, too insignificant to play any part in the struggles of the Mohammedan dynasties in the Dekhan; but when wars unending had weakened the forces of the whole country, they began to appear upon the scene. Their first great chief, Sivajî, commenced his career about 1650, and before his death, in 1682, he had become master of Konkana, the sea-coast province at the base of his native mountains, and had spread the name and the terror of the Mahrattas over half the Dekhan. His son and successor, Sambajî, was taken and put to death with barbarous cruelty by the Emperor, in 1690; but the ravages of the tribe continued; and after his generals had for ten years longer tried in vain to put down and annihilate the Southern Plunderers, as they were called, Aurengzîb was compelled to take the field against them in person. He met with little better success; his foes could never be brought to face him long enough to be beaten; and while he was engaged in besieging their fortresses, desperately defended by a few resolute men, their predatory bands were levying contributions all over his dominions. The last seven years of his life were spent in this inglorious contest: he died in 1707, and with him departed forever the strength and glory of the Mogul empire. Impotence and utter confusion followed; henceforth the titular Emperor was no more than the plaything of a court, the puppet of the great vassals who disputed the right in his name to plunder and oppress the country; at one time, within a period of only eleven years, five emperors were murdered, and six pretenders to the throne set up and pulled down again. It was not the Mahrattas who had brought the empire to this low estate; its dissolution was the effect of a natural process, the same through which all Moslem empires have had to pass; despotic power, when deserted of virtue, energy, and prudence, can lead only to weakness and anarchy. The Mahrattas, however, did their full part in hastening the downfall, and it was they who reaped from it the largest share of benefit.

At the commencement of their career, the Mahrattas represented in some measure a rising of the native Hindu population against its Mohammedan oppressors. Their chiefs were all Hindus, of the various castes; their language, their customs, their religious usages, were of Hindu origin. They made war rather upon the governments than upon the people, sparing or affecting to spare the latter as much as possible, and their incursions were not unfrequently encouraged or invited by the petty Hindu Rajahs, who sought in them a check upon the oppression of the lieutenants of the empire. Their power lay to no small degree in the impossibility of inflicting upon them any harm comparable to that which they could inflict. They had no rich country, no cities to defend; they were possessors of nothing which they could not afford to lose, and of which the loss was not easily to be made up; they were a nation on horseback; their mounted bands roved through the country incumbered only by the spoil they bore away, and what they won was soon spent in adding to their forces new levies of the same lawless soldiery. Had India been in other than a state of defenseless anarchy, the increase of their power might soon have found a limit; as it was, they grew rapidly in might, and extended their ravages on every side, till hardly a nook or a corner of the country had escaped their visitation, or was exempted from the tribute they levied. Their policy was at first only an organized system of pillage; they were accustomed to demand of the provinces they threatened with devastation a certain portion of the public revenue, generally the fourth part; and this, under the name of the *chout*, became the recognized Mahratta tribute, the price of the absence of their plundering hordes. The *chout*, however, was often made a pretext for unlimited exaction, or for such an interference with the administration of a country as ended in their taking entire possession of it. It was in the nature of things that a state so constituted could not long retain its form unaltered; and indeed, the Mahratta state, if it were ever entitled to that name, ran through a rapid succession of changes. Under their early Rajahs, there was among the marauding bands enough of coherence and submission to the central authority to render it possible to direct upon any point force enough to overcome the resistance found there; but the reins of power dropped from the weak hands of the grandson of Sivajî, and while the eastern portion of the dominion which the tribe had won fell off, and formed a separate realm under the chieftain Bhonsla, the Rajah himself was stripped of power and placed in close confinement for life, while his Peshwa, or hereditary prime minister, assumed the direction of affairs in his name, and became the acknowledged head of a loose confederacy of states, founded by the most noted and successful leaders, out of the territories which their arms had won, or which had been assigned them for the support of the troops that fought under their banners.

It was in or about the year 1690 that the Mahrattas first crossed the Nerbudda; the torrent of invasion had never rolled through its valley in that direction before: from this time, the plateau of Malwa, next north of the river, the hills and vales of the Rajput country to the westward, and the rich peninsula of Guzerat, with its dependencies upon the main-land, were brought ever more and more under their influence and authority. Forty years later, they were acknowledged as the dominant power throughout Central India; in 1735, the second Peshwa, Bajerao, after overrunning and plundering for the first time the plains of Hindustan, up to the very gates of Delhi, extorted from the Emperor the appointment of Viceroy of Malwa; and before his death, in 1740, he had levied the *chout*, or tribute of one fourth, upon the whole remaining revenue of the Mogul empire. His successor, Ballají, received the same appointment, his four chief generals, Puar, Holkar, Sindia, and Gaikwar, becoming his sureties for obedience and faithful service. These are names which have still an existence and a value in Indian history; the independent states they founded are yet in the possession of their descendants: the seat of Sindia's government is at Gwalior; Holkar's capital is Indore, near the crest of the Vindhyas; the Gaikwar is ruler of Guzerat; the Puars have territories of less extent in Malwa.

We have left for a season the story of the intrigues and murders, the treasons and rebellions, of which the throne of Delhi was the centre, because the fates of India, during this period, were much more closely linked with the rising fortunes of the Mahrattas than with the decadence of the Mogul empire. But events were now transpiring in the north which require our notice, as indicating the forlorn and helpless condition into which the land had fallen. In 1739, the ferocious Nadir, who, from a shepherd-boy, had become a captain of banditti, then a leader of mercenaries, and finally Shah of Persia, while engaged in subjecting the Afghans of Cabul, received an insult from the Indian monarch. Without delay he marched into India to avenge it. This was the first time that the frontier of the Mogul empire had been passed by a foreign enemy. Nadir easily overthrew the forces which were sent out from Delhi to bar his passage, and entered the city. Massacre and plunder followed; the imperial treasury was robbed and public property seized, to the estimated amount of $150,000,000; then, with horrid cruelties and tortures, the wealth of private individuals was extorted from them; and, leaving the city to famine and pestilence, the Persian returned to his own dominions, restoring to his throne the pillaged emperor, and exacting of him only the cession of all territory west of the Indus. In 1747, Nadir was murdered in his tent, and Afghanistan became an independent state under Ahmed Shah Abdalli, who succeeded his old master as scourge of India. Two years after his accession to the throne, he severed the Penjab from the Mogul empire forever. The next year the Mahrattas were called in to defend Hindustan against Afghan invasion: they were successful in repelling the enemy, but seized themselves upon the country they had rescued. Again, in 1756, Ahmed returned, captured Delhi, and almost reënacted the horrors of Nadir's invasion, when a pestilence which broke out in his camp forced him to retire. After his withdrawal, the Mahrattas had everything their own way, and were threatening to swallow up the last remnants of the empire, when the Afghan was once more called in to the aid of the Mohammedan chiefs, who chose submission to the rule of the foreigner rather than of the infidel. The whole force of the Mahratta states, under their ablest chiefs, was assembled to oppose him. On the old battle-field of Pannipnt was once more disputed the empire of India. The Mahrattas were signally defeated; a hundred thousand fell in the battle, and as many more in the pursuit; the aggressive power of the confederacy was for the time annihilated. No other result, however, followed from the victory of the Afghan monarch; he returned home almost immediately, and never again attempted to interfere in the affairs of India.

The battle of Pannipnt was fought in January, 1761: but already, four years before, the battle of Plassey had laid the foundation of British power in the country. The main interest of Indian history shifts once more, to the two points on its eastern frontier, Madras and Calcutta, where a company of merchants were preparing to become the arbiters of its destinies.

We have given with so much of detail the history of the wars, revolutions, and invasions which preceded and prepared the way for the entrance of the English upon their career of conquest in India, because a full knowledge of the condition of the country, and of the causes which led to it, is the most necessary requisite for judging aright the English occupation. Never was a great country, rich in natural resources of every kind, rich in an inheritance of ancient glories, in a more deplorable condition than India in the middle of the last century. Seven hundred and fifty years, of almost unbroken oppression and misrule, were surely enough to accomplish the destruction of any state. We have seen that, even at the beginning of this period, Indian civilization and the Indian character were in a state of decadence; after Persian, Afghan, Turk, and Mogul had successively pillaged him, trampled upon him, torn him asunder in their struggles for the right to oppress him, the Hindu could not come out otherwise than yet further degraded and brutalized. We are unable to see anything but unmixed evil in the Mohammedan occupation of India. Had the wild tribes of the north come in as did the Goths upon southern Europe, bringing fresh blood and uncorrupted simplicity to infuse a purer life into what was old and effete, or even as did the Normans into England, to blend, after a brief period of oppression and separation, with the mass of the people, contributing only a new element to their language, manners, and institutions, valuable results for both races might perhaps have followed: but it was not so; to the last the two stood distinctly apart as oppressors and victims; there were no grounds for hope that the relation would ever be changed; one or the other must be annihilated or driven from the country, or else both must be rendered harmless and tolerant of one another by subjection to a third power. How little of capacity was left in the country itself to effect its own regeneration appeared clearly from the character of the national uprising which took place at the decay of the Mogul empire: it showed itself incapable of aught but mischief and disorganization, powerless to expel the old enemies of the land, helpless against the attack of new foes. Nowhere was there to be discovered anything which gave promise of improvement. The future was as dark as the present. Was India to be left to herself to work out thus her own destruction, or was she to come into the possession of a new master? She lay there at the mercy of whoever was strong and bold enough to seize upon her: was she to fall into the hands of a barbarian, or of a civilized and Christian nation? These questions were to be answered, and her fate to be finally determined, by the events of the next fifty years.

The English, it is well known, were not the first Europeans to open commerce with India, and gain territorial possessions there. A hundred years before the formation of the East India Company, twenty-seven years before the invasion of Baber, the Portuguese had found their way to the coast of Malabar, and established factories which still subsist. Not a little of the same rapacity, bigotry, and cruelty which marked the Mohammedan invasions characterized the proceedings of this Christian power. Happily, Portugal was too weak a country, and its energy and enterprise declined too speedily, to allow of its affecting seriously the history of India. Before the arrival of the English, a part of its possessions had fallen into the hands of the Dutch, and at the beginning of the last century these three powers were rivals for the gains of Indian trade. The East India Company was organized in 1600: its first factory was established in 1620, at Surat, near the seat of the ancient commerce by sea between India and the west; in 1636, another was set up on the Hoogly, above the present site of Calcutta; in 1640, Madras was acquired; in 1668, Bombay was given to the Company by Charles II., who had received it as part of the dowry of the Portuguese princess he had married; Calcutta was purchased in 1698. Up to this time, and even till fifty years later, the Company was simply a company of traders, neither possessing nor aiming at political power; they were occupied with the endeavor to enrich themselves by means of traffic, and to this end they acquired certain sites, built factories, obtained privileges from the native princes, and sought to exclude their rivals from competition with them. But herein, little as they knew or suspected it, lay the germ of the whole after development of the British Indian empire; they could not maintain themselves, and protect their property and the rights which had been ceded to them, without becoming a power in the land; they could not subsist as a power, and command peace about them, without possessing the supreme authority over the whole country. We will run briefly over the steps of the progress by which this end was reached.

The first foundation of British empire in India was laid by the French; it was they who originated the idea of a great European power in India, and from them the English learned it, or won it by hard blows. The French established themselves in the Carnatic (as the region along the southeastern coast of the peninsula, from Madras southward and northward, was called) much later than the English; and they not only were looked upon by the latter as interlopers, but formed such plans, and carried on such intrigues, for the extension of French power and influence through the country, that it was impossible for them and the English to live peaceably together. The struggle began in 1746, with the capture of Madras by the French; and until 1761, when Pondicherry was taken by the English, and the French power annihilated, there was almost constant war between them. Meantime, in 1756, the Nabob of Bengal made an unprovoked attack upon Calcutta, which ended in the well-known tragedy of the Black Hole. The next year retaliation began; the battle of Plassey overthrew the Nabob, and placed upon his throne a rival, the creature of English power, and the extensive districts of Burdwan, Mednipur, and Chittagong were ceded to the Company. But the difficulties in Bengal continued; and, after a series of changes little creditable to the policy or integrity of the Company's officers, the administration of the three great provinces of Bengal, Behar, and Orissa was directly vested in the English by a grant from the Emperor of Delhi. The successful termination of the French war gave the Company the possession of sundry lesser districts in the Carnatic, and in 1765 an imperial grant placed under its authority the country called the Northern Circars, extending along the coast from the Carnatic to Orissa.

For more than twenty-five years after this, through the noted administration of Warren Hastings (1772–1785), and almost to the close of that of Lord Cornwallis (1786–1793), there were no further important accessions of territory; but it was by no means an interval of peace and quiet; violent dissensions among the Company's servants, disputes and difficulties with all the native Indian powers, a harassing and useless war with the Mahrattas, and a desperate conflict with Hyder Ali of Mysore, marked this, the transition period of British India, the time of half measures and of vacillating policy, resulting in both internal and external weakness.

In 1790 a new war broke out with Mysore. The Sultan of that country was the deadliest and most formidable enemy of the British. At about the time of the great battle of Panniput, Hyder Ali was a low-born freebooter and adventurer in the service of the Hindu

Rajah of Mysore. Being eminent in the qualities which then led to power in India, he had succeeded in overthrowing his master and usurping control of the government, and with all the energy of a new dynasty had established himself in the possession of a great kingdom in the south of the Dekhan, reaching from the Carnatic to the Malabar coast, and growing at the expense of its neighbors on every side. Had it not been for British opposition, Hyder might perhaps have subjugated the whole Dekhan; and he hated the British accordingly. Two wars he had fought against them with varying success, unsubdued, though unsuccessful. He had died before the close of the second, but his son Tippoo inherited his ability, his cruelty, his bigotry, and his animosity. The third conflict terminated most disastrously for Mysore. After two campaigns, Tippoo was reduced to purchase peace by the cession of half his territories to the Company.

Again, from 1793 to 1798, a season of outward tranquillity followed, under the administration of Sir John Shore (Lord Teignmouth); the orders of the home government were strict, and were conscientiously carried out, but the policy of non-intervention, of peace at any price, brought the state to the brink of ruin. The French were then the masters of Europe, and even India was drawn into the magnificent plans of Napoleon for the destruction of England. French influence was predominant in the three great native Indian courts, that of Tippoo, of the Nizam of the Dekhan, hitherto England's faithful ally, and of the Mahrattas, in whose keeping was the Emperor of Delhi. The genius and energy of Lord Wellesley (1798–1805), ably seconded by his brother, afterward Duke of Wellington, who won here his first laurels, turned the scale everywhere in favor of the English. The Nizam was manœuvred into English interests, and his French-trained army disbanded. In 1799, Tippoo's capital was stormed and he himself slain; the ancient Rajahs of Mysore were raised from a dungeon to the throne, as dependents of the Company, with nearly their ancient territory, stripped only of the conquests of Hyder and Tippoo. Then followed a severe conflict with the Mahrattas. It was waged nominally in support of the Peshwa, or head of the confederacy, against his rebellious chiefs, who were contending together for the possession of his person, in order to gain the support of his name and authority. The Mahrattas were everywhere beaten, their French forces annihilated, the Emperor rescued from their custody, and extensive cessions of their territory exacted, both in Hindustan, Central India, and the Dekhan.

It was not in war only that the English extended their dominion under Lord Wellesley. They carried matters with a high hand among their allies and dependents, pulling down, reforming, reconstructing, as it seemed to them that the interests of British India demanded. The Nabob of Surat was deposed and pensioned. The Vizier of Oude was compelled to purchase with half his dominions the security of the other half. With the Nabob of the Carnatic the English had been involved in most complicated relations, which brought distress and confusion on him and his dominions, ever since they had established him on the throne in opposition to the French; the embarrassment was now relieved by his forced withdrawal into private life upon a liberal pension. No such increase of power and responsibility had marked the administration of any former Governor-general. The Company were alarmed; they sent out stringent orders for peace, and replaced Lord Wellesley by Lord Cornwallis, who lived but three months after his arrival at Calcutta. Sir John Barlow succeeded him provisionally, and then Lord Minto, who governed from 1807 to 1813 in almost undisturbed tranquillity.

But the foundations of peace had not yet been securely laid. Hardly had Lord Hastings taken the direction of affairs, in 1813, when hostilities broke out with Nepal, the long narrow district of hill country lying at the base of the Himalaya. The hardy mountaineers, over-confident in their own valor and the strength of their position, provoked a war wantonly, fought it manfully, and were allowed to purchase peace with the loss of but a small portion of their territory, eastward from the upper course of the Ganges. Now followed a more serious struggle. For many years a great system of plunder had been laying waste all the interior of India. Season after season, bands of marauders had burst out from their hiding places in the mountains, ravaging and destroying with a savage ruthlessness which threw into the shade even the old devastation of the Carnatic by Hyder Ali, immortalized by the eloquence of Burke. They fought under no one's name, but were harbored and encouraged by the Mahratta rulers. A system of operations was arranged for their repression, and upon a most extensive scale, for it was well foreseen that the Mahrattas would take up their cause when once the combat was joined. The campaign was conducted with great skill and energy, and with complete success. The defection of Sindia was crushed in its commencement, and only the little province of Ajmîr, in the Rajput country, was taken from him; the Peshwa's perfidy was rewarded with the loss of all his territories, and his exile as a pensioner to Hindustan; the other great Mahratta chieftain, Bhonsla, Rajah of Nagpore and Berar, was stripped of his districts along the Nerbudda, which gave the English a continuous chain of possessions through the heart of India. The bands of the Pindarris, as the marauders were called, were annihilated, and peace so thoroughly established throughout the interior that no general disturbance has since been possible. The supremacy of the Company over the whole land, its right to supervise the relations of all the existing states, to settle disputes, to prevent war and commotion, to dictate peace, was at length solemnly proclaimed. India had become British India.

War and annexation, however, were not yet at an end. Under the administration of Lord Amherst (1823–1827), the Indian government was forced into hostilities with Burma, as the result of which, in 1826, Asam and the long strips of sea-coast in Farther India which border the bay of Bengal, Arracan and Tenasserim, were ceded to the British. In 1834, the Rajah of the little hill district of Kûrg, in the south, formerly saved by English interposition from the vengeance of Tippoo, was deposed, for horrible tyranny and cruelty, and hostility to English interests. After the great catastrophe of the invasion of Afghanistan, in 1843, difficulties occurred with the Emîrs of Sindh, the country bordering on the lower Indus; and Sindh was conquered and annexed. In 1845, the Sikhs, who had maintained peaceful relations with the Company during the life of their great ruler, Ranjit Singh, became turbulent, and invaded the British dominions. Though beaten back, and mulcted of a portion of their territory, their spirit was not quelled; in 1848, war broke out anew, and ended only in the reduction of the whole Penjab under British authority. A new Burman war, in 1852, gave to the Company the province of Pegu, in Farther India. In 1854, Nagpore and Berar, the realm of the Mahratta chief Bhonsla, were taken possession of on the extinction of his line. Finally, in 1856, Oude was annexed, on account of the failure of its rulers to meet their obligations to the Company, and their outrageous tyranny and mismanagement, which rendered it the seat of distress and disorder, and dangerous to the security of its neighbors.

The territory thus immediately subjected to British rule is estimated at 840,000 square miles, and sustains a population of 132,000,000; that which still remains under the authority of its native rulers amounts to 628,000 square miles, with 48,000,000 inhabitants. The native powers, however, have the privilege only of internal administration; they are allowed neither to form treaties nor make war; the Indian government guarantees their security without and tranquillity within, and enjoys either a constant or a contingent right to payment for this protection, and to the service of their armies in case of need.

We have passed thus hastily and lightly over the history of the British dominion in India, sketching only its general features, and entering into no discussion of its details, for more than one reason. In the first place, the subject is too vast and difficult to admit of a full exhibition here. No course of events occurring in modern times, and respecting which information has been at once so abundant and so accessible, has been more variously judged. The public opinion even of England itself has been divided between enthusiastic admiration, hesitating approval, and bitter condemnation. Each separate act is a case of casuistry, requiring for its solution the fullest comprehension of all the conflicting rights and interests which it was destined to affect, of all the circumstances which led to and accompanied it. But again, such an extended discussion is not necessary to our present purpose. In great historical events like those which we are now considering, there comes a time when we have a right to let bygones be bygones, to wipe out the past, and judge the present by what it is and what it promises. We would by no means maintain the right of national interference: that one people may take upon itself the guardianship of another, however much the latter may mismanage its own affairs; or that a part of the earth's surface of which the resources are neglected or wasted by its present occupants may be wrested from them by others who feel that they can better administer the inheritance. But, fearful as were the excesses committed by the Teutonic barbarians, in the first heat of conquest, upon the corrupt races they dispossessed, who does not now rejoice in the invasion which brought about a rejuvenation of Europe? Were there a whole continent now peopled by savage or half-savage tribes, humanity would shudder at the thought of their being deliberately driven out, or swept from existence, to make room for a race of better husbandmen of man's heritage. Yet, the work being once done, as it has been done upon the soil we occupy, on whose conscience presses heavily the burden of the wrongs done to the red man, as we look abroad and see what a wondrous change civilization has wrought upon his wild and gloomy forests? This is what we are wont to call the hand of Providence in human history, bringing good out of evil. Now if we were to go back to the beginning of Indian history, and place under the ban of our condemnation all who have forced their way into the country to the detriment of its earlier possessors, we should, as has been seen, leave few unmolested. But we have accepted the first, the Aryan, conquest, because it was, upon the whole, productive of grand and valuable results; because it made of India a great united country, the seat of an admirable civilization, the scene of events, the birth-place of institutions, which have told powerfully, and for good, upon the history of the world. By a similar judgment we have rejected the Mohammedan occupation, because, undertaken in fanaticism and rapacity, it was consistently carried out under the guidance of the same principles, to its inevitable end in anarchy and confusion; because it produced incalculable misery, and accomplished inappreciable good; because its continuance held out no prospect of improvement, but only of prolonged and increased misery.

By the same rules would we likewise judge the British

conquest. Much of wrong and much of error we can and must allow that there was, both in its inception and in the steps by which it was accomplished. England, it is granted, had no right to subject India to her authority. It must also be granted that she had no will to do so. Had the East India Company, had the English people, seen the end from the beginning, they would have recoiled in fear, if not in horror. It is a fact acknowledged and familiar that they never did foresee the end: every movement forward they hoped would be the last; with every new pacification they believed that a finality had been reached. The consent of the Company and of the nation was always a step, and often a long one, behind the march of events in India: they were forbidding aggression, commanding peace, protesting against aggrandizement; but their servants did not and could not obey, for they were only accomplishing what both Company and nation required of them, that the British possessions, authority, and influence should be maintained, wherever in the country they had been acquired and established. In this necessity of constant advance after a beginning had once been made, a necessity felt and acted upon more than acknowledged, lies the explanation, and the excuse, if not the justification, of the British empire in India. That it was a necessity, we fully believe; the advance of the English to the virtual authority over all India was as natural an effect of the same causes as that of the Anglo-Saxon race to the possession of America, after the first settlements made upon the Atlantic border. They were the one fixed point in a whirlwind of confusion, which could subside into order only under an influence radiating from them. They had acquired property and rights in a country where neither were wont to be sure to their possessors for a day against violence, where treachery and oppression were the normal condition of things, where governments had neither the power nor the will to keep their pledged faith; they had no protection to rely upon save their own stout arms and hearts; if they were bent on preserving what was their own, and repelling insult and injury, they could not but go on, step by step, till their word became the supreme law in every part of the continent of India.

It must be further admitted that the means by which the great end was attained were often far from unexceptionable; that great errors, and not a few great crimes, were committed; that greed of gold, and ambition of authority and distinction, came in as an important element in the contest; that there are many pages in the history of British India which no Briton can read without a blush, no friend of humanity without a shudder. Would that it were not always thus in human history! We have no right, however, to leave out of consideration the peculiar difficulties under which the British labored in their relations with India. It was as an unknown country to them when they first set foot upon its shores; its geography, history, political divisions, institutions, manners and customs, and languages, had all to be learned. If they understood so little what and whom they were dealing with, they understood no better what they were striving after and tending toward. Three concurrent powers were dividing between them the management of Indian affairs — the English Parliament, the East India Company, and the Indian government; each with its own full share of selfishness, party spirit, and shortsightedness, each embarrassing, almost as often as aiding, the action of the others. Much, accordingly, was done unjustly, was done blunderingly and by halves. Had the English nation set out with the avowed determination of subjecting India to its authority, pursuing for that end one consistent and energetic course of action, no doubt a great saving of life and treasure might have been effected, and perhaps — although that is more questionable — more might have been left than is now left of native government under British superintendence. It is clear, however, that there has been from the commencement a steady and marked improvement, both in the wisdom and the humanity which have characterized the action of the British in India. They began as an irresponsible company of individuals, seeking for gain, in competition with greedy and unscrupulous rivals, and in a country of which the wealth, reputed vast beyond conception, was extorted and squandered by governments indescribably vile, corrupt, and oppressive. It is not strange, then, that something of the grasping selfishness and disregard of principle which formed the atmosphere in which they lived and moved infected the British officials, was communicated to the Company, and even showed itself in the first movements of the Parliament toward interference with Indian affairs. But, for the honor of England and the happiness of India, British rapacity and corruption did not grow with British power; the tone of the government rose in the measure of the responsibility it assumed; the pettiness of a trading company was rebuked and vanished, and in its place rose the majesty of a great nation. India was brought more and more under the care of the whole English people, placed under the ægis of that public opinion than which a more enlightened and a more humane protector is nowhere to be found on earth. If great errors and crimes have been committed on Indian soil, so also has it been the arena where eminent abilities and shining virtues have displayed themselves. The record of these hundred years is of startling interest, and pregnant with instruction; and it is all opened before the eyes of the world; nothing is hidden; universal attention and criticism are invited to it; and no nation is more ready than England itself to study and learn, to praise or condemn as the case shall demand, to heed both warning and example.

In estimating, therefore, the present position of the British in India, and in giving or withholding from them our approving sympathy, we are not required to lay to their account the evils caused by the folly and injustice of a past generation. The English of this day have received their Indian empire as a legacy from their ancestors, with all the advantages, and with all the responsibilities, which the possession of such an empire brings; they have received it, also, with the balance of the good or evil which have thus far resulted from English interference in Indian affairs. Our standard of judgment must be: what, on the whole, has England done for India, and what does she promise to do for it? Now if we have read aright the history of India down to the last century, and have sketched a true picture of the miserable anarchy, hopeless of improvement from within, helpless against aggression from without, into which it had fallen, we must allow that there was never a country which more needed to be taken under the charge of some powerful guardian, to be saved both from its own madness and from the malice of its foes. Nor can we rejoice too much that it should have fallen into the hands of the British nation. It is the custom to taunt England with being too grasping in her acquisitiveness, too much devoted to her own material interests, too little regardful of the independent rights of those upon whom she imposes her influence. Doubtless there is much of truth in this: if individuals are selfish, nations are not less so. But there are higher and lower grades of selfishness; and happily the aggrandizement of Great Britain is closely linked with the best good of the human race; she flourishes by virtue of a system which requires for its full development the peace and prosperity of every nation on the earth. The interests of commerce, as interpreted by her, are safer and more beneficent regulators of the relations of states than the desire of national glory, or than zeal for the extension of free institutions, as the latter are understood in some parts of the world. It is our firm conviction that no other nation possesses in the same degree those valuable traits of character — political wisdom, executive capacity, steadiness, energy, integrity, high-toned morality and humanity — which, in combination with her external advantages, make England the best guardian in whose care the welfare and happiness of India could be placed.

The good which the English occupation has accomplished for India already outweighs a hundred times the evil by which it has been accompanied. It has established the sway of the two great principles, toleration to religion and security to property, all over the land from which both had been excluded for ages. The rest which India so pined for, as the first condition of its regeneration, has been given to it. The value of the foundation thus laid for the revival of its material prosperity is incalculable; not less is the value of the check given to the decay of morality, to the dissolution of the bonds which bind society together, by the reëstablishment of order and public faith. While the elevation of the land by its own internal forces has thus been rendered possible, the way has been opened for the introduction into it from abroad of everything which is good. Knowledge of its present condition and past history has been spread out before the eyes of the world. It is indeed wonderful to contemplate the change in this respect which only fifty years have wrought. While the languages, manners, and institutions of India at the beginning of the present century were hardly known even in their latest forms, their development has now been traced up to a period in the past to which the annals or the traditions of hardly another people in the world reach back. This knowledge is one of the most important consequences flowing from the English conquest, for its value to the world, and for its value to India, as laying open the needs of the latter, and showing how they may best be supplied. Not much more than this preparatory work, it is true, has yet been accomplished for the restoration of the country; but it is not reasonable to expect much more. Only forty years ago, the British were still engaged in the struggle to establish themselves; and although since that time they have been in peaceful possession of the country itself, frequent wars upon the frontier have engaged the energies and absorbed the resources of the government. Those who point to the immense works of internal improvement undertaken by some of the Mogul sovereigns, as a reproach to the apathy and negligence of the British, forget whence the means to pay for them were drawn, from heavy burdens levied upon a country yet unexhausted, from wholesale and pitiless plunder of vast regions just reduced to subjection; all India being laid under contribution for the benefit of the one district where the monarch had his residence. Those, again, who taunt the English with the insignificance of the amount expended in the instruction of the people, forget how hard it is for a government of an alien race, a different faith, and ideas and habits of mind so unlike those of its subjects, to make itself at once their teacher. Herein, indeed, lies the great difficulty of the position which the British hold in their eastern empire. It was comparatively easy for them to do what they have done, to redress the sorest of the evils under which the land labored, reinstating order and confidence in the place of anarchy and faithlessness; but if there is any work which calls for the highest wisdom, prudence, and circumspection, it is the revival of a sunken civilization, the elevation of a debased national character. To carry out such a work, not less than the collective intellect of a nation, zealously and earnestly applied, can be sufficient.

The main significance of the present revolt of the native army lies, to our apprehension, in its bearing upon this point, of the future relation of the English nation to its Indian subjects. Let us turn aside for a moment to consider the causes and character of the revolt.

It is not to be supposed that an authority like that whose history we have been reviewing, established by force of arms, and by a strange nation, would be entirely acquiesced in by the whole people of India, whatever the benefits it conferred upon them, and however great a majority might have rejoiced in its extension over them. As the remembrance of the heavy yoke from which it brought deliverance became gradually fainter, and the feeling of grateful relief vanished, an uneasy sense of the burden still remaining, a repugnance to the dominion, however lightly exercised, of a nation of strange color, religion, and manners, could not but by degrees usurp its place, even in the great body of the people. Much more must the Mohammedan, despising alike Hindu and Frank, regarding India as his own by the right of conquest and of near eight centuries of unchecked oppression, and as wrenched from his grasp by the English, feel the bitterness of vengeful hate towards the latter. Nor less would the deposed rulers, Nabobs, Rajahs, chiefs of every kind, stripped of power, and retaining only the pomp and wealth of a mock dignity, long for a revolution which should place them again at the head of affairs. And the crowd of restless characters, old plunderers and banditti, who, though dispersed and repressed, had not been entirely destroyed, would be ready at the first opportunity to join in the overthrow of order and authority.

In spite of the constant ferment of these elements of disaffection, the vigilance and energy of the government, the weakness, isolation, and want of harmony of the malcontents, rendered serious apprehension from them needless. There was another point, however, where lay at once the strength and the weakness of the British empire; it reposed on military power, and the sword and the bayonets to which its keeping was confided were borne by native hands. From the very beginning of the British dominion, it had been the practice to train in the European discipline, and to officer with Englishmen, bodies of native troops, called sepoys. The system had been marvelously successful; no troops of the native powers could stand against the British sepoys; they had been the main instruments by which British victories were won, and British empire extended. It was an age and a country of mercenary warfare, and these hirelings were attached to the flag under which they served by kind and considerate treatment, by the ascendancy of character of British officers, by some sense of the glory and success which attended their arms, and by liberal wages, of which the full and punctual payment was always to be relied upon. The service was greedily sought; the ranks were always full; desertion was unknown; dismissal was itself a recognized punishment for grave offenses against discipline. Almost all the sepoys had families, which they were allowed from time to time to visit, and which were supported meanwhile by a stated portion of their pay, made over to them directly by the government authorities. After a certain term of service the sepoy was allowed a pension to the end of his life; and as everything in India has a strong tendency to become hereditary, so when the old veteran retired he was wont to send his son to take his place in the ranks. It seemed as if every possible means had been used to secure the fidelity of these troops, so to bind them, by affection and interest, to the British cause, that they might be trusted, even in the case of a rebellion; and they had shown themselves fully trustworthy, not only in dangerous conflict, but also in popular outbreaks, which appealed, it seemed, in the strongest manner to their sympathies.

While, however, the sepoys had been in most respects submissive and docile, there was one point upon which the government had always been compelled to consult and humor their prejudices — namely, upon matters connected with religion and caste. It was their weakness to entertain the suspicion that it was intended to convert them, all at once and against their will, into Christians. The feeling was not entirely unnatural: they were so under European influence and authority, the power of discipline was so great; they had been made into brave and orderly soldiers; some mysterious process there might be which should change them into apostates. They looked with extreme jealousy upon any new regulation which seemed to trench in the most distant manner on the usages of caste. These feelings were industriously fostered and artfully exaggerated by the malcontent classes. They had broken out once, in 1806, in the massacre of Vellore, as it is called — a mutiny remarkably like the present one in its causes and attendant circumstances, although upon a scale very much smaller. A number of trivial innovations had roused the sensitive suspicions of the sepoys, and led to general disaffection, treasonable communications, and mutterings of conspiracy. Finally, an order for the introduction of a turban of new shape, which seemed strongly to resemble a European cap, brought matters to a crisis. The government was obliged to retract and conciliate; but it was too late to prevent the outbreak at one station, Vellore, near Madras: the garrison mutinied, murdered its officers, and committed horrible excesses. Help was near and promptly given, and the revolt was quelled without spreading further; but a little want of energy and prudence might have allowed a flame to kindle which would have threatened the utter extinction of the British authority, then only half established in India.

Within the past few years, indications have not been

wanting that the Bengal army was falling into a dangerous state of insubordination. The long peace had loosened the bonds of discipline, the distance between the native corps and its English officers had become much greater than of old, and the command by the latter of the respect and attachment of their men was accordingly weakened; little infringements of military discipline had been treated with a leniency which made the impression of weakness; the whole body of native troops had swung away, in short, from the government, and stood apart as a separate power in the state; the sepoy had become indolent, self-conceited, sensitive, almost openly mutinous; insomuch even, that a year ago acute observers had persuaded themselves that the whole system of management by which the British power was upheld was effete, and must be changed from the foundation. But the government foresaw nothing, took no precautionary measures, heeded not the smouldering disaffection. The spark which lighted the flame, as is well known, was the proposed issue of new cartridges with greased balls, which the sepoys were taught to believe had been smeared with the fat of cows and swine, so that in biting them, as is done in loading, the caste and the purity of Hindu and Mussulman might be destroyed together. Had the troops been in their old state of discipline, and as amenable to the influence of their officers, the trouble might speedily have been allayed; but it was not so. From the time when the first suspicions were aroused, the middle of January, 1857, for near four months, there were constantly recurring difficulties; suspicious communications were detected, conspiracies discovered, attempts at murder and plunder frustrated, and more than one regiment was broken and disbanded. On the tenth of May, at Meerut, forty miles east from Delhi, the mutiny burst out at last with uncontrollable fury; and so unequal to the crisis were the officers at that station, that although it contained a British force even outnumbering the sepoys, the latter were suffered, after murdering their officers and committing fearful atrocities upon all Europeans, men, women, and children, that fell into their hands, to make their escape to the ancient Mohammedan capital hard by, and give to their movement, by the possession of that city and of the person of the emperor, the semblance of a national uprising. We cannot undertake to trace the progress of the mutiny, as the contagion spread from station to station, and from corps to corps, till of the great army of a hundred thousand trusty soldiers only the smallest remnant continued faithful; to describe the fearful suddenness of the rising, the suspicionless security of the victims, the sickening and heartrending outrages perpetrated by the mutineers, and the daring gallantry, worthy of the very best days of England, which her sons have shown in the unequal struggle they have since been maintaining. All these things are fresh in the remembrance of every one, as eagerly gathered from the weekly accounts which have reached this country. We have here to deal rather with the character and the results of the outbreak.

As regards its character, it is to be noted that all attempts to give it a grand significance, as the result of far-reaching intrigues, or of a deeply laid plot, as the expression of the despair and vengeance of a nation, have been given over as futile. It is not the revolt of India against an oppression too heavy to be borne: excepting in the newly annexed and still unregulated province of Oude, the mutineers have met with sympathy and aid from only that part of the population which is the natural enemy of order; the country at large remains quiet, and is ready to help, so far as it dares, the fugitives who are seeking for shelter and succor; the sovereigns of the independent and the dependent native states sympathize with the English, and not with their foes. It is not a deliberate uprising, brought about by special influences, and directed to a distinct object: the time of outbreak, its place, the want of concert, of leaders, of plan of operations, indicate this beyond a question. Russian influence, that bugbear of a part of the British public, is not to be thought of; nor is there the least evidence that any deposed sovereign, as the King of Oude, or the Emperor of Delhi, has been directly active in bringing about the movement—even if such have fallen in with it, or been forced to join it, when it was once in full career. It is simply that which we have described it, a mutiny; vast and terrible beyond any other which history records, it is true, but yet only a mutiny, the revolt of an army against its officers. The triviality of the causes which directly led to it, and the remarkable and appalling character of the circumstances by which it has been accompanied, add to its importance as an event an intense interest as an exhibition of Indian nature. It is strange to see how regiments loud and sincere, so far as can even now be judged, in professions of fidelity, even faithful in action, one day, have the next felt the infection of disloyalty. And what are we to think of the ferocious cruelty manifested in those deeds which have made the world shudder with horror and indignation? They were no work of maddened retaliation; the sepoys had ever been treated with kindness and consideration. Nor do they seem to have been deliberate, and for a purpose; it is possible, indeed, that a wish to anticipate the severe retribution which they knew would be made the penalty of their treason, that an impulse to bind themselves to mutual faithfulness by crimes which could never find forgiveness, that a desire to profane and degrade to the utmost in the eyes of the whole country the British authority, by devoting to shame and torture and death the women and children whom even Oriental fury is wont to spare, regarding them as sacred, may have had some influence in prompting to such atrocities. But we fear that they are yet more the spontaneous outbreak of ferocity in a character which passes at a bound from contented submission to the extreme of deadly hatred, the saddest evidence of what a thousand years' reign of superstition, faithlessness, and oppression can do to efface the better lineaments of a nature originally noble.[1]

The immediate result of the mutiny is too plain to be mistaken: it is destined to be put down with a strong hand, and that right speedily. The sepoys have learned long ere this how sadly they have mistaken the sources of the strength in which they were trusting. Accustomed for a hundred years to constant victory under the British banner, they imagined they should be as invincible when arrayed against it. The superiority of the British native troops over those trained and officered by men of other European nations had always been conspicuous: now it appears how little even the discipline of the British sepoy can effect, when no longer directed by British intellect, and inspired with British courage and spirit. Since 1757, no more brilliant victories have been won by a few against a host than the last year has seen. The small number of English troops upon the spot have shown themselves able to hold in check, and even to make head against, the myriads of the mutineers. The old prestige of English superiority, which had always been one of the most effective agencies in maintaining and extending English power in India, is fully reëstablished. The reinforcements which have since reached the country will have turned the scale completely in their favor; and before the next summer's heat comes, India will be as tranquil as two years ago.

The remoter consequences are not so easy to foresee;

[1] It has been made to appear later that the accounts of Indian atrocities sent home during the mutiny were not a little exaggerated; and the wholesale and undiscriminating severities by which they were requited have left a stain upon British civilization as well.

but some of them may be even now distinctly read. Since the catastrophe is not like a great convulsion of nature, which alters permanently the features of a country, but rather a storm which sweeps for a time with fury over its surface, and passing by leaves it to resume its former condition, there will be few conspicuous political changes following upon it. No new distribution of territory will be made; the government will remain constituted as before; even the sepoy army will have to be reconstructed, for England cannot afford the men, nor India the treasure, to keep on foot a sufficient European force. Yet we are persuaded that many and important changes will take place in the relations of the two countries. In the very first rank of consequence is to be set the increased interest and attention with which those relations will be regarded by the British people. It has long been their reproach that they were too little heedful of their Indian empire, and of their responsibilities toward it; now their indifference is thoroughly broken down, and, we are certain, not for the moment only. During the past year more advance has been made by the public mind of England in the comprehension of all the great interests involved, than in twenty years before. This is precisely what was wanted to insure the faithful execution of that guardianship which she has assumed over India; and its consequences will soon appear in the new spirit of the Indian administration. Half measures will be cast aside: England will herself rule her eastern empire, not through the East India Company and in the name of the Great Mogul. She will not attempt longer to guide only the financial and political concerns of the country, letting its opinions and domestic institutions take care of themselves. She will deal with India more frankly as what it is, a semi-barbarous nation, conquered and governed by one of superior cultivation and endowments. While practicing the utmost toleration in matters of religion, the government will not be afraid to assume its proper character as an enlightened and Christian government, to encourage in all proper ways the spread of its own religion among its subjects, the spread of European ideas, and knowledge, and manners in the land. The impolicy, as well as dishonor, of the position which it has hitherto occupied with regard to this matter, is now fully recognized. A host of erroneous views and false principles of long standing have been cleared up and swept away by this revolt. The nature and strength of the hold which England has upon her Indian dominions is better appreciated. The blow which for years has been dreaded and guarded against with the most sensitive anxiety, as destined, should it come, to lay her empire in the dust, has fallen, and it has not staggered her for a moment: she has never felt firmer in possession than during these past six months. The general justice, integrity, and energy of her administration had grounded her influence throughout the country at large too securely to be shaken, even by such a whirlwind of defection on the part of those whom she had most trusted and most sought to bind to her.

England occupies at this moment a prouder position toward India than ever before in her history. We cannot but admire the political ability, and the moral and physical force, which could found so firmly, maintain so manfully, and reëstablish so speedily her authority over the hundred and eighty millions of her subjects or dependents in the East. It is also a position of more hopeful promise than at any earlier period. The spirit in which English sentiment has met the crisis is worthy of all praise and approval. It has manifested no less humility than firmness; it recognizes as the cause of the calamity its own want of prudence and attention; it is resolved to watch with more devoted care over its charge, for the best good of both. The future must show how these resolutions are kept, and with what result. The object to be striven after is the final regeneration of India, the education of whatever capacities for good there are in her, and her restoration to the full capacity of self-government. There is great danger of failure in the attempt to unite this object with the long guardianship which must precede it; danger of completing the destruction of the national character, by taking away whatever of independence is left, and putting nothing better in its place. But so much as this is certain; no calamity could befall India so great as the withdrawal at present of the British grasp upon her. She is in the hands of her friends; we accept what they have wrought for her already, we accept the spirit which now animates them in the continuance of their work for her. We would wait and hope, we would study and help, that she may some time assume again among the nations of the earth the position to which she is entitled by her blood and by her ancient history.

During the more than sixteen years which have now (1874) elapsed since the foregoing paragraphs were written, nothing has come to light in the relations between England and India which should cause them to be canceled, or seriously altered. Direct control of the country by the English government was assumed by the Queen's proclamation of November 1, 1858; and the whole outward form of administration, rather than its inward character or its spirit, was thus changed. There has followed a long period of peace and of the works of peace, during which all our anticipations of the progress of the country have been realized. The acquiescence of all classes and conditions in the British dominion has never been more complete and hearty. Immense public works have been executed by English skill and capital. Thousands of miles of railway have been carried across the land in all directions, and have exercised the same influence as in other stagnated communities: startling the minds of the people into greater activity and widening their knowledge and interest and sympathies, and giving accessibility and value to the productions of districts formerly isolated; helping also thus to avert or break the dread visitations of famine which have always come, from time to time, upon a country so thickly populated, and living under such peculiar climatal conditions, as does India. The works also of irrigation and of water communication, by which the best rulers in the middle age of Indian history have now and then distinguished themselves, but which had all gone to decay in the anarchy of later times, before the British came upon the scene, have been in part restored, in part added to upon a vastly increased scale, and with the happiest results. New and important branches of agricultural industry have been introduced and nursed into prosperity. Educational interests have been liberally attended to; a vast system of schools of every degree, from the university down to the village pedagogue, is organized and growing in efficiency. In matters of religion and public morality there is a quiet but decided furtherance of what is better and repression of what is worse, without obtrusive meddling. Though fully opened to the permanent settlement of Europeans, the country has not become the resort of permanent immigrants, but only of men who come in for a time to manage enterprises in which English capital is invested. There is still no real mixing of the two races; the Europeans stand over against the natives, and even against the Eurasians, as those of mixed European and Asiatic blood are called, with far too much of that pride and haughty exclusion which characterize the Anglo-Saxon in his intercourse with races whom he deems inferior. Here is the weak point, where a change is most needed, and hardest to bring about. At the central points, the natives are rising in education and enlightenment, and movements toward the reform of their institutions are making some genuine internal progress — a progress, however, which is not marked by any general disposition toward the acceptance of Christianity: young India tends rather to the abandonment of all positive religion. But it is too early still to prophesy what is to be the result on the national character of causes now working; we can only wish that those causes may long continue in operation, under the same ever-improving management.

II.

CHINA AND THE CHINESE.

IT is a singular circumstance,[1] which has not failed to attract remark, that the Atlantic cable seems to have been laid for no other practical end, so far as we on this side the ocean are concerned, than to let us know, a few days earlier than we should otherwise have learned it, that a treaty had been concluded with China by the two greatest European powers; a treaty which promised the attainment, at last, of the purpose of long years of peaceful diplomacy and warlike endeavor, in the laying open of that vast and populous empire to the knowledge of Europe, and the influence of European ideas. Certainly, no other event of the century has had so costly and conspicuous an instrumentality provided for its announcement. And although, in an age of cool-headed reason and contempt of omens like the present, we shall hardly be allowed to draw from this fact the inference that no other event of the century has been of the same importance to us, we may claim, without danger of serious contradiction, that it stands prominently forward among the great events of the time, and that its bearings require to be carefully studied; the more so, on account of the acknowledged difficulty of the subject. More discordant opinions than may be found recorded respecting China, the character of its people, the value of their

[1] The first transatlantic telegraphic cable was laid in August, 1858, and was disabled after a few days of imperfect service.

institutions, their accessibility to trade, their capacity of adopting new ideas and new forms of social and political life, the possibility of their reception into the brotherhood of nations — if it be not impertinence in us, wrangling and mutually exclusive set that we are, to talk of our fraternity, and of admitting into it a member as big, and many times as old, as all the rest of us together — more discordant opinions than have been expressed upon such points as these, even by the well informed, it would not be easy to find put forth upon any other similar subject. We by no means suppose that anything we can say will go far toward reducing this discordance to harmony; but we have a right to have our word upon whatever the world is talking most about, whether it shall prove to be well said or ill said. Perhaps we may be able to bring forward facts, or present views, which will enable some minds to arrive at juster and clearer judgments than they would otherwise form respecting the Celestial Empire and its inhabitants.

We candidly warn our readers, at the outset, that we feel a strong inclination to side with the Chinese in their present difference with the rest of mankind, so far as a regard for the rights of the case shall not forbid it. We desire to take the most favorable view that we can of all that concerns them; to allow them credit for whatever is justly their due, and to look with compassion and indulgence upon their shortcomings and faults; to place ourselves, in short, in as close sympathy with them as shall be found possible. Various potent considerations move us to this. Feelings of gratitude, in the first place, are not without their effect upon us. Who can sit over that cup, of all cups the most social and cheering, and the most harmless withal, and not feel within him a warm glow of something like affectionate good-will toward a country which has given, and which alone continues to supply,[1] such a gift to man and womankind? Can that part of earth's surface, after all, be truly said to have cut itself off from community with the rest, from contributing intimately and efficiently to their pleasures, which in so many and so widely scattered homes fills the steaming urn with its enlivening beverage? What shall we say, further, of silk and porcelain, as contributions to the material comfort of the race? We will not insist too strongly upon the Chinese inventions of the mariner's compass, gunpowder, and the art of printing, since, while some of them may be claimed to have done nearly as much mischief as good in the world, we cannot trace their origin, as possessions of our own, directly and certainly back to China. But a country which has bestowed upon mankind silk, porcelain, and tea, we might almost regard as having done its fair part, and allow to build up as high a fence as it pleased about itself, even at the risk of shutting out much sunlight, and to be happy within in its own chosen way.

Again, we cannot help feeling a great respect and admiration for a country which has had such a history as China. The remarkable character of the spectacle it presents among the nations of the earth is not seldom remarked upon, but cannot be too often or too impressively called to notice. China was one people and one kingdom a thousand years before that dim and half-mythical period when the Greek heroes led their followers to the siege of Troy, and it has maintained ever since, unbroken, the identity of its language, its national character, and its institutions. What changes, what overturnings and reconstructions, has not every other part of the world had to undergo during that interval of four thousand years! There alone upon the earth's face does stability seem to have reigned, while revolution has been

[1] Less exclusively, to be sure, now than fifteen years ago, when this paragraph was written.

elsewhere the normal order of things. We say deliberately stability, not inaction. China has known during all that time as constant action, often as violent commotion as other countries, and in many respects not less real progress; had it been stagnant only, had there not been in it a healthy vital action, it must long since have perished in inanity and putrescence: but, far from that, China has seen within the last two hundred years one of its happiest and most prosperous periods. Here is a problem for the student of history of which the interest cannot easily be overstated. How have the Chinese succeeded in finding and maintaining the stable equilibrium which other races have vainly sought? Is it in their character, or their peculiar external circumstances, or in the wisdom with which they have harmonized the two, that their strength has lain? As we look upon this venerable structure, the sole survivor of all the fabrics of empire reared by the hands of the men of olden time, we can hardly help wishing that it might have been left to stand until it should fall of itself; that the generations to come might have seen whether it yet retained enough of the recuperative energies which had repeatedly raised it from an estate far lower than that into which it was seeming now to have fallen, to give it a renewed lease of its old life, a return to its ancient prosperity and vigor. That is now no longer possible. China was able, by the force of her superior gifts and culture, to overbear and assimilate the wild tribes of the northern and western deserts, her only conquerors hitherto: but now an element is forcibly introduced into the workings of her history which cannot be thus dealt with, which must either leaven or destroy her.

This is another, and a principal reason, why we feel impelled to plead the cause of the Chinese. They are undergoing subjection to an influence which is irresistible, and of which the effect upon their own national prosperity, and even existence, is, to say the least, extremely doubtful. All the power of the West is arrayed together against them, and they are but as infants in the hands of us wise, daring, and rapacious children of Europe, armed with the terrible engines of destruction which our ingenuity has supplied to our combativeness. They must needs yield; it is only a question of time, of the forbearance or the mutual jealousies of their antagonists. And does the right of the question lie so entirely upon our side as we are ready to persuade ourselves? For whose advantage is it that the Western world is striving to break its way into China? Primarily, of course, for its own, and not for that of the Chinese. We want more of their silk, their tea, their thousand articles of pleasant and profitable trade; and we do not wish to pay for these in hard cash, making only one profit; we desire that they in turn should buy what we have to sell. To be sure, we also maintain that China will be the gainer by thus dealing with us. Free trade, brotherhood of nations, spread of civilization, are not these the universal regenerators, the forerunners of the millennium of culture? Are not we vastly richer, stronger, braver, more virtuous, more enlightened, more progressive, than these poor Chinese? Do we not know that they are fools and blind, and have everything to learn of us? But if we say yes to all this, the question is still by no means settled. The Chinese themselves dislike and fear us, and their opinion should not go for nothing in a matter which so nearly concerns them. It is so convenient and easy for us to assume that they are unjust both to us and to themselves in shutting their borders against us, that we ought to be very sure that it is really so before we break down the barrier. Our assumption may savor of that comfortable philosophy which maintains[1] that the African race is to be exalted to Christianity and civilization by association in the capacity

[1] That is, which in 1859 still maintained this.

of bond-servant with its superiors. The exclusiveness of China is no immemorial policy; it is comparatively a recent measure of precaution, suggested and enforced by experience; it may yet prove to have been prompted by the instinct of self-preservation. The history of the past few centuries affords more than one melancholy spectacle of the ruin and annihilation of a race by contact with a higher civilization, which it was itself incapable of adopting. It is upon our heavy responsibility if we crowd ourselves, with all our superior wisdom and virtue, upon a resisting people; and if Chinese nationality goes down in consequence of it, if the race that has maintained itself for four thousand years in such general contentment and prosperity as no other race on earth has known hastens to swift decay and extinction, our guilt will be great indeed.

We do not assert that this is to be the unfortunate result of our more intimate relations with China; we hope the contrary; but we do claim that the possibility of it requires to be taken fully into account. We believe that there is not a little ignorance and arrogance in the popular estimate of the Chinese and of the value of their civilization, and somewhat of selfish inconsiderateness in the plans formed respecting them. We hold that, in virtue of what they have been and still are, they deserve to be treated with more forbearance and generosity than has been wont to be exhibited toward them by the West; that their own welfare ought to be more carefully and more intelligently considered in all the dealings with them of the more enlightened nations. To this end we desire to contribute our mite by a view of the Chinese character, as exhibited in the history of China, its native institutions, and its relations with the rest of the world.

The history, religion, and polity of China, more than that of any other country in the world, centre in a single individual — in the sage Confucius. No man ever stamped his impress more thoroughly upon the character of a whole nation; perhaps none who ever lived has affected more powerfully the fates of a greater number of his fellow-beings. If we are to solve aright the problem of the Chinese nature and its development in history, it must be, in great measure, by comprehending the great Chinese philosopher, his relation to the times that preceded, his influence upon the times that followed him. We can find no better vantage-ground for taking a survey of the Chinese character and history than is afforded us by his life and doctrines.

Kong-tse, or Kong-fu-tse, 'the Sage of the Family of Kong,' was born in the year 551 B. C., which is very nearly the same date with that commonly assigned to the appearance of the no less famous Hindu teacher, Buddha. China was at that period broken up into a number of petty feudatory kingdoms, which owed but a nominal submission to the central authority, and were engaged in perpetual quarrels with one another. The political condition of the country was sad enough, and, in sympathy with it, the bands of social and moral order were also relaxed. Confucius felt keenly the evil character of the times in which his life had been cast, and devoted himself with deliberate purpose to the work of reform. Being called, as all of his genius and learning invariably are called in China, to high political office, he tried first, as chief minister of his native state, the little kingdom of Lu, in the present province of Shan-tung, what he could accomplish by personal interference in the affairs of state. Soon discouraged, however, by the little success which rewarded his efforts, he withdrew into private life, and set himself to infuse into the sum of affairs a leaven which should spread and work through all China, for all time, producing, by an organic process, those results which no effort of his single administrative arm could bring about. In this, his success was complete. His instructions were eagerly resorted to, and he soon saw about him a band, we are told, of three thousand disciples. The affection and reverence with which he inspired them were unbounded, and, through them, his influence soon began to be powerfully felt all over the land. He died B. C. 479, at the age of seventy-three; but he left works, compiled or composed by himself, to represent his doctrines, and his school long survived him, working on in his spirit, promulgating and expounding them. His influence went on steadily increäsing; his own works, and those of his nearest disciples and their followers, became by degrees the moral and political bible of the nation, the fountain of wisdom, the rule of virtuous and useful conduct. Successive dynasties vied with one another in paying honors to his memory; the whole educated class, the aristocracy of China, took him for their patron and model. He has at this day nearly six hundred temples in the different provinces of the empire, in which, at stated seasons, reverential honors, of a kind to be more particularly described hereafter, are paid to his memory. And it should be particularly observed that all these honors have been and are paid to the actual Confucius himself, and for what he really was and did; not to any distorted and glorified image of him, enthroned in the popular mind, and become the recipient of a worship which understands neither itself nor its object. The difference in this respect between Confucius and the great teachers and reformers of other lands is not a little striking and significant. Thus, to cite but an instance or two, the Persians soon made of their Zoroaster a being of supernatural gifts, who in person fought with the powers of darkness, and held converse with the Supreme Being. Thus the Indian monk, Buddha, underwent a yet more wondrous transformation; his life, as related by his followers, is filled *ad nauseam* with preposterous marvels, while his doctrines have been so changed, and perverted, and overlaid, that their identity is almost utterly lost: neither the Buddha nor the Buddhism of the modern Buddhists has any fair title to the name. But Confucius has no more been a subject of mythical and legendary history to the Chinese than Washington to us; he is a man, whose birth, life, opinions, acts, writings, are plainly on record, and incapable of misapprehension. The Chinese have treated him in the spirit of his own character. No one was ever more free from pride, from arrogant assumption of authority, from pretensions to superhuman wisdom, than was Confucius. He would not even lay claim to originality; he professed to be only a reverent student of the past, and a restorer of the principles and practices of the olden and golden time. This is the key-note of his whole philosophy. To extract from the past all that it contained which was best and worthiest of imitation, to combine it into a system of precepts of wise and righteous conduct, and to urge it by every available argument upon the acceptance and observance of the nation — this, and this alone, was what he attempted.

How well Confucius comprehended the work he had to perform, and how wisely he chose his means for its accomplishment, the result bears him witness. We cannot refrain from comparing him here with one of his own contemporaries, the sage Lao-tse, also one of the most eminent men whom China has ever produced. He, too, felt and mourned over the corruption of the times, and endeavored in his own way to set bounds to it, and to restore men to virtue. But his method was an altogether independent and original one. He was a transcendental philosopher, and had arrived at the apprehension of an absolute, spiritual, impersonal being, the cause and principle of the universe, to which he gave the name of Tao, 'the Way;' and he taught that by intimate recognition of this being, and spiritual union with it, through the means of the negation of whatever constitutes the nature and attributes of man, were to be attained virtue and its consequence, happiness. Lao-tse gave origin to a school, or sect, which is not yet extinct. The "religion of Tao" has at times enjoyed a wide popularity throughout China, and the countenance and patronage of its rulers; and it is still counted as one of the three creeds said to divide the homage of the Chinese people: yet not in its original form, as a mystical philosophy; it has been for long centuries corrupted into a low form of idolatrous superstition and necromancy, and its priests and adherents are justly held in contempt by all the more enlightened of the people. Thus the system of Lao-tse, which was not deeply based upon the national character, and met with no genuine response from the national mind, was doomed, despite the genius of its founder, to corruption and virtual extinction; while the philosophy of Confucius so closely adapted itself to the wants and the capacities of the nation, that it commanded and attained universal acceptance. Indeed, we know not how to characterize Confucius more summarily and more truly than by saying that he is the representative man of China, the highest exponent of the national character in its best normal development.

Hence it is that the great philosopher is, as it were, the focus of Chinese history; all the culture and wisdom of the past centre in him, and from him they radiate upon the centuries to come. It is even true that almost all the records which have come down to us of the early history of China, the relics which we have received of its ancient literature, owe to him the form in which they have been preserved, and to his sanction their preservation itself. Of the five canonical works, the King, which stand at the head of the Chinese literature, three were compiled, and one composed by him. The foundation-text of the first, the I-King, or 'Book of Changes,' is ascribed by tradition to the mythical Emperor Fu-hi.

It is simply a number of figures made up of straight lines, entire and broken, variously put together in parallel arrangement. These are regarded as typifying the elements and processes of nature, and the great truths of the moral and intellectual world; in them the earliest cosmical philosophy of the Chinese was pleased to find its expression. To the brief interpretation of these emblematic figures by the earliest founders (1100 B. C.) of the dynasty under which he himself lived, Confucius added his own fuller explication. It tells of the reverence of Confucius for what long tradition had hallowed, that he accepted such a text for his philosophy: his own straightforward common sense would never of itself have led him to so fantastic an invention. Again, the early ages of China, like those of other primitive nations, had not failed to produce popular lyric poetry. And it is curiously characteristic of the elaborate system of polity by which the affairs of the nation were regulated even at so remote a period, that the provincial governors had long had it for their duty to collect the lyrics which sprang up in their respective provinces, and to send them to the capital, as evidences of the state of opinions and morals prevailing among the people: it is clearly no modern discovery that the songs of a people are the most faithful reflection of the popular sentiments. From the material thus assembled, and from the mass of like material otherwise placed within his reach, Confucius selected three hundred and eleven pieces, being those which he deemed most valuable and worthy of preservation, and combined them to form the Shi-King, 'the Canon of Songs:' all the rest have since perished. The third canonical book, the Shu-King, is the most important of all. It is a work of historical character, yet by no means a chronicle of events alone; it is rather a record of the wisdom and virtue of the past; it is made up for the most part of the conversations, the counsels, the decrees, the institutions of the sovereigns of ancient China. It claims to be derived from authentic annals, and must, at any rate, represent the traditional belief of the Chinese at that period respecting the men and deeds of their country's early history. The record is brought down to a time about two hundred years before that of Confucius himself. As its continuation to his own period, the philosopher himself composed the Chun-tsieu, 'Spring and Autumn,' a brief historical compendium, which ranks as the fourth of the canonical books, and is the only work in our possession which comes directly from the mind and hand of Confucius: so faithful was he to his own idea of his mission, as the interpreter and mouth-piece of the past, and so little did he put forward his own personality in connection with his work. The fifth of the canonical books is the Li-Ki, or 'Book of Rites,' a compilation brought into its present form some centuries after Confucius, and made up from material of very different age and character, but a text-book especially of ceremonial and etiquette. An important place in it is occupied by the personal teachings of Confucius himself. The doctrines of the great philosopher are likewise exhibited in the Sze-shu, or Four Classics, which emanated from his school during the course of the first centuries after his death, and which, together with the five King, make up the sacred literature of the Chinese people.

As the Confucian philosophy is thus essentially a digest of the wisdom of the past, it will be well, instead of proceeding to a direct consideration of its character and import, to turn back and contemplate rather the past out of which it sprang.

The origin of the Chinese people is to be sought — if it be possible ever to trace back their movements beyond the limits of their own territory — in the northwest. The mountains of the southwest are yet occupied by wild tribes of another race, which perhaps once possessed the whole country. The earliest history of China has for its theatre only the northern and northwestern provinces. The great event with which its authentic history is generally regarded as commencing is the success of Yu the Great, the founder of the first clearly historical dynasty, that of the Hia, in damming the furious waters of the Great Yellow River, the Hoang-ho, and rescuing its immense and fertile valley, still the richest and most populous part of the empire, from inundation and waste. Yu is said to have commemorated his great work by an inscription cut upon the face of a mountain that overlooks the valley; of this inscription a copy still exists, which is by high authority pronounced unquestionably authentic. The date of the event is variously estimated at from 2200 to 2000 B. C. Its nature, and the employment in recording it of a written character radically akin with that still in use, prove that even at that early period the Chinese nation was no mere aggregate of wandering tribes, but at least beginning to be a great, powerful, and well ordered state, and that it had already passed through no very brief history of growth in knowledge, arts, and institutions. There are, unquestionably, elements of historic truth in the traditional accounts of the dynasties preceding the Hia, although largely mingled with mythological and cosmogonical legends: to their emperors are ascribed the first constitution of society, the invention of the useful arts, and the like. Conspicuous among these founders of the Chinese state and culture are Fu-hi and Hoang-ti; the two latest of them, Yau and Shun, find a place in the earliest, half-legendary accounts of the Shu-King. It is not necessary for us to go into any detail respecting the external history of the first dynasties. The Hia maintained itself upon the throne for about two hundred and fifty years, and then gave place to the Shang; this, in its turn, lasted nearly six hundred and fifty years, when the weakness and tyranny of its princes, and the unhappiness of the people under their rule, caused the revolution which placed upon the throne the heroic Wu-Wang, chief of the illustrious house of Chau. This emperor and his father are two of the brightest examples of wise and good rulers which ancient Chinese history affords, and are among those oftenest held up by Confucius to the admiration and imitation of posterity. They committed, however, the capital political error of dividing the empire into feudal provinces, of which the rulers received, or soon acquired, too much independent power to consist with due subordination to the imperial authority; and the result became, during the six centuries which intervened between the establishment of the dynasty and the manhood of Confucius, that disturbed and anarchical condition of the country which, as above stated, called out his efforts at reform.

It is evident that, at the period of their great philosopher, the Chinese nation had passed through a history abundantly long enough for the full development of a national character, the growth of a creed, the establishment of a system of polity. Indeed, at the epoch of Yu the Great himself, the Chinese were, in all probability, essentially the same as they have ever since remained, and that persistency and stability which have always distinguished them in so marked a manner were even then beginning to find scope for their exercise in the maintenance of past conditions.

Physical ethnologists reckon the Chinese as belonging to the race called Mongolian. That is, however, a classification of them which is of little value, as indicating their actual origin and relationship; for, by the language which they speak, they are severed by a deep gulf from all other people on the face of the earth. The general character of this language is well known to almost every one; it is a language of monosyllables, a root-language, as we may call it, an undeveloped form of human speech, giving in each of its words only the central, the radical idea, and lacking the whole apparatus of derivative and inflective syllables, which, in their infinite variety of form and use, make up an important part of the mechanism of all other known tongues. Order of collocation, and the requirements of the sense, as gathered from the totality of the sentence, are in Chinese obliged to do the whole work of declension and conjugation, and even, in great measure, of the distinction of parts of speech. As an instrument and aid of human thought, then, it is of all known languages the most unmanageable, the most defective and insufficient. Yet, such is the power of the mind independent of, and over, the means of its expression, that this imperfect language has served the ends of a cultivated and thinking people throughout its whole history, has conveyed far nobler and profounder views and reasonings than the greater part of the multitude of inflective dialects spoken by men — dialects strong in their capacity of being applied to high uses, weak in the ignorance and feebleness of the minds which should so apply them. The whole vocabulary of the Chinese spoken language is made up of only about five hundred syllables, each constituting a word; although this number is virtually more than doubled by the use of different tones of utterance, which give the syllables a distinction of meaning. The written language is vastly more complicated: a written language in truth it is, an auxiliary to the spoken, instead of being its reflection merely. The Chinese, like all the other modes of writing of which the history is traceable back to its origin, began with rude pictorial representations of visible objects, with hieroglyphics; but, instead of passing by degrees into a phonetic alphabet, it adapted itself ingeniously to the peculiar needs of the language which it was to represent, and, by combining in its characters a phonetic and an ideographic element, and bringing forth an immense variety of combinations, it was able to remedy in part the defects of the spoken tongue; the relations of the separate ideas, indeed, it could not represent, but it could relieve the ambiguity arising from the host of different significations of which each word, as pronounced, admitted. Thus, for a language of five hundred words, there is an alphabet of which the characters are counted by tens of thousands. Yet only a small part of these, of course, are in constant and familiar use. Dr. Williams's dictionary, one of the latest and most practically useful, gives about eight thousand, as supplying all ordinary needs, and even enabling one to read much of the literature. The style of writing the character has varied greatly at different epochs, and several forms of it, as employed for different purposes, are even now in use.

In the character of the language, as thus described, we find two of the distinguishing features which belong to everything that is Chinese: in the first place, an exceeding simplicity, amounting even to poverty, of means, material, first principles, combined with an astonishing ingenuity and variety in their development and application; and in the second place, a not less remarkable stability. The Chinese is in great measure exempt from the working of those alterative processes which are so active in other languages; its stiff monosyllables admit neither composition nor mutilation; they are exposed only to the slow modifying effects of euphonic laws: and hence it has undergone less alteration, during the four thousand years of its traceable history, than many another living language in four hundred years.

The religion of the ancient Chinese was of the same simplicity as their language; and it, too, seems to be preserved to us from the earliest period, unchanged as to all its essential features, in that body of rites and observances which is wont to be called the state religion, together with one important and prominent popular cultus. the homage paid in each family to the ancestors. Like many other of the primitive religions of the world, it was a worship of the powers of nature. In virtue of its character, it is fairly entitled to be called a religion. It was no mere superstition, no expression of a timorous dread of the powers of evil, seeking refuge in a cringing and deprecatory homage rendered to them; it was the outpouring of a genuine religious feeling, the offering in admiring awe, and gratitude, and trust, to the supposed rulers of the universe, of a worship which exalted and benefited the worshiper. It was, indeed, to a remarkable degree, free from the features which disfigure so many of the ancient religions; it was free from idolatry, from all cruel and bloody rites, from all taint of vicious and lustful indulgence; its ceremonies were of a purity and simplicity almost unexampled. Yet even these its virtues were in part the result of the unideal nature of the Chinese, and of the feebleness and lack of vital energy of religious sentiment which has always distinguished them. The native Chinese religion can hardly be said to have had a history; it has remained stationary at a stage which in other religions has been but the first of a long course of development. The chief objects of its adoration were heaven and earth, and the sun and moon. Now these natural objects have been the germs of the principal divinities of many another ancient religion; but almost everywhere their original identity has been lost in the personal deities which have grown out of them, hidden by the mythology of which these have been made the subject. But the Chinese religion never produced any mythology; it can hardly be said to have had any personal gods; the nation had a devout sense of an overruling power, or powers, under the supreme government and direction of which the affairs of the world went on, and devoutly and decorously they paid it their homage: but this was all. The weakness of their sense of personal relation to the Deity, and individual duty growing out of that relation, the comparative insignificance of the element of religion in the general sum of the affairs of life, is further evidenced by the fact that neither order nor class of priesthood ever grew up among them, charged with the ministry of divine things, and that the offering of worship became an affair of state, the performance of the religious rites of the nation the business of the civil authorities. The object of highest worship, heaven, might be addressed only by the Emperor himself; it was high treason for any one less exalted to offer solemn sacrifice to the Supreme Ruler; and each successive order of officials below him had likewise, in virtue of its official position, religious services to perform, at stated seasons, to the divinities of lower rank.

One class of religious rites, however, remained in the hands of the people at large. It is well known to all who have made any study of early religions, how often the almost universal primitive belief in immortality takes such a form as leads to a kind of worship of deceased ancestors. Their departed spirits are supposed to have entered upon a new life, which in many respects is a counterpart of the old one; they still own the ties and feel the wants of their earthly existence; they maintain intercourse with their living descendants, and are able to confer blessings upon them, while they are also accessible to their pious attentions, and even in a measure dependent upon them for support in the world of shadows. Such was the belief also of the earliest Hindus,[1] a race the most widely removed from the Chinese in place, origin, and character; and the pious Brahman still holds monthly the ancestral feast, at which the fathers are invited to assemble and partake of the food set forth for them, although it is with him only a dead ceremony, inherited from the remote past, while his own present belief has assumed a form with which such rites are wholly

[1] See the preceding volume, Article II., the "Vedic doctrine of a future life."

inconsistent. But this ancestral worship has nowhere else attained to such prominent importance as a part of the national religion as in China; it even constituted, and still constitutes, almost the only religious observance of the common people; and one which no decay of belief, no importation of foreign creeds, no upspringing of superstitious rites, has been able to displace. Every family has its ancestral altar: with the rich, this has a separate building allotted to it; with the poorer, it occupies a room, a closet, a corner, a shelf. There the commemorative tablets are set up, and there, at appointed times, are presented offerings of meats, fruits, flowers, apparel, money. But this part of the Chinese religion has also its public and official side. Although, in general, the ancestors of each family are the care of their own particular descendants, and not of strangers, yet an exception is made in the case of those who have been benefactors of the whole nation: distinguished philosophers and statesmen, patriots who have given their lives for their country, are in a manner canonized by having their memorial tablets removed from the privity of the family mansion, set up in public temples, and honored with official worship. Of this character, and of a prominence befitting his high rank and desert, is the homage paid to the sage Confucius.

The form of the Chinese polity was patriarchal; the state was an expansion of the family. The latter was both its model and its composing element; the individuals of whom the state was made up were heads of families. Neither age, nor property, nor wisdom, conferred political rights. So long as the father lived, the son was a minor; he was incapable even of acquiring real estate, or executing a contract, without the consent of the father, expressed in due form. Heads of families, associated together according to neighborhood, formed the primary political assemblies; and to them, or to their combination into secondary organizations, or to the officers freely elected by them, were committed many and important functions of administration. This, however, was not in virtue of an established constitution, or compact between the nation and its rulers; neither the theory nor the practice of the Chinese recognized any such. They had devised no fine hypotheses respecting the constitution of a state, respecting the rights of the individual, and the checks and balances necessary to maintain them; they knew of no national order different from that of the family. As the family is a natural community, having for its head the father, not by any election or convention, but by the very nature of things, so the nation is a natural community, of which the Emperor is the head; as reverence and implicit submission are due from children to a parent, so also the same are to be paid, with no abatement, by all the members of the national family, to its father and head. The Emperor is, as he is styled, the Son of Heaven. He derives his authority directly from the Supreme Ruler. As he owes his place to no election, he is limited by no human statute. He is the source of all honor and all authority throughout his empire; his word is law. By technical definition, then, the Chinese government is a despotism; and yet it would be unjust to stigmatize it by that term, as ordinarily understood by us. For, in the first place, as regards the theory of the state, the Chinese by no means held that it existed in the Emperor, and was to be administered for his benefit, the people being his vassals and slaves. They believed, no less than we, that governments exist for the benefit of the governed. Their system demanded of the Emperor the strictest devotion to the welfare and happiness of his subjects. He was not exempted from the binding force of any of the principles of morality and justice which were made obligatory upon the private individual. Heaven had made him, it is true, the father of his people, giving him unlimited dominion over them; yet for their good, that he might be their father indeed, and might make his children happy and prosperous. It is easy for us to say that this moral obligation is but a weak restraint, and that despotic power will and must be abused. The Chinese have learned that, too, and by sore experience. And yet this experience has never taught them that their system was radically defective, and required amendment. Over and over again has China passed through frightful convulsions, in its endeavors to rid itself of a corrupt and tyrannous dynasty; but never, so far as we are aware, has it made the attempt, by limitation of authority, by the imposition of checks and the exaction of guarantees, to guard against further tyranny. Content with the ancient constitution, not even imagining the possibility of a different one, the nation has sought only to place its administration in better hands.

But there have not been wanting, in the Chinese system, elements of which the practical working has operated powerfully to check tyranny, and to soften the hard features of absolute power. In the first place, the absence of all disposition, on the part of either the governors or the governed, to find fault with the established order of things, introduce innovations, encroach upon one another's prerogatives, has tended at least to promote tranquillity. Again, no people in the world have ever been more orderly and methodical, more attached to ancient institutions, more unpliable to new ways, than the Chinese. The laws and methods of administration of their great empire became very early an immense and elaborate system, which grew more stable and rigid with every century of its existence, and which no Emperor, no dynasty even, was able essentially to alter. The will of the Emperor was law, it is true; but it was greatly hampered in its exercise by the stiff and unwieldy apparatus of councils, and boards, and courts, through which it was compelled to act. Nor was it possible for the sovereign to win a class or a caste to his personal support, and to fill all offices with his creatures. Of classes and castes there were none; neither rank, nor dignity, nor authority were hereditary. If it were desired, in recompense of extraordinary merit, to extend to the family of the meritorious individual the favors shown to himself, the Chinese have always been used to confer dignity, not on his descendants, but upon his ancestors: an ingenious and happy device, which it is unfortunate that western nations have not imitated. Surely, an aristocracy is not necessary to the stability of the institutions of a country, if the most populous empire in the world has been able to subsist for four thousand years without a noble. The Chinese officials do indeed form a terrible bureaucracy, uplifted above the heads of the people in virtue of the delegation to their hands of part of the heaven-derived authority of the nation's father, proud of their position and presuming upon it, and often weighing heavily upon their plebeian countrymen; yet their general independence of the Emperor, and sympathy with the nation, are assured by the fact that their ranks are recruited directly from the mass of the people, and by a process which really brings, in the main, the best talent of the country to the management of its affairs. It is well known that for ages past the incumbents of office in China have been taken exclusively from the so-called lettered class; the class of those who, having been thoroughly instructed in the various branches of Chinese learning, have exhibited, in a strict competitive examination, the highest capacity and the profoundest acquirements. Access to this examination is denied to no one; the career of honors and dignities is open to every individual in the empire who has the requisite talent and industry. In this provision, and in the primary municipal institutions already referred to above, there is laid a foundation of real democratic equality, and one of no little depth and firmness, for the fabric of absolutism to rest upon. And the general result has been, that the empire has been governed under a system of laws of rare wisdom, equity, and humanity, which need not shrink from a comparison with those of the most favored epochs of the most enlightened nations in the world. When the Chinese have suffered under tyrannical oppression, it has been from the abuse of absolute power, exercised arbitrarily and in contravention of law. Against this they have reserved to themselves but a single remedy, and that is, the right of open rebellion. When matters have been borne with to the utmost, when the corruption or imbecility of the reigning dynasty, and the impossibility that the nation should be happy under its charge, are evident beyond dispute, then it is assumed that the commission of heaven has been withdrawn; pretenders to the virtually vacant office start up, and he who succeeds in crowding himself into the throne, and setting successfully in motion the machine of state, is accepted anew as the nation's parent and absolute lord.

It is not difficult to see the consistency between a political constitution like this, and the form and condition of the national religion, as we have described it. The family being the norm of the state, and the parental relation being held in the highest respect in the one as in the other, it was the more natural and easy to maintain the popular worship of the ancestors: this was hardly more than a transfer of the filial submission, attention, and reverence, always paid to the living parents, to their departed spirits. In the patriarchal state, again, there is no distinct separation of religious from political functions; both belong alike to the head of the family, and to his delegated representatives. The Chinese, indeed, can hardly be said ever to have established a distinction between religious, moral, and political principles, acts, and duties. All were alike incumbent upon the individual, and necessary to the well-being of society: why should they be severed from one another?

We cannot forbear calling attention once more to the fundamental traits of the Chinese character, as displayed in their system of government: the simplicity, the primitiveness in the common order of historical succession, of their form of polity; and, on the other hand, the magnificence of the development which it received, as applied to regulate the affairs of a vast and cultivated empire, instead of the petty concerns of a feeble tribe, or aggregate of tribes, such as those among whom we generally find that form prevailing; and the high measure of success which attended its workings. It never produced a separation of the people into privileged and unprivileged classes, with the discontent and heart-burning, the arrogance on one side and abjectness on the other, which are wont to result from such a separation. The distinction of wealth and poverty, and such others as seem to inhere in the very constitution of human society, did indeed exist in China, as elsewhere, and produced enough of practical inequality; but the law did nothing to aggravate or perpetuate it. Nor did the system degenerate into one of organized oppression, or of galling interference with individual rights. Not a little of personal freedom was enjoyed under it. The individual was left at liberty to go and come, to follow what course of life he would; he was protected in the acquisition and the enjoyment of wealth. There was wanting only that he should be fenced about with those safeguards against arbitrary violence on the part of his rulers, without which civil liberty, as we understand it, does not exist; but this was a want of which he himself, at least, was not conscious; he neither knew nor dreamed of a better system than that under which he lived.

Such we believe to have been, in their main features, the institutions of China at the time of the appearance of

Confucius. We have already briefly characterized the nature of the work which he undertook with reference to them. He came, not to overthrow, but to establish; not to reform, but to restore. He came to rouse the conscience of the nation, and to recall it to the fulfillment of known duty, and the practice of acknowledged virtue; to rescue the national institutions from the destruction with which they were threatened, by self-seeking rapacity on the one side and insubordination on the other, and by the general corruption of morals and manners. He came to give to the national ideas their highest, clearest, and most authoritative expression, that the nation might never forget or neglect them. He was not a religious teacher, because the national spirit, of which he was the reflection, was by no means religious. At his time, indeed, even the modicum of religious faith which had found its expression in the ancient religion seems to have nearly died out, and the ceremonies both of official and private worship to have become the forms which they have since continued to be, tenaciously adhered to and faithfully practiced, but no longer representing a living belief. Confucius accepted these ceremonies, and enjoined their careful observance; but, as it seems, from no higher regard for them than as they formed a part of the system under which virtue had flourished, and happiness reigned, in the ancient times of the empire. He expressly declined to meddle with matters lying beyond the present world and mortal life, in words identical in spirit with those of the famous couplet of Pope. "While I know so little of myself, my fellow beings, and the world which I see about me," he says, "how should I venture to carry my inquiries beyond them?" Accordingly, he bases his system upon no alleged revelation of a divine will; he derives for it no support from the retributions and recompenses of a future state of existence; he reads the will of Heaven only in the love of right and justice and virtue inherent in the human mind, and in the dependence upon these of the happiness of the individual and the welfare of society. These principles he lays down broadly and faithfully enough; the simplicity, dignity, and purity of his moral teachings are unsurpassed. He makes no pretention to metaphysical profundity, or to subtlety of casuistical reasoning: the results he arrives at are reached directly, by the intuition of an enlightened mind and a benevolent heart; they are stated aphoristically, and the sympathy, rather than the intellectual acumen, of the disciple, is trusted to for a favorable response. He contents himself with laying down guiding principles, not following out their application into all the details of life and action.

It would be an ungrateful task to criticise the work of Confucius, and dwell with reprobation upon what he did not accomplish. In the most important point of all he is above the reach of criticism: he did all that was in him to do; so far as we are able to judge him, he was as sincere, as devoted, as disinterested, as any of those who are numbered among the world's great teachers. His deficiencies may be summed up in a word: he was Chinese, and Chinese only. But it is on that very account that his influence over his countrymen has been unbounded. That it has been for good, too, and almost only for good, does not admit of question. That the Chinese system found at that time so noble and unexceptionable an expression was a matter of no slight moment to the nation. It was a critical period in their history. A philosophy specious in appearance, but corrupt at the core, and which cunningly adapted itself to the salient features of the Chinese character, might then have won currency, to promote powerfully the disorganization of society, and to bring down the permanent ruin of the empire. The influence of the Confucian doctrine, on the contrary, has been in a high degree conservative; it has contributed its full share toward the wonderful longevity of the Chinese state. The nation, on its part, deserves not a little credit for having implicitly accepted, and faithfully adhered to, a system of teachings of so pure and elevated a character. Their adoption of it, as we have already seen, was complete. For two thousand years the Confucian doctrines have been the moral basis of the whole fabric of Chinese thought and action. The works which contain them have been the invariable text-books, by and from which each successive generation has been educated. To appreciate the significance of this fact, we need to note the special importance of the system of instruction in a country where instruction is so general and so highly considered, and where eminence in learning is the path to honor and authority; where the educated are the only aristocracy, and form the class from which are drawn the rulers of the nation. And further, we need to note the peculiar character of the process of education in China; how that, owing to the great difficulty of the written language, more and maturer years are devoted to it than with us; how that, by the intense and prolonged toil which the student is compelled to devote to his text-books, in order to answer the requirements of the system of examinations, the native energy of his mind is impaired, and he becomes rather mastered by their contents than himself master of them. All the educated intellect of China has been thus imbued with Confucianism; even those have been schooled in it who were votaries of other religions than that of the state. As the Bible underlies all the varying forms of religion of the Christian world, so Confucianism has underlain all the phases of Chinese doctrine. That it admitted of being overlaid with new growth is not its least virtue. It trammeled the progress neither of religion nor of science, for it was not based upon any system of religious belief, nor identified with any scheme of physical or metaphysical philosophy. If the

Chinese have fallen later into idolatry and superstition, and have made little valuable progress in knowledge, it has not been owing to the enslavement of the national mind by Confucius, but to defects more radical in the national character.

Before going on to present our views of the Chinese character, we will briefly sketch the history of the empire since the epoch of the great philosopher.

The dynasty under which Confucius lived eked out its existence for more than two centuries after his death, or until B. C. 255, without any marked change in the conditions of the country. The Confucian school flourished in high esteem; about one hundred years after the death of its founder it produced its next most eminent sage, Mencius, the record of whose wisdom is included in, and closes, the sacred canon. Under the following dynasty, however, the Confucian doctrines and their representatives suffered a severe persecution, which, had their hold upon the popular mind been less firm, might have extinguished them forever. About 250 B. C., the princes of the kingdom of Tsin, in the northwestern part of the empire, rebelled against the imperial authority, extinguished the dynasty of Chau, and seated themselves upon the throne. The second emperor of the new dynasty of Tsin, Chi-hoang-ti, is one of the most remarkable figures presented by Chinese history. A great statesman and warrior, he destroyed the independent power of the petty sovereigns of provinces, and made the whole empire once more submissive to the imperial sceptre; he carried his arms far to the west, extending the dominion of China over nearly all central Asia; he chased the Huns across the northern frontier, and, to check their incursions for the future, he built the Great Wall, which has ever since remained one of the wonders of the world. But, in spite of his great deeds, his memory is execrated by the Chinese. His temper and spirit were thoroughly un-Chinese. He abhorred the servitude to usage and precedent to which even the imperial power had been wont to be subjected. He detested the authority of the past; he wished to blot out even all memory of it, and to begin on white paper a new history of the empire. To this end he sought to annihilate the existing literature, especially the Confucian, and to destroy its sectaries. The books he burned, all that the strictest requisition could bring into his power; the philosophers he buried alive, or sent to work upon the Wall. This state of things did not, however, endure long. Hardly was the great Emperor dead when his family were hurled from the throne; and one of the first acts of the founder of the dynasty which succeeded was to make a solemn pilgrimage to the grave of Confucius.

The dynasty of Han held the great fabric of the empire together for about four hundred years, or during the two centuries that preceded, and the two that followed, the birth of Christ. Such was the general wisdom of their rule, and the happiness of the country under it, that the Chinese even yet love to call themselves sons of Ḥan. During the first century after Christ, Buddhism was introduced from India, and made immense progress among the people. To this great event in the history of the country we can give but a passing mention here; its fuller consideration belongs to another department of our subject. As had been the case with its predecessors, however, the power and success of the dynasty waned at last, and, about 200 A. D., the empire was rent into three independent kingdoms, and a new era of intestine war and commotion began. Yet even this was not without its glories. The period of the San-Kwo, or 'Three Kingdoms,' is the heroic age of Chinese history, prolific of striking character and startling incident, the source whence the novelists and dramatists of after times have drawn their best materials.

We pass over the five following dynasties, which, together, lasted only a little more than three hundred years, from 264 to 588 A. D., and which held under their dominion only a part, now greater and now less, of the empire, noticing only that the invention of printing from wooden blocks, as at present practiced by the Chinese, was made about the close of this period.

The dynasty of Sui, which next obtained the control of affairs, once more united the dismembered empire, but, after only thirty years of power, was forced to yield the sceptre to the founder of the great dynasty of Tang.

Now followed a period of internal order and prosperity, of outward power and glory. The limits of the empire were again carried to the Caspian. Lyric poetry was revived, and attained its highest perfection. The drama arose. The examinations for literary dignity and political office were placed upon the footing which they have from that time maintained. The Chinese Academy, which has since played a conspicuous and important part in both the literary and political history of the country, was founded. During the reign of the Tang, China was probably the most enlightened and happy country on the face of the earth. But this dynasty, too, degenerated, and, after a period of weakness and misery, became extinct at the beginning of the tenth century. During the fifty-three years of civil war which succeeded, five different dynasties arose and fell. At last, in A. D. 960, the house of Sung seized the reins of authority, and reëstablished peace and order throughout the empire.

A new enemy, however, had appeared, to vex the Chinese state. The Tartar and Mongol tribes of the great plateau of Central Asia were beginning those restless heavings which not long after poured them, like a deluge of destruction, over all the countries of the east, the south, and the west. By the year 1127, they had wrested from the empire the territory north of the Hoang-ho, and were pressing on to the conquest of the rest. In this time of internal and external misery and danger, appeared the last great representative of Chinese philosophy, the sage Chu-hi. In wisdom and virtue he is accounted almost another Confucius; he is universally regarded as the man who has best comprehended, and most truly reproduced, the spirit of the Confucian doctrines; his interpretation and explication of the canonical and classical books has had, for all after time, an authority only inferior to that of those books themselves. Like his master and exemplar, he devoted himself, as statesman and as teacher, to the restoration of virtue and the salvation of the state. But the march of events was not to be arrested; China was doomed to pass, for the first time in her history, under a foreign yoke. The Mongols, under Genghis Khan, invited in at first as auxiliaries against the Tartars, seized upon the empire for themselves; and in 1279, Kublai Khan, the grandson of Genghis, became the first emperor of a new Mongol dynasty, to which he gave the name of Yuen.

That was a splendid vassalage in which the Chinese empire was now held. From his throne at Pekin, Kublai swayed the affairs of all the countries from the eastern seas to the very borders of Germany. The Emperor of China was sovereign of the most enormous empire which the world has ever seen. Kublai was a great ruler, too, and he had especially at heart the welfare of China, the richest and most populous part of his dominions, and his residence. He reformed the abuses which under the Sung had crept into every department of the administration. He executed great and beneficial public works: the Grand Canal is a monument of his wise policy. Literature flourished under him: the period of the Yuen is that of the highest perfection of the drama. Altogether, the country enjoyed greater prosperity under his government than for centuries before. Yet was the nation impatient of foreign rule, and when, under the successors of Kublai, weakness and tyranny began to usurp the place of vigor and justice at the capital, a general insurrection took place, which expelled the intrusive dynasty before it had completed its first century of dominion.

With the dynasty of Ming, which mounted the throne in 1368, begins the modern epoch of Chinese history. Founded by a man of various and remarkable genius, who was the son of a common laborer, and had been a Buddhist priest before he became a soldier of fortune, it upheld for a time the glory and prosperity of the empire, but later, lapsing into imbecility, met with the fate of the Sung. Early in the sixteenth century, the Manchus, another branch of the same family with the Tartars and Mongols, began to harass the northern frontier, and, between foreign invasion and internal oppression and rebellion, the country was reduced to a state of extreme misery. Though the Manchus doubtless aimed at making the whole empire their own, it was not as conquerors that they actually possessed themselves of the throne. They were called in by a faithful servant of the Ming, to save the dynasty from destruction by successful rebellion: but they reached Pekin too late; the last Ming emperor had slain his family and hung himself, to avoid falling into the hands of the rebel leader. Advantage was at once taken of so favorable a conjuncture; the Manchu chief seated himself upon the vacant throne, and China once more saw a dynasty of foreign birth. This was in 1644. The new dynasty gave itself the name of Ta-Tsing, or "Great-Pure." It was not firmly and peaceably established upon the throne until after fifty years of struggle; then, the last grand rebellion was repressed by the wisdom and valor of the illustrious Kang-hi, the greatest of the Manchu line of monarchs, and his descendant is still Emperor of China.

The Manchu conquest is to be looked upon rather as a blessing than as a misfortune to the country. China had never been in such a condition of anarchy and distress as during the last years of the Ming. Civil war and oppression ran riot in the land. It almost makes one's blood run cold to read of horrible massacres and devastations, by which whole provinces were turned into deserts. The Manchus were a hardy race of northern warriors, greatly superior to the Chinese in warlike prowess, and they soon established comparative order throughout the empire. Like the Mongols, they attempted no revolution, no great and sweeping change even, in the order of the state. The submission of these wild tribes to the superior enlightenment of the people whom they had brought under their sway is remarkable. It would have been, indeed, no light undertaking for a horde of warlike barbarians to force into new ways the teeming millions of the Chinese population, more inflexibly attached than any other race on earth to their own institutions, of immemorial antiquity; but we should hardly have expected them so fully to realize this truth, and so wisely to govern themselves by it. Aided by the all-controlling centralism of the Chinese system, they have simply infused an element of their own nationality through all the departments and grades of office, and allowed the great machine to work on as before, only with another engineer. Perhaps — we would not venture to affirm or deny it with confidence — perhaps the vital force of the Chinese race, after an existence so immensely prolonged, was becoming exhausted, and an infusion of new and vigorous blood was needed, in order to the further continuance of healthy life. However that may be, the best period of the Manchu domination, including the reigns of the great Kang-hi and his grandson Kien-lung, each of them of sixty years' length — the former reigned from 1662 to 1723, the latter from 1736 to 1796 — has been not less distinguished by power and consideration abroad, by tranquillity, prosperity, and contentment at home, by the faithful administration of just laws, by the success of industry, by the increase of population, by the activity of literary production, than the best which the Chinese annals can boast. Since the beginning of this century, the vigor and purity of the administration have greatly fallen off; discontent has arisen, to which additional violence has been given by the antagonism of the two nationalities, and many of the signs have appeared which in China are wont to indicate the downfall of an old dynasty, and the accession to power of a new one, with the intervention of a longer or shorter period of confusion and anarchy.

As to what the result is to be, we will not at present trust ourselves to offer an opinion, or even a conjecture. Two questions, of the most important bearing upon the future of the empire, demand first to be settled. Has the national character indeed so fatally degenerated that the country is no longer capable of rising by its own internal forces, as of old, from depression and misery? And again, what will be the effect upon the nation of the intrusion of foreign ideas, foreign arms, and foreign poisons? Both these questions are not a little difficult of solution. As to the first, the testimony of those who speak from personal observation is often very conflicting, even as regards the character of the Chinese of the present day, and generally very unreliable, as regards the comparison of the present with the past. Assignable reasons for this are not wanting. Many have judged the whole nation from a brief knowledge of the inhabitants of the sea-board cities, unquestionably the lowest class of the whole population, representing the native character as most altered for the worse by foreign trade and piracy. Those who know the Chinese most thoroughly, by continued, wide-extended, and familiar intercourse, are generally those whose opinion of them is most favorable. But the Chinese nature must not be too exclusively judged by the impression it makes upon those who at the present day are brought in contact with it. Its deficiencies have always been of such a character as most to offend our tastes, and through them to affect our judgments. There has been in it a dryness, a lack of ideality, of affection, of enthusiasm, which strikes us more strongly and unfavorably than the want in others of many a real sterling quality which the Chinese have possessed. In almost all that they are and do, there is something which spoils its savor for us. Their faces and forms are ugly in our eyes; their elaborate and exaggerated manners, regulated by rules older than all the Occidental literature, seem to us almost a mockery. Their capacities are limited by bounds of which we are so impatient, that we fail to appreciate how admirably they work within those limits. They exhibit in everything a childishness which sits most ungracefully upon their antiquated stiffness. In short, they seem a miraculously preserved relic of antediluvianism, most unlike us, and hardest for us to understand, or feel sympathy with. Their music illustrates the difference in our make and theirs. What to them is delightful harmony, to us is ear-splitting and soul-harrowing discord: we could tolerate it as the accompaniment of a war-dance of savages, but we cannot bear it from a people pretending to culture. Their drawing and painting, too, though showing close and shrewd observation, great faculty of imitation, skill in the use of colors, and a power of expression and artistic freedom of handling which Egyptian art does not even approach, not only is ignorant of perspective, but wants the very vivifying spirit of beauty which should elevate it from a mere talent to the dignity of an art. All this we should find much more tolerable if the Chinese mind were more open to instruction, could be convinced of its deficiencies, and brought to acknowledge the superiority of another culture. And thus it might be, were it only half-grown and still developing. But it has been for these thousands of years fully grown and completely developed; it has virtually worked out whatever of capacity there was in it. During all that time, China has been immensely superior to all the neighboring nations. It has been the source whence these have drawn art, science, and letters. It has brought barbarous hordes under the sway of its regulated polity. Repeatedly overrun and conquered, it has, like Greece, vanquished its victors; and even more truly than Greece, for it has never been ruled under any other than its own institutions. What wonder, then, if it is unable and unwilling truly to appreciate, and ingenuously to accept, what is now offered it from without? Is it not the very essence of the Chinese nature to be fixed and immovable?

The brief historical sketch which we have given will serve to show, we think, that the theory of Chinese quietism and immobility must be held under some restrictions. The outward condition, at least, of the empire, has not been one of tranquil and unbroken uniformity. It has passed through much the same series of convulsions and revolutions, though on a far grander scale of numbers and of years, which has also vexed the petty empires of the West. The grand and striking difference between the two cases is this: in China, the equilibrium has never been quite lost; mighty as the elements of disorder and destruction have been, those of order and conservatism have shown themselves yet more powerful. For this it is impossible to account by any assignment of secondary causes. The reason lies deep in the foundations of the national character itself, in the truly conservative bent of the Chinese mind, which has given to all its productions a form calculated for endurance, and has steadfastly adhered to them, and persistently maintained them upright. The same conservatism is exhibited by the intellectual life of China. There has been vast and unceasing activity, wonderful industry and productiveness, but next to no real advance. But we must never forget, in judging China, that, according to the ordinary march of events in human history, the Chinese empire should have perished from decay, and its culture either have become extinct or passed into the keeping of another race, more than two thousand years ago. It had already reached the limit to its capacity of development. Had it been then swept from existence, it would have left behind, for the unmixed admiration of all after generations, the memory of a nation wise, powerful, and cultivated, beyond almost any other of the olden time. Consider how many nations have died in giving birth to the modern Christian civilization, of the possession of which we are so proud. Where is Egypt now, that most ancient home of so many of the germs of our culture? Where are the two Semitic races, the Phenician and the Hebrew, whose influence on commerce, literature, religion, has been of such exceeding importance? Persia, too, has borne her part, if only subordinately, in the search after light and the struggle for empire: but how short-lived was her glory! And of our own chosen European races, the heirs of all the best wisdom of the past, the depositories of all the best hopes of the future, how has one fallen and another risen! How soon waned the transcendent genius of the Greek! How did the Roman empire become the prey of the barbarian, when over all Europe settled down the gloom of the Dark Ages! How is Spain degraded from the foremost rank she once held! And who shall tell what the future may have in store for those who are now the representatives of the world's best thought and action?

Such considerations as these should make us modest and merciful in passing judgment upon China. If the present is ours, the past is hers. Were it possible to multiply the amount of enlightenment which she has enjoyed by the years of its duration, and the number of human beings who have profited by it, we have little doubt that there would be found to have shone in China, in the aggregate, not much less light than in all the rest of the earth taken together. It is our duty, too, in forming our estimate of the value of a system, to take fully into account its adaptedness to the people who have lived under it, as indicated by its successful working. And we must perforce acknowledge that the Chinese have shown on the grandest scale that practical capacity which they evince in the petty concerns of ordinary life, by giving origin to a system of morality and polity which, however imperfect we may deem it in many respects to be, has proved itself so precisely suited to them. So long a life necessarily implies the presence of sound and healthful qualities. The history of the Chinese proves them to have been distinguished, as a nation, by many saving virtues: by orderliness, by submissiveness, by contentment of spirit, by frugality, by industry, by temperance, by general morality.

We have felt that these aspects of Chinese character, that this method of viewing it as exhibited in the whole history of the country and its institutions, had been too much neglected; that the general opinion did not do justice to its many great and admirable qualities. Hence we have been the more solicitous to set them forth prominently, and in as favorable a light as historic verity would allow. If we shall seem to any to have done them more than justice, we may plead that there are enough to judge harshly the unfortunate Chinese, and to heap contumely upon them, and that they deserve to find also a friendly advocacy. That they have fallen from the normal standard of their national character, we do indeed fully believe: their religious condition is sufficient proof of it: they have passed from that negative state in which we have depicted them, and in which history shows that no nation can long abide, into positive idolatry and superstition. No satisfactory discussion of this point and of its bearings is possible, however, without a much fuller consideration of the intercourse of China with the rest of the world, and its effects upon her, than we have left ourselves room for. We shall return to the subject in a future article.

III.

CHINA AND THE WEST.

In a former article we presented a sketch of the history of China, and a brief and comprehensive view of Chinese institutions. Our design was, by thus exhibiting the character and culture of the Chinese nation in their whole historical development, to lead to more intelligent and juster views of their value, and so to help in solving one of the great questions which must suggest itself to every one who takes even an ordinary interest in the historical events of the day — namely, what is to become of China now, when she is no longer left to work out her own destiny undisturbed, but is forced to feel the potent influence of Western ideas, commercial, social, and religious, backed by Western arms and diplomacy? Reverting at present to the general subject, we take up a portion of the evidence affecting it which was then left untouched — the history of the intercourse hitherto carried on between China and the West, and the influence already exerted by the latter upon the former.

It is only with the nations of the West that we have now to do. Toward the North, the East, and the South, China has always maintained the position of an acknowledged superior, in arms, in culture, or in both. We have seen, while reviewing the annals of Chinese history, that the irruptions of the northern and northwestern barbarians into the Great Central Flowery Kingdom have indeed repeatedly led to their political supremacy, but have also always ended in their intellectual and social subjection. As for Japan and Farther India, they have borrowed from their powerful and enlightened neighbor letters and arts, and have given little or nothing in return. None of these nations stands now in any such relation to China as should lend importance to the history of their former dealings with her. With the remoter West, the case is far otherwise; it has become a matter of no small moment to trace downward, through more than twenty centuries, the successive steps of that intercourse by which the races of our own Indo-European stock — beginning with its most eastern representative, the Indian, and ending with its most western, the English — have affected, and are threatening yet more powerfully to affect, the fates of the great Oriental empire.

The determining motives of intercourse between the West and the extreme East have been from the earliest times, as they are even now, of two kinds, commercial and religious. There was the exhaustless wealth of the empire to be shared in by the rest of the race; there were the teeming millions of its population to be converted to a new faith and a better life. The two motives have operated, sometimes together, more often independently of each other; we shall, in treating of them, follow simply the order of time, tracing their joint and separate workings from the beginning down to the present age.

As commerce has ever been wont to serve as the pioneer of missionary effort, so was it with respect to China also. The attractions of the empire for the trader and merchant have ever been of the most commanding character. The great variety and richness of its natural productions, together with the inventive ingenuity, the mechanical skill, and the unwearying industry of its people, have made it, since the first dawn of history, one of the great bazars of the world's trade. Such a career of industrial preëminence no other nation or country has seen.

How few years have elapsed since the highest ambition of the skilled workmen of Europe was to imitate with success the Chinese porcelain! And hardly does the memory or the tradition of the West reach back to a time when the silk stuffs of China were not the richest articles of apparel and ornament which the earth could afford to the wealthy and luxurious. At precisely what period the products of the Chinese looms and workshops first found their way into western Asia, it is not now possible to say. Vessels of Chinese manufacture are asserted to have been found in Egyptian tombs of not less than fourteen centuries before Christ, but the authenticity of the claim is at least very questionable. The first distinct mention of the country in western literature now extant is supposed to be the well known passage in Isaiah (xlix. 12), "and these from the land of Sinim." At the time of the Jewish prophet, then, at least five hundred years before our era, some dim knowledge of China had reached Palestine—doubtless from Babylon, and as the result of that overland trade to Persia and Assyria which we certainly know to have been actively carried on at a period not much later. The natural position of the empire determined the routes of its early commerce. The ocean was long a barrier, and not a highway, upon its eastern and southern border. There is no evidence that even the adventurous fleets of Phenicia ever reached those shores. The mountains which shut it in upon the west left but a single practicable passage into the interior of Asia, and that was at the northwestern corner of the empire, the entrance way, perhaps, of the Chinese race itself, and near to its earliest historical seats. Through that gate more than one route led across the deserts, amid the wild tribes that infested them, and over lofty chains of mountains, to the valleys of the Oxus and Jaxartes in northeastern Iran, whence the way lay open to Mesopotamia, Syria, and the Mediterranean. A long and perilous route, truly; and if the prize had been less tempting, even the daring traders of those times would not have cared to risk its dangers. We have authentic information from the Chinese annals, that, in the times of the Han dynasty, a century and more before Christ, the resources of the empire were tasked to quell the insolence of the northern nomads, and give freedom and safety to the westward journeys of the caravans. The vigorous and growing China of those heroic times thus took an active part in the commerce which bore its productions to the West. A couple of centuries later, the borders of the empire were also approached upon the other side, by sea; China was drawn into the net of that world-commerce which brought to Rome and her dependencies, through the Red Sea, and by the mart of Alexandria, the wealth and luxury of India and the farthest East. If the current identification of Ptolemy's Kattigara with the modern Canton be well founded, that port began soon after the commencement of our era to play the prominent part in commercial history which has ever since belonged to it.

An indirect consequence, probably, of the trade between China and Bokhara, and one of far greater importance in the ancient history of the empire than any commerce, was the introduction into it of Buddhism. This Hindu religion — of which the author is supposed to have lived in the sixth century before Christ, and so to have been very nearly a contemporary of Confucius — began, three or four hundred years after its origin, to be carried in every direction beyond the borders of India, by the earliest religious missionaries whom the world has ever seen. The countries on the northwest of India soon became, as they long continued to be, a chief seat of the doctrine of Buddha. There the Chinese first made acquaintance with it, and thence, during the first century of our era, it made its way into China itself.

The Chinese have a story of their own respecting the manner in which it was introduced. About A. D. 66, say they, the Han emperor, Ming-ti, had his attention strongly directed by a dream to an expression in one of the works of Confucius, to the effect that "they of the West have a sage." This western sage he determined to discover, and accordingly sent out in search of him an embassy, which, in due time, returned with Buddhist teachers and books from India. We seem to see in this not very probable story an attempt to attribute the introduction of the strange doctrine to imperial agency, and, more remotely, to the influence of the great Chinese teacher himself; thus, on the one hand, giving the foreign religion a more legitimate status within the limits of the empire, and, on the other, relieving the dynasty and the literary class of the imputation of having had it brought in upon them without their consent and participation. But, however it may have come in, it took firm root among the Chinese people, and spread rapidly over the empire; and even now, in the classification of the religions of the globe, the four hundred millions of Chinese are wont to be set down as votaries of Buddha.

It is not difficult to see why Buddhism should have made extensive conquests among the tribes of central Asia. It came to them as one of the matured fruits of a culture vastly superior to their own. It brought with it knowledge, arts, and letters. Its doctrines were in most respects full of attraction. Its morality was all gentleness and purity. It breathed a spirit of toleration, compassion, love, to all living creatures. It was instinct with the sentiment of the universal brotherhood of man, a sentiment then unknown elsewhere in the world. Its motto was peace on earth, good-will to men. Its philosophy was indeed atheistic, and its acknowledged and coveted chief good annihilation. Yet these features of its doctrine, little calculated to recommend it to the acceptance of wild and simple-minded races, were at a very early period greatly modified and concealed, and in its popular aspect hardly appeared at all. Its want of a pantheon and a mythology was supplied by the elevation of its own author into an object of worship, and by the creation of a host of kindred deities about him; its chilling end was hidden by the interminable series of renewed existences, of heavens and hells, interposed between this life and it, or was altogether explained away. No wonder, then, that it spread and flourished among the uncultivated people of Asia. No wonder that it acted upon them as a softening and civilizing influence, and that its results were, upon the whole, eminently happy.

In China the case was far otherwise. China had a civilization and a literature, arts and sciences, of its own, not less developed and worthy of admiration, in their different and peculiar types, than those of India. It had a code of morality as correct and exalted, if less mild and winning, than that which Buddha promulgated. In these respects it had nothing to gain from foreign teachers. And the antithesis of the Chinese and Hindu characters has always been such that it would seem impossible that any product of the one should be heartily accepted by the other. The Chinese are distinguished by hard common sense, by worldliness, thrift, industry, domesticity: the Hindu is imaginative and metaphysical beyond all due measure, careless of the actual and the present, living in and for the future. Not only was the philosophy of Buddhism thoroughly penetrated with the negativeness, the quiescence, the subjectivity of India; its external institutions were in many points repugnant to the principles of Chinese social polity. The assemblage of its special votaries, male and female, in great cloisters, shocked Chinese ideas of propriety; its priests, those who had risen highest in its faith and practice, and had a peculiar title to the rewards it promised, were professed celibates and beggars, two characters alike hateful to the orthodox followers of Confucius. How is it, then, that Buddhism made conquest of China also, as well as of all the countries to the west of it?

We confess that we see no way of answering this question satisfactorily, if the religious condition of the empire at the time be not fully taken into consideration. The Chinese people was, so to speak, without any religion. We have shown in the preceding article how scanty was the content, how meagre the forms, of the ancient Chinese faith; how the whole business of keeping up its ceremonies, saving only the offerings to the dead, had fallen into the hands of the state, and become a matter of official duty only; how Confucius had known no religion and taught none. But it would require a dryness of spirit beyond the measure even of Chinese aridity, a philosophic enlightenment and freedom from superstitious tendencies far greater than China could boast, to maintain a whole nation permanently in this negative condition. It must have a positive and tangible creed and worship. Buddhism, then, as we conceive, was not ill calculated to supply the want. Where such a want was felt, its many claims to admiration and acceptance would be fully appreciated, and its repulsive features overlooked. It was far from exciting enmity and opposition by setting itself up in hostility to the native religion. Everywhere and always tolerant in its character beyond any other religion — the only one, perhaps, which never set on foot a religious persecution — it fully admitted and encouraged the ceremonial observances of the state officials, and the ancestral rites of the common people. It was not above adapting itself to the popular mind, and even making itself the minister of the popular superstition. It came in thus, as it were, and quietly occupied an almost forsaken territory, neither expelling nor disturbing the few original possessors still left there.

Our view of the causes of the success with which the efforts of the Buddhist missionaries in China were attended is supported by the after history of the religion, and by the effects which it produced, and which were produced upon it, in its joint workings with the native institutions. It suffered far more change than it wrought. Greatly altered and corrupted, hollowed out from within and overlaid with strange matter from without, as Buddhism has been everywhere in Asia, in China it soonest and most completely lost its original character and legitimate influence. Not that there were not for a long time among its numerous followers those who were zealous for the purity of the faith. Time and again, through a succession of centuries, enthusiastic and devoted Chinese monks visited India, bringing back from thence fresh supplies of sound doctrine, and great stores of the Buddhistic legendary and controversial literature — the dreariest literature, perhaps, that was ever painfully scored down, and patiently studied, and religiously preserved — which then found Chinese translators and imitators, till the empire was even fuller of Buddhist books than of those of native origin. We still have records of the travels and observations of several of those ancient pilgrims, and they testify not only to the religious zeal of their authors, but to the transforming influence which, in some respects at least, and not for the better, Buddhism could exert upon the Chinese mind. While, in the absence of a native Hindu chronology and history, they are valuable contributions to our knowledge of India — as even bare lists of names, of undoubted authenticity and assignable date, would be — they are yet as barren of aught that could interest any but a zealous Buddhist as it was possible to make them. One cannot help sorely regretting that the travelers had not been genuine Chinese, curious, clear-headed, matter-of-fact followers of Confucius, with eyes for something besides temples and topes and foot-prints of

Buddha, with ears open to something other than legends and lying wonders, with interest in something more human than the controversies of the schools of Buddhistic theology; what priceless information might they not then have handed down to us respecting mediæval India! But when we look for distinct effects of Buddhism upon the general national character, we find next to nothing. Confucianism has maintained since, as before, its mastery over the mind of the nation, its first place in the respect and affection of the most enlightened class, and the religious rites it sanctioned are practiced as faithfully to-day as two thousand years ago. Buddhist sentiments of human brotherhood have not softened the contempt and dislike with which the son of Han regards the "foreign red-haired devils." Buddhist respect for life, in all its manifestations, has not stopped the slaughter of Chinese swine, fowls, and fish. Buddhism has not redeemed the religious indifferentism of the Chinese, nor taught them to care less for this life and more for another, nor provided new and efficient encouragements to virtue or restraints upon vice. While it has thus been no elevating and ennobling element in the intellectual and moral development of the Chinese people, it cannot be relieved of a heavy responsibility in connection with their religious degradation. It has not only opposed no barrier to superstition, it has even adopted and encouraged it, and furnished it a channel in which to run its course; and it has occupied the ground, to the exclusion of better influences, which might otherwise have had more efficiency.

To follow in detail the external history of Buddhism in China is not our intention. At times it has enjoyed the smiles of imperial favor; at times it has been severely persecuted, for the discordance of its institutions with the constitution of the state, and its encouragement of idleness and idolatry; yet persecution came too late, and was too fitfully resorted to, to interfere seriously with its prosperity. It has always been frowned upon and discouraged by the wiser and worthier classes, and occupies at present a low and mean position in presence of the public opinion of the empire. China is, indeed, so far as this Buddhistic, that it is full of Buddhist monasteries and temples, and that few of all its inhabitants would hesitate to have recourse to Buddhist ceremonies, or to the services of Buddhist priests, in mere superstition, for help out of trouble, or for the attainment of some coveted good; but in like manner all are Confucians, all are sectaries of Tao. There is no Buddhist church or body of believers, properly speaking, but only a prelacy and priesthood, ignorant and despised, though tolerated and supported.

No small share of the interest which attaches to the history of Buddhism arises from its relation to the history of Christianity in China. In studying the latter, the light cast upon it by the former may not be neglected. The character and the causes of the lasting success which has attended the proselyting labors of the Indian missionaries must be duly appreciated, if we would rightly understand the failure of the repeated and persevering efforts made for the establishment of Christianity within the limits of the empire.

Leaving out of account, as nothing better than a pious fable, the pretended apostolic labors of St. Thomas in China, we recognize in the Nestorians the missionaries who first carried the Bible and Christianity into the remotest East. This sect, pronounced heretical, and cut off from the communion of the western Catholic church, for denying that Mary was the mother of God as well as the mother of Jesus, and of which the scanty remnants are now themselves the objects of Christian missionary labor — this sect was, for many centuries, the chief representative and the active propagator of Christianity over all the vast continent of Asia. Its missionaries, following at a distance of five or six centuries upon the track of the apostles of Buddhism, preached the Christian faith in almost every country of central and eastern Asia, with equal zeal and success; and it might, had the soil been as receptive and as fertile as that on which fell the seeds of Roman doctrine, have gathered in a harvest not less rich and lasting than was reaped at the same period in Europe. The decay of the Nestorian church in numbers, in power, in energy, in intelligence, has been accompanied by the loss of its records, and almost even of its traditions; and a few scanty notices, gleaned here and there from eastern and western literature, are nearly all the information we possess respecting the labors of its missionaries and their results. When they entered China is not certainly known; it was probably as early as the beginning of the sixth century. The two monks who in the middle of that century brought the eggs of the silk-worm to Constantinople are supposed to have been Nestorians. Happily there has been preserved to our own days one ancient document for the history of the Nestorian missions in China. We refer to the famous monument of Si-ngan-fu, of which the authenticity, long disputed, may now be regarded as fully vindicated. It is an immense marble slab, about ten feet by six, having its surface covered with a long inscription in Chinese, to which are appended a few lines of ancient Syriac. It contains a summary statement and eulogy of the doctrines of the Illustrious Religion, as the Nestorian faith was denominated, a grateful commemoration of the favors shown it by the emperors of the great Tang dynasty, and a general account of the success which had attended its propagation in the empire. It was prepared and set up A. D. 781, during the reign of the Tang, and its record goes no farther back than to the accession of that dynasty to the throne, or to A. D. 635, when the arrival of a certain Alopun from Syria, and the encouragement extended to him, seem to have made an era in the history of the mission. The erectors of the monument claim that the votaries of their doctrine were numerous throughout the empire, and that their churches were to be found in every city; and there is no reason to question the justice of these claims; they are fully supported by all the scattered evidences which we are able to derive from other sources of a later date. At the epoch of the Tang, haughty and ignorant exclusiveness had not come to be a fundamental characteristic of Chinese policy; the empire was hardly less open to foreigners than the freest states of modern Europe, and its sailors and merchants bore an active part in a widely extended foreign commerce. We have in our hands the relations of one or two Arab travelers of the ninth century, which show us that for hundreds of years the intercourse between Chinese ports and the marts of India and the Persian Gulf had been lively and constant. Chinese vessels, far exceeding in size those of the western countries, came to the mouth of the Euphrates for the exchange of valuable commodities. Arabs, Persians, and Jews, as well as Christians, were to be found in great numbers in Chinese cities. According to the Chinese annals, the Arabs and Persians were numerous enough in Canton in A. D. 758 to take advantage of the breaking out of a tumult to burn and plunder the city. Arab tourists penetrated to the capital, and had audiences of the emperor; and the accounts they give us of his familiarity with the geography and politics of the West, and of his freedom from prejudice and national vanity, are almost marvelous. Khan-fu, a port better situated than any which has for centuries past been accessible to European commerce, was then the chief resort of the foreigners. The Mohammedans settled there were judged by one of their own number, appointed by imperial authority to the office. An attractive picture is drawn by our Arab authorities of the then condition of the empire, of its populousness, its wealth, its fertility, its beauty, of the fineness of its silks and its transparent porcelain, of the justice and equity of its government, and of the universal education of its people — every one learning to read and write, and the poor receiving instruction at the public expense. The picture is not too highly colored; we have said before that the enlightenment and prosperity of the Chinese empire at this period were not excelled anywhere upon earth. Toward the end of the ninth century, however, a terrible change came over the scene. The ruling dynasty went down, amid tumult, devastation, and massacre. In 877, Khan-fu was besieged and taken by a ferocious rebel chief, and one hundred and twenty thousand Mussulmans, Christians, Jews, and Pârsîs, are said to have been slaughtered among its inhabitants; we may hope that at least the number is greatly exaggerated. This disaster gave a shock to foreign commerce from which it was slow to recover; for a long time regular intercourse by sea with the West was suspended. The Nestorian missions bore their share in the general suffering of the country; a reinforcement sent out by water in the course of the next century returned, somewhat hastily and faint-heartedly, perhaps, professing to have found no trace of its co-religionists, and announcing that the Christian religion was extinct in China. For a long time the empire was lost sight of and forgotten, as it were, in Europe and the western coasts of Asia; no further mention of it is to be met with in occidental literature until the thirteenth century.

That the proselyting efforts of the Nestorians in High Asia were not in the mean time intermitted, was attested to the West by dim rumors of a mighty potentate in the distant East, who was both a Christian and a priest — rumors which made their way to Europe in the eleventh and twelfth centuries. Our English version of the name by which he was known is Prester John. This was, in fact, an actual personage, the powerful Khan of the Kerait Tartars, converted to Nestorian Christianity early in the eleventh century. The tribe was conquered later by Genghis-Khan, and incorporated into the Mongol empire, but its sovereign was still a Christian when Marco Polo passed through his country on the way to China.

The noted traveler whose name we have just mentioned may almost be said to have discovered to Christian Europe the countries of Central and Eastern Asia. His father and uncle, noble merchants of Venice, had found their way to Peking, the capital of the Mongol emperor Kublai, in 1260; after a brief stay in the country, they were dispatched by Kublai himself upon an embassy to the Pope, and upon their return, in 1276, they took the young Marco with them. Their journeys to and fro were made by the tedious and painful inland route. They resided this time for seventeen years in China, in high favor with Kublai, and even holding at times offices of important trust in his empire, till they at last came back, by water from the mouth of the Pei-ho, a voyage of eighteen months, to the mouth of the Euphrates, and reappeared in Venice in the year 1295. Happily for the world, Marco was soon after taken prisoner by the Genoese, and to while away the tedium of his confinement he made as faithful and complete a record of his travels and observations as his memory and notes could furnish. The work gained a great popularity, and was soon translated into almost all the languages of Europe. Its statements were received with not a little incredulity, but their general correctness has been abundantly established by the better knowledge since obtained. Its author's special object was to describe the wealth, the institutions, the manners and the customs, of the Chinese empire, and the power and grandeur of its sovereign, and he but seldom touches upon matters which concern foreign commerce and foreign religions; yet it is evident from his occasional mention of Christian, Mohammedan, and Jewish communities and churches in the Chinese cities, that both the Nestorian missions and the Arab commerce had recovered from the state of prostration in which the fall of the Tang had left them four hundred years before. The policy of the great founder of the Mongol dynasty himself was eminently liberal and enlightened: foreigners of every race were received by him with kindness, and entire freedom of faith was allowed throughout his dominions.

Fifty years after Marco Polo, the enterprising and indefatigable Arab tourist, Ibn Batuta, who has left us the story of his wanderings over almost every part of the eastern world, reached the southeastern coast of China by sea from India, and made his way by the routes of inland travel to Peking. His account of the empire both supports and supplements that of his Venetian contemporary. He praises it as the most populous, wealthy, and highly cultivated country in the world; he extols the industry and the mechanical and artistic skill of its inhabitants, the beauty and abundance of the porcelain and silk-stuffs, the greatness of the cities, the pomp and splendor of the court and capital. He notices the use of paper money, the care taken of human life, and the unparalleled safety assured to travelers. He tells of Moslem communities in every important city, dwelling and practicing their religion in security, and governed and judged according to their own laws by authorities chosen from among themselves. In the great metropolis of Khansâ (supposed to be the place more recently called Nanking), he describes one of the six quarters of which the city was composed as peopled exclusively by Jews, Pârsîs, and Christians. This is his only mention of Christians; it did not enter into the plan of his story to give details upon such matters; his attention was directed especially to the native inhabitants of the countries he visited, and to the condition of his own co-religionists among them. His exit from the empire was hastened by the internal troubles attending the decadence of the Mongol dynasty.

In the mean time had taken place the first successful attempt of European Christianity to extend its influence into Eastern Asia. The effort was prompted by the instinct of self-preservation. The Mongols, early in the thirteenth century, had broken forth from the mountains and deserts of the great Asiatic plateau, overrunning, devastating, and subjecting alike the east, the south, and the west. Soon their terrible hordes of horsemen were pressing hard the borders of Catholic Europe, and threatening destruction to both culture and religion. In this emergency, while Christian sovereigns were arming for a combined defense of their states, the spiritual guardian of Christendom was likewise moved to send out peaceful embassies to the homes of the fierce nomads, to turn them, if it might be, from their savage spirit of conquest, or to avert their arms from Europe. Repeated missions found their way, between 1245 and 1260, from Rome and France to the camps and capitals of Tartary, and not without a degree of success in establishing an understanding between Christians and Mongols. One tie of common interest united them: both alike were the foes of the Mohammedan sultans of Egypt, Syria, and Asia Minor, who had checked and baffled their plans of aggrandizement. On the one hand, the crusades were just ending in ignominious failure and defeat; on the other hand, here was the rock from which the tide of Mongol conquest was rolled back. The first burst of their strength and fury had spent itself, and Europe was safe. The names of Carpini and Rubruquis are conspicuous among those of the papal emissaries who visited the homes of the Mongol race, and returned, bringing back valuable information to Europe, and pointing out the way to Christian missionaries to a new field of effort. It was at once occupied. Missions were soon scattered here and there over Central Asia; and hardly had Marco Polo left Peking when John of Monte-Corvino, the first Catholic missionary to China, entered it. Complete liberty of preaching and proselyting was allowed him; his mission flourished, in spite of Nestorian opposition; after some years numerous and repeated reinforcements were sent out, and placed under his direction as Archbishop of Peking, and it seemed for a time as if Catholic Christianity had at last taken firm root all over the remote East.

But these flattering prospects were soon eclipsed. The breaking up of the Mongol empire, only a century after its first establishment, was attended with commotions which almost extinguished both eastern and western Christianity in Asia. In China itself, the catastrophe was complete. About the year 1368, after the usual period of distress and civil war, the Mongols were driven out, and a native dynasty, the Ming, seated upon the throne. A great reaction took place in favor of the native institutions, and against everything that was distinctively foreign. The Christian teachers had enjoyed the protection of the expelled dynasty; like it they had come in from the West; their origin and their sympathies were beyond the borders of the empire. With it, then, they were driven out, or their weak establishments went down amid the general confusion, and could not be revived. Parties of missionaries sent out from Europe were never heard from again. Even the Nestorian faith, which had so long survived all revolutions and changes of dynasty, now utterly disappeared. For the first time in eight hundred years, China was free from all remnant or trace of Christianity.

It is greatly to be regretted that, in the absence of all records of the inner history of the Nestorian missions, we are unable to judge respecting the causes of their long success and ultimate failure. We know not what position Nestorian Christianity maintained toward Chinese indifferentism and superstition; whether it was a bold, faithful, and uncompromising representative of Christian doctrine, or inoffensively tolerant of the weakness and errors of those whose good it sought; whether it strove after a show of strength by the accession of crowds of nominal converts, or labored for a real success in the transformation of the hearts and lives of its proselytes. However this may have been, the final result was the same. It passed away, and left no abiding impression. Chinese history ignored it, and all remembrance of its presence in the empire was lost. When the next Christian missionaries appeared, the state of China was as if the name of Christ had never yet been heard within its borders.

More than a full century now elapsed before the renewal of European intercourse with China. The rediscovery, so to speak, of the empire was one of the occurrences which marked the close of the fifteenth and the beginning of the sixteenth centuries, that epoch so rich in great events, when the invention of printing, the application of the compass to its true work, the discovery of America, the discovery of the Cape of Good Hope, changed the aspect of the world, and gave such an impulse to the development of European civilization as it had never before received. It was in 1487 that Diaz returned to Lisbon from his voyage of discovery, and reported that the way eastward around the continent of Africa was open to the maritime enterprise of western Europe. Ten years later a Portuguese colony, never since dislodged, was established under Vasco de Gama on the western coast of the peninsula of India; and in 1517 a Portuguese squadron, tracing backward the route of Marco Polo, entered the port of Canton. This was the commencement of the modern era of Chinese intercourse.

The native dynasty of Ming still sat upon the imperial throne, but had already passed the zenith of its power and prosperity. It had seen the extinction of European influence in the land; it was destined, before its downfall, to behold the renewal of that influence, in more than the former measure. The policy of the dynasty was by no means especially hostile to foreign commerce, or to foreign religions. Jews and Mohammedans were to be found, not only in the sea-board cities, but far in the interior of the empire; and they enjoyed entire toleration, because themselves quiet and inoffensive, and menacing with danger neither the religious nor the civil institutions of the empire. It depended altogether upon the character of the new comers how they should be met. Had the Europeans shown themselves peaceful in their policy and moderate in their demands, and had they awakened no jealous fear by their conduct in other parts of the East, we have no reason to suppose that any restrictions of especial severity would have been imposed upon them.

Unfortunately, they gave the Chinese, at the outset, a very unfavorable impression of their character. The first Portuguese expedition, indeed, conducted itself peaceably, and, being kindly met, effected a satisfactory and profitable exchange of the commodities it brought. But while a Portuguese embassy was on the way to Peking, to arrange terms of future intercourse, a second fleet, newly arrived at Canton, fell to burning, murdering, and plundering, as if a mere band of lawless freebooters. Intelligence of this, as well as of the predatory conquests made by the Portuguese in Malacca, among the very allies and dependents of the empire, reached the capital with the envoys. The result was what might have been expected. The ambassadors were treated as spies and impostors, and sent back in chains to Canton, where, chancing to arrive at the same time with the commission of new outrages, they were put to death, or detained in permanent captivity. Still the visits of the Portuguese were not altogether and permanently interdicted. They formed profitable establishments in many of the ports of the empire, and after 1560 were allowed to establish a kind of colony at Macao, at the mouth of the Canton River, which long continued to be the head-quarters of European commerce, and the chief station of the Catholic missions.

The Spaniards first approached the coast of China in 1575, from the neighboring Philippine Islands, of which their recent conquest was as unfavorable a recommendation to Chinese hospitality as they could possibly have had. The injustice and impolicy of their government of the islands, and especially their cruelty to the numerous Chinese emigrants to Manila, produced later distinctly traceable effects upon the Chinese policy toward all Europeans,

The Dutch, too, did what they could to add to the evil reputation of Europe in China. At their first appearance they came as enemies of the Portuguese, and offended the government by an attack upon Macao, which was still Chinese territory, although tenanted by foreigners; being beaten off there, they seized upon the Pescadores, a cluster of islands lying just off the coast, a little farther to the north.

The first visit of the English, in 1637, was also attended with unfortunate circumstances, ominous of anything but harmony and a good understanding in the future; although, if we may trust the accounts given, the chief blame was this time with the Chinese; since the latter, led astray by the false and malicious representation of their intentions made by the Portuguese, commenced an unprovoked attack upon them. It was fiercely and successfully resented; and after the capture of the forts which had been guilty of the outrage, explanations were entered into, and apologies made, and the intruding vessels were allowed to exchange their cargoes before leaving the river. No further intercourse was had with England or her colonies until 1664.

When we take duly into account all these untoward occurrences attendant upon the reopening of commercial intercourse between the East and the West, and the generally aggressive character, half freebooting, half conquest-making, belonging to the adventurous expeditions of the Western traders, we can hardly think it strange that the Chinese should have met the new foreign commerce in a very different spirit from that with which they had greeted the old. Distrust, fear, and aversion became the determining motives of the policy which they adopted toward their visitors. That it was not based merely upon haughty and contemptuous self-sufficiency, indifference to commerce, and blind intolerance of foreigners and their manners and institutions, is clearly evident from what we have seen above respecting the earlier commercial relations between China and the West, and the long and peaceful occupation, by Moslems, Jews, and Christians, of domiciles in all parts of the empire. Circumstances, however, did enable the government to give its policy a coloring of arrogant contempt. The foreign commerce was, in truth, a matter of relatively small consequence to China. Compared with the domestic trade, which made of the interior of the country one vast market for the exchange of the productions of different provinces, its amount and the revenue it yielded were, especially at the first, quite insignificant. It seemed to be carried on solely for the benefit of the stranger, who came to supply his poverty from the abounding resources of the empire, and was able to offer in return but little of value. It is well known that, until the poisonous drug, opium, was brought in to turn the scale, the balance of exchange was always terribly against the foreign trader, and the hard specie in which he was forced to pay for his purchases was of small account in the public economy of a country which knew no authorized currency save paper and copper. Hence the foreigners appeared as suppliants, begging to be allowed to enjoy and profit by an intercourse which it was a matter of indifference to the other party whether they granted or refused. The Chinese were not slow to perceive and to push the advantage. They habitually tried how much the foreigners would endure of imposition and of indignity under the pressure of a threat to stop the trade. Neither the latter nor the countries from which they came were suffered to make a dignified and imposing figure in Chinese eyes. Any difference between them and the petty half-civilized and barbarous states which bordered upon the empire, was studiously ignored. Their embassies were made puppets of in the hands of a rigorous etiquette, were balked of all valuable results, and treated as acknowledgments of inferiority and vassalage. What, indeed, were the handfuls of subjects who acknowledged the authority of the Western monarchs, to the hundreds of millions who bowed to the throne of the Son of Heaven? And of the energy, knowledge, and capacity which made a few countries of Europe, small as was the space they occupied upon the earth's surface, a power greater than all the rest of the world together, the Chinese had little appreciation. They were content with and proud of their own culture, literature, and social and political institutions, all of immemorial antiquity; and, in the true spirit of a stiffened civilization, they misapprehended and contemned whatever was discordant with it; and what they were compelled to acknowledge only heightened their fear and distrust, and made their exclusive policy more stringent.

The political condition of the empire was not without its influence upon the treatment of the foreigners. The dynasty of Ming had built itself up on the expulsion of a foreign domination, and the reassertion of Chinese nationality; and the Manchu dynasty, which succeeded it, itself intrusive, and conscious of its insecure hold upon power, was naturally jealous of the presence and influence of the races which were overturning and founding empires in so many other parts of Asia.

It was, then, as we conceive, mainly from apprehension, and in self-defense, that impediment after impediment was thrown in the way of free intercourse with Europeans, that the avenues of access were one after another closed, until, just a century since, European commerce was limited to the one port of Canton, and otherwise placed under severe and oppressive restrictions. And we are compelled to acknowledge that, however much there may have been in it of narrow-mindedness and ignorance, there was also political sagacity, and a true instinct of self-preservation. The consequences of a want of like foresight elsewhere are apparent, in the overthrow of native institutions, and the establishment of European supremacy, in the fairest portions of both the Old and New worlds. We can hardly avoid being touched with some compunction, at witnessing the final failure of a plan of national conduct so long and perseveringly pursued, and the forcible intrusion, on a scale that shakes the fabric of Chinese empire to its foundations, of the influence so anxiously excluded.

It remains for us to review the history of the efforts made since the epoch of modern intercourse to introduce Christianity into China, or the history of the Catholic and Protestant missions.

During the sixteenth century, the Catholic church, although feeling at home the staggering effect of the severest blows ever struck at its supremacy, was in the midst of a career of active and successful propagandism abroad. This was especially the case after the foundation of the order of Jesuits, about the middle of the century. Jesuit missionaries accompanied nearly all the fleets which bore Spanish and Portuguese adventurers to the various parts of the newly opened world. One of Loyola's original associates, St. Francis Xavier, the apostle of the Indies and of Japan, made the earliest attempt to establish a mission in China; but he died in 1552, upon the borders of the empire, before he had succeeded in overcoming the difficulties thrown in his way, more by his own countrymen than by the Chinese. The Jesuit Ricci was the first who effected an entrance. He was suffered to pass the frontier about 1580, after years of delay and negotiation, and for a long time he preached and taught in the neighborhood of Canton. This, however, was to him only the school in which to fit himself for a higher and wider field of action. Not content with the precarious toleration which the provincial authorities allowed him, he sought to win for Christian missionaries such a position in the very heart of the country as should command universal toleration, and should recommend Christianity to the acceptance of the masses of the people. He pushed forward from point to point, more than once rebuffed and driven back to his old place, until at last, in 1601, he was admitted to the capital, and was able to found there the Jesuit mission, which, for more than two hundred years, maintained an existence always remarkable and often full of honor and success. The character which he impressed upon the mission it retained through its whole history. He was a man of vast acquirements and no ordinary capacity; he was versed in literature, philosophy, and science, an accomplished representative of the best culture of the West. He felt the vast superiority of European knowledge and skill in its application over those of the Chinese, and his aim was to utilize that superiority in every possible way for the benefit of European religion. His science had won him great consideration at Nanking; the curious instruments which he brought as presents opened to him the gates of the capital and of the court; like influences procured him the imperial permission to remain, spite of the opposition of the Board of Rites, under whose jurisdiction such matters properly fell. Thus it continued to be from that time forth. The Peking mission became a kind of European Academy, filled with men eminent for learning and ability, selected with reference to the wants, and often by the express request, of the emperor; men who placed themselves and their knowledge at the disposal of the state, filled high offices, executed important trusts, and by their usefulness as mathematicians, geographers, astronomers, mechanicians, artists, teachers, and by the respect and influence thereby assured to them, were able to maintain for a long time the struggle in behalf of Christianity against the ever growing fear and jealousy of it on the part of the general government of the empire. This was a bold and brilliant system of tactics, and it held out high hopes of success; had the times and the places been more propitious, it might have won such a triumph in the East as when, in the West, the Roman empire was converted to Christianity. But it was also not without its special dangers, as it brought the new faith and its defenders into more conspicuous opposition with the native institutions and their representatives, and awakened political and scientific, as well as religious, jealousies and hatreds. In the end it failed utterly. Niggardly toleration for a season was the best boon it could obtain for Christianity; the state policy of exclusion of everything foreign, as being valueless to the welfare, and dangerous to the stability, of the empire, held inexorably on its way; while the missionaries were honored at Peking, and suffered to worship as they would, their religion was proscribed and persecuted everywhere else. The mission sank into the unhappy position of a knot of personal satellites of the emperor, and unrewarded servants of the empire, and at last became extinct. We will briefly trace its history during the interval.

As soon as the news of Ricci's success reached the West, he was appointed Superior of all the Chinese missions, and a numerous band of laborers was sent out to work under his direction. For some time all went well. But, shortly after Ricci's death, the opposition of those who were jealous of European influence at the capital prevailed, and an edict was obtained by which the missionaries were expelled from the country, and all exercise of their religion forbidden. Many of them remained in hiding, protected by the friends they had made, both in the court and among the people, and waiting for better times. At this period the troubles and disorders which led to the overthrow of the dynasty were breaking out in every province. The friends of the missionaries succeeded in having them authorized to reappear, as men whose knowledge and capacity might be made useful to the empire. Adam Schall, the most eminent among them, was made chief of the astronomical board, and, about 1640, was set to casting cannon for the imperial use. But the dynasty, oppressed at once by rebellion and foreign invasion, was doomed to fall; in 1644, Peking fell into the hands, first of the rebels, and then of the Manchus: the latter remained its masters, and the masters of the empire.

The change of dynasty made no difference in the condition of the mission, although, of course, the Christian communities suffered, and Christian missionary labor was greatly impeded, by the disturbances and civil wars which desolated the empire. Schall was continued in his offices and dignities, and received unusual marks of favor from the first Manchu emperor, whose attachment to him was excessive, and over whom he wielded a powerful influence. With the regents who, after the death of the emperor, conducted for a time the affairs of state during the minority of his son, afterwards the great Kang-hi, the case was different; and the enemies of the missionaries were able once more to set on foot a persecution more violent than the previous one. In 1665, the Christian religion was placed under ban; the missionaries were thrown into prison, and condemned to deportation into the depths of Tartary, while Schall, the chief mark for jealousy and hatred, was sentenced to an ignominious death. An earthquake prevented the execution of the sentence, and frightened the persecutors. Schall was released, but immediately died. Four others were retained, that they might serve the empire, and the rest, twenty-five in number, were sent to Canton and thrust out of the country.

Science once more raised the missions from their low estate. Their chief persecutor, and Schall's successor as head of the astronomical board, proved himself a terrible ignoramus and bungler in his profession. In constructing the state calendar, a matter of the highest consideration in China, he had even allotted to the new year an intercalary month to which it was not entitled! This and other errors were proved upon him by the missionaries, in presence of the young emperor, who had now assumed the reins of power. Their triumph was complete; their foe was disgraced, and Verbiest installed in his place; and the admiration and confidence of the greatest and ablest monarch who ever sat on the throne of China was given to the missionaries, never to be withdrawn. He became their eager pupil, and their attached friend and protector. The victims of the recent persecution were at once recalled to their old fields of labor; and some years later, in 1692, the emperor's direct and sovereign authority carried through the tribunals, in spite of their reluctance and opposition, a decree which granted full toleration to Christianity throughout the whole empire. The reign of Kang-hi is the period of the greatest prosperity of the Catholic missions in China. It is also the period of the most active and honorable participation of the missionaries in the affairs of the country. Verbiest again founded cannon, for use in the wars against the Tartars. Gerbillon negotiated a treaty of peace and amity with the Russians on the northern frontier. The emperor was cured of a dangerous fever by the use of quinine. The great work of constructing an accurate map of the whole empire was successfully accomplished.

An unfavorable change, which, even before the close of the reign of Kang-hi, came over the condition and prospects of the Chinese mission, was due to dissensions among the missionaries themselves. Ricci had been very tolerant of the weaknesses of Chinese character and the prejudices of Chinese education, and had sought to adapt to them, so far as was possible, the doctrine which he preached. He had seen no sufficient objection to permitting the practice of those ceremonies of official and ancestral worship which made up the substance of the orthodox state and popular religion. He regarded them as the "peculiar institution" of the empire, which had a civil character merely, and upon which it was highly unadvisable to lay a disturbing finger, lest the great work of spreading the gospel among the benighted heathen of the empire should thereby suffer hindrance; for every religion which had as yet obtained permanent foothold in the country had been compelled to respect and adopt those venerable rites. His view was a highly politic, but probably also a sincere, one; and it was correct, at least so far as this, that the Chinese generally performed the ceremonies as mere inherited forms, connecting no idolatrous or other meaning with them. Unquestionably, however, they were by origin, and in their real nature, superstitious and idolatrous, and it could be but a degraded and lifeless Christianity which would permanently tolerate them. Differences of opinion respecting their character and the manner in which they were to be dealt with had prevailed from the beginning among the Jesuits themselves; yet these, as a body, adopted the views of Ricci. The Dominicans and missionaries of other orders as generally condemned them. The dispute, aggravated by the rivalry of the monastic orders, and even by political and national jealousies, long raged high, greatly to the scandal of the unbelievers and the detriment of the missions. Both sides appealed to Rome, and several discordant decisions were, in the course of the seventeenth century, provisionally pronounced by the Holy See, subject to revision upon further examination; yet the scale evidently leaned strongly against the views defended by the Jesuits. The latter were then so indiscreet as vastly to complicate the question by appealing to their friend and patron, the emperor, and making him a party to its adjudication. He, himself an eclectic and an indifferent in matters of religion, as Chinese emperors have long been wont to be, pronounced a decision, as was to be expected, in favor of the Jesuits and of the Chinese rites, declaring the latter to be free from all taint of idolatry, and altogether innocent and praiseworthy. But unfortunately, after the maturest deliberation, the case was decided at Rome the other way. Here were two irresistible forces, the infallibility of the pope and the universal authority of the emperor, formally arrayed in opposition to one another; neither could give way, but the missions had to feel the direful effects of their collision. Repeated embassies from the pope to the emperor only led to violent disputes, and to the exile, imprisonment, and persecution of the legates; while the imperial favor was withdrawn from the missions, and the continued toleration of the missionaries within the borders of the empire made conditional upon their giving a promise in writing to make no opposition to the rites, and to remain all their lives in the country. Hardly, however, had the last papal legate returned from his futile mission, when, in 1722, the great Kang-hi died.

Yung-ching, his son and successor, was a ruler of abilities not unworthy of his father, but a man of stern temper, and who cared little for the society and personal instructions of the missionaries. As the personal protection of the emperor had long been the main defense of the missions, prohibition and persecution now immediately followed. In answer to the expostulations of his European servants at Peking, the emperor gave them, with his own mouth, the explanation of the course which he deemed it for the interests of the empire to pursue, using these remarkable words: "You wish all the Chinese to become Christians, and your law requires it; that I know very well. But in that case, what should we be? the subjects of your kings? Your Christians recognize none but you; in times of trouble they would listen to no voice but yours. I know that at present there is nothing to fear; but when your vessels should come by the thousands and tens of thousands, there would be trouble."

We have here the key to the whole policy of the Chinese, in respect to both the religion and the commerce of the West, as it was gradually developed and established, under the most enlightened sovereigns who have ever ruled over the empire. Their intolerance of Christianity had no religious motive; but they feared the men of Europe. They feared them for the very qualities which they admired in them, and turned to their own profit — for their energy of character and their vastly superior knowledge. They could bear the growth of no such powerful influence as Christianity might be expected to become, to the decay of the native institutions, the ruin of the ruling dynasty, and the final imposition of a foreign domination.

The history of the Chinese missions after the death of Kang-hi may be told in few words. The prohibitory edict of Yung-ching was never repealed. The missionaries at Peking were allowed to remain, to recruit their numbers from time to time, to retain their civil offices and dignities, and to practice by themselves the ceremonies of their religion; but as Christian missionaries they were forbidden to labor, nor was the presence of Europeans tolerated except at the capital. Yet, during this and the following reigns, the exiled laborers stole quietly back to their posts, and continued their old labors in secret, and under the constant dread of discovery. This was, indeed, the best and most heroic epoch of Catholic Christianity in China; the annals of the church can hardly show more noble examples of self-devotion, of persevering labor in the midst of discouragement and danger, of patient endurance of a life of hardships, of fortitude and resignation in meeting torture and death, than were exhibited by the Chinese missionaries. Not a few of the native Christians were also called to yield up life, or to go into distant exile, for their religion; and most of them, if we may believe the accounts handed down to us, worthily stood the test; while the success of the work of proselyting was hardly less than it had been in the halcyon days of European influence at the imperial court.

To the brief rule of Yung-ching succeeded, in 1736, the long and prosperous reign of Kien-lung, ending with his abdication in 1796. The attachment of the latter to his European artists, mechanicians, and astronomers, was very great, but he adhered inflexibly to the established policy of prohibition of Christianity in the empire, and a slight relaxation of the vigilance and violence of the local authorities of the provinces in discovering and punishing its sectaries was the nearest approach to toleration which could be made during all the latter part of the century which had opened with such signs of promise. But now troubles of another kind came to interrupt the progress of the missions. The order of Jesuits was suppressed. The French revolution put an end to the special support which the Chinese mission had long received from the French government, and the troubled state of Europe, and the prostration of the Romish church, cut off other sources of supply, both of laborers and of means of their support. The Peking mission grew weaker and weaker, and in 1820 Tao-kwang, upon his accession to the throne, drove out its last remaining representative. Yet has the Catholic church never relinquished its hold upon China; its numerous missionaries still traverse the empire in disguise, keeping up in every city the long established communities of Christians; and its votaries are still counted even by hundreds of thousands. It would, however, be an error to account Catholic Christianity as a power among the Chinese people, or even as having any vital and self-sustaining force in the empire. There is reason to apprehend that its victories have ever been nominal more than real; that its standard of proselytism has been fixed far lower than would satisfy the requirements of the Protestant missions. It is not especially difficult to win, from a people so little attached to any religion of its own as the Chinese, a verbal acknowledgment of the truth of Christian doctrine, submission to baptism, and partial or occasional compliance with the ceremonial practices of the Romish church; to communicate a real knowledge of Christianity, and the possession of its spirit, is something very different. That the great majority of the millions of converts reckoned by the Catholic missions since their establishment have been converts in form only, is past all reasonable doubt; it were uncharitable to attempt to say just how many may have been of another character. Some appreciation of the spirit in which the later missionary operations are carried on may be won from the fact that a considerable item among them is the baptizing, under false pretenses and by unconsecrated hands, of infants considered to be at the point of death from sickness. At all events, even Catholics can hardly refuse to acknowledge that Catholic Christianity has as completely failed to make conquest of China, or to establish itself firmly and securely within the limits of the empire, as did its predecessor, Nestorian Christianity.

Since the beginning of the present century a new era

of missionary effort has been inaugurated, under the auspices of the Protestant societies of England, Germany, and America. With the history of this movement our readers are already too well acquainted to need that more than the briefest sketch of it should here be presented. The first Protestant missionary was Morrison, who landed in the country in 1807. The contrast between his career and that of Ricci well illustrates the difference in aim and spirit of the two missions of which they were respectively the founders. Morrison established himself in the most quiet manner at Canton, and devoted his attention especially to two works — the preparation of a dictionary, and the translation of the Bible; works intended to serve as auxiliaries to those who should come after him. He maintained a weekly religious service, but founded no church, and sought not to measure the usefulness of his mission by the number of converts made, and the degree of public attention excited. During his whole life — he died in 1834 — he never set foot farther within the interior of the country than Canton. This modest and unaggressive policy was rendered necessary by the changed condition of the empire, taken in connection with the natural limits to the efficiency of Protestant missionaries. To attempt a clandestine entrance into the interior, when every avenue of access was jealously guarded, and open instruction and proselytizing impracticable, would have been useless. The only thing to be done was to begin in confessed weakness and obscurity, and to wait; to lay a foundation, and to hope that better times would build the superstructure. All the ground accessible to the acknowledged missionary was soon occupied, and the expansion of the missions has kept even pace with the unclosing of the empire. During their earlier period, especially, attempts were made to gain influence among the colonies of Chinese emigrants, who are to be found scattered all over the coasts and islands of the Indian and Southern oceans, wherever there is gain to be made by industry and enterprise; but the moderate success met with, and the gradual opening of China itself, have caused them to be for the most part relinquished. More than two hundred men have, during fifty years, been sent out by the various societies. Unlike the Jesuits, they have addressed themselves primarily and chiefly to the common people. They have published numerous editions of the whole or parts of the Bible, in different translations; they have reduced many of the popular colloquial dialects for the first time to a written form, in Chinese or Roman characters, and in these or in the literary language have composed and circulated hosts of tracts, and of elementary text-books in history, geography, natural science, and the like. They have been active and successful in collecting and communicating knowledge of the language, literature, history, and institutions of the empire. If they are not unfrequently sneered at by the Catholics for the limited sphere of their labors, and for their misapplied activity in scattering abroad books which in the great majority of cases must be wasted and lost, the sneer is an undeserved one, and comes moreover with a bad grace from those who have themselves signally failed in an opposite course of policy. The Catholic and Protestant systems have not yet come into competition with one another upon the same ground, as may soon be the case, in order that their relative efficiency may be tested. Great hopes have been built upon the complete opening of access to all parts of the empire, which appears now imminent. Yet it should not fail to be borne in mind that but a small part of the obstacles to penetrating the country with civilizing and Christianizing influences will thus be removed. Of all regions of the world, China is the hardest and least promising field for such labor. The whole character of the people, both in its positive and its negative traits, and, not less, their absorption in the struggle for existence forced upon them by the immense over-populousness of the empire, tell powerfully against the reception of the new doctrines; and no one should be so thoughtless as to expect that, where Nestorian and Roman missionaries have toiled for centuries without any abiding harvest, there is now to be a speedy and notable change for the better. We should ourselves rejoice to see reason to believe that the Chinese are more likely to be penetrated with a new spirit, and to rise in the scale of nations, from free intercourse with Europeans, than to lose what they already have, and to suffer national degradation and extinction.

IV.

MÜLLER'S CHIPS FROM A GERMAN WORKSHOP.[1]

OUR notice of this important work, which was published in England not less than two years ago, comes a little late (1869). But we were willing to await the time when the appearance of the American (authorized) reprint should have put it in the hands or within the reach of more of our readers. Everybody now knows it, at least by repute, as one of the striking books of the decade; as excelled in interest by none of Professor Müller's former publications, great as has been the acceptance which these have won. Their author has so gained the ear of the reading public, that anything which he may send out is sure of a wide circulation and the most favorable consideration. We rejoice that the present volumes come forth with this prestige, for they are worthy to be extensively studied, and cannot fail to exert a valuable influence in moulding the views of thoughtful men. They are in advance of the general opinion, but in the direction in which that opinion seems to be moving. The mode of their usefulness is twofold: as they furnish authentic information respecting the religious ideas and mythical fancies of periods and races lying outside our European Christian civilization; and as they instigate us to view these in

[1] *Chips from a German Workshop.* By Max Müller, M. A., etc. Vol. I. *Essays on the Science of Religion.* Vol. II. *Essays on Mythology, Traditions, and Customs.* New York: Charles Scribner & Co. 1869. 12mo. Pp. xxxv., 374, and 402.

their right relation to one another and to Christianity. No one living, probably, is better qualified than Professor Müller for the task which he has here undertaken. His specialty, the study of the Veda, sets him in the very heart of the myths and creeds and rites of the Indo-European peoples; and hardly any one has studied them more deeply, or in a more original spirit, than he. The circle of Vedic divinities and their Greek correspondents are his most engrossing theme; but he is hardly less full upon the subject of the Zend-Avesta; while the monotheism of the Semites, the dry utilitarian precepts of Confucius, the dizzying doctrines of Buddhism, and the simple beliefs of half-civilized American aborigines, receive also not a little of his attention. Such trustworthy and comprehensive information, so attractively presented within so brief compass, is not elsewhere to be found by the student of the general religious history of mankind. Made up, as it is, of independent essays, collected and reprinted with little change, the work has not the order and completeness of a systematic treatise; but it is more easily read than such a treatise would be; each essay is a whole in itself, and not long enough to fatigue the attention of any one who is capable of deriving profit from the instruction it offers. There is also, it must be confessed, some repetition, which we might wish that the author had been willing, by a little additional labor in rewriting, to avoid; yet the fault is one of trivial consequence in comparison with the solid merits of the work.

So large, and so much the most important, part of the two volumes deals with religions, that the work as a whole is fairly to be reckoned as religious, although only the first volume purports by its title to be such. That title, by the way, is not quite happily chosen: the preface alone is of the nature of an "essay on the science of religion;" the rest are rather essays on specific religions, as contributions to a science of religion. This science the author would fain see constructed after the model of the science of language, and founded upon a comparative study of all the religions which prevail or have prevailed upon the earth, and upon an understanding of them as the diverse products and expressions of one universal religious faculty or instinct. He pleads with much fervor and eloquence for the free and impartial submission of all religions, Christianity included, to this scientific investigation, this historical and comparative examination; urging in its favor the authority of the old Christian Fathers, and the advantage certain to accrue to us in the better comprehension and estimation of our own religion, not less than of those with which it is compared. He earnestly protests, at the same time, against the prevailing judgment of heathen religions as products of human depravity, sacrilegious devil-worships, worthy of unmixed condemnation; and insists upon their claim to be regarded as earnest, though erring, attempts on the part of short-sighted humanity to solve the same great problems to which our own faith is an answer.

Professor Müller fully recognizes the difficulty of persuading the great body of those who hold the Christian religion to let it become the object of a scientific scrutiny, along with the rest, as if it were of like substance with these. Their feelings are almost invincibly opposed to such treatment. Their religion, to them, is no product of a human instinct, but a body of absolute truth, supernaturally revealed, and obtainable in no other way. Nor are Christians alone likely to be found impracticable. The sincere advocates of every creed under heaven will insist on making a similar reservation. You may analyze and compare other men's religions as you will, tracing their various features to certain traits of human nature, or influences of human history and institutions; but each one's own faith is something of a different class. The Moslem has authority for all that he believes, in the infallible inspiration of his prophet; the Brahman claims that his Veda has existed from all eternity, and is itself a foundation of truth, undemonstrable and unassailable; the Buddhist vaunts the superhuman wisdom and power of the dreamy ascetic who taught him to aspire to extinction — and so with the rest. Only the Chinese, who have never arrogated to their great teacher anything but superior insight and purity of heart, will be liberal enough to join heartily with the votaries of the new science, along with those who elsewhere may have risen, or fallen, into a Chinese indifferentism. It is in vain to tell each one that, if his creed really contains the essence of divine wisdom, the most searching and impartial study and comparison will only bring its superiority more clearly to light: he will see an indignity in the very quest.

But even those who allow the impartial comparison of all religions have room to doubt the feasibility of a science of religion. Religion is so intricately intertwined with the whole of human thought and action that it hardly admits of being separated and considered apart, completely and distinctly. Its substance — human opinions and convictions — is of too subjective a character to be easily and safely handled; and the creeds which strive to express it, the rites and observances which it prompts, are wont to be, as our author well shows, untrustworthy witnesses to its true character. They are very unlike the words and forms and phrases of which human speech consists: these have enough of the concrete and objective about them to bear scientific treatment. A science of religion seems almost as little to be looked for as a science of human opinion, or of manners and customs.

These, it may be alleged, are merely difficulties in the way, and the progress of study and of the enlightenment of general opinion will show them not to be insuperable. But we do not see even the possibility of a science of religion upon just the basis which Müller would establish for it. If the bulk of human religions have their origin in the universal facts of human nature and the variety of human character and circumstances, then something like a scientific exposition of their rise and development may be possible; not otherwise. According to what may be called the naturalistic view, now accepted by many of the students of human history, the religious feeling is called forth in the first instance, and guided in its growth, by men's recognition of a power without them and infinitely superior to them, manifested in the phenomena of the world which surrounds them; by their irresistible disposition to attribute to this power an anthropomorphous form or forms, paralleling its action with that which they best understand and see to be most efficient within the sphere of their own consciousness and observation; and by the attempt to settle their own relation to it, and put themselves in communication with it, in order to the obtaining of good and the averting of evil. Man is the only creature capable of forming the fundamental conception of something in nature higher and greater than himself, and of feeling the desire to penetrate its secrets; but he acquires this capacity along with his rise above his primitive and natural condition, his utterly savage state. There are races, even now, so sunken and absorbed in the lowest wants of their animal nature, that no religious idea has ever dawned upon their minds, any more than the idea of beauty, or the love of virtue. In different races such ideas make their appearance at different epochs of mental progress, and assume a very diverse form, with corresponding influence upon life and character. With some, religion is from the outset an ennobling element; it elevates and makes them happy; with others, it begins and remains abject and cringing; it is full of dread, like the fear of children in the dark; it expresses itself in deprecatory rites, and is fertile of superstitions of every kind. On the whole, it follows a certain direction of advance; it makes its way from blinder and more childish views to such as are clearer and stronger; it begins with finding gods and demons everywhere, in its naïve ascription of each class of phenomena to a separate agency; it tends, where character and circumstances favor, toward the apprehension of a unity in all the varying phenomena of the universe, and a oneness of their creator and manager — that is to say, it tends from polytheism toward monotheism.

Now it appears to us that no one who does not take something like the view thus set forth of the rise and growth of the heathen religions has any right to talk of a science of religion at all; and it is at this fundamental point that we deem Professor Müller's science wanting in soundness and consistency. His religious philosophy presents a curious analogy with his linguistic philosophy. In language, he adopts and teaches the current methods of historical research, treating human speech as the product of a continuous process of development from elements the most simple and formless, carried on along with its use, by men who have spoken it, until he gets back to the very beginning: there he assumes a miracle — not precisely a scriptural, but a kind of natural or materialistic miracle; namely, an original instinct, different from anything which men have nowadays, vouchsafed for the express purpose of setting in motion the process of linguistic development, and withdrawn when it had answered that purpose. So also, at the very fountain-head of all religion he finds — we must not say an instinct, since he criticises and rejects that word as used by Renan, but what is equivalent — an intuition and a feeling, "an intuition of God and the immediate feeling of dependence on God," which "could only have been the result of a primitive revelation." This intuition he regards as neither monotheistic nor polytheistic; and its natural expression is simply the dogma, "God is God." Elsewhere he calls it a "feeling of sonship," and qualifies it as *henotheistic*—that is to say, as not apprehending or believing in more gods than one, although at the same time not consciously holding the unity of God.

So far as this is intelligible to us, it is altogether unsatisfactory. If Müller means simply to maintain that, before the distinct and conscious recognition of a plurality of gods, there must have existed in the minds of untutored men a dim and undefined apprehension of an extra-human force or forces at work in the world about them, he is only presenting in a somewhat peculiar form the prevailing view stated above. But his phraseology does not fairly imply this; it seems hardly accordant with any other theory than that of an original paradisiac condition of man, as a being with powers miraculously developed and knowledge stored up by superhuman means, instead of such a one as any of us might have been if flung at birth into a desert land and nurtured by wild beasts. We do not suppose that our author holds such a theory, although he nowhere, that we have noticed, expresses himself distinctly either for or against it. Doubtless he believes in a general upward progress of mankind since the earliest ages, in the gradual development of powers at first possessed unconsciously, in the accumulation of knowledge and the acquisition of the power to use it and reason upon it. That the untaught and undeveloped generations of men were capable of an intuition of God, and a feeling of sonship, seems to us quite inconceivable: we fail to see upon what good ground the assumption can be maintained as plausible. So far as Müller himself attempts to support it by argument and illustration, he is not very successful. Thus, to prove the priority of monotheism, he alleges the fact that "in no language does the plural exist before the singular." But the same fact, it is evident, would equally prove that the existence of one sole tree or bird was believed in before that of many trees or birds; that men were monodruists and monornithists before they became polydruists and polyornithists. If we do not misunderstand him, he would account for the separation of one God into many gods in such ways as this: Men first said *tonat*, βροντᾷ, meaning '*he* thunders'—that is to say, he, the one God. Then, since the thunder came from the sky, they occasionally said also "the sky thunders;" and this mode of speech grew into a habit, so that finally "he" and "the sky" became irretrievably mixed together in their minds, "by the almost irresistible force of language," and they confusedly looked upon the latter as one of the names of the former. And, having committed similar confusions in speaking of other manifestations of the one supreme deity, they found themselves all at once in possession of a set of names for him, as sky (*Jupiter*, Ζεύς) and so on, which they imagined to be names of so many distinct beings. And so they fell into polytheism.

We should be very glad to make an exposition of this peculiar theory which should be less implausible and even self-refuting, but we know not how to do so. It attributes to words a kind of power over the mind which we can only compare to jugglery, and which we cannot but regard as inconsistent with any sound view of human speech. It is not, however, altogether at variance with opinions respecting language which our author has elsewhere expressed. He inclines generally to regard words as the masters rather than the servants of ideas, holding that the former condition the latter, instead of being produced for their service, and that no abstract conception is for a moment possible without a vocable expressing it. Thus, also, in the essay on "Semitic Monotheism," from which we have taken a part of the expressions quoted or referred to above, he combats with much vigor Renan's theory of an original monotheistic tendency in the character of the Semitic races (Hebrews, Arabs, etc.), and ascribes whatever may be peculiar to them in this regard to the peculiarity of their language, the radical meaning in their words being much more persistent than in those of other tongues — a Semitic epithet remaining an epithet merely, while in Indo-European languages, for example, its origin is readily forgotten, and it assumes the value of a specific designation. The Semite could never be cheated into imagining that, in the phrase Ζεὺς βροντᾷ, Ζεὺς signified a being instead of a part of the material creation, because its appellative meaning, 'the bright,' or 'shining,' would not be wholly lost from memory. This characteristic feature of Semitic speech is very suitably brought in as an element in the discussion; but most scholars, we are persuaded, will think that Müller overestimates its importance, and that his solution of the problem is, to say the least, not more satisfactory than that of the author he opposes. The Semites have managed to find real names for all the objects they have wished to designate; and if their mythopœic or theopœic tendency had been as pronounced as that of the leading Indo-European races, we see no reason to believe that they would not have fabricated as many myths, and believed in as many gods. In fact, as our author points out, if all the Semitic races are taken into view, it is found that they have been polytheistic enough; and he ascribes their exalted doctrine of one God directly to the one man Abraham, whom he believes to have received it by divine revelation. So that, after all, it appears that the original intuition of one God, even when aided by the unyielding processes of Semitic word-formation, has not been able to furnish the later world with a single monotheistic religion. It is not without show of reason that Müller rejects Renan's theory of a Semitic "instinct" for monotheism, as refuted by the general Semitic worship of Baal, Moloch, Ashtaroth, and the rest; but what shall we think of his own universal "intuition" of humanity, which in every race under heaven has been blinded and baffled by its own blundering attempt at expression, and of which the appointed office has had to be filled by a later superhuman agency?

The vexed question of Semitic monotheism is much too recondite to be followed out here; we can only touch upon it in passing; and would say to our readers that two more eloquent and interesting articles than those of Renan and Müller upon it are not easily to be found in the whole range of discussion upon this class of subjects.

There is yet another point, closely connected with those already treated, in regard to which our author appears to us not less guilty of exaggerating the influence of expression; and it is a point of prime consequence. Mythology, not less than polytheism, is laid by him at the door of language. His views as to the relation of myths and words are drawn out more fully in the second series of his Lectures on Language than in the present work; yet the second volume of Chips contains his celebrated Oxford Essay on Comparative Mythology, which sketched the outline of his whole system, and even brought forward many of the details which have attracted the attention of scholars, and led to no small comment and controversy. He goes so far as to declare mythology a kind of "disease of language," and to maintain that men were led along into mythic fancies, as into a belief in many gods, without their own knowledge and almost against their own will, by the overpowering influence of the phrases they used. It may be that his expressions do him partial injustice, and that his views are not so different from those of other scholars as they appear to be; but we are persuaded that he at any rate presents the subject in a false light, and lays an unsound and untenable foundation for the whole study of myths. We at the present day say, "The wind dashes the rain against the house," "The cloud darts lightnings at the earth," and so on, in what we call figurative or poetic phrase, without running the least risk of sliding away into a belief that the wind and cloud are superhuman beings, acting after the manner of men. Why is this? Because, says Professor Müller, words have less power over us than over the ancient generations; because our thought is withered; because our language is not suffering under that specific disease: and more of the same sort. But in this he is himself a mythopœist. One of the essential parts of myth-making is the substitution of an analogy for an explanation. To express by a figure something which is only half-understood or wholly obscure, then to dwell upon the figurative expression as if it were a true definition, and let it hide from sight the thing meant to be expressed, is a good process in mythology, though not in science. What is the power of a word? A word is nothing but the sign of a conception; the only force in action is the mind which forms the conception, and uses the word as its sign. We are saved from making gods of the wind and cloud by the fact that we have long since left behind us that stage of development in which we inclined to see in the works of nature the acts, and effects of acts, of beings similar to men. This inclination, now, seems to us to be incontestably the true mythopœic force, and it should receive the first place and consideration in all theoretic discussion of mythologic fancies. The linguist may then go on to show how designation by a word is an important step in the process of personification, how it constitutes an external support for the conceptions to cling to, and furnishes the means whereby the figurative statement is handed down more faithfully than its explanation; so that the two are finally divorced from one another, and there remains a myth, with its proper meaning unintelligible to those who report and credit it. Thus the study of language is proved to have a most important bearing upon that of mythology, although not, as our author is inclined to claim, its actual foundation.

As regards the details of his mythological investigations, it is well known that Müller is at variance with many of the best specialists in this department on the continent, who regard a part of his comparisons and explanations as fanciful and erroneous, and his etymologies as forced. Especially, they refuse to follow him in his identification of almost all mythic figures with the sun or the dawn, and his explanation of numberless myths as growing out of the relation of those two manifestations. Whether, however, he be finally proved wrong or right, it is certain that he has struck a very productive vein and worked it in a most ingenious manner, and that the views he has suggested and the discussions he has stirred up cannot fail to promote the rapid advancement of the study of primitive religions.

The manner and style of these essays of Müller, as of his larger and more serious works heretofore published, are worthy of high praise. No English author in this department has a greater power as a writer of English than he; none writes with more fervid thought or more genuinely eloquent expression. Of course, the essays are not of entirely equal merit in these respects; and it should be especially noted that one who commences his perusal of the work with the first essay in the first volume, the author's lecture at Leeds on the Veda, will gain a too unfavorable idea of the whole, of which it is the heaviest and least attractive portion, though replete with valuable information. The same paper exhibits, to our apprehension, a rather marked tendency to put its author forward as *the* editor of *the* Veda, instead of *an* editor of *a* Veda. The same tendency appears here and there in other essays. That the Rig-Veda is by far the most important work of its class, no one will deny; but this does not justify the assertion that the rest are all of a merely liturgical character, and have no value independent of this one. And if he had made the good people of Leeds fully understand that the bulky quarto which he was at the pains to carry along and exhibit to them contained only about one part Veda and four parts modern Hindu commentary, of disputed worth, they might not have opened their eyes quite so widely with admiration.

Professor Müller informs us that the present volumes contain only a selection from his fugitive writings on the two classes of subjects indicated. The first includes at least one essay which we greatly regret that he did not class with those destined to oblivion. We mean that upon the Aitareya Brâhmana of Professor Haug. It is in all respects unworthy of him, being an unreserved and uncritical encomium of a work which, along with very great merits, has some striking defects, shows signs of hasty preparation, and unduly depreciates the labors of others in the same field. Nor is the inclusion of the essay recommended by any interesting discussion of points of general importance contained in it, or by sound and instructive views upon the period of Hindu antiquity to which it relates; while it is especially objectionable on account of the note which its author has added at the end.

In the article as originally published ("Saturday Review" for March 19, 1864), Professor Müller had been ill-advised enough to insert an attack upon his fellow Sanskritists, the collaborators in the great Sanskrit lexicon published at St. Petersburg, charging them with having formed a mutual-admiration society, with the intent to "sing each other's praises in the literary journals of Russia, Germany, and America," and to "speak slightingly" of all outside of that circle. What had happened to call forth this accusation is hard to discover; unless perhaps that more than one of the scholars referred to had recently (without any apparent or known concert) joined in defending the lexicon and its authors from a very violent and unjust attack made upon them. At any rate,

Dr. Haug (who has quite enough merit to stand alone, and can afford to invite searching criticism instead of indiscriminate commendation) was patted on the back, and assured that, if his book should be spoken of unkindly "in the journals of the Mutual-Praise Society," this should have no effect upon the opinion of anybody whose opinion was worth having. In the "Chips," now, Müller has omitted the offensive paragraph; but he has appended to the essay a note which, instead of mitigating, has trebled the original offense. He first explains the omission, intimating the nature of the accusation made, and averring that he did not originate it, but merely repeated it from others, being convinced that there was foundation for it. He represents it as having been met "by a very loud and boisterous denial." He is sorry if he has given unnecessary pain by what he has done, and hopes that in future no reason for similar complaint will be given; if that result be produced, he will try to bear like a martyr the wrath and resentment which he has provoked. We are at a loss for words to characterize the cool effrontery of this paragraph. Its tone of magisterial assumption is not easily to be paralleled. Müller says, in effect, that a parcel of naughty persons have been caught in their naughtiness; that he has administered to them deserved correction, under which they have cried out lustily; that he is grieved at having had to hurt them so much, and make them so angry; but comforts himself with the belief that it is for their good. And this to men some of whom can show services to Sanskrit literature far superior to his own, and whose reputation for single-mindedness and candor is, to say the least, not less than his!

As regards, indeed, fairness and candor, there are implications and insinuations in this note which are not calculated to increase its author's reputation. There is, in the first place, the "very loud and boisterous denial." It is a pity that we are not informed where such a denial is to be met with; we suspect it to be a figment of Professor Müller's lively imagination. An anonymous criticism, in a periodical so little famed for impartiality and leniency of judgment as the "Saturday Review," was not likely greatly to disturb the peace of whomsoever it might be aimed at; and to those who recognized in it the hand of the Oxford Professor it was doubtless more worthy of attention as an illustration of personal character than in any other way. We are not aware that any one ever took public notice of it, excepting Professor Weber of Berlin. This eminent scholar, being himself the butt at which both Haug and Müller had chiefly aimed their arrows, could hardly remain silent without seeming to confess inability to repel the accusations laid against him; accordingly, in his *Indische Studien* (ix. 2, 1865), he reprinted the article, side by side with another very able and trenchant criticism of Dr. Haug's book, written by a Hindu and first printed in India, for the purpose of contrasting the learning and spirit of the two critics — much to the disadvantage of the Anglo-German; and then, after a few strong but dignified words in answer to the latter's insinuations, he proceeded to a very detailed and careful examination of the work which Müller had volunteered to guaranty especially against any attack he might make upon it — discussing it with a fullness of erudition certainly not at the command of any other European scholar, doing justice to its solid merits, but also pointing out, without passion and without carping, its errors and defects; thus furnishing a running commentary upon it of the highest value, and without the assistance of which no unpracticed student should venture to use the work at all. This was Weber's "denial:" if Müller describes it as "loud and boisterous," we can only infer that it must have rung bodefully in his ears.

Again, the charges of "literary rattening" which our author says that he merely alludes to, and of which he shifts the burden to Dr. Haug's shoulders, are not to be found in the latter's pages at all; they appear rather to emanate from no other person than the scholar whose attack upon the St. Petersburg lexicon was the occasion of all the after-trouble. So that the plain history of the affair seems to be this: some one falls fiercely upon the work of a company of collaborators; they unite in its defense; thereupon the aggressor reviles them as a mutual-admiration society; and Müller repeats the accusation, giving it his own indorsement, and volunteering in addition that of another scholar.

Once more, Müller refers his readers, if they are curious to see the expunged paragraphs, to the *Indische Studien*, where, he says, the review may be seen "reprinted, though, as usual, very incorrectly." It is strange that, writing especially for Englishmen, he does not send them rather to the place of original publication; apparently, he could not resist the temptation to cast in passing an additional slur upon the man whose denial had seemed to him so boisterous. In this, however, he was too little mindful of the requirements of fair dealing; for he leaves any one who may take the trouble to turn to the *Indische Studien*, and compare the version there given with that found among the "Chips," to infer that all the discordances he shall discover are attributable to Weber's "incorrectness;" whereas they are in fact mainly alterations which Müller has made in his own reprint; and the real inaccuracies are perfectly trivial in character and few in number — such printer's blunders as are rarely avoided by Germans who print English, or by English who print German. We should doubtless be doing Müller injustice if we maintained that he deliberately meant Weber to bear the odium of all the discrepancies which a comparer might find; but he is equally responsible for the result, if it is owing only to carelessness on his part.

We regard this note as by far the most discreditable

production of Professor Müller that has ever come under our notice; the epithet "outrageous" is hardly too strong to apply to it. If this is to be his style of carrying on a literary controversy, he cannot much longer claim to be treated with the ordinary courtesies of literary warfare.

It is also not quite fair and above-board that in the body of his article he notes with complacency, as supporting his own view of the matter, that Dr. Haug "calls absurd" the theories of those who hold that the lunar asterisms constituting the old Hindu zodiac were probably devised in some other country than India. For if he had dared to quote Haug's own *dictum*, his readers would have seen how weak a staff it was to lean upon. Haug is speaking of the observation of the solstices recorded in the Jyotisha, and he remarks: "To believe that such an observation was imported from some foreign country, Babylon or China, would be absurd; for there is nothing in it to show that it cannot have been made in the north-western part of India, or a closely adjacent country." That is to say, it is absurd to believe anything the contrary of which does not admit of being proved impossible! Moreover, it will be noticed how far Müller has stretched the bearing of the allegation of absurdity brought by his authority. After these two examples of his ill success in reporting the latter's opinions, we should almost be justified in adding to any further statement of his, "made, as usual, very incorrectly."

In fact, we would call attention to one more very incorrect statement made in the course of the same review. He says, respecting the date of the observation above referred to, that it "has been fixed by the Rev. R. Main at 1186 B. C." (altered in the reprint to "has been accurately fixed," etc.). But this gentleman did nothing whatever toward fixing the date in question except to take a calculation made by Archdeacon Pratt, of Calcutta, and very slightly change the value of one of the factors in it — namely, the precession of the equinoxes. Mr. Pratt had estimated the precession approximately, as is usual in calculations of this character, at one degree in seventy-two years; greater precision than this does not comport with the general conditions of the problem; and the other, by insisting upon its absolute mathematical value, committed a piece of mathematical pedantry, very much as one who should insist on a fraction of a mile in estimating the distance of the sun from us. The whole calculation, to be sure, is little better than worthless, and has been so proved;[1] but if any one is to have credit for it, it is Archdeacon Pratt, and he alone.

Astronomy is not one of Professor Müller's strong points, and it would be easy to show that others of his reasonings in this essay bearing upon astronomical subjects are unsound and without value; but we have surely already said enough to prove our thesis — that the omission of the essay and its appended note from his next edition would be a notable increase of the value of the work. We hope that in the other pair of volumes, promised as the completion of the series, he will be somewhat more tender of his fellows' reputation and of his own.

The third volume of "Chips" was issued by the author in 1870; and neither the fourth, nor any announcement of it, has yet appeared, so that the series appears to be for the present brought to an end. The concluding volume could not expect such a career as its predecessors had, since it deals with subjects comparatively accessible and often treated, and on which the distinguished author has no higher authority to speak to us than a great many of his contemporaries. Its first paper is a really valuable sketch of German literature from the earliest times; it was originally published as introduction to a volume of

[1] See below, p. 381.

selections from German authors. Among the slighter articles that follow is an account of the author's father, Wilhelm Müller, a poet of real merit, though not of wide repute, who died while his more celebrated son was a very young child. The collection is brought to a close by a lively and appreciative sketch of the life, genius, and labors of the author's patron and life-long friend, the Chevalier Bunsen, from which many will be glad to learn something of the many-sided activity and noble spirit of that truly great man. To this biographical notice are added as appendix an extended series of letters from Bunsen to Müller, making up between a quarter and a third of the readable contents of the entire volume. Their interest as materials in the hands of a biographer of Bunsen, or as parts of a special and independent tribute to him, is undeniable; whether it was well judged to put them before the world as so substantial a part of Müller's collected essays, admits of more question.

A more proper continuation of the first two volumes of "Chips" was given by their author early in 1870, in the form of four lectures "On the Science of Religion," produced at the Royal Institution in London, and variously printed and reprinted since.[1] These, however, are chiefly an expansion of the preface to the first volume of "Chips," together with an epitome of part of the information as to particular religions contained in both volumes. They do not show any noteworthy progress in the author's mind toward clear and definite views; they do not advance the plan and ground-work of the new science; and in point of style and interest of presentation they fall short of his usual standard. We venture here a further critical remark or two, on subjects related with those which have been discussed in the preceding pages.

[1] Collected in a volume at New York (Scribner & Co.) in 1872; more recently (1873) by the author himself, at London, with the addition of two later lectures, one on the Philosophy of Mythology, and one on Mistaken Analogies in Comparative Theology.

The one all-important truth, without a recognition of which there can be no foundation for a scientific or fruitful study of religions, is, in our view, clearly this: that the early religious beliefs of every race arise out of the unaided attempts of that race to explain to itself the problem of the universe, as we may call it — the mystery of man's existence, surroundings, and destiny. Every human being finds himself placed in the midst of forces which are vastly more powerful than he, and indefinitely varied in their manifestations, and of which the action, while he can neither understand nor control it, is now helpful and now hurtful to him; his own birth and death are inexplicable phenomena; the influences, in himself and others, which make for his happiness or unhappiness, he does not half comprehend; his longings and his fears seek a support outside of himself; his consciousness of good or evil desert puts itself in relation with those awful powers which seem to govern the whole of nature. No race of men — if sufficiently gifted and sufficiently developed to have a sense for all this, or to be otherwise affected than struck dumb with stupid wonder at it — could possibly help reasoning upon it, and deriving views and theories and beliefs, and framing acts and ceremonies expressing them: and these, in all their variety, depending upon the various endowments and circumstances of the different peoples, are their religions. The religion of a people is even more inseparable at the outset than later from the general mass of its thought and opinion.

If this fundamental truth be accepted, then the true method of investigation is an obvious corollary to it: the religion of each race must be studied as a whole, and in its historical connection and development. It is a historical product, the result of long growth, a structure built upon by generation after generation, one working over, modifying, and adding to that which was bequeathed it by another. The language of every race is a similar product of similar forces, another accompaniment and result of a connected historical development. This being so, those grand continuous communities (whether absolutely pure races or not) which have formed families of connected languages, will have formed related religions also: religions more or less alike, because proceeding from the same basis, but also more or less diverse, because of their discordant later growth. This is the simple ground of the parallelism between religion and language — a parallelism which, in his third lecture, Müller misunderstands and distorts most strangely. Instead of joint results of ethnic unity, twin institutions handed down through the divergent lines of relationship of each race, he makes them the causes of nationality, and dependent each in turn upon the other. It might not be easy to find a more striking example of unclear perception and unsound reasoning in all Müller's works than he exhibits in this lecture; and the views he incidentally puts forth as to the nature and history of language — especially as to its originally wild and chaotic condition, and its concentration, in three special cases, into families of related speech, by an unnatural and exceptional process, originating in the spontaneous act of certain remote generations — are unintelligible and indefensible, at variance with his own soundest teachings hitherto, and subversive of the science of language which he claims to have done so much to establish.

In criticising and setting aside certain superficial classifications of religions (which were, perhaps, hardly worth so much attention, since they would disappear of themselves in presence of a right method), Müller has forgotten to notice the most important distinction of all — that between, on the one hand, ethnic religions, which have grown up by the gradual accumulation of beliefs and practices in a whole community, innumerable individuals bearing a part in their formation; and, on the other hand, individual religions, products each of the deeper insight and uncompromising independence of some one person, who breaks the shackles of traditional faith and practice, clears away narrow superstitions and effete ceremonies, and founds upon a new basis of perceived truth a new system. Religions of the latter class, of course, can arise only in later times, and can succeed in establishing themselves only where the forms of the old religion have become hollow, and no longer faithfully represent the better insight of the times. They, too, are alone capable of extension and transfer from one race to another, of becoming "missionary religions;" for, though they have their roots in the whole body of the national faith, and for their comprehension need the most careful study of the latter, they also in a degree cut loose from it, and plant themselves on grounds which men of other races can accept and occupy.

The spirit in which the study of religions is to be pursued is equally evident from the view we have taken: it is the spirit of liberal and tolerant inquiry, of interest, of consideration and respect; often, perhaps, of pity and sorrow, but without intermixture of holy horror and indignation at the depth of human depravity displayed. If human nature has proved itself, on the whole, so weak and short-sighted, so selfish and impure, as to have won only faint glimpses of truth, and to have clothed them in wild and abhorrent forms, it is very sad; and we ought to be the more grateful for the light which we enjoy, and by which, in the same weakness of human nature, we walk but fitfully and unfaithfully. All the higher and better religions of the world confess this weakness, for they all claim to found themselves on a revelation: that is to say, they imply the impotence of man, without supernatural aid, to understand whence he comes, how he is to live, and what is to be his end. And a hearty charity and kindly compassion should be among the most trustworthy and valuable signs of a true illumination.

We may look for valuable results from Professor Müller's lectures in the directing of more enlightened attention to the study of religions, and we may expect from his wide scholarship and liberality of spirit important additions to our knowledge of religions; but we are hardly disposed to recognize him as the founder and promulgator of a new science.

V.

COX'S ARYAN MYTHOLOGY.[1]

In this work Mr. Cox has followed up a beginning which he made some years ago (1867) with his little "Manual of Mythology." The latter, in its brevity and one-sidedness, hardly merited so large a name; and it was somewhat overpraised by the adherents of the special school to which it belonged, and by those who take their cue from them. The present is a much more ambitious and elaborate effort; and it well deserves, as it will doubtless receive, general and careful attention. It is the extreme working-out, in one direction, of a tendency in mythological study which has been for some time growing in force, and has quite recently made itself very conspicuous: the tendency, namely, to shift the basis of investigation of any special mythology within the circle of the Indo-European family to the more general ground of Indo-European mythology; to treat it as a developed branch of an older stock, requiring comparison with the other branches from the same stock; at once to expand the field and to change and deepen the methods of mythologic research. This tendency began to show itself with the first establishment of Indo-European unity, and was its necessary result. When once it was impregnably demonstrated that a single community had laid the foundation of Greek, Latin, Celtic, Germanic, Slavic, Iranian,

[1] *The Mythology of the Aryan Nations.* By George W. Cox, M. A., late Scholar of Trinity College, Oxford. In two volumes. London. 8vo. 1870.

and Indian language, and had developed that language to á high degree of structural perfection, under traceable conditions of culture which were far in advance of utter barbarism, the inference was a natural one that the same community must have developed, also, a common religion: that is to say, that it must have arrived at certain apprehensions of the nature of the powers existing and at work in the world outside of man; of their modes of action and their connection with man; of man's relation to them, his origin, duties, and destiny; that it must have framed some common expression, by word, myth, and ceremony, of its religious views; and that, accordingly, some relics of this primitive faith might be plausibly looked for among the early beliefs and myths of the Indo-European nations; just as relics of their ancient tongue had been discovered, abundant and unmistakable, in even their most modern idioms. Of course, only investigation could show whether the presumed relics were actually to be found; and, if found, of what extent and value they would prove to be; and whether any one people would appear to have saved so much of the faith once shared by all that it would offer, as it were, a key to the whole. But there were indications lying upon the very surface, which awakened hope of abundant results to reward the investigator. Thus, to refer to only one or two of the most conspicuous, quoted by way of illustration a hundred times—the correspondence of *deus* and θεος with the Sanskrit *devas*, and of *Jupiter* and Ζευ(πατερ) with the Sanskrit *Dyu(pitar)*, taken in connection with the fact that *dyu* in Sanskrit signified unequivocally the bright 'sky,' or the shining 'day,' and that *deva*, its regular derivative, meant 'shining' or 'heavenly,' was like the outcrop of a rich vein, tempting the miner to explore its hidden depths. And those who entered upon the investigation soon convinced themselves that ancient India had preserved the primitive conditions with a faithfulness which was in vain to be sought elsewhere. On the one hand, the Sanskrit language offered in general, as in the examples just quoted, the clearest explanation of those names to know which is often to know the things themselves; on the other hand, the very earliest recorded period of Indian antiquity, the Vedic, wore an aspect almost to be called Indo-European. The former was to be expected, considering the recognized exceptional value of the Sanskrit as the means of Indo-European etymological research; but the other was in no wise its necessary accompaniment and counterpart; it was rather a special and exceptional piece of good fortune for the student. Indeed, by the time that Indian history had fairly begun, the state of things was entirely changed; while the classical Sanskrit retained most of its Vedic primitiveness, the religion which it expressed had gone further from the old Indo-European basis than the Greek, for example, ever went. It is because hardly even the germs of the distinctive institutions of India are to be found in the Vedas, that these are so fertile of illustration for the antehistorical Indo-European period.

Every Vedic student, then, became, almost of necessity, a student of primitive religions and a comparative mythologist. He could not help setting side by side what he found in the Veda and the analogous facts from other quarters of the world, within or without the Indo-European domain, and trying to make the one explain the other. The general theory of the early stages of religious development made rapid advance, and a host of points in the special history of Indo-European religions were brought clearly to light. Some scholars have been more active in this direction than others. Burnouf, Roth, and Kuhn were very prominent among the early investigators, and of these Kuhn has worked most continuously and most deeply. The names of others, whose activity is more recent or less effective, we need not stay to mention.

The solidity of the basis which these men have established, and the real value of the results they have built upon it, are beyond all reach of denial or cavil. The conclusions of the comparative mythologists are, within their narrow limits, not less firm than those of the comparative philologists; and they require to be carefully heeded by all who would study any part of Indo-European antiquity. When such a new field of pertinent material is thrown open, he is an unfaithful worker who does not resort to it. It is no longer possible to undertake the interpretation of Greek myths, for example, from Greek sources alone, any more than to study Greek derivations without regard to the other Indo-European tongues. There runs a constant analogy between these two departments of inquiry, and we are all the time tempted to draw upon the one for the illustration of the other. The root of a word is like the natural phenomenon in which a myth or personification takes its origin. If the latter is to be fully understood, the former must be traced out, or approached as nearly as may be. Either word or myth may have become the embodiment of special national life and feeling, to any degree: it may be, for example, instinct with the very spirit of Greek individuality; it may have so racy and local a flavor as to seem to have grown up out of the soil of Hellas: and yet it contains an inheritance from an older time, and its present aspect is the final result of a history of change and adaptation, which has to be read or our comprehension of it is imperfect. Behind the splendid pageant of Greek mythology, as behind the wonderful development of Greek speech, there lies a past of a very different character, bare and even poor in its simplicity, possessing few attractions, save for the historical student, though for him replete with the highest interest. And of that past a more faithful picture is to be found in India than the most careful and cunning search can catch and set forth from the records of the hoariest Greek antiquity. The natural conservatism of classical scholars long resisted the intrusion of the new light from the East in grammar and etymology; but the contest is now nearly over; the comparative method, through the whole extent of Indo-European speech, is acknowledged as the only true and fertile one; and the time is doubtless not far distant when the same accordance will be reached in the department of mythology and religion.

But if the main principle of the comparative method is thus sound, the details of its application are more intricate and questionable. When we come to inquire how much and what the Vedic hymns teach respecting the origin of Greek myths, there is room for all the differences of individual capacity and tendency to manifest themselves. No such bright and convincing light is cast that he who runs may read, and that error is impossible. The ante-mythical period is more fully illustrated than formerly, and the mode in which myths originate made more distinctly apprehensible. Some names are explained, and many hints toward direct interpretation are given; hardly more. Nothing stands in the way of exaggeration and abuse on the part of the upholders of the new method. Here, again, the parallelism with the study of language is close and instructive. When the Sanskrit was first brought in to the aid of Indo-European philology, there were not a few who overrated its importance, who applied it where it was not pertinent, who set it up as supreme where it should have stood second, who, without profound knowledge or critical method, were ready to solve every obscure or doubtful question by reference to a Sanskrit dictionary. The influence of such advocates was, of necessity, hurtful to the cause they espoused, strengthening the aversion of all who were inclined to shut their eyes to the new light; but for the aid and comfort thus given to the enemy, the contest would have been sooner and more absolutely settled. In a like manner, the Vedas have been, and will be, handled as a kind of spell for clearing up the darkness of Indo-European antiquity; their myths and germs of myths strained far beyond what they will bear as means of interpretation, or pressed into the service of some favorite theory; Indian material of late growth and doubtful authenticity treated as primitive, and what is exclusively Hindu put forward as belonging to the whole family. Continued study, the consenting labor of many minds, and conscientious criticism, will by degrees correct these aberrations, and save the true method, with the grand principles it involves, even out of the hands of those whose ill-judged advocacy does it present harm.

In the study of which we have thus concisely and imperfectly sketched the basis, the labors of Professor Max Müller have made a new era. His article on Comparative Mythology, in the "Oxford Essays" for 1856 (reproduced in the second volume of his "Chips from a German Workshop"), made a great sensation among English readers on both sides of the Atlantic, being to many the revelation of a field of research of which the possibility had been before unsuspected. Some of its themes he elaborated more fully in the second volume of his "Lectures on the Science of Language;" and his "Chips" contain other essays of kindred character and object. The principal significance of his work lies in two directions. In the first place, he has set forth, in his peculiarly happy style, with attractive eloquence and rich and varied illustration, the leading principles of the study, drawing toward them the public attention in a manner and to a degree that was within the reach, probably, of no other living writer. To regard him, however, as father and founder of the science (as many, especially in England, seem inclined to do), is an injustice to the great scholars who were his predecessors. He cannot fairly be claimed even to have deepened and strengthened its basis. It is precisely in his fundamental views that he is most open to adverse criticism, as being at variance with the approved tendencies of the science of the day. His assumption of a special religious faculty in man, a primitive intuition of the infinite and divine, an innate craving and recognition of a heavenly Father, instead of a capacity to see the Creator in the works of creation, a power to feel and be impressed by the supernatural, and to rise, by constant observation, comparison, and inference, higher and higher in the apprehension of spiritual truth, is not greatly different from the old assumption of a primitive revelation, with the later religions as its alterations and debasements, which he himself contends against, and would fain refute. It inverts the true order of development, putting that at the starting-point which ought to be the goal. In accordance with this, he looks upon monotheism as earlier than polytheism, and even goes so far as to find an antecedent and underlying recognition of one God in the simple naturalism of the old Vedic faith — a radical perversion, in the opinion of most students of the Veda, of its real meaning. Müller, too, believes in a corruption and depravation of earlier and purer doctrines as the ordinary course of development in religion; but he is original in making the *word* the instrument of the depravation. His peculiar views of the way in which men have blundered into error on the most vital points of belief, through simple forgetfulness of the proper meaning of the terms they were using, have been already noticed and combated,[1] and need not be dwelt upon here. They stand in legitimate connection with his theory as to the general relation of language to mind and thought. To him, the word is not the servant and instrument of the thought, but the thought itself; and speech is reason; so that errors of speech naturally turn to unreason. No one will think of denying that such errors play their part in the

[1] See above, p. 133 *seq.*

grand history of the aberrations of the human mind; but that part is far from being the leading one which Müller claims. Coming down from religion to mythology, the same tendency to exaggeration of the word is seen in his theory of "mythical phrases," as the germs of developed myths, in which we are convinced that whatever is new is ill-founded. So long as a phrase is the real expression of a conception of its utterer, so long it has a living force within itself, and is capable of growing into something else; but the moment it becomes a phrase merely, it is dead, and can only drop into oblivion.

The other, and the more striking and original part of Müller's work, lies in his actual contributions to the interpretation of myths; in the details of his application of the principles of comparative mythologic study; in the way in which he has turned Vedic elements to account for the explanation of points, especially in Greek mythology, hitherto obscure or wrongly treated. He has brought forward into the first rank of importance two personifications, of the sun and of the dawn, of which comparatively little had been made before, and has furnished a series of certainly very brilliant and attractive interpretations. The number of mythical figures under which he finds these two natural phenomena, and of mythical situations representing their various relations, mutual or other, is quite surprising. He is himself startled at it, and asks whether it can be, after all, that everything is the dawn or the sun. We may, indeed, question a part of his identifications; we may regard some of his combinations as implausible, and criticise here and there an etymology as over-venturesome; we may, in brief, think that he has a hobby and rides it too hard; yet we cannot refuse him the credit of having thrown open and exploited a vein of which his predecessors had failed to discover the wealth, and given a new and promising turn to the whole subject of mythical interpretation.

A striking feature in this part of Müller's work is the extent to which he resolves the early mythical history and heroic tradition into purely mythical elements. Common opinion has heretofore inclined to see in those grand figures which loom up on the threshold of a nation's story as it lies in the nation's mind, veritable men, only magnified and adorned by the admiration of posterity. Even the gods have been taken for deifications. Better and deeper knowledge, however, has long been turning the minds of students of antiquity in the other direction, and showing them that beings of supernatural origin are drawn to earth and made men of, by excess of anthropomorphism, much more often than the contrary. Müller has only carried this tendency farther than his predecessors; startling, for example, the classical scholar by maintaining that even the war of Troy is only a form of the contest waged in the East to recover the treasures of which the powers of darkness have robbed the day in the West; that Helen is the dawn, and Achilles a solar figure, in whose beauty and prowess, in whose wrath and sullen retiracy, in whose triumph and vengeance, in whose brief career and early death, are to be seen merely one set of variations of the theme which has engaged bard and poet since the first dawn of the poetic faculty.

There were two ways, now, of continuing the work thus begun by Müller. It might be gone over again, in a thoroughly independent and critical spirit, by some one possessed of learning and acuteness enough to test it in all its parts — examining the alleged basis of Indo-European mythical fancy laid before us in the Veda; weighing anew the value of the prominent elements there, and tracing out their development by the livelier fancy of the Greeks; striving after such a comprehensive view of both as should bring their relations into clearer light; questioning identifications and correcting etymologies. Or, on the other hand, its leading ideas and methods might be taken up and pushed on by one whose whole soul was possessed by them, with the single design of seeing how far they could be carried, and how much could be brought within their reach.

To return, then, to the work which formed the starting-point of this exposition (and of which we are more solicitous to point out clearly the position and connections than to give a detailed and exhaustive criticism) — Mr. Cox, it cannot be questioned, has followed the latter of these two ways; or rather, his mind has been taken possession of by Müller's researches, and he cannot help urging them forward with all his powers. We do not often meet with so implicit a disciple, so enthusiastic a sectary. All that Müller has said upon the subject is to him the law and the gospel; each of the master's opinions is taken up and dwelt upon and illustrated and worked out by the pupil, with a hearty assent and admiration which are not a little interesting to see. Mr. Cox does not feel that there can be any real doubt, or need be any serious discussion, of the principal points involved in Müller's theories. To him, they are already supported by an array of evidence "which will not long hence be regarded as excessive;" and they need only to be stated and illustrated in order to be received by others with the same delighted conviction with which his own mind has accepted them.

Probably there are few who will go this whole length with Mr. Cox. Many, rather, will be in some measure repelled by the fervor of his advocacy, which will seem to them more indicative of obsequiousness of mind than of independent critical judgment. We must take his work, however, for what it is, and we shall not fail to find much to admire in it, and to gain from it valuable light. There is always something winning in the earnestness of full persuasion; and the assent of many, and the interest of more, will be carried onward by the mere force of the author's current. His volumes are doubtless more picturesque, sparkling, and readable than if his nature had been cooler and his style more scientific. Mr. Cox's mind, like his master's, hardly has the scientific habit; it is genial, imaginative, constructive. In his early chapters, it is true, he commends and urges the scientific method; but he does not define it, or show us its foundation; and he does not exemplify it, if, besides a faithful resort to every available source of evidence, it demands a calm and dispassionate judgment, unbiassed by a favorite theory, and a logical and orderly plan, a progress from one established point to another. It were useless to attempt giving an analysis of the contents of the book, which is a gush of exposition and illustration of one leading idea in various forms, and, in part, seems to have been divided into chapters by an afterthought. An extract of twenty pages almost anywhere would furnish a kind of ideal section of the whole, showing all its different strata of thought and argument, and yielding specimens of its staple constituents. In a work so written there cannot but be a great deal of repetition; and we imagine that from this one a full third might be removed without omitting anything. The same myth is explained over and over again, with varying fullness; objections are answered half a dozen times; and difficulties already laid to rest arise once more to vex our souls and to be exorcised anew. A facility of ornate and eloquent expression is the author's most conspicuous quality; and it is less held in check and guided by logical closeness and accuracy than were to be desired. He lays no claim to original scholarship, excepting in the classical department of his subject; and he is neither too careful in the selection of the sources on which he relies nor too conscientious in using them. In matters of etymology he is least of all trustworthy. Take, for example, his statement (i. 171) that "Argynnis and Phoroneus, Brisêis and Achilleus, Paris and Helen, names of persons in Hellenic legend, are in the earliest songs of the Aryan family found still in their original application as names of the morning, of the sun, or of darkness." Here are a number of Müller's most venturesome conjectures, which he himself puts forth with diffidence, elevated into first-rate facts. The first two of the names quoted are somewhat doubtfully identifiable with certain common adjectives in Sanskrit, which have not in the least the character of appellatives, though, as meaning 'shining' and the like, variously applicable to the phenomena of light. To explain *Brisêis*, we have twice in the Veda the word *Bṛsaya*, as name of a (male) demon apparently. To *Achilleus* the Veda furnishes no correspondent whatever, and it is only by setting sound etymology at defiance that it can be brought into even distant connection with anything found there. And as for Paris and Helen, their oneness with the *paṇi's* and Saramâ (the former, in the Veda, the thieves of Indra's kine, the latter his messenger to reclaim them), is very far from being established; even Müller holds it but doubtfully; and it will take, we think, a much stronger internal probability than can be made out for the identification to overcome the external difficulties, in the forms of the words compared. And because *ahanâ* occurs once, and once only, in the Veda, as an epithet of the dawn — being of wholly doubtful meaning and derivation, although, but for its lack of *d*, it would be identifiable with *dahanâ*, which has a derivation, and might well enough also have been applied to the dawn, only it unfortunately is not — therefore to Mr. Cox (Preface, p. x.), "the affinity of Athênê with the Sanskrit Ahanâ and Dahanâ and the Greek Daphnê" is so clear that Liddell and Scott are to be seriously blamed for not admitting it into their Greek lexicon as a satisfactory etymology. And if he suggests a new etymology of his own, it is some such impossibility as the correspondence of the Latin Consus and the Sanskrit Gaṇeça (i. 347, note).

Nor is Mr. Cox always mindful of consistency in the interpretation he gives to mythic elements. The poisoned robe of Dejanira, in which Hercules expires, is sometimes (*e. g.* i. 56) the mantle of cloud in which the sun sinks to rest at the close of day; at other times (*e. g.* i. 56 again!), it is the representative of "the piercing rays which burn in the tropical noon-day;" and yet again (i. 66, note), the boar's tusk, which cuts short the life of Adonis, and "reappears in the myth of Odysseus, is but the thorn of winter and the poisoned robe of Herakles." The "thorn of winter," namely, because the death of summer, under the baleful influence of winter, is not only inseparably connected with the overwhelming of day by night, so that either can be substituted for the other to help out an interpretation, but — strangely enough — the destroying power is most fitly represented by the fatal weapon which wounds the hero in his one vulnerable spot. It is the arrow that pierces the heel of Achilles; it is the sword which is thrust into Siegfried's back; it is the spindle that pricks the finger of the maiden shut up in the tower; it is the poisoned fragment of finger-nail that the malignant dwarfs have left in the crack of the door; and various other things. Mr. Cox's circle of comparisons is a wide one, and sometimes brings together strange bedfellows. Thus (i. 410, note), the gray-haired chief in Scott's ballad of Erlinton, who alone is left alive to tell the tale, and the immortal sisters of the slain snaky-haired Medusa, and Phrixos, who lives on while Hellê dies, and the youngest child of Kronos, who is not swallowed, and the youngest goat (in Grimm's story of the Wolf and the Seven Little Goats), whom the wolf does n't eat, are all the same thing, and brought in in connection with the trials of Cupid and Psyche. And (ii. 330, note) the burning up of Blue-Beard in his own house, with all his wealth and accomplices, "is manifestly the destruction of Ilion" — Blue-Beard, like Paris, being a power of darkness, that steals dawns, or Helens, till he meets with one who is too cunning for him, and brings about his destruction — a form of the myth, we would suggest, that must have grown up near the Arctic circle, since that is the only quarter of the world where the twilight sometimes gets the better of night altogether.

This extreme extension of the ground of mythologic research and comparison is one of the specialties of Mr. Cox's system; although here, as elsewhere, he is only pushing boldly forward where Müller had led the way. To him, the Odyssey has but the same story to tell as the Iliad; it is the sun, wandering and suffering through his ten hours of toil, while the powers of darkness (the suitors) worry and distress the bride (the dawn) whom he left at evening, and whom he will find again, as young and fair as ever, when he returns in early morning. The German *Nibelungen Lied* is palpably the same tale, under another aspect. Arthur and Roland came out of no other crucible. And, yet further, the tales and stories with which we made acquaintance in childhood are solar and dawny in their essential texture: wherever there is an irresistible hero doing wonderful deeds, it is the sun; where there is a lovely damsel waiting for a deliverer, it is the dawn, expectant of the return of the great luminary after his day's toil or his night's eclipse. But the heroes of a humbler class are of the same lineage: Boots, and the Shifty Lad, and Jack the Giant-killer, and doubtless Tom Thumb, although we do not remember his name in the list. Mr. Cox has drawn up (in various places: most briefly and comprehensively, perhaps, at i. 43, 44) a scheme of the elements which may enter into a solar myth, or of the "mythical phrases" in which the Indo-Europeans of the earliest age must have incorporated their impressions of "the daily or yearly course of the lord of day," and which afterwards, when the proper sense of the terms used had been forgotten, grew up into a wild luxuriance of myth and story. Wherever, now, he detects the presence of any of these, there he is ready to assume that a solar myth lies hidden. And we have seen, by the examples cited, how keen is his sense for such prey, and with what slight indications he is satisfied. We should call it easy credulity, if it did not merit a better name. He is, in fact, wholly dominated by his theory; he has established in his own mind so immense an antecedent probability in favor of this mode of interpretation of heroic incident, that he is prepared to find occasion for it everywhere. The general community of scholars, however, we believe, will long continue skeptical, and will only yield its assent, if yield it must, to a cooler and more logical advocate. They will not readily believe that the ancient Indo-European people treated this one theme with such an exuberant fertility of imagination as nearly to exhaust themselves upon it, and to sing and tell of nothing else. They will not believe that elements originally mythical had a power of self-preservation and propagation so exceptional that even those who for thousands of years had entirely lost the underlying mythical sense could not but reproduce them with faithful iteration. The correspondences, in parts, of the nursery and narrative literature of many nations of Europe and Asia are, indeed, very remarkable; and it remains to be determined by comprehensive and wary inquiry, how much of them is accidental or due to the like working out of tendencies common to all human nature, how much is the result of transmission from one people to another, and how much, if any, is to be traced to a common tradition from the remote ages of unity. We cannot consent to have the whole question settled for us in advance so summarily.

Mr. Cox's method palpably invites to burlesque and caricature. We might almost say that he himself sets us the example of caricaturing it, so exaggerated is, in many cases, his valuation of the coincidences which he thinks to find, so great his ingenuity in discovering them where no one else would have suspected their existence. An instance is his exposition (i. 151 *seq.*) of the story of Ahmed, as told by Irving in the "Alhambra;" it is much too long to repeat here; but we could hardly ask a better model to follow, if we would learn the art of interpreting stories into solar myths. And caricatures have begun to appear; hardly any critic of the work has been able to refrain from them; the most elaborate and artful one we have seen, worked out with immense ingenuity and learning, and with a surprising command of countenance, is found in No. 5 of "Kottabos" (an organ of the erudition and wit of Trinity College, Dublin), where Max Müller himself is proved to be a solar myth, and one as compared with which "few are so detailed and various; and perhaps there is none which brings together in so concentrated a focus the special characteristics of Sanskrit, Hellenic, and Norse fable." We, on our part, see capabilities in General Grant, from which we refrain our hands only unwillingly. His famous resolution "to fight it out on this line, *if it takes all summer*," has the true solar ring, announcing a myth of the northern variety, where the yearly instead of the daily career of the orb of day is the theme; and if we add the long winter of inaction and fruitless effort before Richmond, and the final resistless outbreak and conquest, as soon as the vernal equinox was past, we have a more than usually abundant capital of evident solar elements with which to begin our interpretation.

But though we may permit ourselves a laugh at Mr. Cox's exaggerations, we ought to laugh good-humoredly, and without refusing him our full respect as an earnest scholar and a powerful and ingenious writer. His work deserves, as we have said, to be widely studied; and it will do valuable service, doubtless, in advancing the cause he has at heart, if only by exciting public attention and stimulating research and discussion, which shall tend toward the final establishment of truth. Under and along with the exaggerations, we, for our part, are confident that there is a great deal which is solid and valuable.

Only a part of the preparatory work needful to be done in order to make the Veda yield its full harvest of results for Indo-European antiquity has been yet accomplished. When the internal content of that venerable document shall have been as thoroughly laid open as its speech has been analyzed, and shall have engaged the labors of as many careful students, we may hope — not, perhaps, for so abundant and certain results as some are even now promising themselves, and hastening forward to gather; but, at least, for much more than is now within our reach, and enough to more than repay all that it shall cost. Just at present, tilling should be more the occupation of the day than reaping; and we cannot help regarding such works as the great St. Petersburg Sanskrit lexicon (now nearly completed) and Muir's Original Sanskrit Texts (especially the last published volume, "Contributions to a Knowledge of the Cosmogony, Mythology, Religious Ideas, Life, and Manners of the Indians of the Vedic Age") as more likely than any others to do permanent service to the study of the mythology of the Aryan nations.

VI.

ALFORD'S QUEEN'S ENGLISH.[1]

It may seem late to undertake the criticism of a book the second edition of which has been already some time before the public. But the first edition, which appeared a few years since (in 1863), although not passing without some slight notice in our literary journals, attained no American circulation, and made no impression upon our community. The enterprise of the publisher has succeeded in procuring for the work in its new form so wide a currency among us, and in attracting to it so much attention, that it becomes worth while seriously to inquire into its merits, and estimate its right to be accepted as an authority. This, however, as much for the sake of challenging a popularity and consideration which may turn out undeserved, as from regard to the good or harm which the book is likely to do. For it makes no great pretentions to a wide scope, or to philosophic method and profundity. It styles itself "Stray Notes on Speaking and Spelling," and is composed of desultory and loosely connected remarks on errors and controverted points in orthography, orthoëpy, and grammar, written in part, as its author takes pains to inform us, at chance moments of leisure, in cars and eating-houses and other such places. Criticism, however, it is plain, should not be disarmed

1 *A Plea for the Queen's English; Stray Notes on Speaking and Spelling.* By Henry Alford, D. D., Dean of Canterbury. Second Edition. London and New York: Alexander Strahan. 1865. 16mo. Pp. xvi., 287.

by such acknowledgments, since no man has a right to thrust his odd thoughts before us who cannot make them fully worth our acceptance. The Stray Notes grew by degrees into their present form. They were put together first into lectures, and then became a series of articles in a weekly newspaper. These attracted much notice, and called out abundant correspondence and comment, so that the successive papers took on a shape in part controversial and replicatory. The same was their fate after their collection into a volume; and the second edition is not a little altered from the first, under the process of criticism and reply. They have had, it will be seen, a rather peculiar history, calculated to provoke our curiosity. The author is an English divine, of considerable note as critical editor and commentator of the Greek text of the New Testament, and also acquired some fame in his earlier years as a writer of verses. We should naturally, then, explain to ourselves the popularity which the work has won by the critical and scholarly ability and the elegant style it is found to display. Such qualities, added to the general and attractive interest of the subject, ought to be enough to insure a notable career to even a heavier volume.

It is unfortunate, however, for the American student who may be desirous to draw from this source valuable instruction as to the best usage of his mother-tongue, that he finds himself repelled, almost at the start, by a violent ebullition of spite against his native country. The reverend author, namely, is engaged in magnifying his office as polisher of the habits of speech of English speakers, by showing the exceeding and deep-reaching importance of attention to niceties of diction; and he holds up Americans to reprobation for "the character and history of the nation, its blunted sense of moral obligation and duty to man, its open disregard of conventional right where aggrandizement is to be obtained, and, I may now say, its reckless and fruitless maintenance of the most cruel and unprincipled war in the history of the world" (p. 6). This, it is true, was written before Lee's surrender. Since the end of 1864 we have changed all that; and, in our zeal after self-improvement, we can well afford to pardon a few hard words to a "dignitary of the Church of England" who has given his ardent sympathies to the cause of Secession and Slavery, provided only he shall make good his claim to be our instructor in his proper department. Still, we cannot but form the suspicion that our author is somewhat under the dominion of class and national prejudices, and either careless of seeking information as to subjects upon which he is very ready to offer his opinion, or not acute in judging and profiting by information obtained. And further, it cannot but seriously shake our confidence in his philological acumen to find that our dreadful example is intended to "serve to show" the horrified British nation "that language is no trifle!" Our astonished inquiries into the connection of such a warning with such a lesson bring us to see that the Dean attributes our viciousness to the infelicities of our speech, since "every important feature in a people's language is reflected in its character and history." We had always thought, it must be owned, that the "reflection" was in the opposite direction — that character and history determined language. It is perhaps allowable to say, by a kind of figure, that a man's image in the glass is reflected in his person; and it is certain that, if we can make the image transcendently lovely, the man himself will be sure to turn out as handsome; only we cannot well reach the image save through the man himself. In like manner, if we can train the masses of a people to speak elegantly, doubtless we shall change their character vastly for the better; but the improvement will be only in a very subordinate degree due to the reflex action of language; it will rather be the direct effect of the process of education.

Our suspicions of the soundness of our philological authority, thus aroused, are not precisely lulled to sleep by an examination of the other incentives he offers to exactness of speech. We are pointed to the example of the Apostle Peter, when he was accused by the bystanders of being a Galilean, on the ground of his Galilean dialect. "So that," says our author, "the fact of a provincial pronunciation was made use of to bring about the repentance of an erring Apostle." It is not easy to see the point of the argument here made. One might rather be tempted to infer that a provincial pronunciation is a good thing, and deserves encouragement, if it could become the means of so important a conversion; who knows but that our own local idioms, carefully nursed and duly displayed, may somehow be made to work out our salvation? But there is a worse difficulty behind; and really, if Mr. Alford were not a Dean, and an editor of the New Testament text, we should be inclined to accuse him of neglecting his Bible. According to the received reading of the Evangelists (we have not examined Dean Alford's edition), the charge brought against the saint that he did not talk good Jerusalem Chaldee had for its sole effect to draw from him a repetition of his former lying denial, along with a volley of oaths and curses (luckless Peter! he forgot that his native dialect would only show more distinctly in such an outbreak of passion); and it was the crowing of the cock that brought about his repentance. So that, after all, the lesson we are to learn must be that, if we will only repress our local peculiarities of speech, we shall be less exposed to being detected in our wickedness; or else, that we must beware of accusing any one of dialectic inaccuracies, lest thereby we drive him to greater enormity of sin. Our author has perverted, yet without appreciable gain, a text which would not bend to his purpose in its true form.

We are now tempted to examine the other case cited

by the Dean in this department, and see whether it will not, perhaps, give us a higher idea of his qualifications as a critic of language. He speaks (p. 7, *seq.*) of the spurious poems of Rowley as having been in part detected by their containing the word *its* — a word which was not in good use in Rowley's time. So far all is well. But then he goes on to discourse concerning the infrequency of *its* in early English, and the employment of *his* for it, evidently in total ignorance of the reason: namely, that *his* was in Anglo-Saxon, and hence also for a long time in English, the regular genitive case of *it* (A. S. *hit*), not less than of *he;* and that the introduction of *its* was a popular inaccuracy, a grammatical blunder, such as the introduction of *she's* for *her* would be now. To the general apprehension, *his* stood in the usual relation of a possessive case, formed by an added '*s*, to *he*, and had nothing to do with *it;* and so popular use manufactured a new "regular" possessive for *it*, which was finally, after a protracted struggle, received into cultivated and literary styles, and made good English. Hear, on the other hand, our author's explanation of the rarity of *its* during the period from Shakespeare to Milton: "The reason, I suppose, being, that possession, indicated by the possessive case *its*, seemed to imply a certain life or personality, which things neuter could hardly be thought of as having." A more fantastic and baseless suggestion is rarely made; it is so empty of meaning that we can hardly forbear to call it silly. There was not at that period a neuter noun in the language that did not form a possessive in '*s* with perfect freedom. Who can fancy Shakespeare doubting whether a table really had or possessed legs, as well as a horse or a man; or as being willing to say "a table's legs," but questioning the propriety of "a table on *its* legs"? Or how were the Bible translators avoiding the ascription of possession to things inanimate by talking of "the candlestick, *his* shaft and *his* branch," and so forth, instead of "*its* shaft and *its* branch"?

If these, then, are fair specimens of our author's learning and method, we must expect to find his book characterized by ignorance of the history of English speech, inaccuracy, loose and unsound reasoning, and weakness of linguistic insight. And we are constrained to acknowledge that such expectations will be abundantly realized in the course of a further perusal of the work. Let us cite a few more specimens.

Perhaps the most striking example we can select of the Dean's want of knowledge on philological subjects is his treatment of the word *neighbor*. "This," he says (p. 12), "has come from the German *nachbar*"! but he adds in a foot-note that the derivation has been questioned; that a Danish correspondent thinks it should be referred to the Danish or Norse *nabo;* and he has himself chanced to observe "that the dictionaries derive it from the Anglo-Saxon *nehyebur*." He does not venture to judge a matter of such intricacy and difficulty, and simply leaves in the text his original etymology from the German. This is very much as if we were to be in doubt whether to trace a friend's descent from his grandfather, or from one or other of his second-cousins, finally inclining to a certain cousin, because with him we ourselves happened to be somewhat acquainted. Certainly, one who can display such ignorance of the first principles of English etymology ought to be condemned to hold his peace forever on all questions concerning the English language.

The case is the same wherever a knowledge of the history of English words ought to be made of avail in discussing and deciding points of varying usage. Thus, when inquiring (p. 46 *seq.*) whether we ought to say *a historian* or *an historian*, and instancing the Bible use of *an* before initial *h* in almost all cases, he omits to point out that *an* is the original form, once used before both consonants and vowels, and that, when it came by degrees to be dropped before consonants, for the sake of a more rapid and easy utterance, it maintained itself longest before the somewhat equivocal aspiration, *h*. He is right, we think, in not regarding the rule for using *an* before the initial *h* of an unaccented syllable as a peremptory one. The better reason is on the side of the more popular colloquial usage; if the *h* of *historian*, like that of *history*, is to be really pronounced, made audible, *a* ought properly to stand before it, as before the other. But no Biblical support can make of such a combination as *an hero* aught but the indefensible revival of an antique and discarded way of speaking.

So also, Dean Alford (p. 48) fails to see and to point out that, in the antiquated phrase *such an one*, we have a legacy from the time when *one* had not yet acquired its anomalous pronunciation *wŭn*, but was sounded *ōne* (as it still is in its compounds *ōnly*, *alōne*, *atōne*, etc.). As we now utter the word, *such an one* is not less absurd and worthy of summary rejection from usage than would be *such an wonder*.

The discussion, again, of "better than *I*" or "better than *me*" is carried on (p. 152 *seq.*) without an allusion to the fact that *than* is historically an adverb only, the same word with *then*, and has no hereditary right to govern an accusative, as if it were a preposition. "He is better *than* I" is, by origin, "he is better, *then* I" — that is to say, "I next after him." Linguistic usage has, indeed, a perfect right to turn the adverbial construction into a prepositional; but, as the former is still in almost every case not only admissible, but more usual, the tendency to convert the word into a preposition is not one to be encouraged, but rather, and decidedly, the contrary.

It might be deemed unfair to blame our author for his equally faulty discussion of the question between the two forms of locution, "it is *I*" and "it is *me*," because his correspondents and the correspondents of some of the English literary journals (which have been the arena of a controversy upon the subject much more ardent than able, within no long time past) are just as far as he is from doing themselves credit in connection with it. What he cites from Latham and (in a note) from Ellis is of very little account. It may well enough be that "it is *me*" is now already so firmly established in colloquial usage, and even in written, that the attempt to oust it will be vain; but the expression is none the less in its origin a simple blunder, a popular inaccuracy. It is neither to be justified nor palliated by theoretical considerations—as by alleging a special predicative construction, or citing French and Danish parallels. There was a time when to say "*us* did it" for "*we* did it," "*them* did it" for "*they* did it," was just as correct as to say "*you* did it" for "*ye* did it;" but usage, to which we must all bow as the only and indisputable authority in language, has ratified the last corruption and made it good English, while rejecting the other two. He would be a pedant who should insist in these days that we ought to say *ye* instead of *you* in the nominative; but he would also have been worthy of ridicule who, while the change was in progress, should have supported it on the ground of a tendency to the subjective use of the accusative, and cited in its favor the example of the Italian *loro*, 'them,' for *elleno*, 'they,' as plural of respectful address. And so long as it is still vulgar to say "it is *him*, it is *her*, it is *us*, it is *them*," and still proper and usual to say "it is *I*," our duty as favorers of good English requires us to oppose and discountenance "it is *me*," with the rest of its tribe, as all unlike regretable and avoidable solecisms.

Of course the Dean puts his veto (p. 253) upon *reliable;* men of his stamp always do. He alleges the staple argument of his class, that *rely-upon-able* would be the only legitimate form of such a derivative from *rely*. They ought fairly to put the case somewhat thus: "It is *unaccount-for-able*, not to say *laugh-at-able*, that men will try to force upon the language a word so *take-objection-to-able*, so little *avail-of-able*, and so far from *indispense-with-able*, as *reliable;*" then we should see more clearly how much the plea is worth.

Of course, again, our author sets his face like flint against writing *or* instead of *our* at the end of such words as *honor* and *favor;* and that, upon the high and commanding consideration that to simplify the termination thus "is part of a movement to reduce our spelling to uniform rule as opposed to usage" (p. 10); that it "is an approach to that wretched attempt to destroy all the historic interest of our language, which is known by the name of *phonetic* spelling" (p. 14) — and upon the phonetic movement he proceeds to pour out the vials of his ponderous wit and feeble denunciation. On the whole, we think the phonetists are to be congratulated on having the Dean for an adversary; his hostility is more a credit to them than would be his support. There are a host of difficulties in the way of the phonetic spellers which they themselves, or many of them, are far from appreciating; but they are not of the kind which Mr. Alford seeks to raise. No one wants to set up rule against usage, but only to change usage from a bad rule to a good one. And our language has a store of historic interest which would not be perceptibly trenched upon, even if we were to take the extraordinary liberty of writing our words just as we speak them. Our present spelling is of the nature of a great and long-established institution, so intimately bound up with the habits and associations of the community that it is well-nigh or quite impregnable. But a philologist ought to be ashamed to defend it on principle, on theoretical grounds. He, at any rate, ought to know that a mode of writing is no proper repository for interesting historical reminiscences; that an alphabetic system has for its office simply and solely to represent faithfully a spoken language, and is perfect in proportion as it fulfills that office, without attempting to do also the duty of Egyptian hieroglyphs and Chinese ideographs. No other so great linguistic blessing could be conferred upon the English language and the people who speak it as a consistent phonetic orthography.[1]

It is calculated profoundly to stagger our faith in Dean Alford's capacity as an interpreter and expositor of difficult texts to find him guilty of explaining (p. 105) the reflexive verb *to endeavor one's self* by 'to consider one's self in duty bound,' and of asserting that this "appears clearly" from the answer made by the candidate for ordination to the bishop's exhortation to diligence in prayer and other holy exercises, "I will *endeavor myself* so to do, the Lord being my helper." Not only does this answer exact no such interpretation of the phrase as the one given by the Dean, but it even directly and obviously suggests the true meaning, 'to exert one's self, to do one's endeavor.'

A similar paucity of insight is exhibited in our author's theory (p. 86), that the origin of the double comparative *lesser*, for *less*, is to be traced to the "attraction" of the dissyllabic word *greater*, with which it is not infrequently found connected in use. No such effect of attraction as this, we are sure, can be found in any part of our English speech. The true reason of the form is not hard to discover: it lies in the extension of a prevailing analogy to one or two exceptional cases. *Less* and *worse* are the only comparatives in our language which do not end in *r*; and *er* is accordingly so distinctly present to the apprehension of the language-users as sign of comparative meaning that they have gone on, naturally

[1] This subject is more fully discussed in the next article.

enough, to apply it to these two also, thus assimilating them to the rest of their class. The only difference in the result is, that *lesser* has been fully adopted, in certain connections, into good usage, while *worser* is still almost a vulgarism, though employed now and then by writers of undoubted authority.

Nor can we ascribe any greater merit to the Dean's treatment of the preposition *on to* or *onto*, used to denote motion, as distinguished from locality or place, denoted by the simple preposition *on:* thus, "The cat jumped *on to* the table, and danced about *on* the table." Such a distinction, as every one knows, is often made in colloquial style, but is not yet, and perhaps may never be, admitted in good writing; this tolerates only *on*. Our author is not content with denying that *on to* is now good writable English; he tries to make out that there is no reason or propriety in attempting to express any such difference of relation as is signified by the two separate forms. His argument is this: if we say "The cat jumped *on* the table," or if the tired school-boy, begging a lift on his way, gets from the coachman the permission, "All right, jump *on* the box," will there be any danger of a failure to understand what is meant? Of course not, we reply; but neither should we fail to understand "The dog jumped *in* the water, and brought out the stick;" nor would Tom be slow in taking, and acting on, coachee's meaning, if the reply were "Jump *in* the carriage." The question is not one of mere intelligibility, but of the desirableness of giving formal expression to a real difference of relation — as we have actually done in the case of *in* and *into*. *On to*, says our author (p. 181), is not so good English as *into*, "because *on* is ordinarily a preposition of motion as well as of rest, whereas *in* is almost entirely a preposition of rest." This is an amusingly absurd inversion of the real relations of the case: in fact, *in* is a preposition of rest only, because we have *into* in good usage as corresponding preposition of motion; *on* is obliged to be both, because *onto* has not won its way to general acceptance. The double form would be just as proper and just as expressive in the one case as in the other, and there is no good reason why we should not heartily wish that *onto* were as unexceptionable English as *into*, whether we believe or not that it will ever become so, and whether or not we are disposed to take the responsibility of joining to make it so. Every German scholar knows how nice and full of meaning are the distinctions made in the German language, as regards these two and a few other prepositions, by the use after them of a dative to denote locality and an accusative to denote motion. The Anglo-Saxon was able to accomplish the same object by the same means; but we have, in losing our dative case, lost the power to do so, and have only partially made up the loss, by coining, during the modern period, such secondary words as *into* and *onto*, that they may bear a part of the office of *in* and *on*.

We will barely allude to one or two more instances of a like character: such are our author's conjecture (p. 52) that our separation of *mănifold* in pronunciation from *many* is due to the influence of its felt analogy with *mănifest;* his attempt (p. 91) to find an etymological reason for the translation "Our Father *which* art in heaven," instead of "*who* art;" his theory (p. 42) that the conjunction of the two words "humble and hearty" in the Prayer-Book is good ground for holding that the first as well as the second was pronounced with an aspirated *h;* his apparent assumption (p. 25) that the *'s* of *senator's* represents the Latin *is* of *senatoris* (or is it only his confused expression that is to blame here?) — and so forth.

These are but the more prominent and striking illustrations of Dean Alford's general method. We may say without exaggeration that — especially in the first half of the book, where questions are more often dealt with that involve historical considerations and call for some scholarship — there is hardly a single topic brought under discussion which is treated in a thorough and satisfactory manner, in creditable style and spirit: even where we are agreed with our author's conclusions, he repels us by a superficial, or incomplete, or prejudiced, or blundering statement of the reasons that should guide us to them. It is almost an impertinence in one so little versed in English studies to attempt to teach his countrymen how they ought to speak, and why.

The last half of the work deals prevailingly with syntactical points, requiring to be argued rather upon rhetorical than grammatical grounds. But, though in a measure exempt from the class of criticisms which we have found occasion to make above, it is not without its own faults. The Dean's chief hobby throughout is the depreciation of "laws," whether of the rhetorician or of the grammarian, and the exaltation of "usage" as opposed to them. He has, of course, a certain right on his side, yet not precisely as he understands it. The laws he rejects are only meant to stand as expressions of good usage; nor do those who set them up arrogate to them peremptory and universal force, but rather a value as guiding principles, attention to which will save from many faults the less wary and skillful. No one holds that he who has not native capacity and educated taste can become by their aid an elegant writer; no one denies that he who has capacity and taste may cast them to the winds, sure that his own sense of what is right will lead him to clear and forcible expression. But we have all heard of a class of people who inveigh against "laws," and would fain escape judgment by them; and the very vigor of the Dean's recalcitrations inspires us with suspicions that there may be good cause for his uneasiness. And so it is; he has not in any eminent degree that fine sense which enables one to write without rule a pure and flowing English. His style is always heavy and ungraceful, and often marked with infelicities and even inaccuracies. As many of our readers are aware, he has received on this score a severe scathing from Mr. Moon, in a little work happily entitled "The Dean's English," by way of answer to "The Queen's English." To this we refer any one who may be curious to see the other side of his claim to set himself up as a critic of good English properly exposed. The professed general views he puts forth are in no small part special pleadings, rather, against the criticisms of his censors. He appears to suppose that any somewhat inaccurate or slovenly phrase or construction of his for which he can find parallels in our Bible translation and in Shakespeare is, thereby hallowed and made secure against attack — unmindful that our style of expression has in many points tended toward precision and nicety during the last centuries, so that not everything which was allowed in Shakespeare's time will be tolerated now; and further, and more especially, that great writers may be pardoned in taking now and then liberties which, if ventured on by little men, like him and ourselves, will be justly visited with reprobation.

It is our opinion, therefore, upon the whole, that the English-speaking public would have lost little had our author's lucubrations been confined to the "Church of England Young Men's Literary Association," for which they were originally intended, and which doubtless received them with unquestioning faith, and had he never brought them out where Dissenters and other irreverent outsiders should carp at them. The circulation and credit they have won in this country are mainly a reflection of the unusual attention which has been paid them in England; and the latter is partly fortuitous, the result of a combination of favoring circumstances, partly due to the general interest felt in the subject of the work, and curiosity to hear what a man of high position and repute for scholarship has to say upon it; and in part it is an indication of the general low state of philological culture in the British Isles. We cannot wish "The Queen's English" a continued currency, unless it be understood and received by all for just what it is — a simple expression of the views and prejudices of a single educated Englishman respecting matters of language; having, doubtless, a certain interest and value as such, but possessing no more authority than would belong to a like expression on the part of any one among thousands of its readers. Its true character is that of a sample of private opinion, not a guide and model of general usage.

VII.

HOW SHALL WE SPELL?

HOW our English words shall be spelt is a matter concerning which the great mass of those to whom the language is native appear to have pretty fully made up their minds. They intend to tolerate no change in the present orthography. Those who put forth proposals for its alteration, whether in certain words and classes of words only, or upon a wider scale, are set down and laughed at without mercy. The public sentiment is perhaps stronger and more unanimous upon the subject than ever before. There was a time when the movement toward a consistent spelling, of which the *Fonetik Nuz* was a conspicuous exponent, wore in the eyes of many persons a threatening aspect; but it now seems dangerous to nobody. Reaction, even, is the order of the day. The orthographical "improvements" made by that unscrupulous radical, Noah Webster, have been one by one abandoned and ignored by his editors. The writing of *honor* for *honour*, and the like, was once pretty well established throughout America, and making progress in England itself; at present it is quite crushed out in the latter country, and many American scholars and publishers are giving it up, in shame and confusion of face. And yet there are, from time to time, voices raised also upon the other side of the question; even efforts seriously made — doubtless with some hope of a successful issue — to bring about that sweeping revolution which we, the English-speakers at large, are determined neither to encourage nor to allow. To mention only one or two of those which have last come under our notice: a company has been formed at Mendota, in Illinois, "with a capital of $35,000," for carrying through the great national reform in spelling, and introducing a new and strictly phonetic alphabet; the American Philological Society[1] (in and of New York) has put forth, as a feeler of the public pulse, if not as the direct suggestion of reform, a phonetic allegory on the late war and its causes, the "History of Magnus Maharba" (Abraham); and a senator of the United States has moved to devote a part of the superfluous public funds to paying a mixed commission, which shall devise and report a plan for a consistent orthography. The subject, then, is still in some degree an open one before the public mind. Or, if we are to regard the influence of these few unquiet spirits as too insignificant to be made much account of, we may at any rate take a satisfaction in reviewing the position we hold against them, and realizing anew its strength and security.

No one, we presume, will be found to question that one very important reason why we cleave to our present modes of spelling is the simple fact that they are ours. We have learned them, by dint of diligent study, if not of painful effort; we are used to them; our spoken words in any other garb would look to us strange and quaint, or even ridiculous. To give them up would imply a revolution — such an overthrow of a grand institution, firmly rooted in the usages and predilections of a wide community, as no race or generation has ever yet been willing to permit, save under the pressure of some great and profoundly felt necessity. And we acknowledge no such necessity; far from this, we think we see a variety of reasons why our favorite institution is preferable to any

[1] A private organization, not to be confounded with the American Philological Association.

that could be put in its place. Precisely here, however, we ought to feel most distrustful of the ground we stand upon. It is so easy to overvalue, or even wholly to misinterpret, reasons apparently favoring conclusions which we are already determined to reach! Let us, then, enter into a summary examination of the alleged advantages of our present English orthography, for the purpose of determining both what is their actual worth, and how far we rely upon them in our defense of the institution.

First to be noticed among the advantages referred to is the convenient discrimination to the eye of homonyms, or words which are pronounced alike, but have a different origin and meaning. A familiar example is afforded us in the written distinction of *meet*, *meat*, and *mete;* and another that of *to*, *too*, and *two;* such triplets, as every one knows, are not very rare in our language, and couples of the same sort are to be counted by scores. Now, we have to observe that any credit which is given to our written language in this particular must be taken away from our spoken language. We gain nothing by writing the uttered syllables *meet* and *too* in a variety of ways, unless, when uttered, they are of ambiguous meaning. If our minds are for even the briefest moment puzzled by such expressions as "he goes *to* Boston," "he goes *two* miles," "he goes *too* far," not knowing which *too* is meant in either case, then it is worth while to avoid a like difficulty in our reading by spelling the word differently. But who will consent to make so damaging an admission? There is a language in the world, the Chinese, where the words are so few, and their meanings so many, that orthographic differences are brought in as an important aid to comprehension, and the writing follows, upon a grand scale, not the utterance alone, but the signification also. Thus, there are more than eleven hundred ways of writing the word *ē*, and other words count their representatives by hundreds, by scores, or by tens.

A host of devices have to be resorted to there in spoken speech to get rid of ambiguities which are wholly avoided in written. Our English, however, is not afflicted with such poverty of expression as to be brought to this strait. We have also three different *founds* — *found* from *find*, *found* meaning 'establish,' and *found* meaning 'cast, mould' — between which, we venture to say, no soul ever thought of making a confusion, though they are all spelt with the same letters. Is there any one who cannot tell, by the ear or by the eye, when *cleave* means 'stick together,' and when it means 'part asunder?' Who ever finds any more difficulty in separating *bear*, 'bruin,' from *bear*, 'carry,' than in separating either of these from *bare*, 'naked'? Of how infinitesimal value, then, is the Chinese principle, as introduced into English usage! We may blot out every vestige of it from our vocabulary to-morrow, and it will never be missed; the written language will still continue to be as good as the spoken; and if any one is not content with that, let him migrate and learn another tongue. If the principle is to be kept and made much of, let us agree to give it a more consistent application: let us not spell alike words so different in history and use as the three *founds;* when the same vocable diverges into meanings widely dissimilar, let us vary its spelling a little to match, not writing in the same way "she *became* ill" and "her dress *became* her," nor letting the lawyer and the lover go to *court* in the same orthographic fashion — yet more, when there has been a divergence of pronunciation as well, as when a *minúte* portion of time has become a *mínute.* Let us separate he *rĕad* from he *rēads*, as we have separated he *lĕd* from he *lēads;* above all, let us not confound together in spelling words distinct in every respect — derivation, sense, and utterance — like the verb *lēad* and the metal *lĕad.*

Consistency, however, of any kind in English spelling we have taught ourselves to regard as of little or no consequence; its value is quite overborne and thrown into the shade for us by that of the "historic" principle. If there is any one thing more than another that makes us content with, even proud of, our orthography, it is the fact that it is "historic." But wherein, again, lies the worth of the historic principle? Why, in its interesting suggestiveness, of course; in its exceeding importance to etymology. Very extreme claims have been made in its behalf in this latter respect by the enemies of the *Fonetik Nuz* party. Thus, an English Quarterly reviewer, taking Max Müller to task for the few words in favor of the inherent desirableness of a phonetic mode of spelling boldly spoken by him in the last series of his lectures on language, asks "who would have either time or energy enough to master the history of this single language" if we strike out the traces of the origin of its words still preserved in their spelling? and he adds that the introduction of a phonetic system "in the second generation would break the backs of philological students, and in the third render their existence impossible" (the latter catastrophe, as we may remark, being a very natural consequence of the former). And a very recent American writer on the English language echoes these sentiments, maintaining that, "if the form were to follow the sound, there would soon not a single trace be left of the language used by our forefathers;" and that, "if the *Fonetik Nuz* had been started a thousand years ago, it is safe to assert that nobody would have had either the courage or the time to attempt mastering the history of our language." Now, we doubt not that these gentlemen conceived themselves to be making a stout fight in defense of the guild of etymologists, threatened with the cutting off of one of its chief sources of gain, and to be winning a title to its collective and profound gratitude. But save us from such champions! They may be allowed to speak for themselves, since they know best their own infirmity of back and need of braces; the rest of the guild, however, will thank them for nothing. If the English were like the Tibetan, for example, a dialect of unknown history and of exceedingly obscure character and relations, the philologists who first came upon it would naturally be delighted to find its words, like the Tibetan, crowded full of silent consonants and built about mispronounced vowels — all relics, or at least presumed ones, of former modes of utterance. But the two cases are not, in fact, altogether parallel. Of the English we have abundant monuments coming from nearly every century since before the time of Alfred, or say for eleven or twelve hundred years; and the chief fault which we have to find with them as illustrations of the history of the language is that they are so little regardful of the phonetic principle. The confused orthography of the Anglo-Saxon itself is an obstacle in the way of our fully understanding its orthoëpic aspect, and the difficulty grows constantly worse from that time to the present. Painful researches into the history of the changes in English pronunciation are now in progress which would be rendered unnecessary if the written literature of each period had represented in an orderly and consistent manner its own modes of utterance. There is in existence a manuscript poem, the "Ormulum," of the "Semi-Saxon" period of our literature (A. D. 1150–1250), apparently in the author's own hand, no one else having ever thought well enough of it to copy it; and a tedious work it is, indeed; but for us it has a high and peculiar value, just for the reason that its author was a phonetic fanatic, and wrote it out in a consistent mode of spelling of his own devising, one that throws a deal of light upon the condition of the spoken language of his time. While we have the sources of our English fully within our reach in the Anglo-Saxon and Old French literatures, it is the height of unreason to assert that our reading of English etymologies is in any manner dependent upon the current "historic" orthography.

But further, were this dependence as great as is claimed, we are still puzzled to see how it should have any bearing upon the present practical question of a reform in spelling. Should even the Tibetan people desire to carry through such a reform — to write, for example, *dag* instead of *bsgrags*, *mre* instead of *smras* — the philologist would rather admire their good sense than quarrel with its results; having once obtained a record of the old written form, he is indifferent as to whether it be or be not longer kept up in popular usage. Do the writers whom we have quoted above imagine that, the moment we adopt a new mode of spelling, all the literature written in the old is to pass in a twinkling out of existence and out of memory? Certainly there are agencies which might be made use of to avert so bewildering a catastrophe. A Society for the Preservation of English Etymologies might perhaps be organized, which should make a provident selection of old-style dictionaries and grammars, and store them away in a triply fire-proof library, for the young philologists of future times to be nursed upon until they could bear stronger food. It might even be found practicable, by ingenious and careful management, to procure the construction of a dictionary of the new-fangled idiom in which the former spelling of every word should be set alongside its modern substitute, in order to render possible the historic comprehension of the latter. Thus, to take an extreme case or two, the new word *sam* (*a* as in *far*), by having the explanation "anciently, *psalm*" added to it, would be sufficiently insured against any such shocking suppositions on the part of the future student of English as that it pointed to Samuel instead of David as author of the sacred lyrics, or that it was a development out of the mystical letters "S. M." placed in the singing-books at the head of so many of their number; *him* (*hymn*) would be, by like means, saved from confusion with the personal pronoun — and so on. We do not wish to show an unbecoming levity or disrespect, but it is very hard to answer with anything approaching to seriousness such arguments as those we are combating; "absurd" and "preposterous," and such impolite epithets, fit them better than any others we can find in the English vocabulary. They are extreme examples of the fallacies to which learned men will sometimes resort in support of a favorite prejudice.

Many, however, who have too much insight and caution to put their advocacy of the "historic" or Tibetan principle in English orthography upon the false ground of its indispensableness to etymologic science, will yet defend it as calculated to lead on the writer or speaker of our language to inquire into the history of the words he uses, thus favoring the development of an etymologizing tendency. He who now pronounces *sam* and *him*, they think, would be liable, if he also wrote those syllables phonetically, to just simply accept them as names of the things they designate, like *pig* and *pen*, without giving a thought to their derivation; whereas, if he knows that they are and must be spelt *psalm* and *hymn*, his natural curiosity to discover the cause of so singular a phenomenon may plunge him into the Greek language, and make a philologist of him almost before he suspects what he is about. There is more show of reason in this argument; but whether more reason, admits of doubt. The anomalies of our orthography, unfortunately, are far from being calculated, in the gross, to guide the unlearned to etymological research. For one of them which is of value in the way of incitement and instruction, there are many which can only confuse and discourage. In the first place, there are not a few downright blunders among them. Thus, to cite a familiar instance or two, the *g* of *sovereign* (French *souverain*, Italian *sovrano*) has no business there, since the word has nothing whatever to with *reigning; island* (from Anglo-Saxon *ealand*) is spelt with an *s* out of ignorant imitation of *isle* (Latin *insula*), with which it is wholly unconnected; in like manner, an *l* has stumbled into *could*, in order to assimilate it in look to its comrades in office, *would* and *should; women* is for an original *wif-men*, and its phonetic spelling would be also more truly historical. Again, another part, and not a small one, seem to the ordinary speller the merest confusion (and are often, in fact, nothing better), calculated to lead him to nothing but lamentation over his hard lot, that he is compelled to master them. Take a series of words like *believer*, *receiver*, *weaver*, *fever*, *reever*, and try how many of the community are even accessible to proof that their orthographic discordances are bottomed on anything tangible. There is in some persons, as we well know, an exquisite etymologic sensibility which can feel and relish a historical reminiscence wholly imperceptible to men of common mould; to which, for instance, the *u* of *honour* is a precious and never-to-be-relinquished token that the word is derived from the Latin *honor* not directly, but through the medium of the French *honneur:* and we look upon it with a kind of wondering awe, as we do upon the superhuman delicacy of organization of the "true princess" in Andersen's story, who felt the pea so painfully through twenty mattresses and twenty eider-down beds; but it is so far beyond us that we cannot pretend to sympathize with it, or even to covet its possession. If we are to use a suggestive historic orthography, we should like to have our words remodeled a little in its favor: if we must retain and value the *b* of *doubt* (Latin *dubitare*), as sign of its descent, we crave also a *p* in *count* (French *compter*, Latin *computare*), and at least a *b*, if not an *r* also, in *priest* (Greek *presbuteros*); we are not content with but one silent letter in *alms*, as relic of the stately Greek word *eleēmosunē;* we contemplate with only partial satisfaction the *l* of *calm* and *walk*, while we miss it in *such* and *which* (derivatives from *so-*

like and *who-like*). Why, too, should we limit the suggestiveness of our terms to the latest stages of their history? Now that the modern school of linguistic science, with the aid of the Sanskrit and other distant and barbarous tongues, claims to have penetrated back to the very earliest roots out of which our language has grown, let us take due account of its results, and cunningly convert our English spelling into a complete course of philological training.

We have, however, no intention of taking upon ourselves here the character of reformers or of proposers of reforms; only, when this and the other principle are put forward as valuable, we cannot well help stepping aside a moment to see where we should be led to if, like true men, we attempted to carry out our principles. As regards the historic element in English orthography, we think it evident enough that its worth and interest do not at all lie in its instructing effect upon the general public who use the language, but rather in its tendency to call up pleasing associations in the minds of the learned, of those who are already more or less familiar with the sources from which our words come. It is much more an aristocratic luxury than a popular benefit. To the instrument which is in every one's hands for constant use it adds a new kind of suggestiveness for those who know what it means, and gives them the satisfaction of feeling that, though they may not wield the instrument more successfully than others, there are peculiarities in its structure which they alone appreciate. Such a satisfaction is a selfish one, and improperly and wrongly obtained, if bought by a sacrifice of any measure of convenience or advantage to the great public of speakers and writers.

What may be the general loss in these respects we will not now stop to inquire. For it is incontrovertibly true that, whether the natural merits of the two principles we have been considering — the Chinese and the Tibetan, the differentiation of homonymous words and the retention in writing of former modes of utterance — be greater or less, they are practically held in the most complete subordination to another, namely a simple conservation of the modes of spelling now current. All that is said in their defense is as much aside from the true point as were the pleas put forth a few years since by the Southern slave-owners respecting the curse of Canaan and the separate origin and inferior endowments of the negro race. Those pleas were urged, no doubt, with a certain kind of sincerity; but we have yet to hear of the ethnologically learned or the devout Southerner who ever set a slave free because the blood of the superior race predominated in him, or because only the sixteenth part of his lineage was to be traced to Ham, while the rest went back to Shem or Japhet, or both. "Possession is nine points of the law" and "*partus sequitur ventrem*" were the true proof-texts and scientific principles on which the master's right reposed; and so also "whatever is, is right" constitutes the complete ethical code of him who is defending English spelling. Anything else is mere casuistry, a casting of dust in the eyes of the objector. The paramount consideration, which really decides every case, is that the existing orthography must be perpetuated; if for this and that word any other apparently supporting considerations of any kind soever can be found, they may be made the most of — yet without creating a precedent, or establishing a principle which is to be heeded in any other case, where it would make in favor of a change. The advocate of "historic" spelling insists as strongly upon retaining the *l* of *could* as that of *would*, and fights against a *p* in *count* not less vehemently than in favor of a *b* in *doubt;* the difference of *receive* and *believe* is no more sacred in his eyes than the sameness of *cleave* and *cleave*. Now, we have no quarrel with any one who plants himself squarely and openly upon the conservative ground, and declares that our English spelling is, with all its faults and inconsistencies, good enough for its purpose, that every item of it is consecrated by usage and enshrined in predilections, and therefore must and shall be maintained. What we cannot abide is that he who means this, and this only, should give himself the airs of one who is defending important principles, and keeping off from the fabric of English speech rude hands that would fain mar its beauty and usefulness. Orthographic purism is, of all kinds of purism, the lowest and the cheapest, as is verbal criticism of all kinds of criticism, and word-faith of all kinds of orthodoxy. As Mephistopheles urges upon the Student, when persuading him to pin his belief upon the letter, —

Von einem Wort lässt sich kein Iota rauben,

'every iota of the written word may be fought for' — and that, too, even by the tyro who has well conned his spelling-book, though his knowledge of his native speech end chiefly there. Many a man who could not put together a single paragraph of nervous, idiomatic English, nor ever had ideas enough to fill a paragraph of any kind, whose opinion on a matter of nice phraseology or even of disputed pronunciation would be of use to no living being, fancies himself entitled to add after his name "defender of the English language," because he is always strict to write *honour* instead of *honor*, and *travelled* instead of *traveled*, and never misses an opportunity, public or private, to sneer at those who do otherwise.

In what we have said, we have been solicitous only to put the defense of our present modes of spelling upon its true ground, showing that it is a pure and simple conservatism, which by no means founds itself upon useful principles, historical or other, but only in certain cases hides itself behind them. We may next inquire what reasons we have for finding fault with this conservatism and its results, and for wishing and attempting to overthrow them.

In the first place, English orthography violates the true ideal of the relation of written language to spoken, and of an alphabetic mode of writing. To those who have never looked into the subject, it may seem that a phonetic spelling, giving one sign to every sound and one sound to every sign, is a rude and simple device, which an enlightened ingenuity might well enough be tempted to enrich and adorn by mixing it with elements of higher significance. But the student of language knows that the case is far otherwise; that an alphabet is the final result of centuries, even ages, of education and practice in the use of written characters. As a historical fact, writing began, not with representing spoken language, but with trying to do over again what language does — to put occurrences and ideas directly before the mind by intelligible symbols. Only later, and by an indirect process, were men brought to see that, having already produced one system of means, namely words, for bodying forth thought and knowledge, it was needless to devise another and independent one for the same purpose; that their written tongue might best undertake simply to place before the eye their spoken tongue. The great step toward the perfection of writing was taken when it was fully subordinated to speech, and made to represent the names of things instead of things themselves. But even this brought it out of the purely pictorial into a hieroglyphic stage, where it long continued, awkward and unmanageable; and another difficult and protracted process of development was necessary, in order to impart to it a phonetic character, so that it should signify words no longer by simple indivisible symbols, but by characters representing sounds. Our best illustration of the whole history is furnished in the Egyptian monuments, where we see signs of every kind — purely didactic pictures, figures of objects representing those objects themselves, other figures standing for the names of the objects they depict, others for some part, as the consonants, of those names, others, finally, as single letters for the initial sound of their names — all mingled together and exchanging with one another, making up a system of writing not less inconsistent than the English, and infinitely more intricate and troublesome. The Egyptians were too conservative to seize upon the one practically valuable principle which their system contained, and to carry it out consistently, casting aside its inherited incumbrances. But what they could not do was within the power of another people. Every one knows that our own alphabet goes back, through the Latin and Greek, to the Phenician; and it is at least exceedingly probable, though far from admitting of demonstration, that the Phenicians learned to write of the Egyptians. Either of the Egyptian or of some other analogous history of alphabetic development the Phenicians inherited the results, and their alphabet was a simple scheme of twenty-two characters, the names of which (*aleph*, 'bull,' *beth*, 'house,' etc.; whence the Greek *alpha*, *beta*, etc.) began respectively with the sound which each represented. Yet this system, while it discarded everything but the purely phonetic part of the Egyptian, was no complete phonetic alphabet; it wrote the consonants alone, leaving the vowels to be supplied by the reader. It received its full perfection only upon passing into the keeping of the Greeks; they converted some of its superfluous characters into vowel-signs, added others, and produced at last an instrumentality which could and did set faithfully before the sight the whole structure of spoken speech. Among all the alphabets of the world, ancient and modern, there are few, excepting the Greek and its derivatives, which have attained this completeness — to which there does not cleave some taint of a pictorial or a syllabic character.

The Latin alphabet, taken from the Greek, fully accepted and carried out the phonetic principle, rejecting some of the Greek signs and devising new, so as to make an exact adaptation of its modes of writing to its modes of utterance. Nor have its descendants, in their turn, meant to do otherwise. But it is very difficult to maintain the principle in perfect purity, because the spoken forms of words change more insidiously than the written; all tongues which have had a long written history have become more or less "historic" in their spelling, change of orthography lagging ever behind the heels of change of pronunciation. And peculiarly unfavorable circumstances, which in no small part can be distinctly pointed out, have suffered to grow up a greater discordance between the written and the spoken speech among us than in any other community of equal enlightenment. This is the whole truth; and any attempt to make it appear otherwise savors only of the wisdom of the noted fox who lost his brush in a trap, and wanted to persuade himself and the world that the curtailment was a benefit and a decoration. Every departure from the rule that writing is the handmaid of speech is a dereliction of principle, and an abandonment of advantages which seemed to have been long ago assured to us by the protracted labors of many generations of the most gifted races known to history. The handmaid has no right to set up to be wiser and better than her mistress in a single particular. That the written word in any case deviates from the spoken is a fault; which may, indeed, admit of palliation, even amounting to excuse, but which it is an offense against all true science and sound sense to extol as a merit.

We have, of course, no intention of bringing forward the unfaithfulness of our orthography to the highest ideal of a mode of writing as a sufficient reason for an orthographic revolution. A grand practical question, which touches so nearly the interests of so many millions of writers and speakers, is not to be settled by sentimental considerations — any more by this which we have adduced upon the one side, than, upon the other, by the gratification of the small class of curious heads who may delight themselves with seeing Greek and Latin and Old English utterances dimly reflected in our modern spelling. But it was desirable, and even necessary, to draw out the exposition, in order to show that the phonetists have the advantage upon their side, not less in regard to the principle involved in the cause they are defending than in regard to the convenience and enlightenment of the historical student of language.

It is upon practical grounds that our final judgment of the value of English orthography must mainly rest. The written language is a universal possession, an instrument of communication for the whole immense community of English speakers, and anything which impairs its convenience and manageableness as an instrument is such a defect as demands active measures for removal. Now, no one can question that the practical use of our tongue is rendered more difficult by the anomalies of its written form. We do not, indeed, easily realize how much of the learning-time of each rising generation is taken up with mastering orthographical intricacies; how much harder it is for us to learn to read at all, and to read and write readily and correctly, than it would be if we wrote as we speak. We accomplished the task so long ago, most of us, that we have forgotten its severity, and decline to see any reason why others should ask to be relieved from it. Teachers, however, know what it is, as do those who for want of a sufficiently severe early drilling, or from defect of native capacity, continue all their lives to be inaccurate spellers. Such may fairly plead that their orthographical sins are to be imputed, in great part, not to themselves, but to the community, which has established and sustains an institution so unnecessarily cumbrous. We may see yet more clearly the nature of the burden it imposes by considering what it is to foreigners. Our language, from the simplicity of its grammatical structure, would be one of the easiest in the world to learn if it were not loaded with its anomalous orthography. As the matter stands, a stranger may acquire the spoken tongue by training of the mouth and ear, or the written by help of grammar and dictionary, and in either case the other tongue will be nearly as strange to him as if it belonged to an unknown race. It is doubtless within bounds to say that the difficulty of his task is thus doubled. And this item must count for not a little in determining the currency which the English shall win as a world-language — a destiny for which it seems more decidedly marked out than any other cultivated speech. In view of what we expect and wish it to become, we have hardly the right to hand it down to posterity with such a millstone about its neck as its present orthography.

It is, moreover, to be noted that a phonetic spelling, far from contributing, as its enemies claim, to the alteration and decay of the language, would exercise an appreciable conserving influence, and make for uniformity and fixedness of pronunciation. So loose and indefinite is now the tie between writing and utterance, that existing differences of utterance hide themselves under cover of an orthography which fits them all equally well, while others spring up unchecked. No small part of the conservative force expends itself upon the visible form alone; whereas, if the visible and audible form were more strictly accordant, it would have its effect upon the latter also. The establishment of a phonetic orthography would imply the establishment and maintenance of a single authoritative and intelligible standard of pronunciation, the removal of the more marked differences of usage between the cultivated speakers of different localities, and the reduction of those of less account; and it would hold in check — though nothing can wholly restrain — those slow and insidious changes which creep unawares into the utterance of every tongue.

One more thing is worthy of at least a brief reference — namely, that a consistent spelling would awaken and educate the phonetic sense of the community. As things are now, the English speaker comes to the study of a foreign written language, and to the examination of phonetic questions generally, at a disadvantage when compared with those to whom other tongues are native. He has been accustomed to regard it as only natural and proper that any given sound should be written in a variety of different ways, that any given sign should possess a number of different values; and it requires a special education to give him an inkling of the truth that every letter of our alphabet had originally, and still preserves in the main, outside of his own language, a single unvarying sound. His ideas of the relations of the vowels are hopelessly awry; he sees nothing strange in the designation of the vowel-sounds of *pin* and *pine*, or of *pat* and *pate*, or of *pun* and *pure*, as corresponding short and long, although we might as well assert that *dog* and *cat*, or that *horse* and *cow*, or that *sun* and *moon*, are corresponding male and female. And he reads off his Latin and Greek in tones that would have driven frantic any Roman or Athenian who suspected it to be his own tongue that was so murdered, with unsuspecting complacency, even flattering himself that he appreciates their rhythm and melody. It is not the least telling of the indications he furnishes of a sense for the fitness of things debauched by a vicious training, that he is capable of regarding a historical spelling as preferable to a phonetic — that is to say, of thinking it better to write our words as we imagine that some one else pronounced them a long time ago than as we pronounce them ourselves.

A thoroughly consistent spelling would be a far more valuable means of philological education than such a one as we now follow, were the latter twice as full as it is of etymological suggestiveness.

We are, then, clearly of opinion that a phonetic orthography is, of itself, in all respects desirable, and that there is no good reason against introducing it save the inconvenience of so great a change. Every theoretical and practical consideration makes in its favor. At the same time, our hope of a reform is exceedingly faint. No reform is possible until the community at large — or at least, the greater body of the learned and highly educated — shall see clearly that the advantage to be gained by it is worth the trouble it will entail: and whether and when they will be brought to do so is very doubtful. At present the public mind is in a most unnaturally sensitive condition upon the subject; it will listen to no suggestion of a change from any quarter, in any word or class of words. The great need now is to enlighten it, to show that its action is the result of a blind prejudice alone, and really founded on none of the reasons which are usually alleged in its support; that there is nothing sacred in the written word; that language is speech, not spelling; and that practical convenience is the only true test of the value of an orthographic system. Until this work is accomplished, all reformers will be likely to meet the fate of Noah Webster, one of the best abused men of his generation, and for one of the most creditable of his deeds, the attempt to amend in a few particulars our English spelling — an attempt for which (however fragmentary it may have been, and ill-judged in some of its parts) we ourselves feel inclined to forgive him many of his false etymologies and defective definitions. We have read in the story-books that a certain Prince Nosey was condemned by a malevolent fairy to wear a portentously long nose until he should himself become convinced that it was too long, which salutary but unpalatable truth was kept indefinitely concealed from him by the flattery of his courtiers. The English-speaking people are in somewhat the same case; and though fairy days are now over, and we can no longer hope that our superfluous nasal inches will drop off the moment we recognize their superfluity, we know that at any rate we shall not lose them sooner, because we shall not sooner be willing to set about the work of ridding ourselves of them. Of course our words would look very oddly to us now in a phonetic dress; but that is merely because we are used to them in another. So our friends the ladies, if they should suddenly appear before our sight in the head-gear which they are going to wear five years hence, would shock us and provoke the cut direct; yet we shall by that time be looking back to the bonnets of this season as the height of absurdity. If once brought to the adoption of a consistent orthography, we should soon begin to regard with aversion our present ideographs and historiographs, and wonder that we could ever have preferred, or even tolerated them. It is easy now to raise a general laugh against the man who writes *news* "*nuz;*" but so the Englishman can count upon an admiring and sympathizing audience among his own countrymen when he turns against the Frenchman that crushing question, "What can you think of a man who calls a *hat* a '*shappo?*'" — and the appeal is really to the same narrow prejudice and vulgar ignorance in the one case as in the other.

The future is a very long period, and a great deal is possible in the course of it. There is no telling, spite of present appearances, that the public temper may not come to admit, some time, the introduction of improvements of one kind and another into our orthography, which shall prepare the way for a more thorough reform. Meanwhile we look with interest and respect upon the effort of every one who is laboring toward that end, since, however little he may seem to accomplish, he is at least contributing his mite toward the arousing of public attention to the subject, and helping perhaps to inaugurate a change of feeling.

Respecting the further difficulties — many and serious, and only partially apprehended by the greater part of those who undertake the making of phonetic systems — which beset the labors of the orthographic reformer, and render his success doubtful, even supposing the preliminary obstacle of which we have been treating to be cleared away, we cannot, here and now, undertake to speak.

VIII.

THE ELEMENTS OF ENGLISH PRONUNCIATION.

IT is a fact well known to the students of language that no living tongue is spoken in an entirely accordant manner by the whole body of those to whom it is native. Differences of utterance (along with differences of phraseology and signification) sometimes rise to such a degree as to produce strongly defined dialects, the speakers of which can hardly, if at all, understand one another. The existence of such "dialects," alongside the approved speech of the cultivated, is as general as the existence of a cultivated speech. But even in the utterance of the latter the same discordances occur; on a smaller scale, indeed, yet marked enough to allow the various locality of different well-educated speakers to be detected by one who has the requisite quickness of ear, and a sufficiently wide experience. We could not expect it to be otherwise. The same effects are due to the same causes, in the one case as in the other; they only differ in degree with the different efficiency and length of action of the causes. The universally inherent tendency of language to vary in the usage of various individual speakers can be kept well under, but it cannot be entirely repressed, by the counteracting influence of communication in its various forms, of instruction, of the imitation of accepted models. Even educated usage has never been made precisely accordant, down to the last particular; and if it were once by a miracle made so, it could not be kept so; the lapse of a certain time would show the old state of things brought back again. Discordant pronunciation, within certain narrowly defined limits, is the inevitable condition of existence of even the best regulated language. Recognizing this truth, the student of language is not too much disturbed by his observation of deviations from the strictest norm of fashionable utterance — not even if he observes them in himself; they are all matter for interested scientific curiosity; they are indications of what has been, or of what is going to be, or of what is trying to be but will not succeed in becoming, good and approved speech; they are part and parcel of that pervading and ceaseless play and change which makes the life of language.

If I endeavor, then, to give in this paper an analysis and description of the elements of my own native pronunciation of English, it is partly in order to furnish a small contribution to the subject of English dialectic utterance — a subject which is now receiving more attention than ever hitherto,[1] and is entitled to much more than it receives. In faithfully reporting my own peculiarities of utterance, I shall have to make, at one and another point, what may be called the "confessions of a provincial;" but this, for the reason already stated, I shall not allow to daunt me. For aught that I know, my speech may be taken as a fair specimen of that of the ordinarily educated New Englander from the interior; a region where (to characterize it by a single trait) the proper distinction of *shall* and *will* was as strictly maintained, and a slip in the use of the one for the other as rare, and as immediately noticeable and offensive (unfortunately, that is the case no longer), as in the best society of London.[2]

[1] Especially from English scholars, under the lead of Mr. Ellis and the London Philological Society.

[2] My place of residence and education, up to sixteen years old, was in Massachusetts, on the Connecticut river, at Northampton — a shire-town of long standing, which in my youth had not lost its ancient and well-established repu-

But my object is also in part to incite and help some who are speakers of English to a better comprehension of the phonetics of their own language. The study of phonetics has also long been coming forward into more and more prominence as an essential part of the study of language; a thorough understanding of the mode of production of alphabetic sounds, and of their relations to one another as determined by their physical character, has become an indispensable qualification of a linguistic scholar. And he who cannot take to pieces his own native utterance, and give a tolerably accurate account of every item in it, lacks the true foundation on which everything else should repose. In order the better to advance this object, I shall take up the elements of utterance in systematic order, with reference to their mutual relations, and their character as members of a unitary and harmonious scheme.[1]

tation as a home of "old families," and a scene of special culture and high-bred society; the birthplace of President Timothy Dwight, and long the home of President Jonathan Edwards. My father was a merchant and banker, not himself a college-taught man, but son of a graduate of Harvard; my mother's parents were from the shore of Connecticut, her father a clergyman and graduate of Yale.

[1] The profoundest phonetist of the day, and especially the highest authority on matters of English pronunciation, is Alexander J. Ellis, lately President of the London Philological Society. Under his influence and instruction, there is growing up in England a most promising school of phonetic science. The last issued part of his great work on *Early English Pronunciation*, received after most of this paper was written, contains a vast mass of observations, determinations, and discussions in phonology, which no one who wishes to penetrate deeply into the subject should leave unstudied. If it had reached me earlier, I should perhaps have laid it at the basis of my own exposition, only noting such deviations from the author's scheme as I found it necessary to make. As things are, I have preferred to go on in my own independent way, without detailed reference to or criticism of other authorities. I have especially in view, on the one hand, the needs of the beginner or less practiced student; and, on the other hand, the working out and presentation of a single connected scheme of the English spoken alphabet, according to its physical relations.

I have not added pictorial representations of the defined positions of the mouth-organs, such as are given by Max Müller in the third lecture of his second course on language, and by A. M. Bell in his "Visible Speech," mainly because they seem to me of only subordinate value; they illustrate, rather than help define or teach. No cross-section of the mouth can be more than a rude

As preliminary to our descriptions, we need to note only briefly, and in its simplest form, the theory of articulate utterance. Our lungs act as bellows, sending a column of air with more or less of force through the windpipe, to find exit at the mouth or nose. At the upper extremity of the windpipe, in the box of complicated construction called the larynx, are a pair of membranes, which in their ordinary relaxed state leave a wide triangular opening for the breath to traverse freely; but which can be by voluntary action brought close together and stretched, so that their tense edges, the vocal cords, vibrate under the impulses of the passing column of air, like the reed of an organ-pipe, and produce sound, of various pitch. Then the pharynx (the upper back cavity, continuous with the esophagus, into which the larynx opens), the cavity of the mouth, and the passages of the nose, constitute together a sounding-box set over the resonant organ of the larynx, and by their changes of size and form they give variety of audible character to the fundamental tone of the organ. Wherein lies the separate audible character of each articulate utterance, and how it depends upon the muscular action of the throat and mouth, are matters of acoustic rather than of phonetic science; the latter attempts only to trace out and define the muscular action which actually produces the utterance.

1. In any discussion of the alphabet, the first place must necessarily be given to the *a* of *far*, *father*. It is the fundamental vowel-tone of the human voice, the sound which is emitted from the larynx when mouth and throat are widely opened, when all obstructing and modifying influences are put as much as possible out of the way of the issuing column of intoned breath. No other

and insufficient depiction of the mouth-action; and the very considerable discordance between Müller's figures and Bell's (the latter, to be sure, are in general far the better) shows the great difficulty of attaining to anything like accuracy of representation.

definition of it than this is correct and properly characteristic. It is the sound which the sign *a* was at the outset made in order to represent, and which regularly and usually belongs to that sign in other languages than English. We call it the "Italian *a*," taking the Italian as representative of the languages which have preserved to the written character its true original sound; we might just as well call it the German, or Latin, or Greek. In the earliest Indo-European speech, this *a* was by far the most common of articulate utterances; in the Sanskrit, in its long and short forms, it makes over seventy per cent. of the vowels, and about thirty per cent. of the whole alphabet; in the oldest Germanic dialect, the Mœso-Gothic, it is still fourteen per cent. of the alphabet; in the German, only about five per cent.; and in my utterance of English, little more than half of one per cent., being almost the rarest of the simple vowel sounds.[1] The tendency of speech has been to reduce this openest of vowels to a closer form, by substituting for it a variety of utterances requiring less expansion of the articulating organs. But there is hardly another language, if there be any other, which has carried this tendency so far, and retained so little of the *a*-sound, as ours. An *r* following it in the same syllable has been with us the most efficient means of its preservation: thus, in *are*, *debar*, *art*, *margin*, *harp*, *carnation*. And it is almost only in this class of words that the most approved modern usage sanctions it. Until quite recently, it was admitted in other classes also: thus, in *calm*, *calf*, *halve*; in *answer*, *chance*, *blanch*, *pant*, *can't*, *aunt*; in *alas*, *pass*, *bask*, *clasp*, *blaspheme*, *last*; in *path*, *lath*; in *laugh*, *staff*, *raft*, *after*; and in many other words like these. In all of them the leading orthoëpists now require a "flattened"

1 Respecting the English percentages given here and later, see the table and its explanation at the end of this article; those of the other languages named I take from Förstemann, in Kuhn's *Zeitschrift*, ii. 35 *seq*.

a, which is described either as identical with the *a* of *fat* and *fan*, or, more often, as intermediate between *far* and *fat*. But local usage (I cannot say how extensively) still retains the old open *a* in these words; and, in my opinion, is justified in clinging to it as long as possible. In my own mouth, certainly, they are all still uttered with the *a* of *far;* and in my natural utterance I have absolutely no knowledge of anything intermediate between *far* and *fat*. Whether English pronunciation is likely to establish such an intermediate as a permanent constituent of our spoken alphabet, or whether the words which have fallen from the stage of *far* will end with becoming completely and confessedly like *fat*, I would not undertake to pronounce, although I confess to inclining toward the latter view.

The interjection *ah!* and *father* are examples of a small class of sporadic cases in which the true *a*-sound appears; I learned to pronounce *gape* with the same; and *plant* is, I believe, the only word in which I ever hear it without myself pronouncing it. The subtraction of all the classes specified would reduce the occurrence of the sound in English to a quarter of one per cent.

We are accustomed to reckon the *a* of *far* as a "long" vowel. But the distinction in actual quantity of long and short vowels in English is less marked and less consistently maintained than in some other languages, because our longs differ decidedly also in quality from our shorts.

Starting, now, from the indifferent or neutral openness of *a* (in *far*), and beginning to narrow the current of breath by approaching the flat of the tongue toward the palate, we produce by gradually increasing degrees of closure a series of vowels to which we may conveniently (though rather loosely) give the name of "palatal." The three principal degrees of approach give, in their order, the vowel-sounds of *pan*, *pen*, and *pin*.

2. To the *a* of *pan* we give the name of "short *a*," from its greatly superior frequency among the short sounds given to that character, and from its standing often in the relation of corresponding short to our "long *a*" (see below, No. 5), as in *defāme dĕfămatory*, *grāteful grătitude*, *nāture nătural*. We also call it "flat *a*," by a figure of questionable propriety; and we are wont to speak of the reduction of the proper *a*-sound (*far*) to or toward it (not infrequent in parts of the English-speaking community, as also in Parisian French: it is absolutely unknown in my dialect, as has been pointed out above) as a "flattening" of the vowel. A slight exaggeration and prolongation of the flat *a* gives a peculiarly disagreeable and vulgar effect. The sound is among the most common of English vowels, forming about three and one third per cent. of our utterance. Lepsius writes it by an *a* with subscript *e* (thus, *a̦*), thus marking it, very suitably, as an *a* slightly verging toward *e*. Its sign in Ellis's "Palæotype"[1] is *æ*; and this, for lack of type for the other, I shall use when necessary.

3. This "short *a*" has, according to the approved pronunciation, no corresponding long vowel. In my own usage, however, the vowels of such words as *pare*, *pair*, *prayer*, *there*, *their*, *wear*, have the same sound, a little protracted, and followed by the vanishing-sound of "short *u*" (*but*) which other long vowels take in a like situation, before *r* (e. g. *hear*, *mire*, *sour*, *cure*, *soar*: see below, under *r*). The orthoëpists require in this class of words an *ē*-sound (as in *they*): it would, however, have to be described and reckoned as a separate alphabetic element in English speech, because it lacks the *ī* vanish of the usual *ē*. The utterance as "short *a*" (*æ*) is not infrequently mentioned as a dialectic variation, on both sides of the ocean; I have no information as to the extent of its occurrence. The difference between the two

[1] See the Introduction to his *Early English Pronunciation*.

pronunciations in acoustic effect is so slight as to escape any other than an acute and attentive ear.

I write this longer sound, for distinction from the other, with Æ.

The double sound which we have been considering is, as it seems to me, a true intermediate between *a* (*far*) and *e* (*they*, *met*), and thus markedly different from the French *è* and *ê* or the German *ä*, with which it is sometimes identified. These are merely opener varieties of *e*; our *æ* is no more an *e* than it is an *a*.

4. The "short *e*" of *met* is in fact the sound which the name indicates: that is to say, it is a short variety of that sound, intermediate between *a* (*far*) and *i* (*pique*), which the sign *e* was originally made to represent. The *e* is the most Protean of the vowels, the most variously and nicely shaded in different languages, the hardest to seize and reproduce with absolute exactness. Its sign (as we may express it) designates a space rather than a point in the transition from *a* to *i*; it belongs to a whole class or series of sounds, differing slightly from one another in point of closeness. Our "short *e*" is a pretty open member of the series, agreeing with the French *è* or *ê* rather than *é*. It is one of our commonest sounds, forming, like the *æ* (*fat*), just about three and one third per cent. of our utterance.

There is little discordance in general among English speakers as to the words in which this vowel-sound occurs. Examples of it are *let*, *felt*, *flesh*; *bread*, *said*, *says*, *jeopard*, *treachery*, *any*. So far as I know, *any* and *many* are the only words in which an *a* is allowed to be pronounced as "short *e*;" but, until I overcame the habit by a conscious effort, I always gave it the same sound in *plague*, *snake*, *naked*; nor did I escape the pronunciation of *catch* as *ketch* — a deeply rooted error, almost universal among children in this part of the world. *Deaf* I heard so constantly as both *dĭf* and *dĕf* that I cannot now tell which was more "natural" to me; *leisure* I always called *lĕisure*, as do, I believe, most Americans.

5. The vowel in *fate*, *fail*, *great*, *they*, we call "long *a*," by a regretable misnomer, growing out of the fact that a large proportion of the true long *a*'s of the language have undergone transformation into it; it is an *e*-sound, our nearest long correspondent to the short *ĕ* of *met*. It is not, however, a pure vowel-sound; it only begins with *e*, and slides off into *i* (*pin*, *pique*). In our ordinary use, it seems to me a real slide from beginning to end, starting with *e* but not dwelling upon it;[1] if, however, we protract it by an effort, as in singing, we lengthen the first element and wind up with the vanish.[2] A more accurate representation of it, then, would be *ei*, or e^i; but, for simplicity's sake, I shall take the liberty of using *ē*. To compare the quality of its initial element with the *ĕ* of *met* is not easy, since, if one protracts it in order to examine it more closely, one runs great risk of unwittingly distorting it a little. But I think the *ē* begins with a closer utterance, in conformity with the usual relation between our short and long vowels. The difference, at any rate, is very slight, and of little account as compared with the distinction of the two sounds as homogeneous and as transitional.

The *ē* averages only half as frequent as *ĕ*, its percentage in our utterance being but one and two thirds.

6. What we call "short *i*"—as in *pin*, *hit*, *kick*—is also really a short *i*, and properly representable by *i* (or, where fuller distinction is necessary, *ĭ*). Like our other short vowels, however, it is very noticeably different in quality as well as quantity from the long *ī* (which we call "long *e*:" see the next number); being, as I should de-

[1] That is to say, representable figuratively by *e*⟩*i*, not by *e*⟩*i*.

[2] Of course, in all such cases, I say "we" and "our" on the assumption, recognized as liable to error, that my utterance is like that of other speakers, and under correction from those who shall be satisfied that they pronounce differently.

scribe it, a somewhat opener sound than the latter; the tongue, in order to form it, is not brought quite so close to the palate. A. M. Bell, on the contrary,[1] holds here, as in some other like cases, that the actual aperture between tongue and palate is the same for both sounds; and he distinguishes the ī as "primary" and the ĭ as "wide," — the latter term implying an expanded condition of the pharynx behind the aperture. To me, the action of a slight removal of tongue from palate in passing from ī to ĭ, and of a slight approximation in passing from ĭ to ī, seems distinctly apparent. The eminent German physiologist, Dr. Brücke of Vienna,[2] calls our "short *i*," as well as the vowels of *not*, *full*, and *but*, "imperfectly formed." Such a definition of their character is by no means to be approved. Every vowel, if simple, is an utterance through a single definite position of the mouth organs; and I know not what should justify us in declaring any one position more "perfect" or "complete" than any other. The ĭ is not less capable of being continued without change of quality than the ī. Thus, in singing, no English ear would fail to detect in a moment the performer who, in giving a long note to an ĭ, should change its tone to ī — putting *seen*, for example, in place of *sin*. Foreign phonetists are to be expected to find difficulty in dealing with the sound, because it is not native to them. The shortest *i* in French, for instance, is not a particle less close than our "long *e*;" and the point is one on which a teacher of French pronunciation to English pupils has most strongly to insist.

The short ĭ is the most common of English vowel-sounds, constituting nearly six per cent. of our articulations. It is represented almost exclusively by *i*: there is a small class of cases of *y* with this value, as in *abyss*; but other words like *busy* and *minute*, like *women*, *sieve*,

1 See below, p. 303.

2 In his *Grundzüge der Phys. und Syst. der Sprachlaute*, p. 23.

been, *guilt*, and *build*, are only sporadic. *Been* is often uttered as *bĕn* in New England, as doubtless elsewhere: I am not sure that I did not have to unlearn that pronunciation in early boyhood.

7. What we call "long *e*," as in *meet*, *mete*, *meat*, *pique*, is, as has been already pointed out, the long sound which *i* was made to represent and still almost everywhere represents. It is curious that our short palatal vowels, *ĕ* and *ĭ*, have kept very nearly their ancient sounds, while short *a* has been generally "flattened" or palatalized, into the *æ* of *pan*, and while long *a* has been pushed a step farther down the palatal declivity, to the proper *e*-position, and long *e* a like step, to the proper *i*-position; long *i*, finally, being raised to a diphthongal value, which will be discussed later (No. 16). As to the quality of this articulation (which we will call and write long *ī*), there is, I believe, no question; nor as to its correspondence with the kindred sounds of other tongues: it is the French, German, Italian — in short, the universal — long *ī*, the closest vowel-sound that can be produced between the flat of the tongue and the palate: one may bring these organs so near together that a frication, a consonantal rustling, begins to appear, and what of vowel-sound remains will still be *ī*.

The most frequent representatives of *ī* in English, besides those instanced above, are *ie*, as in *yield*, *grief*, or *ei* after *c*, as in *receive*, *conceit*, or *ey* final, as in *key*. There are a few sporadic cases like *people*, *ægis*. Words like *pique*, *fatigue*, *machine*, *shire* (in America), in which the sound has its own proper sign, are very few, hardly a dozen in all. The long *ī* is only half as common as the short *ĭ*; its percentage is less than three (2⅓).

With *ī* ends, as we have seen, the series of vowels produced by an approximation of the flat of the tongue to the palate; we have next to take up a like series, also beginning from the neutral openness of *a*, and involving an action of the lips. The series is illustrated, in the order of progressive closeness, by the vowels of *what*, *war*, *hole*, *full*, *fool*: any one can see for himself, by uttering these vowels in rapid succession, that they require a constantly increasing rounding of the lips, which reaches its extreme in *oo*, and that they tend to run together into a continuous slide. The lip action, however, as we must not fail also to notice, is not the only element in their production: there is an accompanying movement of approach also between the base of the tongue and the back part of the palate, or the pharynx. One may hold his lips fixed immovably in a single position (that, for instance, in which *e* or *i* is naturally pronounced), and yet utter the vowels of *what* and *all* with perfect distinctness; one can also, by an effort, make an *o* and *oo*, clearly recognizable as such and nothing else, although wanting the smoothness of quality which belongs to our usual *o* and *oo*. And, on the other hand, one can fix the lips in the *oo*-position, and yet, by a violent and exaggerated opening action at the base of the tongue, say an unexceptionable *a* (*far*). Change in the form of the resonant cavity which determines the vowel-sound is perhaps more effective, the nearer it is to the vibrating instrument in the larynx, and the deficient action at the orifice is capable of being at least mainly compensated by additional action farther back: we may possibly even have to attribute more essential importance to the lingual than to the labial movement in the formation of our series; yet, as the lips are the organs which we consciously and observably move, and the tongue moves accordantly by an involuntary association which only close attention and study can discover, and as the vowels produced show abundant historical relations with the labial consonants, we are, as I think, fully justified in calling the series "labial."

8. The "short *o*" of *not*, *what*, is the first of the labial series. It gets its ordinary name from the fact

that so many of the short *o*'s of our language have been raised to it. It is often described and reckoned as the corresponding short sound to the vowel of *all*, *for*, etc.: and so, undoubtedly, it is in a certain sense; only, like all our other short vowels, it differs from its correspondent in being also of opener quality. And, to my apprehension, the difference is even greater than is usual between our longs and shorts; the sound in question occupies so nearly a medial position between the *a* of *far* and that of *war* that it might with equal propriety be regarded as the short sound of either. It verges, therefore, very closely upon the true short *a*, as of German *mann*, *alt*, French *ma*, *chat*, and is acoustically much nearer to *a* (*far*) — though always sharply and accurately distinguished from it — than is the so-called "short *a*" (*æ*) of *pan*, etc. For the sake of convenience, therefore, I shall represent it by *ă̆*.[1] It is among the more common members of our alphabetic system, constituting more than two and one half per cent. of our sounds. Besides *o*, and such substitutes for *o* as the *ou* of *hough* and the *ow* of *knowledge*, it has a not unfrequent representative in *a*, but only after a *w*-sound: thus, *what*, *was*, *wan*, *quarry*, *squad*. This last is a plain case of consonantal influence on the vowel tone; the labial semivowel has communicated a slight labial tinge to its successor.

9. The next degree of labial closure gives the "broad *a*" of *all*, or the *au*-sound. It is a step farther from the neutral *a* (*far*), and a true intermediate between it and *o*, as the *æ* of *pan* between *a* and *e* (*they*). That the intermediate sound on the labial side should be a long vowel, while on the palatal it is a short, is in accordance with the fact (to be noticed later) that in the labial series the old long vowels have retained prevailingly their

[1] Ellis, in his *Palæotype*, uses a turned *c* (ɔ) for the "short *o*" of *not*, *on*, etc., and treats the vowel of *what*, etc., as distinct, and as the precise abbreviation of that of *all*.

original value. It much less common than the sound last discussed, making only one and one half per cent. of our articulate utterance. I write it (after Ellis's example, in his "Palæotype") with a small capital ᴀ. It has in our ordinary orthography a considerable variety of written repesentatives: thus, *a* before *l*, as in *ball*, *bald*, *salt*, *false*, and also where the *l* is silenced, as in *talk* and *walk*; *a* after *w* (a case of assimilation, like that noted just above), before *r*, as in *war*, *ward*, *warm*, *dwarf*, and before *n* in *want*; very frequently *o*, as in *for*, *form*, *absorb*, *off*, *often*, *loss*, *lost*, *cloth*, *song*; regularly *au* and always *aw*, as in *haul*, *daub*, *caught*, *law*, *fawn*; *ou* in *bought* and its like; and a few scattering cases like *broad*, *extraordinary*. As regards this sound, there would be found more of individual difference, I believe, in the treatment of the *o*-class than of any other. In my own usage, I am perfectly persuaded that all the words I have given, with many others of which they are examples, have precisely the same "*au*-sound"—although it would be easy, by drawling and distorting the utterance even a very little, to make some of them seem ungraceful and vulgar; and I would say the same of *God*, *dog*, and their like, in which many persons certainly give the "short *o*" (*ă*) sound of *not*.

10. In the regular and authorized pronunciation of English there is no such thing, in accented syllables, as a true short *o*. The sound, however, is a well-recognized element of New England utterance, in a very small number of words—whether and how far outside of New England and its colonies, and whether at all among the educated on the other side of the ocean, I cannot say. By it, *nŏne* is as perfectly distinguished from *knōwn*, and *whŏle* from *hōle*, as is *full* from *fool*, and *sin* from *seen*: and in these two words (though *none* is often pronounced like *nun*, even in New England) the sound in question most clearly and frequently appears. The list of words in

which it is given varies, I think, not a little in different individuals: in my own practice, it is nearly or quite[1] restricted to *none*, *whole*, *home*, *stone*, *smoke*, *folks*, *coat*, *cloak*, *toad*, *throat*; I have heard most often from others, in addition, *bŏne* and *bŏat*. It makes, of course, a hardly appreciable percentage of English utterance.

Much as the orthoëpists may discard and stigmatize this sound, a phonologist can hardly help wishing well in his secret heart to a tendency which would relieve the English spoken alphabet of such an anomaly and reproach as the absence of a true short *ŏ*.

11. The "long *o*" of *note*, *moat*, etc., differs from the sound just treated in being a longer and a somewhat closer utterance, and especially in having a vanish of *u*, precisely as *ē* (*they*) has a vanish of *ī*. It is a little more common than *ĕ*, as constituent of our utterance, making up one and three fourths per cent. Its written forms are numerous: besides those already instanced, it has frequently *ow* and *ou*, as in *low*, *own*, *dough*, *four*, *shoulder*; sometimes *oo*, as in *door*; and sporadically such as *beau*, *yeoman*, *memoir*, *sew*.

12. The true short *u*, as heard in *full*, *bosom*, *could*, *good*, stands related to its corresponding long, in *fool*, *rule*, *move*, etc., precisely as the *i* of *sin* to that of *seen*; that is to say (as I should define it), it has a slightly opener quality. One may, it seems to me, convince himself even more readily and certainly here than in the case of *ĭ* and *ī* that the difference is one of approach in the articulating organs rather than of expansion of the pharynx behind them; in passing from *ŭ* to *ū*, I, at least, am conscious of a very perceptible impulse to round and close the lips a little more. The sound is one of the rarest in English utterance, being less than half of one per cent. Of its four written representatives, the *u* is by far the

[1] I have lost the record which I made twenty-five years ago for the *ŏ*-sound, and do not feel quite certain that I have restored it entire.

most common, the others having but a few words apiece. A part of them, at least, are recent corruptions from the "long *u*" or *oo*-sound, by a process like that which, as above noticed, has converted *whōle* and *hōme* into *whŏle* and *hŏme;* and the change appears to be still going on: *rood*, *roof*, and *root* are words in which one often hears the short instead of the long sound; and *root*, especially, is very widely and commonly pronounced like *foot;* I learned it so, and still give it so, unless by a conscious effort. I also naturally give the same vowel-sound to *does;* and it is evidently historically older here than the present approved utterance (rhyming to *buzz*).

The difference in the treatment by the language of its long and short vowels on the palatal and on the labial side is quite a marked feature in English phonology. Among the palatals it is the short *e* and *i* which have been so generally retained that we still call them by their proper names, and they are more than twice as numerous as the corresponding long sounds; among the labials, the long *o* and *u* are comparatively unchanged, and they are many times more numerous than the corresponding shorts. And whereas the long vowels on the one side have become more palatal, the short vowels on the other have declined in point of labiality, the *ŏ* becoming the almost neutral *ă* of *not*, and the *ŭ* the wholly neutral vowel of *but*, *fun*, etc.

13. The pure long *u*-sound of *food*, *move*, *rule*, etc., is the closest possible labial vowel, and verges, like *ī* (*pique*), closely upon the consonants; nor is it, I believe, distinguished by any even slight tinge of utterance from the "long *u*'s" of other languages in general. It has two principal classes of written representatives, the *o*-class and the *u*-class. The former, which have evidently changed their *o*-sound for an *u* only in comparatively recent times, are *o* and *oo*, as in *do*, *to*, *lose*, *womb*, and *room*, *fool;* *ou* is used very little except in recent impor-

tations from the French, like *route*, *routine;* the Saxon *uncouth* is an almost isolated case; *wound* (not from *wind*) is a bone of contention; its partial retention to modern times of the old *u*-sound is probably in part due to the euphonic influence of the *w*, and to the disposition to establish a distinction of utterance between it and *wound* from *wind*, and for the latter reason, at least, deserves to be encouraged: I have heard it so constantly given both ways that neither is more natural to me than the other. The other class is made up of *u*, *ue* (final), *ui*, *ew*, *eu;* as in *duty*, *pure*, *due*, *fruit*, *rheum*, *feud*, *brew*, *few*, *stew*. The *u*-sound in the first class, now, is preserved always pure; but in the other it is more or less mixed with a preceding *i* or *y*-sound, and this mixture constitutes one of the more striking anomalies and difficulties of English pronunciation. The matter is one upon which common usage, both in this country and in England, is considerably at variance, and modes of pronunciation unsanctioned by the orthoëpic authorities are widely current, even among the educated. Heretical practices are, I believe, particularly prevalent in New England, and my own is an example of them. What my own is, I wish to describe here as accurately as I can; at the same time confessing that I have never been willing to exchange it for such as was more in accordance with approved rules. It has so definite and regular a character, and reposes upon so reasonable a foundation, that I am not sure that it may not be the good English pronunciation of the future, while it has, I believe, a great deal of respectable support even at present, on both sides of the ocean.

In my usage, and in that of those who pronounce with me, there is no intermediate sound or compromise whatever between a pure *u*, the vowel-sound of *food* and *move*, and an absolute *yu*, in which the *y*-element is as distinctly uttered as it would be if it were written. The general rule, with us as with the rest, is that the *y*-sound is prefixed ; and the exceptional cases, in which the *y* is omitted and the *u* left pure, are those in which the *u* is so preceded that the insertion of the semivowel between it and its predecessor is phonetically difficult.

The *y* (as will be more particularly pointed out below) is a palatal semivowel, produced nearly in the articulating position of ī (*pique*), or by an approximation of the flat of the tongue to the roof of the mouth in its after part. It is only, then, those consonants in forming which the tongue is called into action in some other way — that is to say, the lingual consonants — which present an obstacle to the insertion of the *y*.

Hence, if the ū (or *eu*, *ew*) be either initial, or preceded by the neutral aspiration *h*, or by the palatal mutes *k* and *g*, or by the labial consonants *p*, *b*, *f*, *v*, and *m*, it is pronounced as *yu* : examples are *use*, *unite*, *eulogy*, *ewe* ; *huge*, *exhume*, *hew* ; *cube*, *acute*, *accurate* ; *figure*, *gewgaw* ; *pure*, *compute*, *suppurate*, *spew* ; *bureau*, *abuse*, *fabulous* ; *fume*, *perfume*, *feud*, *few*, *nephew* ; *ovule* ; *mute*, *munition*, *emulate*, *mew*. In all the classes of words here instanced, there is probably no discordance among English speakers, as regards the way in which the *u*-sound is uttered.

When we come, however, to the lingual consonants — namely, *t*, *d*, *th* (both kinds), *s*, *z*, *n*, *r*, *l* — in forming which the tongue is already employed at its tip, the interpolation of a new action at its base between the consonant and the following vowel becomes a matter of more difficulty, and there is a tendency to get rid of it.

And this tendency is much the strongest in the case of the *r*, in uttering which the tongue is even rolled back at its tip into the roof of the mouth : to release it and bring the flat surface of the tongue up to nearly the same point requires so much movement and effort that the language generally has abandoned the attempt, and even the best authorities declare that after *r*, in any situation, the *u* is to be pronounced pure, like *oo:* thus, in *rule*, *rude*, *rue*, *accrue*, *construe*, *congruous*, *erudition*. There are, however, those who do not observe this rule exactly; though they may not quite introduce a *y*, they yet make a difference between the *u* and *oo*, altering the sound a little in the direction of the *u* of *burn*. As for myself, my *u* in *rude* is precisely that in *rood;* and so in all other cases.

After the other lingual consonants, English orthoëpy is regarded as calling for the inserted *y*-sound, in all situations: and here it is that the principal discordance in popular usage manifests itself, as regards both the fact and the nature of the insertion. Some introduce a full *y* before the *oo*-sound, just as after a palatal or labial (even allowing it to coalesce with preceding *t* and *d* into the *ch* and *j* sounds, pronouncing *duke* as *juke*, and *Tuesday* as *chusday*); others abbreviate it into a slight prefix which has the quality of *ĭ* (*pin*) rather than of *ī* (*pique*) or *y;* and finally, the faction to which I belong exclude the prefix entirely in a large class of cases, as follows:

No initial lingual followed by *ū* allows the intrusive *y*, whether the syllable be accented or unaccented: thus, the *u* is pure in *tube*, *tuition*, *Teutonic;* in *dupe*, *duration*, *dew;* in *nude*, *nutation*, *new*, *neuter;* in *thuriferous*, *thew;* in *sue*, *superb*, *sewer;* in *zeugma;* in *lute*, *lunation*, *lewd*, *leucoma*. The only exceptions I have noticed are *sure* and *sugar*, in both which the *s* and the *y*-prefix have combined, as usual, into the *sh*-sound: *sugar* is further anomalous in having a short *ŭ* (as in *full*); this shortening has obviously been made recently, since the iotization was fixed by being absorbed into the *sh*-sound.

Again, neither is the *u* iotized after a lingual in the interior of a word, provided the syllable in which it occurs is accented. Examples are *attune*, *mature*, *multitudinous;* *endure*, *indubitable*, *produce*, *adieu;* *assume*, *pursue*, *insuperable;* *presume;* *enthusiasm;* *anew*, *denude;*

illume, *convolution*, *diluvial*. I find but a very few exceptions to this rule: namely, the compounds of *sure*, as *assure*, *insure; luxurious*, which is a case of the same kind; and *inure*, for which I can give no reason.

If, however, the syllable containing the *u* be immediately preceded by the accent, its initial consonant (or sometimes more than one) is treated as if belonging to the accented syllable; it is, as it were, lifted off the *u*, which then becomes *yu*, just as if it were initial. Instances are '*statue*, *saturate*, *venture*, *century* (but *centurion* with pure *u*, as if *-too-*), *fortune* (but *fortuitous* with *-too-*); *modulate*, *arduous*, *credulous* (but *credulity* with *-doo-*); *tissue*, *sensuous; pleasure*, *azure; annual* (but *annuity* with *-noo-*), *ingenuous* (but *ingenuity* with *-noo-*), *penury* (but *penurious* with *-noo-*); *volume* (but *voluminous* with *-loo-*), *soluble*, *value*, *failure*.[1] Of exceptions to this rule, however, my own usage presents a more considerable number: there are, in the first place, cases of more difficult combinations before the *u*, of which the weight is not sufficiently lifted off by the accent to permit the insertion of the *y:* such are *obdurate*, *septuagint*, *abluent*, *affluent* and its like, *superfluous*, *capsule;* and perhaps *indurated*, *contumacy*, *contumely*, may be reckoned with them; and I have also noted *produce*, *prelude*, *sinew*, as apparently mere sporadic irregularities, excesses of a retroactive tendency against iotization after a lingual.

In the not numerous class of words which have a secondary accent only on the syllable before the *u*, its effect is in general the same with that of the primary accent. Thus, the *y*-sound is inserted in *adulation*, *education*, *denudation*, *mensuration*, *accentuation*, *attenuation*, *actuality*, *casuistical*, *manufactory*, *amanuensis*. Here also

[1] It should be noticed here that with *t*, *d*, *s*, and *z* the *y*-sound becomes blended, transforming them respectively into the *ch*, *j*, *sh*, and *zh*-sounds: see the discussion of these sounds below.

there are a few exceptions: I have noted only *intuition* (like *intuitive*) and *deglutition;* they are analogous with those mentioned under the preceding rule.

But finally, when the principal accent does not immediately precede, but is separated by an intervening syllable from that in which the *u* occurs, the latter getting itself a certain degree of secondary stress, there is some variety of treatment. Generally, the *u* is kept pure, as in a syllable with primary accent; it is thus with the considerable classes of words ending in *-tude*, *-tute*, *-lude*, *-lute*, etc.: as *solitude*, *institute*, *interlude*, *dissolute*, and their like; it is thus also with *avenue*, *retinue*, *residue*, (but *residual* with *-yu-*), with *mameluke*, *demilune*, *involucre*, *pentateuch*, *hypothenuse:* in all such words the *u* in my mouth is free from all mixture with a *y*. But the ending *ture* forms a general exception, always admitting the iotization: thus, *furniture*, *investiture*, *ligature*, and so on (of course, in *agriculture*, where the secondary accent precedes the *u*-syllable); although I think we sometimes hear the pronunciation *-toor* in such words.

With those who follow the method of pronunciation thus explained, this peculiar modification of the *u*-sound (into the question of the origin and age of which I must forbear here to enter) introduces no additional element into the English spoken alphabet: whatever is not pure *u* (*oo*) is *yu*, to be reckoned as divisible into *y* and *ū*.

We come next to a quite peculiar pair of vowels, short and long: namely, the "short *u*" of *but*, *son*, *flood*, *double*, and the *u* of *burn*. They are more nearly akin with the open *a* of *far* than with any other of our vowels: that is to say, whereas in the palatal and labial series, which we have been considering, there is a distinct approximation of the mouth-organs at certain definable points, in these two there is rather a general closure of the aperture of the mouth, along the whole line of the tongue. In *a*, the organs are expanded, to give full and clear exit to the sound; in these, they are left in the way, to dim the tone; they are quiescent instead of active; the product is the pure intonated breathing, the grunt or murmur. It is, then, with much propriety, often named the "neutral vowel." It appears in many languages as results of the de-articulation, as we may call it, of other more positive utterances: thus, in most of modern India, the old *a*, when short, has sunk to this sound, becoming what the Sanskrit grammarians call the "covered up (*samvrita*) *a*;" in French, the "mute *e*," when not absolutely mute, has the neutral tone; and the nasal *u* (in *un*, *brun*, etc.) and even the *eu* are very closely related to it; in part of Germany, the unaccented final *e* takes the same sound; the German *ö*, though not far removed, is of different quality and of very different origin, being a mixture of the medial palatal position of *e* with the medial labial position of *o*. The dimming action of the mouth-organs is capable of degrees, like any other articulating action, and a series of vowels between the *a* of *far* and the *u* of *burn* must be admitted as theoretically possible; but the only two which we actually use are very definite in their character, and as necessary to be uttered with exactness as the *i* or *u*-sounds; and, as usual elsewhere, the short *u* of *but* is a little opener than the long of *burn*, differing from it as the vowel of *full* from that of *fool*, as the vowel of *sin* from that of *seen*.

14. The "short *u*" of *but*, *love*, *flood*, *touch*, as found in accented syllables, is a vowel of medial frequency, making a little more than two per cent. of our utterance. Our unaccented vowels, however, tend to run into it on such a scale as nearly to treble its actual occurrence: see below, where this tendency will be discussed and illustrated. Its most common representative by far is *u*, whence the name by which we are accustomed to call it. The signs *o* and *ou* are also found in a considerable number of words; *oo* is much more rare, and any other sporadic only: I have noted only the *i* of *squirrel* (according to the only pro-

nunciation of that word which I have ever heard in America) and the *oe* of *does:* which latter, however (as mentioned above), I myself, with many others, grew up to pronounce naturally with the real short *ŭ* of *full*, the true and natural abbreviation of the long *ū* of *do* — like *says* (*sĕz*) from *say* (*sē*). Lepsius represents the sound by an *e* with a small circle below — thus, *e̥;* in Ellis's "Palæotype," it is written with a turned *e* — thus, *ə;* and, for the sake of convenience, I shall use the latter when necessary.[1]

15. The longer and closer shade of neutral vowel utterance is found in our language only before an *r*, and is the indifferent middle sound into which have passed, before *r*, a number of vowels which, not very long ago, were distinguished from one another. Examples are the following (given nearly in the order of frequency of each representative letter): *urn*, *fur*, *murky*, *disturb; bird*, *dirty*, *astir*, *irksome; err*, *were*, *fern*, *determine; heard*, *learning*, *search; work*, *worship*, *attorney; adjourn*, *scourge; tierce*. In all these classes, according to my pronunciation and that of the immense majority of those whom I hear, there is absolutely no difference in the vowel-sound uttered: instances are rare of those who still make a distinction among them — almost solely, I believe, by giving something of a real *e*-quality to *e* and *ea*. Notwithstanding its restriction to syllables containing *r*, this sound is not very much rarer than the one last treated (in accented syllables); it forms nearly two per cent. of our utterance. I shall represent it, for the sake of analogy with its corresponding short vowel, by a turned small capital E — thus, ᴲ.

The peculiar relation in which our neutral vowels stand to the *r* will render it necessary to make them the subject of further remark when we come to consider the *r*.

[1] A turned *a* would be theoretically preferable, considering the kinship of the sound designated with *a;* but a turned italic *a* is too indistinct in form to be available for use.

We have now to take up the diphthongs, or combinations of more than one vowel sound within the limits of the same syllable. In strictness, our *ē* (*they*) and *ō* *note*) are diphthongal, since they do not maintain to the end the tone with which they are begun; and much the same thing is true, as will be pointed out below, of many of our long vowels before an *r;* but such cases are sufficiently different from the true diphthongs to make it not only allowable but preferable to regard them rather as vowels with a vanishing sound added to them, and to treat the diphthongs as a separate class.

The first two of our three diphthongs—namely, the *ai* of *aisle*, or the "long *ī*" of *bite*, and the *ou* or *ow* sound of *mouth*, *down*—are very obviously and closely akin in character. They are not, as it appears to me, so much combinations of two distinct sounds, as slides: movements of transition from the indifferent openness of *a* (*far*) through the whole series of palatal and lingual positions, as we have called them, to *i* (*pique*) and *u* (*rule*) respectively. The mouth-organs do not rest an instant in the *a*-position at their beginning, but use it merely as a starting-point. This distinguishes our *ai*, for example, from the German's *ei* or *ai*: the German dwells long enough upon the initial *a*-sound to give to the ear a distinct apprehension of *a* as an element in the combination.[1] Hence the peculiar impression of unity which the sounds make. Exceedingly few of those who use them, even with attention particularly called to their character, will recognize them as other than simple. And the transitional movement by which they are produced is performed so rapidly and easily that they hardly require more than the time of a short vowel.

It is matter of dispute among English phonetists, whether the initial position in these diphthongal slides is

[1] That is to say, our sound, if represented by a figure, would be neither *a*  *i*, nor *a*  *i*, but *a* 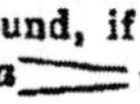 *i*.

that of *a* (*far*) or that of the neutral vowel (*but*), and some of the best authorities (as Ellis) favor the latter. Very probably there is an actual difference of usage in different parts of the English-speaking community. The fact that, as we have seen, there is in ordinary speaking no prolongation of the initial element, makes a satisfactory determination of the point difficult. For my own part, I am fully persuaded that I begin with the *a* of *far*.

16. The first diphthong, then, is that which we ordinarily call "long *i*," because, by a phonetic change which is very peculiar though not without its analogies elsewhere, the real long *i* (pronounced as in *pique*) of Anglo-Saxon and early English has been changed into it. Its usual representative is *i*, as in *mine*, *desire*, *design*, *night*; or *y*, as in *type*, *try*, and *ie*, as in *pie*, *relied*; others are only sporadic, as *eye*, *buy* and *guy*, and *height* and *sleight*. These last two are the only English words in which *ei* has had the diphthongal sound; which, however, is beginning to be extensively heard in *either* and *neither*. Whatever actual foundation this last may have in the native usage of any part of the English-speaking people, it has spread in recent times far beyond that foundation, by a kind of reasonless and senseless infection, which can only be condemned and ought to be stoutly opposed and put down. I have no quarrel with those to whom *aither* and *naither* are a genuine part of their English dialect, who heard the pronunciation in their childhood and grew up to use it unconsciously; but that vastly larger class who originally said *eether* and *neether*, and have since gone about deliberately to change it, ought to realize with shame the folly of which they have been guilty, and to reform.

There is a class of words from the classical languages, of which *isolate* and *microscope* are perhaps the two most frequent examples, where common usage wavers between the "short" and "long" sounds of the *i* — that is, between *ĭ* and *ai*, the lightest and heaviest of vowel utterances; and apparently with a tendency to settle upon *ai*: a regretable tendency, I think, as involving so great a distortion of the original and proper sound of the vowel. In any such case, where usage still gives us the right to make our individual choice, it is well to choose what is most in accordance with the habits of other communities who use the same word. Germans, French, Italians, and all the other nations of Europe, would understand our *mīcroscope*, while *maicroscope* appears plainly to their ears the barbarous distortion which it actually is.

This diphthong is, of course, most naturally and correctly represented by *ai*. It is of more frequent occurrence than many of the simple vowels, forming nearly two per cent. of the whole body of our articulations.

17. The second diphthong is written in English only by *ou* and *ow*, as in *mouth*, *doughty*, *abounding*, *now*, *brown*. It is most accurately written by *au*. If its first element is not a pure *a* (*far*), it is, I think, rather the slightly labialized *ă* of *what* than the neutral ə of *but*, with which latter Ellis identifies it. A flattening of the initial element into *æ* (*pan*) gives it that disagreeable and vulgar sound which the English are wont to regard as American, the Americans as Yankee, the New Englander as Pennsylvanian or Southern, and so on — every locality shoving off the responsibility of it upon some other. In point of fact, it is, I imagine, more or less current everywhere among vulgar speakers; the most marked illustrations of it that I have ever chanced to hear were from persons of English birth. To regard it as in any degree characterizing the utterance of educated New Englanders is wholly unfounded and unjust.

Like the *ai*-diphthong, the *au* is for the most part historically the alteration of a simple long vowel, namely *u*. It is less than half as common in use as *ai*, its proportional utterance being only about four fifths of one per cent.

18. The third diphthong, that in *coil*, *boy*, and their like, is of a quite different character from the other two;

while they are mixtures, it is a mere juxtaposition, a union, by abbreviated utterance, of two distinct vowel-sounds within the compass of one syllable, the two being no more blended with one another than if they constituted two separate syllables. Their uncombinability is due to their belonging to different series: the first element is labial, the "broad *a*" (*ʌ*) of *all;* the second is palatal, the short *i* of *pin;* and the former is the longer and stronger of the two.[1] Their greater separability may be shown by comparing *loyal* with *trial, avowal;* in the first, we might question whether the utterance is more *loi-al* or *lo-yal;* in the others, the *al* is a plain addition to the *ai* and *au* sounds, which maintain their character unimpaired. The *ʌi*-diphthong is the rarest of English vowel-sounds; its share is only the eighth part of one per cent.

These are all the vowel utterances which I should ever think of distinguishing from one another in my pronunciation of English, as found in accented syllables.[2] That they do not vary in quantity in different styles of speaking, and that some of them do not suffer slight modifications of quality in rapid utterance, by an influence proceeding from the other sounds in connection with which they are uttered, I would by no means venture to maintain; but such modification would be unintended, or contrary to intention, and would disappear if the syllable were uttered reflectively and deliberately.

In unaccented syllables, however, our English vowels undergo a change of quality, a reduction to indistinctness and neutrality, beyond what is known in any other cultivated European tongue. No actually new constituents of the spoken alphabet, I believe, are produced in this way; none which the ear and mouth acknowledge, and which are entitled to notice and separate designation in the scale on which the present analysis of English utterance

1 A graphic representation of the compound would be *ʌ* 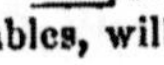 *i*.

2 The *n* and *l* vowels, occurring in unaccented syllables, will be treated a little farther on (Nos. 19 and 20).

is made: for even if, in rapid speaking, some new intermediate grades of vowel-sound may be struck, the moment we turn our attention upon them they will disappear, the sound falling under some one of the categories already established, taking on the semblance of one of our common longs or shorts. It would cost a whole article, or volume, to discuss this subject exhaustively, with full illustration; I can here only sketch briefly some of its chief outlines.

The general modifying influence is of twofold character: either, in the first place, it consists in shortening the quantity and lightening the force of the vowel, cutting off any vanishing-sound it may have, but not altering its quality otherwise than by putting short quality in place of long; or, in the second place, it is a substitution of the neutral vowel, the "short *u*" (ə) of *but*, for the proper sound of the vowel affected. To what degree either of these effects takes place, and even, within certain limits, whether the one or the other of them takes place, depends in part upon variable and wholly undefinable conditions: not only on the dialectic habit of the speaker, but also upon his personal habit, and upon the distinctness which he is at the time consciously putting into his utterance, the rapidity or deliberateness with which he speaks. There is a whole class, too, of shades of modification introduced by the educated speaker's consciousness of the way his words are spelled, and the more or less acknowledged feeling that what is distinguished to the eye ought also to be distinguished to the ear: these help notably to blur the line to be drawn between distinct utterance and orthoëpic affectation and pedantry.

To consider first the reduction to the neutral vowel: there are large classes of cases in which it has been so thoroughly made, and by so general usage, that the syllable no longer has an alternative sound; to pronounce it otherwise than with the *u* of *but* would be a simple affectation. It is so with syllables coming after the accent and containing an *a* which if fully pronounced would be *æ* (*pan*), or an *o* that would be *ă* (*what*): thus, *an* in *woman*, *pagan*, etc.; *ant*, *ance*, *ancy* in *distant*, *errant*, in *distance*, *hindrance*, in *infancy*, *pregnancy*; *al* in *penal*, *eternal*, and *alty* in *penalty*; more sporadic cases are *husband*, *stomach*, etc.; thus, *on* in *nation*, *derision*, and also, of course, in *national*, in *harmony*, etc.; *om* in *kingdom*, *bosom*; *ol* in *carol*, *carolling*; *or* and *ory* in *prior*, *honor*, and *priory*; and scattering cases like *diamond*, *bullock*. The *a* of *ar* is treated in the same way, as in *templar*, *peculiar*, *beggar*; and of *ary*, as in *beggary*; also that of *ard*, as in *drunkard*, *forward*; and the *o* of *some* when ending — thus, *handsome* — as well as when independent word. *U* becomes neutral in *ure*, as *treasure*, *nature*. The vowel *e* has the neutral quality (like *or* and *ar*) in *er*, as *miller*, *robber*; in *ery*, as *robbery*; and in the few cases of *erd*, as *shepherd*. The endings *ent*, *ence*, *ency* follow the same rule, as *patent*, *present*, *presence*, *decency*; and even, I believe, when they stand second from the accent, and so have a degree of secondary accent themselves, as in *penitent*, *innocent*, *penitence*, *innocency*; though in these last cases some will doubtless hold that the *ĕ* sound should be favored a little in careful utterance. But *ent* when radical preserves its *ĕ*-sound, as in *accent*, *comment*. And *en*, *el*, *et*, and most other final syllables with *e*, do the same: thus, *linen*, *chicken*,[1] *woolen*, *vowel*, *camel*, *velvet*, *secret*, *carpet*; and *boundless*, *interest*, *sweetness*, *learned*, *princes*, *acknowledge*, *manifest*, and so on. There are those who in such words as these turn the *ĕ*-sound into *ĭ*, saying *linĭn*, *vowĭl*, *princĭz*, etc.; and even some orthoëpical authorities countenance it; but I find no tendency to the change in my own mouth, and it appears to me a thing to be contended against. And *i*

[1] There are exceptions among words in *en*, as *children*, *heathen*, where the *but* sound prevails.

maintains itself still more sturdily than *e*, being nowhere regularly and confessedly convertible into the neutral sound. The decidedly palatal vowels, partly as being less akin with the neutral, partly perhaps as being themselves very light and easy sounds, offer greater resistance to the process of conversion.

Of final vowels, the *a* is the only one that passes distinctly into ə (*but*): thus, *idea*, *Asia*, *America*.

The cases are very numerous in which, although the *but* sound is allowed and frequent in rapid colloquial utterance, more deliberate pronunciation retains the more distinctive sound. Such are especially the vowels of open syllables in the interior of a word: thus, the *a* of *company*, *separate* (second syllable), *oracle*, *lovable* (though it can hardly be said that in any of these cases, least of all in the ending *-able*, the *a* is ever anything but a "short *u*"); the *o* of *clamorous*, *honorable*, *philosopher* (third syllable); the *e* of *enemy*, *tolerate*, *funeral*, *ceremony;* and even the *i* of *velocity*, *credible*, *indivisibility* (fourth and sixth syllables, *-si-* and *-li-*), *originate*. The gradual diminution of the tendency to conversion in this series, dependent on the character of the vowels as already pointed out, is very clear; probably some will refuse to acknowledge or sanction the change of *i* at all; but, for all that, it is real, and common enough. In the same category of admissible but not required conversions belong a host of syllables that precede the accent in a word: instances are *above*, *again*, *ability*, *habitual*, *pavilion; obey*, *obscure*, *occasion*, *confusion*, *compare*, *forsake*, *to-morrow*, *propose:* I think we also sometimes treat in the same way an *e*, or even an *i*, but only in especially careless utterance; and I do not venture to give any examples, lest they be cried out against.

It can hardly be claimed, I suppose, that we ever pronounce a long vowel with absolute completeness in an unaccented syllable, in our natural and unforced utterance; we rather cut it down into its naturally corresponding short vowel. Even a real short ŏ would have to be acknowledged in the medium pronunciation (medial between the elaborate ō, vanish and all, and the careless ə) of *obey*, *opinion*, and their like. And the abbreviated vowel is liable to be sometimes altered in quality still farther, to a neutral utterance. There are classes of words, also, in which a shortened ĕ is allowed by the orthoëpists to be lightened into ĭ: such are especially the words in *tain*, as *mountain*, *certain*, *captain*: those in *age* and *ace*, as *cabbage*, *village*, *palace*; those in *ege*, as *college*, *knowledge*; and so on. Reference has been made above to final *ness*, *es*, *ed*, as treated in the same manner. To me, this change of ĕ to ĭ seems always to be worse than easy and familiar; to be slovenly, rather, and unworthy of recognition on the part of the orthoëpists.

Not only unaccented syllables, but unemphatic words, are liable to this dimming and changing of quality. The article *the*, as a striking example, is abbreviated to *thĭ* before a vowel, and before a consonant takes the full *but*-sound; and its colleague *a* suffers the same reduction. *From*, *was*, *of*, are further instances of reduction to the neutral vowel in rapid combination with other words; even *to*, though its ū-sound is more persistent, does not always escape the same fate.[1]

The true method for a pronouncing dictionary of English to follow in marking these varieties of utterance seems not difficult to establish in theory, although its carrying out in detail would be much harder, because

[1] Ellis treats this subject of unaccented syllables and unemphatic words with greater fullness, on pp. 1161–1167 of his great work. I find my utterance accordant with his on almost every point; but I think American usage goes farther than English in letting the secondary accent, after the primary, exercise a conserving influence upon the vowel of the syllable: for example, upon the *o* of *territory*, *preparatory*, *testimony*; the *a* of *literary*, *secondary*, *circumstance*; and so on. The last word, which Ellis gives somewhere as having the same vowel-sound in every syllable, is to me, even in rapid utterance, pronounced with three different vowels, æ (*hurt*), ə (*but*), and æ (*pan*).

the various classes distinguished actually pass into one another, across undefinable boundaries. Those vowels which have absolutely and irrecoverably passed over into the neutral sound of *but*, and those which more persistently maintain their quality, with abbreviation and lightening only, might be plainly enough indicated by appropriate diacritical marks; and then a separate mark would be required for those which are allowed to be reduced to neutrality in fluent utterance; and it might even be twofold, so as to point out the varying degree of permissibility, as between the more usual and the rarer cases. No existing dictionary, that I know of, gives the learner of the language any valuable help with regard to the varying quality of unaccented vowels.

I have estimated that the occurrence of the short neutral sound (*but*) in the way of substitution for vowels which an elaborate pronunciation would give with distinctness is more frequent than its independent occurrence, or about three and one half per cent.

We have to note finally, in connection with this subject, that in a considerable class of unaccented syllables containing an *n* or *l*, the vowel, instead of being merely weakened or neutralized, is omitted entirely, the *n* or *l* remaining as "vowel" of the syllable: so in *reckon*, *button*, *liken*, *fatten*, *deaden*, *chasten*, *venison*, *seven*, *often*; so in *tackle*, *bungle*, *apple*, *able*, *little*, *handle*, *bustle*, *evil*. This arises from the peculiar character of the two sounds, standing, as they do (as elsewhere explained, in this and the following article), on the border-line between consonant and vowel, and so capable of being put to use with either value. Though among the rarest sounds in our spoken alphabet, they are both more frequent than the *oi*-diphthong; in ten thousand sounds, I have found the *l*-vowel thirty-five times and the *n*-vowel sixteen times. It is necessary, then, to complete our scheme of English vowel-sounds by adding these two.

19. The *l*-vowel of *tackle*, etc., is almost always written *le*, with the silent vowel following it. And when a syllable is added, as in *bungler*, *ablest*, *bundling*, the *l* entirely loses its vocalic character, and makes no intermediate syllable. There are a few words in which written *el* has confessedly the same character — for example, *hazel*, and (as it seems to me) *morsel* and *parcel*; and a much larger class in which a careless pronunciation gives *l* only, while the authorities still properly require *ĕl*: such are *angel*, *rebel*, *model*, *quarrel*, *level*, etc. The same abbreviating tendency is contended against in a few *il*, *al*, and *ol* words, as *civil*, *medal*, *idol*: in *evil* and *devil*, however, the corruption has established itself beyond remedy, as also perhaps (though I think not) in *metal*.

20. The *n*-vowel of *reckon*, etc., has the silent vowel written before it, and there are few if any words in which this is not sometimes restored in deliberate pronunciation. And when a formative syllable is added, as in *reckoner*, *gluttony*, *fattening*, the orthoëpists differ in opinion as to whether the *n* should be left as sole vowel of the intermediate syllable, or whether the preceding vowel should also be uttered, with neutral sound. In my view, both ways are proper, each in its own style of utterance.

We come now to consider the consonants, the closer articulations of the alphabetic system. Indeed, we have already touched upon the consonantal domain, in treating of the last pair of vowels, which are more usually consonantal sounds, though capable, under special circumstances, of doing duty as vowels also. And first among them we will take up *r*.

21. The *r* is a sound which is formed between the tip of the tongue and the upper part or roof of the mouth, the approach of the two organs not being so close as to produce a rubbing or buzzing sound — which, if produced, would be a *z* or *zh*, instead of *r*. It may be thus

formed along the whole line of the roof of the mouth, from close behind the front teeth to as far back as the tip of the tongue can be turned; varying somewhat in its coloring as it is transferred backward or forward, but everywhere unmistakably an *r*. At its foremost point of production, with the tongue stretched directly forward and nearly reaching the front teeth, it can be trilled or vibrated: that is to say, the tip of the tongue can be made to swing rapidly up and down, alternately narrowing (or closing) and widening the passage; if the tongue be retracted, or its tip turned upward, this action is impossible. As an actual fact, trilling accompanies the pronunciation of the *r* in most of the languages which possess that letter; insomuch that it is common among phonetists to define *r* as a trill or vibration of the tip of the tongue. Whether it be proper or not to do so is in great part a verbal question merely: to me, I must confess, the place of the organs seems to be the main characteristic of the sound, and the vibration one of subordinate or secondary value. If only that is an *r* which possesses vibration, the question arises what we shall call our ordinary English *r;* for this is certainly not trilled. We shall, I am sure, do best to call it still an *r*, though a smooth or untrilled *r*. We pronounce it (if I may judge by comparing the action in my own mouth with what I hear from my neighbors' mouths) with the tip of the tongue reverted into the dome of the mouth, where vibration is impossible. That is to say, we the great body of English speakers, and in our ordinary utterance; for, on the one hand, there are doubtless localities where the letter is still trilled as in the olden time (the Irish have retained this, among other characteristics of a more ancient style of utterance); and, on the other hand, there are individuals among us who, from whatever cause, regularly give the trill; while any of us may, in an effort at peculiarly distinct, emphatic, or orotund utterance, at times do the same thing.

It is very common among English orthoëpists to distinguish in English speech a "rough *r*" and a "smooth *r*," the former being that which is heard before a vowel, the latter when no vowel follows, when the *r* is either final or has a consonant after it. It does not seem to me, however, that such a distinction can be maintained; as regards my own pronunciation, at any rate, it is utterly destitute of foundation: I have never trilled an *r* except by a conscious effort or in connection with an attempt at unusual distinctness of articulation; nor have I any double method of utterance of the letter; to me the variation is not between rough and smooth, but between smooth and nothing. In my natural and unregenerate state, namely, before I had begun to school my utterance to conformity with orthographical and orthoëpical rule, I never pronounced at all an *r* that was not followed by a vowel; I fear that I hardly do so now except when I am thinking of it. I can confess and assert this in the most confident manner, because my attention was directed to the subject before I had any theories as to what was or what should be. And I have taught French and German pronunciation to pupils enough, from all parts of the country, to be convinced that this absence of utterance, and of trill when uttered, is a very general characteristic of American pronunciation. As to that of England, it is enough to note that Mr. Ellis makes the same acknowledgment, in the most explicit manner, respecting his English. It is, indeed, natural that the silencing of the *r*, under circumstances less favorable to its utterance, should form part of that same process of general weakening which has robbed it elsewhere of its vibration.

If the *r* be pronounced wherever it is written, it is, according to my reckoning, the most common of English sounds, reaching a frequency of nearly seven and a half per cent.; but the cases in which it is followed by a vowel are only just about one half of that number.

Between *r* and the neutral vowel-sound there exists a peculiar relation, which must not be passed without notice. I am by no means confident that I fully understand its physical grounds; but I have been accustomed to explain it to myself somewhat in this way. The *r* is a letter of unusually laborious production, as requiring some retraction of the tongue with a reversion of its tip into the dome of the palate. The tongue-position from which its utterance is most readily reached is that inactive one which gives the neutral vowels. These last, then, lie as natural intermediates between any other vowel and *r*. The voice is perfectly able, to be sure, to make the transition so rapidly that no intermediate stage is audible; and it does so after a short vowel; but in the greater deliberateness of a long vowel or diphthong it gives the transitional sound a chance to appear. At any rate, in the whole classes of words like *care*, *fear*, *sore*, *cure*, *fire*, *sour*, a neutral vowel (ɜ) follows the other vowel-sound in a manner which is perfectly palpable to the ear; it is far more noticeable than, for example, the ī and ū vanish of the common ē (*they*) and ō, and almost or quite as plain as the final element of the *oi*-diphthong. If the same insertion is to be theoretically recognized as made after the other two long vowels, *a* and ʌ (in *far* and *war*), it is at any rate wholly inconspicuous, a virtually inaudible glide. In that style of pronunciation, then, in which (as explained just above) the *r* has come to be not uttered at all, the transition-sound is left as its substitute, and is alone heard. *Care*, for example, becomes *kœɜ*, instead of *kœɜr*, and *cared* becomes *kœɜd;* and so with the rest; while *caring* has both the transition-sound and the smooth or untrilled *r*, and is *kœɜring*.

With this phenomenon stands in evident connection the substitution of the long neutral vowel for a more original sound in such words as *worth*, *mirth*, *earth*, *curse*, *scourge*, *tierce* (see above, No. 15, p. 224); the formerly distinct vowel has been overpowered and replaced by the transitional sound at first developed after it. Wherever the *r* is found, it tends to give the preceding vowel a neutral color; and association with it helps to convert the vowels of unaccented syllables to the neutral *ə*.

It is because of its tendency to develop the neutral vowel, and then itself to disappear, in English pronunciation, that the *r* never becomes in English (as it does in various other languages, more fully than any other consonantal sound) the actual vowel of a syllable, like *l* and *n*. In situations where these two would be left alone, with vocalic office, *r* is replaced by a brief *ə* (*but*); or, if itself pronounced, it has such a vowel prefixed: *acre*, for example, is *ēkə* or else *ēkər*. There is, however, one word in the language, where, according to a common (and, as it seems to me, the best) pronunciation, *r* is the vowel of an accented syllable; it is *pretty* (the books mostly prescribe *prĭtĭ*; one hears also *prĕtĭ* and *pŭtĭ*).

22. The nearest relative of the *r* is the *l*. In the latter the tongue touches the roof of the mouth, either by its tip or its upper surface, while there is a passage left open at the sides of the tongue, through which the sonant breath finds free exit. Here, again, the tongue may take any position along the roof of the mouth, just as in making *r*; and even, as is not the case with *r*, the flat of the tongue, instead of its tip, may be the part used: the different *l*'s thus produced are of more diverse quality than the *r*'s, and some of them are used in other languages as regular members of the alphabet, separate from the common *l*: so the palatal *l*, or *l mouillé*, of the French, made with the flat of the tongue against the roof of the mouth, nearly in the *y*-position; and the "cerebral" *l* of the Vedic Sanskrit, with the tip well retracted into the dome of the palate. Our own *l* probably enough varies a little in place, under the influence of the consonants in connection with which it appears; when unconstrained,

the tip of the tongue with me is pretty close behind the upper front teeth, considerably farther forward than in uttering *r*. I have never been able to discover, in my own mouth or in that of others, the slightest vestige of that vibratory or trilling quality which is claimed as its characteristic by some phonetists. Nor does it seem to me a matter of importance whether the vocal breath streams out on both sides of the tongue or only on one side; and, in the latter case, whether on the right side or the left: my own practice appears to vary between the three methods.

The *l* is a common sound in English, making nearly four per cent. of our utterance. Its (not frequent) use as a vowel has been already considered. It is hardly necessary to add that between the vocalic and the consonantal *l* there is not the slightest shade of difference in physical character, in the articulating position and mode of utterance; what difference there is consists only in quantity and stress.

In *r* and *l* we have two consonants which verge closely upon the character of vowels, and are in various languages sometimes used as vowels. In ī (*pique*) and ū (*fool*), on the other hand, we have vowels of so close position that they verge upon the consonants. If we fix the organs to say ī, and then, instead of prolonging the sound, utter it with utmost brevity before another vowel-sound, as *a*, hardly making the position more than a starting-point from which to reach the latter, we shall have an unmistakable and perfect *ya*. An ū if treated in like manner will give us a *wa*. The same effect may in fact be given, only with a little less distinctness, by transition from the ĭ and ŭ (*full*) positions — nay, recognizably even from the *e* (*they*) and *o* positions. On the other hand, the organs may be even more closed for *y* and *w* than for the ordinary utterance of ī and ū, so as almost to give an audible frication, a rubbing or buzzing sound, at the place of closure; and it thus becomes possible to produce the semivowel effect even when ī or ū follows, as in the pronunciation of *ye* and *woo*. I say, almost a frication, because I think it does not quite reach that character; a prolongation of the position will still yield a (turbid) *i* or *u* sound, one far more vocalic than fricative. Moreover, I am not at all sure that, in order to make the *y* and *w* sounds distinct in such combinations, I do not open the closure first upon the short vowel (which is, as already explained, an opener utterance than the long), then immediately shutting it again to the long: thus really saying *yĭī*, *wŭū*. In the ordinary processes of rapid utterance, I believe that we use, according to circumstances, different degrees of closure; and that a true and unexceptionable description of these sounds is that they are ī and ū sounds abbreviated, reduced to consonantal value by being used as mere starting-points from which to reach the vowel that follows. Any dwelling upon them would give them a vocalic effect, and make them diphthongize with the succeeding vowel, or form a separate prefixed syllable. And even in their closest possible shape, they are not more different from ī and ū than these are from ĭ and ŭ. Here, then, as well as in the *r* and *l* sounds, the vowel and consonant systems inosculate; and there is good and sufficient reason for classing the four sounds together, and calling them "semivowels." To put *r* and *l* together with *n* and *m*, as "liquids," is a far more objectionable classification; the *n* and *m* are too peculiar in character and connections to admit such treatment.

23. The *y*-sound is shared by the English with many languages, probably even with the majority. It is far from being a frequent sound with us; even including the cases in which, as explained above (under ū, No. 13), it occurs as first element of the "long *u*," I have found it to average only two thirds of one per cent.

24. With the *w*-sound the case is quite different; the English is the only modern European literary language which has retained it as a full member of the alphabet; in the others, it has generally passed into a *v*, which is a sound of a very different class, a sonant fricative, a spirant (see below, No. 37). One consequence of this has been that the existence of such a sound as *w* has been almost ignored by continental European philologists, who have treated *v* instead as a semivowel — about as gross a phonetic blunder as it is possible to commit.

The *w* is a very much more common sound than *y* in English utterance, its percentage rising to two and one third.

It will be advisable, for convenience of exposition of the systematic relations of sounds, to pass next to the other extremity of the alphabetic system, and consider the mutes.

We began our scheme, it will be remembered, with the openest and freest of human utterances, the *a* (*far*), in which no hindrance is placed by throat or mouth in the way of the expulsion of intonated breath through the larynx. At the farthest remove from this is a series of articulations in which the interference of the mouth-organs with the flow of breath is carried so far as to stop that flow altogether, by producing a complete closure of the mouth. Such articulations are, then, properly enough called "mutes;" also contact-letters, stops, checks. In our language (as likewise in most other tongues) there are three such mutes, the closure being made at three different points in the mouth: either at the lips, or between the tip of the tongue and the fore part of the palate, or between the back part of the tongue and the back palate: they are, respectively, *p*, *t*, and *k*. An indefinite number of different mute contacts is capable of being formed by the various mouth-organs, in various positions; and some languages make use of four, or five, or even more; but

16

these three, which we may call the labial, the lingual, and the palatal contacts, are the only ones found to occur in the great majority of human dialects. The name of mute is appropriate to them, inasmuch as, so long as the contact lasts, there is absolute silence; it is only as the contact is broken that its effect upon the following opener utterance shows what it has been. The products are also sometimes, and very suitably, styled "explosives;" the explosion, or sudden breach of contact, is their characteristic. For the making of the contact, by shutting off a preceding vowel — *ap*, *at*, *ak* — is an utterance of the mute so much less distinct and audible as fairly to be called imperfect; and we are accordingly accustomed, when a mute comes at the end of a sentence, or before a pause, to break the contact again, with a little expulsion of mere breath, in order to make clear the nature of the final: we may represent it by *ap*ʻ, *at*ʻ, *ak*ʻ. Some phonetists claim that to make a whole *p*, for example, both a closure and a breach are required — thus, *apa* — either *ap* or *pa* being only a half or incomplete utterance; others, again, claim that *ap* is complete, and *pa* is complete, and so that *apa* is really double, and ought (I infer) to be written *appa*, a single mute between vowels being an impossibility: but I see no sufficient ground for either opinion.

It is, again, asserted by some (notably by Lepsius) that our usual *p*, *t*, *k* are not simple mutes, but rather aspirates — that is to say, that a bit of breath, a brief *h*, is slipped out between the breach of mute contact and the beginning of a following vowel or other more open sound. This also I should confidently deny, so far as our ordinary pronunciation is concerned; the relaxation of the contact and the beginning of the following sound are so closely fitted together, made so truly simultaneous, that nothing perceptible comes between them. If, indeed, we make the breach with labored energy, with violence, the case appears to be different; I myself, at any rate, in such an utterance, cannot help the escape of a little puff of *flatus* between the mute and the vowel—as is shown most clearly by holding the palm of the hand a little way in front of the mouth during the utterance.

25. The labial surd mute, *p*, is plainly enough produced by the closure of the two lips; and no difference in the usage of individuals or of peoples has, so far as I know, been pointed out as regards the nature of the contact. It is the least common sound of its class in English, falling short of one and three quarters per cent.

26. As to the precise place of the contact by which is formed the lingual mute, *t*, the case is different; and so, as we shall see later, as to that of the *k*. Both these two are generated between the tongue and the roof of the mouth; but there is a considerable range of choice in the precise part of either organ that shall be used. Speaking most generally, the *t*-position is farther forward than the *k*-position. And it should be carefully noted here, as a principle which we shall have occasion more than once hereafter to apply, that the point on the roof of the mouth at which a mute or fricative is produced is decidedly more essentially distinctive than the part of the tongue with which it is produced. For instance, one may turn the tongue so far back as with the reverted tip of it (against the soft palate) to utter an unmistakable *k*; and, on the other hand, one may thrust the tongue half-way out of the mouth, and yet make a perfectly clear *t* by a contact behind the teeth. No small variety, then, especially of *t*'s, is capable of being produced, each clearly a *t*, but distinguishable from all the rest by a slight difference of quality. And a considerable number of them are actually produced, either in the same or in different languages. If the tip of the tongue be laid full against the backside of the upper front teeth, perhaps even reaching below their points, the *t* has a decided tinge of the

th-sound (in *thin*); the difference being that in the *t* the determining contact is still made on the gums behind the teeth, and not upon the teeth themselves; in the latter situation a complete closure is not possible, and only the fricative *th* could result. This seems, according to the descriptions given, to be the character of the modern Hindu "dental" *t*. Again, if the tip of the tongue be turned up into the roof of the mouth, a *t* of different tone (we might describe it as hollower) is produced; and this is the Hindu "cerebral," or "cacuminal," or "lingual" *t*. I should infer from Mr. Ellis's latest descriptions (less certainly from Mr. Bell's figure) that a reverted or cacuminal character belongs to the English pronunciation of *t* to a degree which I had not thought of. My own *t* is made directly behind the teeth, with the tip of the tongue not in the least turned up, but laid forward, and at least grazing the teeth, if it does not fairly touch them; even in pronouncing *tr*, I find in my mouth no assimilation of the *t* to the *r* in respect to position, but a distinct slipping of the tongue backward from the one to the other.

Inasmuch, then, as the teeth have no real part in the production of a *t*, I think the name "dental" as applied to that letter and its immediate relatives a misnomer, and would call the contact in general a "lingual" one, reserving the names "dental," "palatal," "cacuminal," and so on, for characterizing its special varieties. The *t* which I utter deserves none of these names, but, as being made upon the gums of the upper front teeth, it might be denominated (by a term which has sometimes been used for such purpose) a "gingival" *t*.

The *t* is third in frequency among all the sounds of our alphabet, rising nearly to six per cent.

27. The third surd mute, the *k*, is formed, as already stated, by a contact of the back part of the tongue with the palate: at what precise point on the latter is much more difficult to determine than in the case of the *t*; nor

is the matter one of much consequence — especially, as there is good reason for holding that the place varies somewhat, according to the letter in connection with which the *k* is uttered; the *k* of *ki*, for example, being farther forward than that of *ka*, or *ko*, or *ku* (*coo*). The Semitic languages (and something like it is now claimed for the early Indo-European) had a double *k*, one deeper and more emphatic than the other — deeper than anything that we are in the habit of producing, though not very hard for us to imitate. It would be a sufficient definition to say that our *k* is produced upon the roof of the mouth either at or behind the junction of the hard and soft palate. For this reason, we may best call it "palatal;" the name "guttural" is not free from grave objection.

Our *k* is a little more frequent of utterance than our *p*, its percentage being two and one sixth. We shall find through the whole consonantal system that the articulations formed by the back of the tongue and by the lips, added together, are less than half as frequent as those made by the tip or front of the tongue.

I have called these three mutes "surds," by a name which is now quite widely used, and which is intended to describe them as produced without any tone, any sonorous vibration of the vocal cords. Other terms signifying the same thing are atonic, aphthongal, non-vocal, unintonated, and so on, any one of which is free from serious objection, if "surd" (which is offensive to some) be rejected. To call them, however, "hard," or "sharp," or "strong," or by any other such scientifically inaccurate and merely fanciful or blundering title, is altogether to be condemned.

By the same positions of the mouth-organs as those already described are produced, with added action of the throat, three other members of the alphabet, namely *b*, *d*, *g*, which are also ordinarily called "mutes," although not in the same measure entitled to bear the name. In them, there is actual production of sound in the larynx, the utterance of an audible buzz, as it were, while the mute contact is still maintained. Inasmuch, now, as this buzz implies the passage of a column of air through the glottis, setting in vibration the vocal cords on its way, some persons have found it very hard to understand its possibility, and have been led to deny that this is the true account of the difference between, for example, a *b* and *p*. But the explanation is perfectly easy. The cavity of the closed mouth acts for a time as a receiving-box, into which is forced a current of air until it is full and can receive no more. Any one may convince himself of this by trying to prolong a *b;* the sound in the throat continues audible for a while, the cheeks gradually puffing out by distention of the breath forced upward, till at last they are stretched to their utmost, and then the sound ceases; one can, however, then "swallow" the breath, or return it to the lungs, and repeat the process; and so on, over and over, as long as one can bear it without taking a new breath. I find that I can prolong the tone with the *b*-position more than two seconds, with the *d*-position less than two, with the *g*-position hardly one, the difference depending, of course, on the greater or less extent of the available mouth-cavity; but any one of them is time enough for the utterance of a whole series of consonants.

In *ba*, therefore, as distinguished from *pa*, the expulsion of intonated breath and production of sound begins before the unclosure of the lips, instead of simultaneously with the unclosure; in *ab*, it continues in like manner after the closure is made; in *aba*, there is no interruption of the continuity of sound, no instant of silence, as in *apa*. And this is the sole characteristic distinction of the two letters. We should call *b*, then, as compared with the surd *p*, a "sonant" (or tonic, phthongal, vocal, intonated) mute. It is impossible for me to discover on what foundation, even of fancied analogy, reposes the name of "flat," which is used by some. It is easier to see on what misapprehension the much more common "soft" is founded. By the closing of the vocal cords, in order to the production of sonant utterance, the column of expelled air is, of course, narrowed; there is, in a certain sense, a thinner current waiting for the breach of mute contact behind a *b* than behind a *p*. Yet, after all, only in a certain sense; for as the vocal cords are brought together for the production of a vowel at the very instant the contact is broken (unless, indeed, an aspirate, a *p'*, is uttered, instead of a simple surd, a *p*), there is no "harder" or "stronger" expenditure of breath in the surd letter than in the sonant; one may even say, not so much expenditure; for in *b* the loss of breath to the lungs by expulsion beyond the glottis begins before the breach of contact; in *p*, only at the breach of contact.

So far as I can see, there is no ground whatever on which the use of the terms "strong" or "hard," and "soft" or "weak," as applied respectively to surd and sonant letters, can be successfully defended. They began in ignorance, and are continued in heedless imitation or in misapprehension. They have had, and still have, their stronghold in the usage of Germans; among whom, in general, the distinctions of surd and sonant are less observed and less understood than elsewhere. The persistency with which even the greatest German philologists cling to them, and make them the foundation of the phonetic doctrine that, for example, the alteration of *p* to *b* is a process of weakening, and that from *b* to *p* a process of strengthening, is something truly wonderful. A weakening of the utterance of a *p* has not, that I can discover, the slightest tendency to make a *b* of it; nor *vice versâ*; for the *b* contains an element which the *p* does not, and one which may be intensified indefinitely without being lost, but rather the contrary. Either a *p* or a *b* may be struck with unusual energy, even violence, and, again, dropped from the lips with the faintest practicable effort, without in either case losing a jot of its distinctive character.[1]

The question of what distinguishes a sonant letter from a surd in whispering, when no real sonant utterance at all is produced, is one of no small difficulty, and much controverted. It is not easy to determine, in the first place, how far the distinction is actually made to the ear, and how far its apprehension is merely subjective, the hearer understanding by the connection which sound is really intended; nor, in the second place, of what nature the distinctions actually made are. But if the vowels, which in our common utterance are essentially sonant letters, can be imitated in whispering by an imperfect resonance which falls short of true sonancy, there is clearly no difficulty in supposing that similar means may supply the omitted element in sonant consonants also. It seems to me that the surd mutes are distinguished from the sonant by being slightly aspirated. But I have not studied the subject enough to arrive at conclusions worth setting down here; and I refer to it only for the purpose of pointing out that it involves no objection against the explanation of the distinction between surd and sonant which has been given above.

These sonants, as has been already remarked, have not so good a title as their surd correlatives to the name of "mutes." Nor can it be fairly said that the breach of contact constitutes their sole substance; for the tone which they contain is distinctive enough to be recognized by the ear, even before the breach. This tone also makes them more clearly audible at the end of a word than the surds, even without the subsequent breach with *flatus* —

[1] Except, indeed, so far as, in the manner pointed out above, a violent *p* tends to become aspirated, turning to *p'*.

which, however, I think we are in the habit of giving after a sonant final as well as after a surd. Yet no one, probably, will question that the breach of contact or explosion is an essential element of their character, and that they are therefore of one class with the surds.

28. The *b*-sound, then, is the sonant counterpart of the *p*, identical with it in position of the mouth-organs, differing only in the laryngal action. It is very slightly less frequent than *p*, amounting to nearly one and two thirds per cent.

29. In the same manner, the *d* corresponds with the *t* in everything but the element of sonancy, and occurs somewhat less often, though still forming nearly five per cent. of our utterance.

30. The *g*, however, the intonated *k*, is not much more than a third as common as its surd correspondent, making only about three quarters of one per cent.

There is yet another class of three sounds, uttered in the same three positions which have been already described, and with sonant or intonated expulsion of breath, like *b*, *g*, and *d*, but differing from them by the unclosure of the nasal passages. The *velum palati*, 'veil of the palate,' which in most of our speaking is pressed up against the exit from the pharynx into the nose, forcing the breath to find its way out into or through the mouth, is for these three utterances dropped, leaving the breath free exit through the nostrils. Thus are produced the "nasals," *m*, *n*, and *ng* (as in *singing*).[1] In virtue of their mode of formation, they are of a curiously mixed character: on the one hand, as implying complete closure of the mouth-organs, they are "mutes," or contact let-

[1] It is awkward to have to use digraphs for the representation of unitary sounds, and if my object were alphabetic rather than phonetic, to suggest a system of signs for English sounds rather than to analyze and describe the sounds themselves, I should carefully avoid such. As the case stands, the habits and preferences of the general English reader and the convenience of the printer forbid the use of more carefully adapted signs. Lepsius represents the sound in question by *ṅ*; Ellis, in his *Palæotype*, by *q*.

ters, explosives; on the other hand, as involving freedom of exit through the nose to the expelled column of air, they are even of a vocalic character, open, sonorous, indefinitely continuable, capable of being sung to — as indeed, our "humming" is, at least usually, the singing of a continuous *m*. It has, then, naturally enough, been made a matter of dispute whether the breach of mute contact is an essential element in the utterance of the nasals, whether they are or are not properly explosives. There is good reason to be brought forward on both sides. Every one must acknowledge at least as much as this, that in actual fact the explosion is there, that an *m* without either an introductory closure or a succeeding unclosure is not to be found, and that hence to withdraw that element from the utterance would make it less than what it now is, and so far imperfect. But the importance of the explosive element is a matter of degree, of more and of less, in different classes of sounds: in *p* it is all; in *b* it is still much, but not all; and in *m* it is reduced, I think, to quite subordinate value. Even *r* and *l* (especially the latter), even the fricatives, have a partial closure, the making and unmaking of which are appreciable, though no one would think of regarding them as to be given weight in a description of those sounds. *M*, *n*, and *ng* are by no means indefinite nasal utterances to which certain explosions give definite character; they are as distinct and recognizable as the vowels, even, in their continuable murmur, without aid from the explosion; and if it were possible to put the murmur and the following vowel directly side by side, skipping the intervening element, we should not feel the lack of anything — any more than we now recognize anything as wanting to the character of the nasal when we say *imp*, or *ant*, or *ink*.

31. The *m*-sound, then, is a *b* to which the element of nasal resonance has been added, an element which so predominates in its character as to make of it a "reso-

nant" (as Brücke appropriately enough calls it) rather than a mute. It is a pretty frequent sound, forming more than three per cent. of our utterance. That we do not use it as a vowel, like the *n* (except in the vulgarism *yes'm*, for "yes, ma'am!"), is not owing to anything inherent in the character of the sound, but to historical causes: we have not learned to slight and omit the vowel in any of our rare final unaccented syllables ending in *m*. If we were to treat *bosom* and *besom* and *seldom* and *custom* as we treat *lessen* and *reckon*, we should have an *m*-vowel; indeed, I have little doubt that slovenly speakers sometimes pronounce *bosom* as *bŭ-zm*. But the vulgar tendency is in general rather the other way, toward turning even *elm* into *ĕl-əm*.

32. The *n*-sound is related to *d* as *m* to *b*. Of its occasional conversion to vowel value we have already taken sufficient notice (above, No. 20). Its physical character is precisely the same, whether it be consonant or vowel; no element save time and stress is added or subtracted to make the one out of the other. It is by far the most common of the nasals; and, indeed, the most common (with the equivocal exception of the *r*) of all our articulations, forming fully six and three quarters per cent. of our average utterance.

33. Very different, in this respect, is the *ng*-sound (of *singing*), which is related to *g* precisely as *n* to *d* and as *m* to *b*, and is a not less simple and indivisible sound than either of them. It rises to an average of only about three quarters of one per cent. It is never found beginning a syllable, but always either precedes a *g* or *k*, or is the remnant of a group in which a *g* was formerly pronounced after it — whence the use of *ng* to represent it. It has a similar subordinate value in all the languages of our kindred; as, indeed, in nearly all the languages of the earth. Almost everywhere, *m* and *n* are the only nasals of independent and various use. Yet also, in any language,

there will be, regularly or almost unavoidably, as many nasals as there are surd or sonant mutes, or one for every position of mute closure.

Before quitting the subject of the three mute closures, each with its trio of sounds — surd, sonant, and nasal — we should note the relation in which they stand to the semivowels, already described. The *d* is nearly related to the *l* and *r*, all being alike tongue-point letters: a relaxation of the contact at the tip of the tongue converts the *d* into an *r*; a like relaxation at the side or sides of the tongue converts it into an *l*. All, especially the *l* and *r*, interchange frequently with one another in the history of language. So also, the flat of the tongue is so close to the roof of the mouth in *y* that a very slight further approximation, without change of place, brings it to the closure producing *k* or *g*. Hence the ease with which a *y*-sound is inserted after the palatal mutes: an insertion which is a well-recognized beginning of corruption in many languages, leading to the change of *k* and *g* to *ch* and *j*. One of the latest downward steps in English orthoëpy has been the intrusion of this *y*-sound after *k* and *g*, in a not very large class of words, by a certain part of the community. Examples are *kind* (*kyaind*), *guard* (*gya*[*r*]*d*), *girl* (*gyɜ*[*r*]*l*), and so on. To those with whom this mode of pronunciation is not natural, and who have not acquired it later — myself, for example — it has a peculiarly affected and disagreeable sound; and it certainly is on general grounds to be discouraged. Once more, in *b*, we have the lips just brought together which in *w* are on the very verge of closure — only here, it is true, there is the difference that the *w* involves also a rounding action, a drawing together of the corners of the mouth, which is wanting in the *b*. The two, however, show abundantly by historical transitions that their relationship is a real one; and there is, as will be pointed out later, an intermediate between them.

We next take up a class of sounds of which the characteristic quality is a rustling or friction through a narrowed aperture, left between the closely approximated organs at one and another point in the mouth: examples are *s*, *z*, *f*, *v*, *th*. Like the mutes, they go in pairs, surd and sonant, according as simple breath, or sound, intonated breath, is expelled through the same position of the organs; but, like the vowels, semivowels, and nasals, they are indefinitely continuable, because the breath finds escape from the mouth during their utterance. The name "fricative," which is frequently applied to them (especially by Lepsius), is probably as characteristically descriptive as any that could be selected for them.

Let us notice first the pair of *th*-sounds, the surd *th* of *thin* and the sonant *th* of *then*. They are formed between the tongue and the upper front teeth. We have seen already that if, in uttering a *t*, the tongue be laid well against the teeth, even though a real contact be made upon the gums immediately behind them, the *t* has a perceptible tinge of *th*. Let the contact behind be severed, so that the tongue in front touches the teeth only, and *th* is the necessary result. For there can be no tight closure upon the teeth; and whether the breath find its escape through the interstices of the teeth, or between tongue and teeth, the articulated result is the same. So also it is the same, whether the tip be kept inside the teeth, or whether it be taken and held between the two rows of teeth, or even thrust far out, so that the middle of the upper surface of the tongue touches the teeth. That is to say, in all these positions the product is an unmistakable *th*-sound, its modifications of tone being of entirely subordinate value. The breath, it may be added, makes its way out just where it can, along the whole contact: usually, I think, its chief avenue is between the teeth themselves; but if these are exceptionally tight, or if they be made artificially tight by closing the interstices with bits of wax, the exit is in larger measure, or wholly, between the tips and the tongue. The truly descriptive name, then, for the pair would be "dentilingual," or "linguo-dental."

34. The surd *th*-sound of *thin*, *path*, *filthy* is, accordingly, an expulsion of unintonated breath between the tongue and the upper front teeth, laid directly in contact. Although found in a not inconsiderable list of words, it is practically one of the rarest consonantal elements in English utterance, averaging little more than a half of one per cent. The tendency of English speech has long been toward its conversion into its sonant counterpart.

35. The sonant *th*-sound of *the*, *breathe*, *father*, is an expulsion of intonated breath through precisely the same position. Since it is related to the other as *d* to *t*, it may be very fitly and conveniently represented by *dh* — which is its sign in Ellis's "Palæotype;" Lepsius writes the surd and sonant sounds by the Greek letters θ and δ, respectively. Unlike the other, it is one of the commonest consonants in the language, being exceeded by only half a dozen others; its proportion rises to nearly four per cent. This is especially on account of the great frequency of occurrence of the pronominal words which contain it, like *the*, *that*, *this*, *they*, *then*, *there:* that it is found in a much greater number of separate words than the surd *th*, is doubtful; in Old English, with its forms like *hath* and *loveth*, the advantage in point of separate words would doubtless be on the side of the surd sound, while yet in practical occurrence the sonant would be in advance.

As noticed above, English usage tends to vocalize the *th*, converting it into *dh*. The familiar relation of the derivative verb to its noun-theme — as in *bath bathe*, (*bĕdh*), *cloth clothe*, *sheath sheathe*, and so on — is uniformly observed by all. More anomalous is the change of the final surd to the sonant before the plural ending *s;* and here, accordingly, there is much more diversity in popular usage, and the orthoëpic manuals are obliged to point out the right sound in each case, and insist upon its observance. Thus, they tell us that we must give the sonant sound in *baths* (*badhz*), *oaths*, *moths*, *mouths*, *sheaths*, and many more, and must give the surd in *cloths*, *truths*, *youths*, and a few others. I do not take pains to report my own usage with regard to this class of words, because I have nothing worth reporting; I have heard both sounds so often that to my ear, in a large number of cases, the one seems just as correct as the other, and it is only by the artificial process of consulting authorities (if at all) that I rectify my pronunciation.

Very nearly akin with this pair are the *f* and *v* sounds. The latter, like the former, bring the upper front teeth into action, but their contact is made upon the edge of the lower lip instead of upon the tongue. As *th* and *dh*, then, were dentilinguals, *f* and *v* are "dentilabials." Respecting the nature of the contact and the mode of issue of the escaping breath, precisely the same thing may be said which was said above in treating of the *th*-sounds.

36. The surd *f*-sound, accordingly, is produced by touching the edge of the lower lip with the tips of the upper teeth, and expelling through the contact a stream of unintonated breath. The two organs may be pressed together as closely as one pleases, since the interstices of the teeth take care that no actual mute closure is produced. The sound is represented in English not only by *f*, but also by *ph* and *gh* (see below, p. 257). It averages in frequency a little more than two per cent. of our utterance.

37. The *v* differs from the *f* only in being produced with tone, or intonated breath. It is a little more common than its twin surd utterance, its average rising above two and one third per cent. It is to a certain extent produced from the *f*, as the *dh*-sound from the *th*: so in deriv-

ative verbs, *halve* from *half*, like *breathe* from *breath;* and in plurals, *staff staves*, *loaf loaves*, like *path paths* (*padhz*), *oath oaths* (*ōdhz*); only here, as our mode of writing has different representatives for the two sounds, the orthography comes in to aid the orthoëpy, and there is no important discordance in general usage with regard to the change. The words in which *f* (or *ph*) is still written but *v* pronounced are very few, hardly more than *of* and *Stephen:* recent British usage has added *nephew*, which, however, is in America still almost universally spoken with the *f*-sound; I never heard the *v* until comparatively recently. But a considerable part of our *v*'s are of French extraction, being alterations (as referred to above, under *w*) of the old Latin *w*-sound (of *vox*, *venio*, *vivus*, etc.).

Articulations like *f* and *v* do not absolutely require the aid of the teeth in order to their formation; by a fricative contact between the edges of the lips alone may be produced sounds which no one would think of calling by any other name, and which an unaccustomed ear, indeed, would hardly distinguish from those we make. This purely labial pair of fricatives are usual in many tongues: both are found, for example, in German, in the combinations *pf* (*pfund*, *pfropfen*, etc.) and *schw*, *zw* (*schwer*, *zwei*, etc.); and German orthoëpists are at variance as to whether in other situations also the purely labial or the dentilabial utterance is the more normal and less provincial.[1] It is interesting, as bearing on the character of our *w* as a true semivowel and not a fricative, to compare its mode of formation with that of the purely labial *v;* in the latter, the approximation of the lips is in their ordinary position, without rounding; the buzz in the larynx is wholly neutral, and is obviously overborne by the labial rustling or frication, as giving character to

[1] Lepsius and Brücke both favor the dentilingual; but Ellis has shown (p. 1101 *seq.*) that the other is more common and better supported than they had been aware.

the resulting sound; in the former, the corners of the lips are drawn in and their extremities protruded, just as in the vowel *ū* (*rule*), and the tongue is also fixed for producing the same vowel; an *ū*-tone is actually generated, and may be prolonged as such, there being no frication which sensibly mars its quality.

To a great extent these fricatives — *th*, *dh*, *f*, *v* — arise historically out of aspirates: that is, by the phonetic alteration of former mutes in which the breach of contact was followed by an audible, though very slight, expulsion of breath, a brief *h*. Hence their frequent or regular representation by the compound characters *th*, *ph* — to which the German adds *ch*, as a palatal correspondent of the same class. Our own language once possessed the palatal fricative, and it is still written in many of our words, by the kindred digraph *gh*. But, taking a distaste to the sound, and refusing longer to utter it, we have in part simply silenced it, as in *nigh*, *light*, *plough*, and in part have converted it into the dentilabial of the same class, *f*, as in *laugh*, *tough*. And there is at least one word (I know of no other), namely *trough*, in which a popular mispronunciation gives instead the dentilingual fricative, saying *trʌth:* this was my own "natural" way of speaking the word; and I presume that it is a peculiarity dating back in origin to the first transfer of the palatal fricative to another organ.

The sounds thus far considered form so distinctly a single class of utterances, generally akin in origin, and dividing themselves approximately between the three principal positions of the articulating organs, that they are very suitably ranked together as a sub-class of fricatives, and may be called by the special name of "spirants."

There remains, then, another sub-class, the sounds universally known as "sibilants." There are two pairs of them: the surd *s* and its sonant counterpart *z*, and the surd *sh* (which is just as simple a sound as *s*) and its sonant counterpart in *azure*, *vision*, which we may distinguish as the *zh*-sound.[1]

All these four sounds are linguals, in the sense that they are produced between the tongue and the roof of the mouth. But there is, if I am not mistaken, a greater diversity among English speakers as regards their precise mode of utterance than is to be found in the case of any other letters. It necessary, therefore, to determine with care the essential distinction between them. And this consists, I believe, solely in the region of the roof of the mouth at which they are brought forth: the *s* is made farther forward, close behind the upper teeth; the *sh* is made farther back. The division-line between the two may be best tested by passing the tip of the tongue along the palate, from the base of the upper front teeth backward. At the teeth, the sibilant is an *s*, and so a very little way from them, until an angle or ridge is reached from which the roof rises more rapidly to the dome of the palate; and that ridge is the dividing line: the moment the tongue begins to ascend toward the dome, the *sh* character prevails, and continues prevalent as far as the tongue can reach. But here, again, as in the case of the spirants, it is comparatively a matter of indifference what part of the tongue makes the determinative approach to the palate; it may be the tip, or a part of the upper surface, as far back of the tip as can be brought to the right place against the palate — or even a part of the under surface, applied by retroversion.

38. The *s*-sound is, I believe, in actual practice formed in two quite different ways: in the one, the tip of the tongue is applied to the roof of the mouth close behind the upper front teeth, with a degree of approach slightly less than that which produced an *r*, and the unintonated breath is forced through the narrow aperture, causing that peculiar kind and degree of frication or rustling

[1] Ellis, in his *Palæotype*, uses *sh* and *zh*; Lepsius gives instead *š* and *ž*.

which we call hissing; in the other, the tongue is stretched farther forward, so that its tip rests squarely against the inner face of the *lower* front teeth, and the articulating aperture, though at the same point of the palate as before, is made with the flat upper surface of the tongue. Of the two, the former has, I doubt not, the better title to be deemed and called normal. Max Müller's and A. M. Bell's figures, though differing not a little from one another,[1] both point decidedly to it, nor does Ellis, if, I understand him, describe any other; but my own method is the other, and I have found it not uncommon among those persons whom I have examined upon the point. As to the numerical relation between the two parties, I have no sufficient data for giving even a guess at it; I conjecture that all those persons who lisp in early childhood, because of thrusting the tongue too far forward, grow up to produce this second variety of *s*. I presume that a sufficiently acute and practiced ear would readily distinguish the two from one another by their audible quality; they seem perceptibly different to me in my own mouth, though I have not learned to note them in others' mouths.

The *s* is one of the commonest of our utterances, its average rising to above four and two thirds per cent.; that of its sonant counterpart, the *z*, falls short of three per cent.

39. The *z*-sound is, of course, produced by every one with the same position as the *s*, differing from it only in the expulsion of intonated breath, which turns the hiss into a buzz. The difference of articulation between *z* and *r* is very slight indeed; and one may even utter a *z* through the same position in which an *r* has just been produced, by driving out more breath than can find exit without a rustling at the tip of the tongue. Hence, in many lan-

[1] Mr. Bell's is, as usual, far the more accurate; Müller's position, if it gave any definable sound, would, I think, give a *th*.

guages which have not yet acquired a *z*, the *s*, when it yields to a tendency to become sonant, is converted into *r*: the Latin and Germanic languages are conspicuous examples of this tendency in its historical workings, and in Sanskrit it forms part of the ordinary euphony of combination of word with word in the sentence.

A considerable share of our *z*'s are comparatively recent corruptions of the *s*-sound: so, especially, of the final *s* of the possessives and plurals of nouns, and of the third persons singular of verbs: the exceptions being those forms in which a surd final of the theme is pronounced immediately before the *s* — and even there, in such cases as *wolves*, *oaths* (referred to above), the tendency to make the *s* sonant has overpowered and involved in the same change even the preceding final. The change is one recently and still in active progress; and consequently there are many words, and even whole classes of words, with regard to which usage is yet unsettled. My own pronunciation, in almost all such cases, adheres to the older *s*-sound. So, for example, in the classes beginning with the prefixes *dis-* and *ex-*: I naturally say *disable*, *disband*, *disdain*, *disgust*, *dishonest*, *dismiss*, *disoblige*, *disrobe*, etc., with a real *s* (not, however, *discern*, *disease*, *dissolve*); and I believe there is not a single word in which I pronounce *ex-* as *egz-*, without an effort specially directed to that end; what I say, however, is rather *ekz-* than *eks-* — that is to say, the sonant character of the following vowel infects the close of the consonant combination, though not the whole of it: and that, without regard to whether the syllable is unaccented, as in *exert*, or accented, as in *exercise*. Among other words in which the *z*-sound is an abomination to my native ear, I will mention only such as *Chinese* and *manganese*, as *Asia* and *Persia* (in which, I believe, the orthoëpists still approve the *s*), as *gooseberry*, as *grease* (verb) and *greasy*, as *vase* (*vēs*), as *nasal* (more doubtful). Nor did I ever hear the (first) *ss* of *possess* uttered as *z* till I had long learned to give it the other way.

As for the conversion of *s* and *z* into *sh* and *zh*, it will be spoken of under the latter pair of sounds.

We have seen that the *sh*-sound is restricted to no such narrow limits as the *s*; it is a similar articulation, of a strongly sibilant or hissing character, producible between either the tip or the upper flat surface, or even the under surface, of the tongue, by near approximation to the roof of the mouth at a point behind the *s*-point, but capable of indefinite protraction backward. Bell describes and figures it as made with the tongue retracted a little from his *s*-position, yet not at all turned up at the point; on the contrary, still applying a good piece of its upper surface behind the point to the roof of the mouth: and this I presume to be the prevailing mode of English pronunciation. But Max Müller turns the point sharply up, bringing it within the dome of the palate, into our usual *r*-position. This is precisely the position in which the Sanskrit "cerebral" or "cacuminal" sibilant was unquestionably produced, but I am by no means prepared to believe on Müller's authority that any considerable part of the English-speaking community form their *sh* thus; I have not in any of my inquiries met with such a case, and nothing could be more inconsistent with the common derivation of the sound in our language from an *sy*-sound. But there is yet another method, which I presume to be followed by all those who pronounce the *s* as I have described above, and which is my own method. In my *sh*, namely, the tip of the tongue touches the inner side of the lower front teeth, precisely as in *s*; the only difference between the two is that in the former the articulating position is made a little farther back, and therefore with a somewhat posterior part of the tongue. In changing from the one to the other, the tip does not vary its position a particle; but in passing from *s* to *sh* the upper surface is pressed up behind and relaxed in front, while in passing from *sh* to *s* it is relaxed behind and pressed up in front; the point of nearest approach is shifted.

40. The *sh*-sound, made in one or other of the ways described, is among the rarer English articulations, its average being about five sixths of one per cent. Its being written with *sh* is for a like reason with the writing of *th* and *ph*, as explained above; it arises historically, in a large class of cases, out of the combination of an *s* with a following palatal spirant (compare the German *sch*). The physical explanation of the change is not difficult: in the fusing of the two sounds together into one, the palatal element has attracted the sibilant to a more palatal position. But the same influence is also exerted by the *y*, the palatal semivowel; and, according to our present habits of speech, nothing leads so directly to an *sh*-sound as the combination of *s* and *y*. In hasty and careless (not necessarily slovenly) utterance, *sh* is even made out of an *s* and *y* that meet in two successive words: as in "thus you see," "bless your sweet face." And a large share of the acknowledged and approved *sh*-sounds of the language come from a similar combination: either where the *y* has a written representative, as in *nation*, *gracious*, *anxious*, *ocean*, *conscience;* or where a "long *u*" (*yu*) follows the sibilant, as in *sure*, *insurance*.

By sound theory, when an *s*-sound has been converted into *sh* by thus absorbing into itself, as it were, a following *y*-sound, the vowel representing the latter ought not to be pronounced in addition and form a separate syllable. Thus, we ought to say either *pro-nun-ci-(=sĭ)-a-tion* or *pro-nun-cia-(=shē)-tion*. Good usage, however, accepts no such theory as binding, and the utterance especially of *ciate* and *tiate* as *shĭ-ēt* (as in *officiate*, *substantiate*) is not only approved by authority but well-nigh universal. Yet there is also a class of words in which usage is fluctuating, and the orthoëpists more categorical in their decisions than either analogy or usage warrants; we may take as examples (not the best, perhaps, that could be found) *nausea*, *nauseate*, *nauseous*, in which *si-a*, *shi-a*, and *sha* are all in good common currency. To me it is natural to say *pro-nun-ci-a-tion*, *ne-go-ti-(=sĭ)-a-tion*, and their like.

41. The corresponding sonant to *sh*, the *zh*-sound of *occasion*, *pleasure*, *glazier*, *azure*, is the rarest in the language; I have found but two cases of it in 10,000 sounds (a fiftieth of one per cent.): though one may well enough chance to fall in with passages where it is much more frequent, since the words in which it occurs form a respectable body, and some of them are quite familiar. It is no long-established member of our alphabet, but has in every instance grown out of a *z*-sound followed by a *y*, precisely as *sh* out of *s* and *y*, in the manner just explained: we may also hear it in careless utterance where *z* and *y* meet in the sentence, as in "he loves you well," "it is usual."

The *zh* and *sh* sounds, however, are likewise found in a quite considerable class of cases in close combination with a preceding mute, forming what we know as the *ch* and *j* sounds, in *church* and *judge*. If we write the pure sibilants with *sh* and *zh*, it is perfectly proper to write these compounds with *tsh* and *dzh*.[1] Yet this representation would require in one respect a little explanation, inasmuch as the *t* and *d* are not precisely those which we usually utter, but are produced by a contact just at that point where a near approximation produces the sibilant; they are a more palatal *t* and *d*. The compounds are closely akin in character with the *ts* (written *z*) and *pf* of the Germans: a mute with its corresponding fricative appended, implying a relaxation of the contact before its complete abandonment, a dwelling upon a transitional sound

[1] It is thus that Ellis represents them in his *Palæotype*; Lepsius prefers *č* and *ǰ*.

or glide, and bringing it to distinct audibility. And so close is, to the ear, the union of the two elements, that many English speakers, even writers upon orthoëpy, believe and teach that the *ch* and *j* sounds are simple and indivisible. I would not deny the possibility that here, as in some other similarly contested cases, an actual diversity of pronunciation may underlie the difference of analysis and definition; yet I should be more disposed to question it here than anywhere else.

In making a numerical analysis of English utterance, I have — I confess, with questionable judgment — reckoned the *ch* and *j* sounds as independent elements, because of their distinct origin and etymological value, and especially because they are after all not accurately represented by writing them with *t* and *d* and accompanying sibilant. The *ch*, so far as it is more ancient and Saxon, comes mainly from an earlier surd palatal, as in *choose*, *much*, *teach*, *catch*; the *j*-sound belongs to the Romanic side of our language, and comes either from a Latin *y*-sound, as in *just*, *joy*, *June*, or from a sonant palatal mute, as in *agent*, *origin*. But, apart from this whole earlier class of cases, both are abundantly derived in modern usage from combinations of *t* and *d* with a following *y*-sound — just as the simple *sh* and *zh* from *s-y* and *z-y*; and, like the latter, they have their analogies in the careless combinations of the sentence, as in "did you go?" "what you saw." Examples are *question*, *Christian*, *righteous*, *nature*, *virtue*, *actual*; and *soldier* (some people say also *hideous*, *odious* in the same way), *grandeur*, *arduous*, *individual*. The consent of the orthoëpical authorities is far behind the popular usage in these words: but one may precisely as soon think of denying the *sh* and *zh* of *nation* and *pleasure* as the *ch* and *j* of *nature* and *grandeur*.

42. Reckoning the *ch* as only one sound, I find it to average just above a half of one per cent. in English

usage. Analyzing it into its constituents, it would give a palatal *t* of that frequency, and would raise the occurrence of *sh* to nearly one and a half per cent.

43. The *j*-sound, in like manner, averages just below a half of one per cent. The *zh*, therefore, is vastly more frequent in this combination than as an independent sound.

We must not pass without notice the fact that in such words as *inch* and *hinge*, where a nasal precedes the *ch* or *j* sound, it is assimilated to their first element, and becomes a more palatal *n*. If, then, we were to reckon the *ch* and *j* as contributing each a palatal *t* and *d* to the enumeration of English sounds, we should have to acknowledge this *n* also, and assign it a certain percentage.[1]

The English is sometimes accused of an unpleasant predominance of hissing or sibilant sounds; and not without some reason, since the sum of sibilant elements amounts to nine and a half per cent., or nearly one tenth of our whole utterance. In French, however, according to my reckoning, the proportion is even a shade larger, and in ancient Greek it was over twelve per cent.; of our modern Germanic relatives, the German and the Swedish have each about six per cent.

There remains, of our English sounds, only that one which we write by the sign *h*. It never occurs in our utterance excepting before a vowel, or before one of the semivowels *w* and *y*, as in *whip* and *hue* (according to my pronunciation of them: see below). It is a sound of very peculiar character, in that it is not, like all the other members of the alphabet, limited to a particular position of the mouth-organs, but is an audible expulsion of unintonated breath, of *flatus*, through the same articulating position in which the following letter, whatever it be, is uttered. In pronouncing *ha*, for example, the mouth-or-

[1] It occurs, in the 10,000 sounds which I have counted, thirteen times, or forms of them one eighth of one per cent.

gans are first fixed to say *a*, and then a rush of air through them, before the *a* begins, is heard as the *h*. In pronouncing *he* (*hī*), again, the *ī*-position is assumed before the utterance begins; in *who* (*hū*), in like manner, the *ū*-position. There is a difference between this audible rush of air and the mere passage of breath, which may be effected so gently as to produce nothing audible, in all the various articulating positions, fricative as well as vocalic. There is also a difference between it and a whispered vowel, in which a very distinctly characterized, though imperfectly intoned, vowel-sound is produced in the larynx itself, by an imperfect tension and vibration of the vocal cords: like the imperfectly resonant tone, yet of distinct pitch, which can be drawn from a pipe or flute by blowing rudely upon it. The audible quality of the *h* seems to be produced simply by forcing through a fuller and more rapid current of air than can pass unnoticed, one of which the general friction against the walls of the throat and mouth is sufficient to be perceptible to the ear: whence the *h* is, as every singer knows, more exhaustive of the breath than any other utterance. Even if, however, there be sometimes an accompanying and auxiliary narrowing of the passage from the throat in any part, made for the sake of plainer and easier audibleness, and varying with the different styles of utterance (as I do not think that there is), it is not of the nature of an articulation, but only of a modification of the material furnished to the articulating position; it would be analogous with the resonant utterance which makes the sonant consonants and vowels, with the flatus which makes the other surd consonants, with the nasal tone which makes the nasals, with that peculiar modification of resonance which makes the whisper, and so on — the kinds of material which are expelled through a variety of mouth-positions, and which, in virtue of those positions, take the value of distinct articulations, or "letters." It would still remain the characteristic property of the *h* that it alone has no definite mouth-position, but is spoken indifferently through the whole series of vowel and semivowel positions. By historical descent, the *h*, or pure aspiration, comes usually from a guttural spirant, an utterance in which there is a real fricative approach of the organs to one another in the back part of the mouth, a definite position which the organs assume, and from which they make a transition to that for the following letter. When this fricative approach is abandoned, when there takes place only the rush of air, wholly governed in respect to its articulating position by the next letter, then the spirant has become an aspiration, the *kh* or *ch* (German) or χ has become an *h*. This indefinitizing process has gone on in many languages; and it is apt to be followed by an evanescent process, in which the *h* itself becomes silent and disappears to the ear.

There is a difference perfectly appreciable between the various expulsions of breath which we group together under the sign *h*. Only pronounce them by themselves, and dwell upon and watch them, and their discordant character is clearly apparent. But the difference is of a subordinate value only, like that, for instance, between the *k* of *ki* and that of *ku*; it is so slight that the ear overlooks it, and apprehends them all as virtually one. The peculiarity may be formulated somewhat thus: in the closer consonantal positions of the mouth-organs, an expulsion even of unintonated breath yields a sufficiently individualized and characterized sound to be apprehended as a distinct alphabetic element, and the letters consequently go in pairs, one surd and one sonant for each articulating position; but in the openest consonantal positions and the yet opener vowels, the unintonated expulsion is so imperfectly characterized that its differences are disregarded, and they all together add only one element to the system of sounds.

To this class of opener positions, which alike produce an *h*, belong not only all the vowels and the two semivowels *w* and *y*, but also the other two semivowels, *r* and *l*, and the whole class of nasals. In other languages (as the Anglo-Saxon, Gothic, Sanskrit), though not in English, these too may be preceded by *h;* and when we produce the combinations *hl*, *hr*, *hm*, *hn*, as there found, we never think of doing otherwise than fix the organs for the utterance of the following letter before the *h* itself is uttered.

I define *h*, then, as a collective sign under which are comprehended the various but not essentially different surd correspondents of the vowels, semi-vowels, and nasals: these three opener classes of sonants have but a single common surd, while, of the closer sibilants, spirants, and mutes, every sonant letter has its own corresponding surd.

Of course, the nearer we approach in articulating position to the degree of closeness which makes the pairs, surd and sonant, of fricatives and mutes, the nearer does the corresponding aspiration come to being a distinct and independent sound, able to maintain its value as such in an alphabetical scheme. And it is claimed by some phonetists of great eminence (as Ellis and Bell) that in *when* and *hue*, as in all the other words pronounced like them, the *w* and *y* elements have become obliterated, and that there remains before the vowel in either case only a surd *w* and a surd *y*. This would be a parallel to the history of the *ng*-sound; an element which at first appeared only in a dependent character, conditioned by the following sound, had finally, by the removal of that upon which it formerly leaned, assumed a degree of independence. In my view of the essential character of the *h*-sound there is nothing whatever which should stand in the way of the possibility of this; and I have perhaps been too reluctant hitherto to admit it as an actuality in the present utterance of English.[1] I will only be positively certain that I myself say *hwen* and *hyu*, and very confident also that I have heard and hear the same pronunciation from those about me ; how the case may be in other divisions of the great and not too accordant community of English speakers, I will leave to others to determine. But I am sure that many persons who are uninformed as to the true character of the aspiration are without any reason, and unfairly, driven off their well-founded opinion that their *when* is really *hwĕn*, in some such way as by being told to set their mouths for the initial of *hen*, and then try to say *when*. Of course, they fail, because the *h* of *hwen* is not at all the same sound as that of *hen ;* but then the *h* of *hen* is equally not the same with that of *hat* or *harp* or *hot* or *hind ;* and if one were to set his mouth for any one of the five, he would equally fail in striking any of the others without changing his set. If it is proper to call all those five varying initials *an* "aspiration," and to write them with *h*, it is equally proper to call the initials of *when* and *hue* by the same name, and to represent them by the same sign. There are very few persons whose own word I would take as to whether they do or do not say *hwen*.

That those who say *hwen* and *hyu* have preserved an earlier and fuller sound, which has suffered corruption and abbreviation in the mouths of the other party, admits no serious question. In the case of the *hue* class, the sound is obviously made up of the same *yu* which we have as the pronunciation of "long *u*" in *use*, *pure*, *muse*, *beauty*, *cure*, and so on, with the initial *h*. If there are any who do not now sound the *y*-element, it has been dropped out. As to the other class, the fact is equally indisputable, though less obvious. The Germanic (including English) *h* comes in general from a pal-

[1] See the first volume of these Studies, p. 270, and Ellis's remarks in his *Early English Pronunciation*, p. 1142 *seq.*

atal mute, a *k*-sound, of the older Indo-European language: thus, for example, our *heart* corresponds to Latin *cord-*, Greek καρδία; and *horn* to Latin *cornu*, Greek κερατ-, and so on. And so it is also with the *hw* words: *what* (Anglo-Saxon *hwæt*), for example, is the correlative of Latin *quod*, and owes its *h*-sound, as do *heart* and *horn*, to the conversion, first into a spirant and then into the aspiration, of the *k* which preceded the *w*. There is no reason whatever for supposing that the Anglo-Saxons did not pronounce *hwæt*, etc., just as they spelled them; and if a considerable part of the present users of English still give the same sound to the combination which, by a curious orthographic blunder, we have now come to write with *wh* instead of *hw*, it is because they are faithful to the more complete utterance. With a great part of the vulgar speakers of English, the tendency is toward eliminating the surd instead of the sonant element of the combination which ought to contain both, converting *when* into *wen;* I do not see why, in theory, the one mutilation is any worse or better than the other.

44. In adding, therefore, the simple aspiration *h* to complete the alphabet of English as it is in my mouth, I do not distinguish the initial elements of *when* and *hue* from the other numerous varieties of aspiration which that character is used to designate. Including these, the *h* is one of the more usual English sounds, its average rising to two and one third per cent of our utterance.[1]

As regards the small class of words respecting which good usage is undecided whether to omit or retain the *h*, I may mention that my natural pronunciation gives the *h* to *humble* and *humor* (in all senses), but refuses it to *herb* (and its immediate derivatives) and *homage*.

Another matter of discordant usage in connection with

[1] A little more than the odd third of one per cent. is contributed by the semivowel aspirates: with exactness, 43 in 10,000; 39 of these are cases like *when*, and only four like *hue*.

h is, what form the indefinite article shall take before words beginning with it. *An* being the older form of the article, and its reduction to *a* before a consonant being a more recent abbreviation, the light and half-vocalic *h* has been the slowest and latest to exert its full consonantal influence. In our English Bible-version, as in other works of the same period, and even much later, *an* is very commonly retained before an *h* of any kind; and by most modern orthoëpists the rule is laid down that *a* be employed before the (pronounced) initial *h* of an accented syllable, but *an* before that of an unaccented syllable: that we say, therefore, *a history*, but *an harangue*, *an historical tract*, and so on. Writers of excellent standing, however, on both sides of the Atlantic, ignore this rule, and use only *a* before an actually uttered *h*, whether in an accented or an unaccented syllable. And such is the popular usage in the section of English speakers to which I belong; it was formerly not a particle less strange and unnatural to me to say *an harangue* or *an hotel* than *an heart* or *an handkerchief*.[1]

The sounds thus recognized as constituting the English spoken alphabet may be arranged, by their physical characteristics and relations, in the scheme on the following page, which begins with the openest sound and ends with the closest sounds, exhibiting the various classes and series in accordance with the description which has been already given of them.

The reasons of this arrangement will have been in the main made evident by the foregoing exposition: some points in it will be the subject of further remark in the next article.[2]

[1] See also p. 172.

[2] And the table is repeated, in a somewhat modified form, on p. 286.

PHYSICAL SCHEME OF THE ENGLISH SPOKEN ALPHABET.

	Palatal Series.	Lingual Series.	Labial Series.	
Sonant.		*a*		Vowels.
	æ		*ă*	
	Æ		*ʌ*	
	e	*ə*	*ŏ*	
	ē	[illegible]	*o*	
	i *ai*, *ʌi*		*au* *u*	
	ī	*n̥*, *l̥*	*ū*	
	y	*r*, *l*	*w*	Semivowels.
	ng	*n*	*m*	Nasals.
Surd.	*h*			Aspiration.
Sonant.	*zh*	*z*		Sibilants.
Surd.	*sh*	*s*		
Sonant.		*dh*	*v*	Spirants.
Surd.		*th*	*f*	
Sonant.	*g*	*d*	*b*	Mutes.
Surd.	*k*	*t*	*p*	
Sonant.	*j*			Compound.
Surd.	*ch*			

In judging, now, the general character of English pronunciation, it is of considerable interest to know how frequently the various articulations make their appearance in the sum of utterance. I have endeavored to determine this,[1] upon a sufficiently wide basis of selected passages to furnish a trustworthy average; and I have reported the results above, in treating of each sound. It remains to explain here the method adopted, and to present the results reached in a compact and tabular form together.

I made a selection of ten passages, five in poetry and five in prose, from as many authors, of various periods, and separated and counted the individual sounds as met

[1] Of course, for my own pronunciation; but the principal data may be taken as belonging, nearly as given, to the general language.

with in each, until the number of 1,000 sounds was reached. The passages were as follows: —

I. From Shakespeare's "Julius Cæsar," Antony's speech over the body of Cæsar, nearly 38 lines, 288 words, 373 syllables;

II. From Milton's "Paradise Lost," at the beginning, 35½ lines, 274 words, 358 syllables;

III. From Gray's "Elegy in a Country Churchyard," at the beginning, nearly 9 verses, 272 words, 357 syllables;

IV. From Bryant's "Thanatopsis," at the beginning, nearly 36 lines, 283 words, 364 syllables;

V. From Tennyson's "In Memoriam," section lxxxiii., a little more than 11 verses, 284 words, 358 syllables;

VI. From the Bible, in King James's version, Psalm xxvii., nearly 13 verses, 319 words, 396 syllables;

VII. From Dr. Johnson's "Rasselas," at the beginning, 263 words, 388 syllables;

VIII. From Goldsmith's "Vicar of Wakefield," the beginning, 269 words, 390 syllables;

IX. From Carlyle's "Sartor Resartus," book ii., chapter 8, eighth paragraph (on "the net purport and upshot of war"), 258 words, 371 syllables;

X. From Macaulay's essay on Milton, part of the passage relating to the Puritans, 236 words, 374 syllables.

The main results are given in the table on the next page. I did not think it worth while to present them in all their detail for every passage, but give for each sound the general average, drawn from all the passages, and in the order of frequency of occurrence, so arranged that it may be read as a scale of frequency for the whole alphabet, or for the consonantal and vowel systems taken separately. And as it is of interest to note the limits of variation of each sound, I add in the last two columns the least and the greatest number found in any one passage, with specification of the passage or passages in which it is found. The variation is for the most part a natural one, such as

SCALE AND RATE OF FREQUENCY OF ENGLISH SOUNDS.

Consonant.	Vowel.	Per Cent.	Per Cent.	Minimum.		Maximum.	
r	..	7.44	..	VI.	5.4	VIII.	9.3
n	..	6.76	..	III.	5.7	IX.	7.9
t	..	5.93	..	VI.	4.6	II.	8.9
..	*i*	..	5.90	VI.	4.7	VII.	7.4
..	*ə*	..	5.66	II.	4.3	I., VII.	6.9
d	..	4.94	..	I.	4.0	V.	5.8
s	..	4.69	..	III., VIII.	3.7	I., II.	5.8
l	..	3.84	..	I., VII.	2.5	III.	6.2
dh	..	3.83	..	VIII.	2.4	III.	5.1
..	*ĕ*	..	3.34	I.–III.	2.6	IX.	4.7
..	*æ*	..	3.32	III.	2.4	VIII.	4.0
m	..	3.06	..	VIII.	1.8	I.	4.1
z	..	2.92	..	VI.	2.2	I.	4.3
..	*ī*	..	2.80	VII., IX.	1.5	VI.	4.8
..	*ă*	..	2.59	IV., IX.	1.8	VII.	4.2
v	..	2.37	..	I.	1.4	VII.	3.5
h	..	2.34	..	IX.	1.2	V.	3.1
w	..	2.31	..	III.	1.6	VIII.	3.0
k	..	2.17	..	II.	1.1	X.	3.1
f	..	2.06	..	IV., VII.	1.2	II.	2.8
..	*ū*	..	2.00	VI.	1.1	I.	3.5
..	*ai*	..	1.91	IX.	.9	VI.	4.8
..	*ɜ*	..	1.85	I.	.9	VIII.	2.5
..	*ō*	..	1.76	X.	.9	III.	2.6
p	..	1.71	..	V.	1.0	VII.	2.6
b	..	1.64	..	IX.	1.0	I.	3.4
..	*ē*	..	1.61	I.	.5	X.	2.7
..	*ʌ*	..	1.54	X.	.8	II.	2.2
sh	..	.86	..	II.	.1	IV.	1.8
..	*au*	..	.83	X.	.3	III., IV.	1.3
g	..	.79	..	VII., IX.	.3	VIII.	1.6
ng	..	.79	..	I.	.1	III., VIII.	1.4
y	..	.66	..	IX.	.3	IV.	1.1
th	..	.58	..	VIII.	.2	IV.	1.0
..	*a*	..	.56	VIII., X.	.1	IX.	1.2
ch	..	.53	..	I., II.	.1	VIII.	1.2
..	*Æ*	..	.47	VII.	.0	III.	1.4
j	..	.47	..	VI.	.1	IX.	.9
..	*ŭ*	..	.44	IX., X.	.2	VIII.	1.2
..	*l̥*	..	.35	VII.	.1	I.	.7
..	*n̥*	..	.16	I., III., X.	.0	II., VII., IX.	.3
..	*ʌi*	..	.12	I., II., VIII.	.0	III.–VI., IX.	.2
..	*ŏ*	..	.08	II., IV., VI., VII.	.0	I., III.	.2
zh	..	.02	..	I.–VIII.	.0	IX., X.	.1
		62.71	37.29				

might be found anywhere on comparing one extract with another, as I endeavored not to take any extracts which showed a prevalence of a particular word or words: but this could not always be avoided; and the *Brutus* of the Shakespeare passage, for instance, and the *I* and *my* of that from the Bible, exhibit their effects clearly in the numbers given. The figures of the first two columns, as read without the decimal point, give the whole number of occurrences in the 10,000 sounds; those of the last two, read in the same way, the number in each 1,000; the decimal point converts all alike into an expression of percentage.

It should be noted that the number given for *r* represents the more accepted pronunciation, rather than my own natural one (which would leave, as explained above, 370 of the 744 cases unpronounced). As for the unaccented vowels, I have estimated them as well as I could, according to a good and careful reading style, not a colloquial one; no one, I presume, could go over the same passages twice and reach precisely the same results both times.

The proportion of vowels to consonants in English speech appears to be as 37.3 to 62.7. The percentage of vowels is, I believe, a little less in German, a little more in Swedish (38.3), yet more in French (over 40), 41 in Gothic, 42 in Sanskrit, 44 in Latin, 46 in Greek.

The number of words in all the ten passages being 2,746, it appears that the average number of syllables in an English word is (3729÷2746) 1.358;[1] that of sounds to a word is (10,000÷2746) 3.642; that of consonants to a syllable is (6271÷3729) 1.682.

[1] The actual number of monosyllables in the ten passages is 2028, or 73.8 per cent., the range of variation of percentage being between 65.4 (VII.) and 81.2 (VI.); the dissyllables are 510, or 18.6 per cent.; the trisyllables are 146, or 5.3 per cent.; the words of four syllables are 50, or 1.8 per cent.; and there are 11 words of five syllables, and 1 of six.

A few more general combinations and comparisons may be worth making.

First, of the vowels; the classes are as follows: —

Palatal	17.44	Openest (*a*)	.56
Labial . . .	8.41	Next degree (*æ*, *ă*, *ʌ*) .	7.92
Lingual (*l̥*, *n̥*) . .	.51	Medial (*e*, *o*) . .	6.79
Neutral (including *a*)	8.07	Closest (*i*, *u*) . .	11.14
Diphthongs . . .	2.86		

Again, for the consonants: —

Palatal			6.29
Lingual			40.93
Labial			13.15
Neutral (*h*)			2.34
Mutes [1] .	Sonant, Surd,	7.84 10.34	18.18
Spirants .	Sonant, Surd,	6.20 2.64	8.84
Sibilants [1] .	Sonant, Surd,	3.41 6.08	9.49
Fricatives	Sonant, Surd,	9.61 8.72	18.33
Nasals			10.61
Semivowels			14.25
Aspiration			2.34

Finally, comparing the surd and sonant elements, we have —

	Of pairs of cons.	Of all cons.	Of whole alphabet.
Surds,	18.53	20.87	20.87
Sonants,	16.98	41.84	79.13

[1] In this combination, the compounds *ch* and *j* are counted twice, once as mute and once as sibilant.

IX.

THE RELATION OF VOWEL AND CONSONANT.

GREAT progress has been made in phonological science during the past score or two of years, and it is hardly too much to say that the mode of production of the ordinary articulate sounds composing human language is now understood in all its main features. This is especially true of the consonants, which are easier of investigation. The vowels are more difficult; and only the most recent researches of the ablest phonetists and physicists have succeeded in giving anything like an exact scientific definition of what makes an *a*, an *i*, an *u*, etc., as distinguished from one another; and, approximately, by what muscular action in the organs of speech they receive their characteristic quality. As regards this last matter, it can very probably never be determined otherwise than approximately; the processes are too complicated and obscure to allow of more than that.

I do not mean that phonetic science has not still before it a great task to accomplish, and a great career to run. So, for one thing, in the way of gaining diffusion. There are a host of discordant and indefensible views, or half-views, current among philologists on phonetic subjects, which are due simply to an unenlightened or prejudiced disregard of truths in phonology already well established — a disregard which another generation, probably, will see removed. Then there is well-nigh an infinity of living dialects as yet unexamined or insufficiently examined, and the exact study of the sounds they use will in every case have its contributions to make to the comprehension of human utterance, and to the solution of the problems of its past history. And to solve these problems will be the last and hardest task, a task to which the science will return again and again, as it gets a wider and firmer grasp of its facts, and a clearer insight into their connections and causes. But there will be a great deal in the perfected science of phonology which will have only a slighter and more indirect bearing on the historical science of language. There is, if I mistake not, a tendency on the part of some of the eminent phonetists of the day to exaggerate the importance of their special department of linguistic study, almost to hold that the history of language is the history of articulate sounds, their combinations and changes. It is in fact a great deal more than this: this is even, however important, only a subordinate department of the study. The history of language includes also, and especially, the history of words as representing thought, of words with meanings, of vocabularies; the history of parts of speech, of grammatical structure, of forms and their uses, of syntactical combinations. If there were a language of written and visible signs alone, it would still be as worthy an object of the linguistic scholar's study as if every stroke in every sign were a sound addressed to the ear. And the phonetist's work is not destitute of analogy with what would be the work of a student of the visible sign if language in general were written instead of spoken. We are not cut off from fruitful knowledge of a tongue by not being able to read under its written form the exact tones in which its speakers gave it; not even though our misrepresentation of its spoken form be as gross as that which we are actually guilty of in the case of ancient Greek. To lose its phonetic reality and history is to lose a great deal, to be sure; yet, after all, only a minor part. The highest practical office of phonetics is to cast such light on the changes of sounds as shall help the identification of related words and forms, giving an increased degree of precision to the processes of the etymologist and of certainty to his results. The gradual improvement and perfection of the study will increase its value in this regard. But it will also become by itself a definite science, or department of study, having its close and important relations to physiology and acoustics, as well as to philology. There will always continue to be, as there are at present, great philologists who are poor phonologists.[1]

A not unimportant part, in my view, of the process of reducing the results of physical study of the alphabet to a form useful for the historical philologist is the construction of a scheme of arrangement for alphabetic sounds which shall exhibit their relations most clearly and fully. The spoken alphabet of any language is a more or less orderly and well-proportioned system, with lines of connection running through it in various directions; and it requires to be viewed as such, if its history of development is to be well understood. The subject is one which is overlooked by many phonetists and philologists, and which has, as I think, been imperfectly treated by others; I propose, therefore, to submit it here to a new examination — and especially, with regard to the fundamental point of the relation of vowels and consonants.[2]

The triangular arrangement of the vowels, with *a* (*far*) at its apex, as openest and least orally modified of

[1] And this, notwithstanding the opinions of those who hold, with Key, that observations on the *chordæ vocales* lie at the foundation of the whole study of human speech; or, with Farrar, that "the physiology of the human voice is the true basis upon which all inquiries into the origin of language and the mutual connection of languages should be built." (*Comparative Grammar*, London, 1869, p. 1.)

[2] I have discussed the matter at some length in two articles on the *Standard Alphabet* of Professor Lepsius, published in the seventh and eighth volumes (1863–65) of the *Journ. Am. Oriental Society*; and upon them the present essay is in great measure founded.

vowel-sounds, and with ī (*pique*) and ū (*rule*) at the two extremities of its base, as the closest and most orally modified (by action in two different parts of the mouth) of possible vowel-sounds, is so widely known and so generally adopted among philologists that its value may be taken for granted without many words spent upon it. To the historical student in various and widely discordant families of language, it takes cognizance of and helps to explain a fact of prime importance — the greater originality of these three vowels, and the development of others from them and between them. Few, if any, existing languages fail to possess at least the intermediate sounds *e* (*they*) and *o* (*tone*); a very large proportion have no other than these five.

Usually, however, those who study the spoken alphabet have been content to treat vowel and consonant as two independent entities, partners in the work of articulate expression, indissolubly married together for the uses of speech, yet distinct individuals, to be classified and arranged in separate systems. Now it may be theoretically conceivable that the products of the organs of articulation should be thus of two diverse kinds: just as the human race is composed of two distinct sexes, each having its own part to play in the work of the race; any true intermediate form or combination of the two being impossible, any apparent one a monstrosity. But is this actually the case in the spoken alphabet? I think decidedly not. The simple fact of the occurrence in our phonological vocabulary of the term *semivowel* is enough to shake such a theory to its foundation. Think of a woman who should be a "semi-man"! There is, on the one hand, a not inconsiderable body of sounds, known by various names — as semivowels, liquids, nasals — in which, though we reckon them as consonants, we recognize a special kindred with the vowels, insomuch that they even sometimes assume vocalic value: as do, for example, in our own language, *l* and *n* (see above, p. 233). On the other hand, there are two vowels, *ī* and *ū*, which are so closely allied to consonants that, when we put them in the same syllable before another vowel, we can hardly keep them from passing into sounds which we are accustomed to represent by *y* and *w*, regarding them as consonantal and not vocalic (see above, p. 239). These are the prominent facts which seem to oppose the theory of the independence of vowel and consonant, and compel us to inquire more narrowly into what we are to understand respectively by a vocalic and a consonantal character. We do not need to supersede or alter any of the definitions of single sounds, or even of the principal groups of sounds, already prevailing; we only want to find the tie which unites them into more comprehensive classes, and even, if possible, a principle on which the whole alphabet of articulated products may be arranged as a single system, without distortion or disguise of the relations borne by its different members to one another.

It does not appear to me that this needed principle is difficult to find, nor, when found, of doubtful application. It consists in the antithesis of material and form, in the respective part played in the production of the different alphabetic sounds by the organs of the lungs and throat, and by the organs of the mouth — the former furnishing the column of air, the breath or tone, the latter modifying this breath or tone and giving it various individuality. Those sounds in which the material, the element of tone, predominates, are vowels; those in which the other element, the oral modification, predominates, are consonants; but there is no absolute line of division between the two great classes; each has its degrees whereby it approaches the other; there is a continuous line of progression from the openest and purest vowel to the closest and most absolute consonant, and a border-territory between, where the sounds are of doubtful or double character.

The starting-point of the various lines of progression is the vowel *a* (*far*); *a* is the simplest and purest tone-sound which, in virtue of its peculiar structure, the human throat brings forth. This is its true phonetic description. To determine the fundamental and secondary vibrations which give to *a* its acoustic character, to ascertain the length of pipe, or the degree and kind of orificial closure, needful to produce it when the tones of human organs are imitated by means of artificial constructions — these and other like investigations have a high theoretic interest, while yet, in their bearing on linguistic phonology, they are of only subordinate consequence: sounds are produced for the purposes of human speech by the voluntary efforts of human organs, and are to be estimated and classified according to those efforts.

If, now, from that position in which *a* is uttered, we raise the upper flat surface of the tongue toward the roof of the mouth, at the highest point of the latter and farther back, successive degrees of elevation and approach will give us the vowels of *fat* (*æ*), *they* (*e*), and *pique* (*ī*). The accompanying closure of the jaws and lips is here absolutely unessential, contributing nothing to the characterization of the sounds; it is made merely for the convenience of the tongue, helping its access to the palate. The closest sound with predominating tone producible by this method is *ī*; a next further degree of approximation, giving rise to a frication or rustling which overpowers and makes subordinate the tone-element, and is itself plain and distinctive enough, whether made with tone or with breath, produces a pair of fricatives, spirants, the German *ch* of *ich*, *pech*, etc., and its corresponding sonant (which is a very rare constituent of the alphabet): we may write them *kh* and *gh*. Then follow, by complete closure, the intonated and unintonated mutes *g* and *k*. Thus we have a palatal series *a*, *æ*, *e*, *i*, *gh*–*kh*, *g*–*k*.[1]

[1] If any one insists that *y* is closer than ī, and to be distinguished from the

If, again, from the same open position of *a*, we round and protrude the lips a very little, the result is the *a* of *all* (ᴀ); and further degrees of the same action give *o* and *u*.[1] Here the *ū* is the closest tone-sound or vowel; a complete closure of the already closely approximated lips gives the pair of mutes *p* and *b*; and intermediate between the two lies the pair of purely labial spirants (see above, p. 256); which, in order to distinguish them from our nearly related dentilabial spirants, *f* and *v*, we may (with Ellis's "Palæotype") represent by *ph* and *bh*. The labial series, then, will be *a*, ᴀ, *o*, *u*,[2] *bh-ph*, *b-p*.

These two, I maintain, are real series throughout, and no schematic arrangement of the alphabet can be accepted as satisfactory which does not present them as such. They are wont to be so presented, as far as to the *i* and *u* respectively, in the vowel triangle or pyramid, already spoken of. But why stop at these limits? As regards their articulating position, there is no greater difference between *i* and *gh*, between *u* and *bh*, than between *i* and *e*, or *u* and *o*, or between *gh* and *g*, *bh* and *b*; not so great as between either *i* or *u* and *a*. It is true that, in passing from *i* to *gh*, or from *u* to *bh*, we have to cross an important and well marked division-line — the line on the one side of which the tone or throat-product is the main audible element, while on the other side of it the friction of the expelled column of air against the obstacles that so nearly confine it is the main audible element. But the line is not on that account anything more than a mark of division in a series, like the equally well marked one which separates the fricatives from the explosive sounds, or mutes. It simply represents the undeniable truth that, with the same organs, approxima-

latter, he may insert it between *i* and *gh-kh* in the series: so far as the matter here under discussion is concerned, the result is the same.

[1] See the preceding article (p. 213) for the question as to a supplementary action in the throat in the formation of these letters.

[2] Here a *w* may be inserted by those who choose, as a *y* in the palatal series.

tion short of a certain degree produces vowels, and beyond a certain degree produces consonants; and it joins not less than it separates; while it holds the two classes apart, it at the same time combines them into one system.

Besides the two series, composed of vowels and consonants, which have been already described in detail, the ordinary alphabets contain another, of a more prevailingly consonantal character. It is produced by the tip of the tongue, seeking approach and contact with the roof of the mouth in its forward part. It contains, properly speaking, no vowels: as the tongue is turned up at the tip, and brought gradually toward the parts at or behind the upper front gums, no series of gradually changing tone-sounds is heard; but the dimmed *a*, the neutral vowel of *but* and *burn* (see above, p. 222), is an intermediate of convenience; and in English habit of utterance, especially, it bears such close relation to the *r* as almost to require to be ranked as a vowel standing between *a* and *r*. When the approach is near enough, the *r* is generated; and, as was explained in the foregoing article (above, p. 235), it may be either trilled or left smooth. The next degree of approach, at the same place and with the same organs, gives rise to a fricative sound, a *z* (or, if far enough back in the mouth, a *zh*), in which the rustling or buzzing is very conspicuous, and which has, like *gh* and *bh*, its surd counterpart, *s* (or *sh*). And complete closure produces the pair of mutes *t* and *d*. But the tip of the tongue generates two sounds of its own openest class: the *r*, uttered with the tongue closed at the sides and open at the tip; and the *l*, uttered with the tongue open at the sides and closed at the tip. The mutual convertibility of these two sounds in the history of language is a familiar fact, nor would any one think of putting them into different classes. Though not vowels, they are also not properly fricatives; they are the openest, most resonant, and most continuable, of all the consonantal sounds; they have not, like the sonant fricatives and mutes, their surd counterparts, employable with equal frequency and freedom for the uses of articulate speech. No name is so applicable to them as that of *semivowels*, by which they are also most frequently called: they do, in fact, stand as nearly as possible upon the division-line between vowels and consonants. Whether, in their production, the part taken by the throat or by the mouth-organs should be regarded as predominant, seems to me a debatable question; I should not dare to say with confidence whether there is in them more tone or more form. Hence their special capacity of being employed as vowels, and their frequent appearance in that character. The use of *l* as vowel in English has been sufficiently considered already (above, p. 233); and the reason has also been noticed why *r* is differently treated with us. The Sanskrit furnishes the readiest exemplification of a vocalic *r*. The sound may stand with that value in any situation, not being restricted, like *l* in our speech, to unaccented syllables: it receives the accent, as in *karmakr′t;* it is the sole vowel of a word, as in *hrd;* it forms an initial syllable, as in *r-tu.*

The lingual series, then, is [*a*, *ə*, *ɪ*] *r-l*, *z-s*, *d-t*.

There is yet another class of sounds, the nasals, whose relations to the other classes, and their consequent position in the alphabetic system, require a little special discussion. As regards the position assumed by the mouth-organs in their utterance, they stand upon the footing of full mutes, the closure of the oral passage being complete. They are far, however, from being mute sounds, because in pronouncing them the nasal passages are open, and this circumstance gives them no small degree of openness, resonance, and continuability. Their classification, then, is not to be determined by their mouth-position alone — which would rank them with the mutes — but by their general character. And this places them next to the semivowels, between the latter and the fricatives. For, in the first place, they are, like the semivowels, capable of employment with the value of vowels; and one of them, the *n*, is actually so employed in our language (see above, p. 233). And, in the second place, they have not, like fricatives and mutes, each of them its own surd counterpart: they share, rather, with the vowels and semivowels the possession of *h* as common surd. An *f* has fully as good a right in the alphabet as a *v*, an *s* as a *z*, a *k* as a *g*: but the surd expirations through the positions of *m* and *n*, as through those of *l* and *r*, of *y* and *w*, of *a* and *i* and *u*, are too little different to be worth distinguishing, and we should write *hna* and *hma*, just as *hla* or *hra*, as *hyu* (*hue*) and *hwen* (*when*), as *harp* and *heap* and *hoop*. These characteristics sufficiently prove that the contact and its closure or unclosure are in the nasals an element of only inferior and subordinate value.

The sounds which we have thus discussed will, when arranged according to the relations we have noted as belonging to them, form the following scheme:—

Sonant.			*a*			Vowels.	
		æ		*ʌ*			
		e		*o*			
	i		*ə*		*u*		
	y		*r*, *l*		*w*	Semivowels.	Consonants.
	ng		*n*		*m*	Nasals.	
Surd.	*h*					Aspiration.	
Sonant.	*gh*		*z*		*bh*	Fricatives.	
Surd.	*kh*		*s*		*ph*		
Sonant.	*g*		*d*		*b*	Mutes.	
Surd.	*k*		*t*		*p*		
	Palatal Series.		Lingual Series.		Labial Series.		

Such an arrangment as this exhibits, I am fully persuaded, more of the relations, both physical and historical, of the alphabetic sounds, and exhibits them more truly, than any other which can be devised, and upon it as a basis the alphabets of different languages may be most advantageously compared and judged. In the preceding article (p. 272) I have given, upon the same plan, a fuller scheme, embracing all the sounds which make up the English alphabet.

Upon the principal point involved in it, however, the definition of vowel and consonant in their relations to one another, I desire to dwell longer, in order to test its necessity and practical availability.

That some new definition of a consonant is called for seems clearly enough indicated by the discordance and indefiniteness and insufficiency of the definitions hitherto furnished by phonetists. To Professor Max Müller, for example,[1] vowels are tones, and consonants merely noises. Of the latter he speaks as follows: —

> "All consonants fall under the category of noises, and there are certain noises that could hardly be avoided even in a language which was meant to consist of vowels only. If we watch any musical instruments, we can easily perceive that their sounds are always preceded by certain noises, arising from the first impulses imparted to the air before it can produce really musical sensations. We hear the puffing and panting of the siren, the scratching of the violin, the hammering of the pianoforte, the spitting of the flute. The same in speaking. If we send out our breath, intending it to be vocalized, we hear the rushing out, the initial impulse produced by the inner air as it reaches the outer."

This is all that Müller offers upon the subject, and any one can see at a glance how barren of instruction it is. To compare consonants, those essential and characteristic parts of our articulate speech, with the unmusical noises of musical instruments, which are overborne and silenced altogether in good execution, is palpably futile. What is there in the *b* and *l*, the *n* and *d*, of *blend*, for instance, to assimilate them to such noises? Are they, or any other of the twenty or thirty consonants which may

[1] Lectures, second series, third lecture: p. 139 of the American edition, 138 of the sixth (altered) English edition.

gather in groups, even to the number of five or six at once, about each of the vowels, in the least degree dependent for their being on the latter, or generated by it? Is not each one as distinct a product of the voluntary action of the articulating organs, consciously directed to its production, as is the vowel itself? Is there any difficulty in uttering a clear vowel, free from such prefatory (or sequent) appendages? And are those sounds entitled to the appellation of noises only, as distinguished from tones, which can themselves — as is the case especially with the opener consonants — be indefinitely prolonged and musically intoned? The asserted analogy fails of application in every particular.

Dr. Brücke of Vienna, than whom no German phonetist enjoys a higher reputation and more consideration as an authority, explains the distinction of vowel and consonant as follows:[1] "In all consonants, there takes place somewhere in the mouth-canal a closure, or a contraction which gives rise to a plainly audible and self-subsistent rustling, which is independent of the tone of the voice; while in the vowels neither of these things is the case."

To the correctness of this statement less exception is to be taken than to its character as a sufficient definition. It appears to me hardly entitled to be regarded as a definition at all: it is rather a catalogue, a specification of the two principal sub-classes into which consonants are divided, and a description of their respective characteristics. Some consonants, it declares, are produced by a complete closure of the mouth-organs, others by such an approximation of them as gives rise to an audible rustling. The specification, however, is not quite exhaustive. The nasals — or "resonants," as Dr. Brücke, with much reason, prefers to call them — are too unlike the mutes to be included in one sub-class with them, and they involve no

[1] *Grundzüge der Physiologie und Systematik der Sprachlaute* (Wien, 1856), p. 29.

audible rustling dependent on a contraction of the mouth-canal. All the three sub-classes, then — of mutes, resonants, and fricatives — should have been enumerated as making up the class of consonants; and our account of the alphabetic system would be virtually this: sounds possessing such and such characteristics, of three kinds, are consonants; the rest, not possessing any of them, are vowels. This is surely a superficial account of the matter. What common characteristic belongs to our consonantal subdivisions, combining them into a class together, and distinguishing them from the vowels? Why do we set up the vowels as a distinct grand division of the alphabet, and not as well, for example, the mutes: saying, The alphabet is divided into mutes and non-mutes; the non-mutes being continuable sounds, and accompanied with the expulsion of breath through either the lips or the nose; the mutes implying the closure of both, and being explosive only? And if the superior practical value of the distinction of vowels and consonants were pleaded, we should allege the convertibility of *ī* and *ū* into consonants, and of *l*, *r*, *n* into vowels, as facts which find no explanation whatever in Dr. Brücke's definition of a consonant.[1]

Mr. A. M. Bell, again, the eminent author of "Visible Speech,"[2] gives in that work (pp. 12, 13) an account of vowel and consonant which seems more nearly to imply the distinction as I have laid it down. He says: "In forming consonants, the breath or voice is stopped or squeezed, with an effect of percussion, sibilation, buzzing, or vibration, in some part of the guttural or oral passage;

[1] Lepsius, in his *Standard Alphabet*, gives the usual vowel-pyramid, though without any explanation of the reasons on which it is founded, and treats the consonants as a separate system, not attempting to define the distinction or relation of the two systems; and later (in *Jour. Am. Oriental Soc.* viii. 340, 1865) he insists upon the separation, but still without explaining himself as to the subject.

[2] See the next article.

and in forming vowels, the breath or voice flows through similar but more open and 'fixed' configurations, which merely shape or mould the breath, without impeding its emission." But the quality of "more open" configuration, ascribed here to the vowel, is made uncertain and unclear by being combined with "fixedness;" and I gather that the author regards this latter as the more essential part of his definition, for Mr. Peile [1] quotes from another work of his the definition "a vowel is the result of an open *position* of the oral organs; an articulation [*i. e.* consonant] is the result of an opening *action* of the organ." I cannot see that this distinction is a tenable one, as applied to the consonants in general; there are plenty among them — as *f*, *s*, *th*, *ng* — which are capable of being indefinitely prolonged without losing their consonantal character, and only the surd mutes are absolutely instantaneous. And Mr. Bell is involved in other difficulties, as to the occasional vocalic value of consonants and the theory of syllabication,[2] by the same faulty definition.

It is, indeed, by its capability of being applied to explain the nature of the syllable that the value of any definition of vowel and consonant must be tried; since the terms vowel and consonant themselves have significance only in their relation to the syllable. *Consonant* means 'sounding along with' — that is, 'with' a letter of the other class, a vowel. By this is not at all intended, however, that a consonant cannot be uttered except in combination with a vowel: every consonant can be so uttered; the semivowels and fricatives are continuable sounds, not less than the vowels; and even the mutes may be made distinctly audible by explosion with breath alone, with a mere puff of unarticulated air. The epithet is a historical one, not a theoretical. In the actual usage

[1] In his *Introduction to Greek and Latin Etymology*, second edition, p. 57.

[2] They are pointed out in the next article, at p. 300 *seq.*

of language, consonants never do occur independently; no word is composed of consonants alone. The same is true of the lesser entities into which part of our words are divided, namely syllables; every syllable also must contain a vowel — either a sound that is always a vowel, or one here doing duty as such; and a word contains as many syllables as it contains vowels. What, then, is a syllable; and what the real phonetic distinction between a monosyllabic and a polysyllabic combination of sounds?

The ordinary definition of a syllable, repeated over and over in grammars and orthographical or orthoëpical treatises, is or amounts to this: a syllable is that part of a word which is uttered by a single effort or impulse of the voice. Such an account of the matter is of only the smallest value. Just as much is a word of many syllables, or a whole sentence, uttered by a single effort of the voice, when the speaker knows beforehand what he is going to say, and says it at once in conscious connection. It takes a certain amount of instruction and reflection to recognize a word as composed of separate syllables. The speaker unused to examine and theorize about what he says puts it forth without any thought of analyzing it into parts, without feeling a succession of efforts as necessary to the enunciation of the separate syllables, any more than of the separate letters. Indeed, even upon reflection, it is much more proper to speak of the letters than of the syllables as formed by so many efforts of enunciation. We are far from realizing the number, complexity, and exactness of the movements that go on in our mouths in the process of utterance. Let us look, for example, at the word *blend*. Though syllabically a unit, it is a unit of a highly composite character; for its production, the organs of the mouth change their positions five times, by as many separate efforts of the will. First, with the lips closed, a little breath is forced up from the lungs into the closed cavity of the mouth, and intonated on its way through the larynx by being made to set the vocal cords in vibration. This lasts but for the briefest moment; before the cavity is filled so as to stop the expulsion, the lips are unclosed, and *b* is heard. At the same instant, the tongue has been made to touch the roof of the mouth at its tip, while the unintermitted current of sonant breath streams out at its sides, giving the *l*-sound. Next, the tongue changes its position; its point is released from contact and depressed in the mouth, resting against the lower teeth; its upper flat surface approaches the palate, and the *e* makes itself audible. Once more the tongue shifts place; its tip is again applied as in forming the *l*; but this time no opening is left at the side; contact along its whole length prohibits all emission of air through the mouth; but the passage from the mouth through the nose, hitherto closed, is thrown open, and the stream finds exit there: and the sound is *n*. And lastly, with no change of place on the part of any of the other organs, the passage into the nose is shut again; the intonated breath is expelled a moment longer into the closed cavity of the mouth, and the syllable is closed with a *d* — which, however, if not followed by another utterance, requires a supplemental unclosure of the organs in order to be made distinctly audible. All these changes, which it has taken so long to describe, are performed with such rapidity and precision, one position of the organs succeeds another so closely and accurately, that no intermediate transitional sounds, no "glides," are apprehended by the ear; it hears the five utterances and nothing more. In what true sense, now, can this complicated process be called a single effort of the voice? One element of unity, it is true, there is in the word: from its beginning to its end, there has been an uninterrupted emission of intonated breath through the larynx. But, in the first place, this is not necessary in order to make the unity of a syllable: *strength* is also a single syllable, composed of six different sounds; but the intonation begins with the third element, *r*, and continues only through the fourth and fifth, *e* and *ng;* the first two, *s* and *t*, and the sixth, *th*, are produced with breath unintonated. In the second place, unbroken continuity of intonation does not suffice to make syllabic unity; the word *any*, for example, requires but three successive positions of the organs of articulation, and is intonated or sonant from beginning to end; yet it is a word of two syllables. And we might take the self-same elements of which *blend* is composed, and rearrange them into combinations which should be dissyllabic: thus, *bledn* (like *deaden*) and *bendl* (like *bundle*).

The governing principle, it seems plain to me, which determines these and all other like cases, is that same antithesis of opener and closer sounds upon which the distinction of vowel and consonant is founded. The vowel elements of *any* are practically identical with those which compose our *ē* (the "long *a*" of *they:* it has, as explained in the preceding article, a "vanish" of *i*); and *ē* may be protracted so as to occupy the whole time of *any*, without giving the impression of more than a single syllable; but put between the two opener vowel elements the closer consonantal *n*, and the effect is to divide them into two parts: the ear apprehends the series of utterances as a double impulse of sound. So in *lap* there are three articulated elements, of three different degrees of closeness; but the *a* (*æ*) is so much more open than either of the others that they are felt only as its introductory and closing appendages; there is a *crescendo-diminuendo* effect, but no violation of unity. And *alp* and *pla*, in like manner, are a *crescendo* and *diminuendo* respectively, equally without dual character. But *apl* (i. e. *apple*) is two opener sounds separated by a closer, and the effect is distinctly dual; and *lpa* is fully capable of assuming the same character (like the Sanskrit word *r-tu*, quoted above), if only we were accustomed to making such combinations.

Syllabic effect, then, depends upon this: that, among the articulations of which any pronounceable series is composed, there are some which are so much more open and more sonorous than the rest that they make upon the ear the impression of distinct phonetic impulses, separated and at the same time connected by the closer utterances which come between them. The distinction of syllables is more in the ear of the hearer than in the mouth of the speaker; the articulating organs are engaged, in the enunciation of a word or phrase, in an unintermitted series of changes of position, from the first letter to the last, and are conscious of no relaxation of effort; the ear apprehends the products of the different positions as so many successive entities, but also at once classifies them, arranging them in separate groups, in which the closer sounds are subordinated to the opener.

Not, indeed, that the impression of divided parts is capable of being given only in this way. An instant of silence, a hiatus, is equally effective. Take, for example, the ĭ-sound, and prolong it through the time of seven ordinary syllables, and it is but a single long syllable; utter it seven times in quick succession, and it becomes seven ĭ's, seven syllables; speak *indivisibility*, and, though the utterance is one continuous effort, the seven-fold effect, the division into seven syllables, is equally conspicuous.[1]

[1] I neglect here, as unessential, the fact that, in our ordinary pronunciation of this word, the fourth and sixth syllables would receive the neutral vowel-sound. We may represent the three effects rudely to the eye in the following manner: —

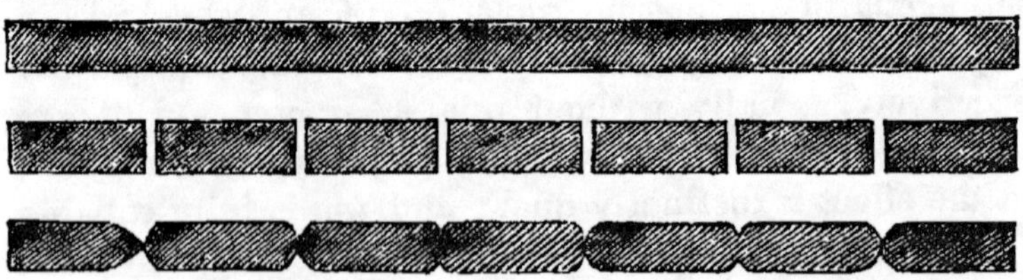

This graphical method may be profitably employed in considerable detail in the illustration of the combination of articulate elements, and of syllabication.

Herein, above all, lies the peculiar character of our speech as *articulated*, jointed, broken up into distinct yet flexible members. It would be possible to have a language of mere vowel utterances, tones, which should follow and blend with one another in a manner not wholly wanting in articulate effect, yet possessing it only unclearly — rather, flexible without articulation, like a rope or rod. It would be possible also to have a language of consonants only, of mutes and fricatives and nasals. But both would be greatly deficient, as compared with the language we actually use, in distinctness, in euphony, in variety, in the qualities which make utterance the serviceable representative and instrument of thought. The one would be sing-song; the other would be sputter; the due combination of the two is the universal articulate speech of men; everywhere alike in general character, notwithstanding its great and numerous differences in different communities, as regards both the articulate sounds employed and the proportion and manner of their combination.

Into the details of these differences, of the construction of syllables as practiced and tolerated in various languages, our present purpose does not require us to enter. I will only remark that, when it comes to allotting to the one or the other syllable the closer sounds which intervene between the opener, there is room for much difference of opinion — partly because one opinion is as good as another, and the question is to be settled by practical convenience rather than by principle. Thus, for example, in *any*, the intervention of the *n* between the two vowels makes the dissyllable; but the *n* itself belongs as much to the one syllable as to the other: whether we should write *an-y* (*ĕn-ĭ*) or *a-ny* (*ĕ-nĭ*) is a matter of indifference. There is, on the other hand, more reason for assigning the *p* of *apple* (*æ-pl*) to the second syllable, because (as was pointed out above, p. 242) the breach of the closure of the *p* by the following vowel is much more sensible to the ear than the formation of its closure upon the preceding vowel.

Now, in the system of spoken sounds, there are some which are of so close position, so little clear and resonant, that they are never used save as consonants: that is, they appear in actual speech only as combined in the same syllable with opener sounds. Such are, above all, the mutes; and the two classes of fricatives, the spirants and sibilants, are in a like case. We may utter or reiterate a *v*, a *th*, an *s*, a *zh*, as much as we please; we shall not succeed in making upon any ear the impression of syllables. Although the mode of formation of the sibilants is such as to allow of their easy and frequent prefixion or affixion to other consonants, of every class (that is, according to our habits of utterance; there are languages which would regard all such combinations as unpronounceable), they are not syllabic, even when separated from a vowel by full contact-letters. Whatever force and quantity we may give to the hissing sound in *tacks*, *adze*, *stain*, *sky*, we cannot make the words into dissyllables. While the *l* of *draggled* is just as distinctly a vowel as the *e* of *draggeth*, nothing that we can do will confer the same value on the *s* of *drag'st*, though its position, between two mutes, is the most favorable that can be devised for the development of vocalic capacity. On the contrary, the power possessed by the semivowels and nasals — especially by *l*, *r*, *n* — in virtue of their superior degree of openness and resonance, to assume vocalic value and office under favoring circumstances, has been already sufficiently pointed out and illustrated; and we have here only to notice in addition that even then they are not always inevitably vocalic; as affixes even to a mute, a certain amount of stress and quantity is required to make vowels of them; they may be so abbreviated and slighted, so subordinated to the preceding syllable, as to form to the ear only a harsh and difficult consonantal appendage to that syllable. So in French, in the prose pronunciation of such words as *sabre*, *table*, where the "mute *e*" is really mute, and the words are monosyllables. While predominantly consonantal, they have so much vocalic quality as this: that they are capable of receiving, and in certain situations do receive, in many languages, without any change of articulate form, the full office of a vowel in making syllables.

The same thing, in its way, is true of the vowels also. There are among them sounds so open that they are always vowels, never occupying the position of adjuncts in the same syllable to another sound which is apprehended as the vowel of the syllable. Such is especially *a*; and *e* and *o* are of the same character. But *i* and *u*, in their closest form, become *y* and *w* on being abbreviated and slighted in utterance; to maintain their vocalic character, they require something of that protraction and stress which, on occasion, give the vocalic character to *l* and *n*. Put *u* and *i* side by side, and whether their combination shall require to be written *ui*, or *wi*, or *uy*, will depend upon the force and time which are allotted to each respectively. Nor is it impossible, by an effort, to pronounce *y* and *w* with consonantal value after the somewhat closer semivowels *r*, *l* (in such combinations as *ary*, *alw*), in a manner truly analogous with *sabre*, *table*, as above instanced.

The discussion of the syllable, therefore, while it shows the high practical importance of the distinction implied in the terms vowel and consonant, at the same time shows that distinction to be not absolute, but only a matter of degree and circumstance. Vowel and consonant are the two poles of a compound series, in which are included all the articulate sounds ordinarily employed by human beings for the purposes of speech.

An additional reason for appreciating correctly the distinction in question, and especially for arranging and regarding the whole alphabet as a series, is to be found in the light thus cast upon the historic development of the alphabet in the Indo-European family of languages. It is well known to all comparative philologists that *a* and the mutes were the greatly prevailing elements in the earliest speech of this family. That speech had no fricative except *s*; *r* and *l* were present, but probably undistinguished from one another; *y* and *w* were even less separate from *i* and *u* than at present. So likewise in the vowel-system, the only elements besides *a* were *i* and *u*, at the farthest remove from it; and they were of vastly less common occurrence than *a*; in the Sanskrit, *a* still makes over seventy per cent. of the whole vowel utterance. It appears, then, that both in the alphabet as a whole and in its vocalic division, the sounds of extreme position, those most broadly and markedly distinguished from one another, were the first to be put to use; and the tendency has been to fill in the intermediate positions, to add the sounds of less differentiation. There has been, as we may fairly express it, a progress made in the command obtained over the organs of speech, whereby they have been enabled to do finer and nicer work. And, just as obviously, the movement of phonetic transition has been from the two extremities of the alphabet toward the middle: the opener vowels have been changed to closer, the closer consonants to opener; only in special and exceptional cases the opposite way. Now what has been the governing motive in all this development and transition? The tendency to ease of utterance, is the common answer; and doubtless, so far as it goes, the true one; only, when we come to ask further wherein lies the greater ease of the new sounds, we get no satisfactory reply, but rather a set of special pleadings: it is found in actual practice that such and such sounds do result from and succeed such and such others; and, as the tendency to ease is the only admissible explanation, the former must be easier than the latter. Hence the words *light* and *heavy*, *hard* and *soft*, *strong* and *weak*, and their like, are glibly employed and sagely pleaded as explanations by people who can give no intelligible account of what they mean, and, on attempting it, bring forward only what is arbitrary and indefensible. Boldly to declare *f* and *v*, for example, "easier" than *p* and *b*, on any ground of their physical difference, is open to the most serious objection. Certainly, young children find *p* and *b* the easier, and are apt to require considerable experience in speaking before they master the others. And it is not likely that the organs of the race in old time, any more than of each new member of it nowadays, would begin with producing the more difficult sounds, and would learn later by practice to produce the easier ones. The experience of other races seems to show the same thing: for, in human languages in general, *p* and *b* are more frequent constituents of the alphabet than *f* and *v*. It is only when we take duly into account the antithesis of opener and closer sounds, and the constant and rapid transition from the one to the other in articulate utterance, in the formation of syllables, that we find an available principle. The transitions between very close and very open positions are longer and more difficult, they require a greater expenditure of muscular force, than those between more medial positions; this is (of course, unconsciously) learned by experience, and the organs gradually find out for themselves those medial positions. What is easier to the practiced speaker, in the rapid combinations of the phrase, becomes thus the norm of speech: sounds come into being which are harder for the child, but which he by degrees learns to produce, after the example of those whose experience has suggested their advantage. The general stream of utterance is narrowed, and the divisions by which it is broken into joints are made less penetrating and separating. Or, as we may express it, the consonants and vowels become to a certain extent assimilated to one another: the consonant is vocalized, or receives an opener position; and the vowel is consonantized, or receives a closer position. Something of the distinctness of articulated utterance is thus sacrificed; the ruggedness of strong contrasts is exchanged for smoother and more flexible transitions; grace is won at the expense of force. The process may be carried so far as to amount to an emasculation of the audible part of language: how far it has actually gone in English, the numerical estimates given at the end of the preceding article, if taken in comparison with similar estimates made for other languages, ancient and modern, will give us the means of determining.

X.

BELL'S VISIBLE SPEECH.[1]

OF the many attempts at an exact physical analysis and description of the processes of articulate utterance, and their complete and consistent representation in an alphabet, no one has come before the English-speaking public with such claims as this. Its author, who has long been an esteemed elocutionist and trainer of the voice in London, exhibits perfect confidence in it, and unbounded expectation of results to be accomplished by it. The degree of his faith is shown by the offer — a liberal one, from his point of view, and creditable to his disinterestedness and patriotism — made by him to the British government, to give up the advantage which he might expect to draw from its copyright, and present it freely to the nation, if the government, on its side, would bear the expense of the inaugural publication, and enable him for a time to act as public teacher of the system, thus introducing it more rapidly and thoroughly to general currency. The proposal was not accepted; red tape, if nothing else, was in the way; the Ministry declared itself to be in possession of no funds which were available for

[1] 1. *Visible Speech: the Science of Universal Alphabets; or, Self-interpreting Physiological Letters, for the Writing of all Languages in one Alphabet. Illustrated by Tables, Diagrams, and Examples.* By Alex. Melville Bell, F. E. I. S., F. R. S. S. A., Professor of Vocal Physiology, etc., etc. Inaugural Edition. London: Simpkins, Marshall, & Co. 1867. 4to. Pp. 126, and 16 plates.

2. *English Visible Speech for the Million; for communicating the exact Pronunciation of the Language to Native or Foreign Learners, and for teaching Children and Illiterate Adults to read in a few days.* By the same. 4to. Pp. 16.

such a purpose. Mr. Bell details the course and end of the negotiation in his introductory chapter, confident that his readers will lament with him the narrowness of a policy which could suffer such an opportunity to pass unimproved. Still, we are too much used to the sight of inventors aggrieved by the stolid indifference of governments and communities to the transcendent merits of their pet devices, to be won over to Mr. Bell's side on his own showing alone. But he is strongly backed by supporters of high rank and unimpeachable character. More than one much-esteemed authority in phonetic science, inventors of alphabetic schemes which the new system comes to rival and supplant, have given it, with praiseworthy candor and liberality, their unqualified indorsement. Among these, our countryman, Professor Haldeman, and Mr. Alexander J. Ellis, especially the latter, are conspicuous. Hardly any other English writer upon such themes, if any, has won so high a reputation as Mr. Ellis; and when he declares that, having in view not only his own investigations, but also those of the principal Continental scholars, whom he names, he yet is obliged to say that he had no knowledge of alphabetics as a science until he was made acquainted with Mr. Bell's system, and that he unequivocally abandons his own in its favor, we see that it is at least deserving of the most careful examination. Mr. Bell further rests its merits upon the results of practical experiments undertaken with it, and described in his book by Mr. Ellis and other disinterested persons. They were conducted after the following fashion. A number of gentlemen — philologists, foreigners, men acquainted with strange tongues, or strange dialects of familiar tongues — were assembled at Mr. Bell's rooms, and dictated to him a series of specimens of languages unknown to him — specimens made in part as idiomatic in character and difficult of reproduction as possible. These he wrote carefully down in his alphabet. His sons, who had had a few weeks' training in the use of the system, were now called in, and the records placed before them, and the young men read them off almost immediately, with the most surprising faithfulness, appearing to reproduce each articulation, tone, and peculiarity of utterance, precisely as it had been originally given. No other alphabet that was ever devised, so far as we know, could have stood such a test as this: none, in fact, has ever attempted so comprehensive a task. For there is nothing uttered by human organs which Mr. Bell does not claim to represent with equal fidelity. In the pages of his book we find the written equivalents, along with articulate sounds, of sighs, groans, sobs, coughs, sneezes, hiccoughs, laughs, chuckles, kisses, sneers, hems and haws, etc.; nay, he even attempts an imitation of the noise of grinding, and of planing and sawing wood. At the same time, the means resorted to are simple and easily learned. Their peculiarity consists in their being throughout representatives of physical acts. Each sign, or element of a compound sign, indicates a position or act of the organs of utterance, and is founded upon an ingenious and natural symbolism. After a thorough preliminary study, therefore, the system of characters is self-interpreting; and it is sufficiently broad and extensible to be capable of depicting to the eye everything, or nearly everything, which the voice of man can utter to the ear. It is a universal alphabet, resting on a true and solid basis; it renders speech visible.

If all these claims are well founded, every one can see that Mr. Bell's alphabet ought to be made known as soon and as widely as possible; and whether they are so, is the question we propose to discuss here. Of course, in the space at our command, and without the type representing Mr. Bell's characters, we cannot, by any means, treat the subject in all its parts and all its relations; but perhaps enough can be said to give our readers the means of forming a tolerably clear and correct opinion respecting it.

There are obviously three principal points to which our inquiries must be directed: first, is Mr. Bell's physical analysis complete and accurate? second, is his system of written characters plain and convenient? and third, supposing both these questions to be answered in the affirmative, what is the practical value of the device, its sphere of profitable application? Without attempting to take up the points stated in systematic order, we will endeavor to keep them all distinctly in view.

Our examination of our author's alphabet will best begin with the consonants, since they are the vastly easier part to be dealt with of the system of articulate sounds, their mode of production being, for the most part, within reach of our observation, when a little trained and practiced, of our own organs of utterance.

The fundamental consonant symbol chosen by Mr. Bell is a curve open on one side—a C. This typifies an obstruction to the free passage of the breath, effected within the oral cavity by the approximation of the mouth-organs—of tongue and palate, or of lip and lip. In the position of a C, it signifies an approach of the back part of the tongue to the soft palatė, such as produces the German sound of *ch* in *ach;* turned over, with the curve up, a like approach of a point on the forward surface of the tongue (Mr. Bell gives it the technical name of "front") to the neighboring hard palate, producing the German *ch*-sound in *ich;* with the curve turned under, the near application of the point of the tongue behind the teeth; with the curve to the right, the approach of lip to lip. If the opening of the curve is closed by a straight line drawn across its ends, complete closure of the organs, forming a surd mute, is intimated; in the C-position, a *k;* in the ◡-position, a *t;* in the Ɔ-position, a *p*. These are made sonant, or converted respectively into *g*, *d*, *b*, by a line drawn from the middle of the curve within, towards its opening; such a line symbolizing here, as elsewhere, that position of the vocal cords in which sonant utterance is produced. Once more, the same characters are made nasal, signs for *ng*, *n*, *m*, by substituting for the straight closing line a bent one, closing only at one end, to represent the uvula, whose pendency opens the channel from the mouth to the nostrils. Here are already sixteen letters of the new alphabet, in part standing for the sounds most common in all languages, of most distinct formation and easiest systematic representation; no exception can be taken to them in any way. But the foundation-sign admits two further modifications, in connection with which certain weaknesses appear. In the first place, by indenting the consonantal curve at its back (like a figure 3), Mr. Bell typifies a close contact of the organs along the middle line of closure, with passage left for the breath at the sides. Of sounds so formed, our *l* is the model, being produced, as every one has noticed, by an application of the tip of the tongue to the roof of the mouth, while the intonated breath finds exit on both sides of the contact; and with our author's designation of this sound, as well as of the palatal *l*, its next of kin, no fault can be found. When, however, we are asked to believe that our *th*-sounds (in *thin* and *then*), and our *f* and *v*, are of the same quality — sounds of central closure and lateral opening — and therefore to be written with analogous characters, we at once demur, and begin to suspect that our author is not incapable of being misled into wrongly apprehending and falsely describing the formation of spoken letters by the facility of thus finding for them a ready place in his system. We are as sure as we can wish to be that the quality claimed for these sounds in no wise belongs to them; nor has it been ascribed to them, so far as we are aware, by any previous authority. But Mr. Bell's signs for *th* involve, we think, another false element, which they share with the sibilant signs. By attaching, namely, recurved ends to his fundamental consonant character, he intimates a mixture of the main articulation with its opposite; and sounds of such mixed articulation, according to him, are our *s* and *sh*, the former produced mainly by the "front" of the tongue, but with aid from the tip; the latter, by the tip of the tongue, with aid from the front. Here, certainly, he is incontestably wrong; the essential character of these two sounds is due to a near approximation of the tongue to two points on the front palate; their difference, to the different situation of the two points, that for *s* being farther forward; it is comparatively a matter of indifference whether they be produced by the point or the front of the tongue; and when we form them, as we may, with either point or front, the other part has nothing whatever to do with them; we may envelop the point, for example, or push it away from its ordinary position, by artificial means, without at all affecting the character of the articulation.[1]

This same character of "mixture"—namely, of the front and point of the tongue—is attributed by Mr. Bell to the *th*-sounds. In fact, his signs for *th* and *s* differ only by the curve of the former being "divided," or modified to show central closure. The real distinction between the two, however, is, that the *s* is produced just back of the teeth, at a point where a close contact, giving a *t*, is possible; while the *th* is the closest contact which can be formed between the tongue and the teeth themselves.[2]

If there are any sounds in our spoken alphabet which ought to be distinctly recognized as "mixed," they are our usual *f* and *v*, and the *th*, since these bring into action the teeth, a set of organs which are not elsewhere directly active. Mr. Bell's system, however, provides no sign for

[1] See above, p. 258.

[2] See above, p. 253.

such mixture as this. The *th*, accordingly, he treats as we have just seen; and, in his ordinary designation of *f* and *v*, he takes no notice of their being otherwise than purely labial.

There are other points in our author's scheme of consonants where we deem him wrong in theory and unsuccessful in designation; but we cannot dwell upon them. We have picked out the most palpable errors — enough to show, as we think, that his alphabet, even upon this side, is open to serious objection; that it is not, as he claims, the complete and undistorted reflection to the eye of the physical processes of utterance, but does violence to nature, both by introducing symbols for unreal acts, and by omitting to symbolize others having a real existence and importance.

We come, then, with an unfavorable presumption against Mr. Bell's absolute accuracy to the examination of what he has done for the infinitely more difficult theory of the vowels. His vowel system has a general analogy with his consonant system. He assumes three fundamental positions of the tongue — one with its back part, one with its front, one with both back and front, brought toward the palate; and three degrees of approach, "high," "mid," and "low," for each of the three positions, "front," "back," and "mixed." Each of these nine configurations he doubles, by applying to it the "rounding" action of the lips; each of these eighteen he doubles again, by claiming that two different sounds are given forth through any "configurative aperture," according as the condition of the tube or cavity behind it is "primary" or "wide" — that is to say, left negative or positively distended. Thus he obtains thirty-six vowel positions, for as many vowels, and he claims that practically they are found sufficient; although, in the shape of certain diacritical modifiers to the three fundamental postures of the tongue and the three degrees of approach, he holds in reserve the means of increasing them, if desirable, to three hundred and twenty-four!

The means by which all this is intimated to the eye is very simple and ingenious. The fundamental vowel character is an I, symbolizing (as above noticed) the position of the vocal cords in sonant vibration. Subsidiary signs attached to this show the action of the tongue and lips. A transverse mark across the middle is the unvarying sign of labial modification. The marks of lingual approach are fastened on at the top and bottom; at the top for "high" approach, at the bottom for "low," at both top and bottom for "mid;" on the right for "front" position, on the left for "back," on both right and left for "mixed." All vowel signs are thus long and slender, all consonant ones broad and round; and it is intended that the former, in their ordinary lower-case forms, shall, like our *l* and *j*, rise above or fall below the line which the others occupy.

Notwithstanding the fullness and regularity of this scheme, and its unquestionable advantages as a mode of notation, we cannot but regard it as essentially an artificial one, not so much growing out of the facts as imposed upon them, ingeniously incorporating many of the obvious features of physical production, but not involving that minute and absolute knowledge of details to which it makes pretense. One weak point, in our opinion, is its distinction of the "primary" and "wide" conditions of the organs, furnishing two different vowels, behind each "configurative aperture;" we cannot persuade ourselves that this is the true explanation of the differences it is used to account for. As examples of vowels related to one another in the manner claimed (the first "primary," the second "wide"), he gives us *up* and *ask*, *eel* and *ill*, *pool* and *pull*, *ell* and *man*, *all* and *on;* all of which, however, we regard as produced by positions of the organs differing notably from one another in the ordinary manner, or by changes of the "configurative aperture" itself. Another objectionable feature is the treatment of the labial modification as in itself of one and the same degree and value in all vowels, or as governed in respect to closeness by the degree of lingual approximation which it accompanies. This "rounding" effect, as our author terms it, does not depend, according to him, upon the lips alone, but involves a "rounding" of the buccal cavity also, and even of the lingual and faucal tube below; whence the possibility, already referred to, of producing it without the lips. Such a change in the form of the tube is to us quite unintelligible; and we are distinctly conscious, when the lips are released from service in forming an *o* or *oo*, of a decided compensating action at the base of the tongue. We are not satisfied with the defined relations, internal or external, of the group of vowels of "mixed" position (made by action both of front and back of tongue), variations — sometimes, we think, trivial or imaginary — of the "neutral" vowel, as it has been commonly styled. And we cannot consent to regard the open vowel *a* (in *far*) as "back low wide" — that is, as involving retraction of the back of the tongue toward the palate, to low degree only, with expanded organs behind the aperture. Whatever removal of the tongue from the position of quiescence it implies is really in the direction of openness rather than of closure; this vowel is only negatively characterized; it is the natural utterance of the human throat when most expanded.

Without pretending, therefore, to understand otherwise than imperfectly the intricacies of vowel formation, we are yet confident that Mr. Bell's labors do not set upon a firm basis the general theory of vowels. The old pyramidal arrangement of them, with *a* (in *far*) at the apex, and *i* and *u* (in *pique* and *rule*) at the sides of the base, which he conceives himself to have outgrown and superseded, contains more truth, and more valuable for the uses of the historic student of language, than his trilinear scheme with its multiplications. His system affords no ground for a unitary arrangement of the alphabet, vowels and consonants together, in all their mutual relations as parts of a whole. His definitions of vowel and consonant are, to be sure, taken by themselves, nearly unexceptionable. He says (pp. 12, 13): "In forming consonants, the breath or voice is stopped or squeezed, with an effect of percussion, sibilation, buzzing, or vibration, in some part of the guttural or oral passage; and in forming vowels, the breath or voice flows through similar but more open and 'fixed' configurations, which merely shape or mould the breath, without impeding its emission" — and to a like effect elsewhere; which is nearly equivalent to saying that the vowels are sounds of opener position, involving less interference on the part of the mouth-organs, than the consonants; that in the one class the element of material, of tone, predominates; in the other the element of form, of articulating action. But he leaves us to suppose that all vowels (that is to say, all "primary" vowels; though why they should be thought to differ in this respect from "wide" ones is not clear to us) are equally akin with consonants; while, in truth, *a* (in *far*) is at the farthest possible remove from them, while *i* and *u* (in *pique* and *rule*) are close upon them, being only infinitesimally and evanescently distinct from *y* and *w*. And he equally fails to apprehend and state clearly the great difference in the approach made by different classes of consonants to a vowel value. Hence he is unable to explain satisfactorily why and when certain consonants in English take on a vowel office (as *n* and *l* in *token* and *able*), and gives us such an account of the matter as would imply the possibility of turning the word *legs* into a trisyllable by simply dwelling a little upon the initial *l* and final *s* (*z*). As a further consequence, the nature and structure of the syllable are obscure to him, and when he comes to the subject of syllabication, he has nothing better to give us as a fundamental principle than the arbitrary *dictum* that "the natural action of the organs of speech is always from close to open, or from consonants to vowels." Considering that in all our actual speech we are constantly passing from open to close, as well as in the contrary direction, we may well ask what is meant by this. When we say *man* and *God*, is only the first part of each utterance natural? Are we guilty of unnatural conduct in pronouncing *up*, *end*, *arms*, or, yet worse, *strands*, in which we shift direction twice, both before and after the vowel? What is "nature," then, and what do we go by when we have abandoned her?

There are other classes of signs, forming important complementary parts of the general system, to which we have not alluded, and which we cannot undertake to describe. Such are the "glides" — vanishing sounds, transition steps between consonant and vowel, which do essential service in representing the niceties of pronunciation, either general or individual; and a long series of "definers," sparingly used in describing ordinary speech, but especially necessary in dealing with half-articulate or inarticulate utterances.

So far, then, as regards the first of our three leading points of inquiry — the completeness and accuracy of the phonetic analysis represented by it — we are not disposed to concede to Mr. Bell's alphabet the transcendent merit to which it lays claim; indeed, notwithstanding its acute and penetrating discriminations, we do not see that it has notably advanced the general scientific comprehension of the processes of utterance. And inasmuch as upon this mainly depends the "science of alphabetics," we cannot but think that Mr. Ellis, in pronouncing it the first realization of that science, overestimates its value, and does injustice to the other eminent men who have labored in the same department — only he is saved from any complaint on their part by having included himself in the same unjust condemnation. Mr. Bell's deserts lie in the line of the art, rather than the science, of alphabetic notation.

To assert this is, of course, to deny to the system that absolute and unique value which it arrogates to itself, and to class it with other schemes of the same character, more or less elaborate and ingenious. It does not stand so entirely alone as its author appears to imagine, even as regards its fundamental principle, of indicating in each sign all the physical acts which produce the sound signified. The distinguished physiologist and phonetist, Dr. Brücke of Vienna, has worked out a similar "Method of Phonetic Transcription"[1] — very different in aspect from Mr. Bell's, as was naturally to be expected; but essentially unlike it only in adopting a more arbitrary and less directly symbolical set of elementary signs, and in undertaking a less complete depiction of all the phenomena of utterance, articulate and inarticulate. In these respects, as well as in general clearness, legibility, and gratefulness to the eye, the Englishman's system seems to us to have the decided advantage of the German's. As an instrumentality for rendering possible the exact reproduction of spoken speech, we presume that its equal has never been devised; perhaps its superior may never be devised. Mr. Bell's experience as a professed elocutionist and trainer of the voice has come admirably to his aid in the construction of his alphabet.

It may seem, at first glance, as if the acknowledged success of the experiments of reproduction tried with this alphabet proved the truth of the physical basis upon which it rests. But a moment's consideration will show that the case is otherwise. For practical use it makes no difference whether a certain sign represents an exact

[1] To be found in the *Proceedings of the Vienna Academy of Sciences*, vol. xli. (1863), p. 223 *seq.*

phonetic analysis of the sound it signifies, or whether it stands conventionally for that sound. Mr. Bell places before our eyes, we will say, a scratch on paper which directs us to approximate the back and front of the tongue together toward the palate to a medium degree, to open the organs behind the configurative aperture, and to apply a rounding effect. Now who in the world (in this world, where even the most practiced phonologists are still disputing over the mode of production of vowel sounds) is going to give him the sound he expects? Not we, certainly; we will not even undertake to find by means of the description the precise American pronunciation of the vowel of *stone*, which he finally gives us as its original. Nor, we presume, would the young men whom he made use of in his experiments as readers have been more successful. If, however, he gives us the sound intended to be signified, we can reproduce that, at once or after sufficient practice; and we can so associate it with the sign as to utter it whenever the sign is shown us; and equally well, whether we do or do not make the attempt to find out for ourselves that the sign has a right to stand for the sound, or even whether, having made the attempt, we conclude that it has or that it has not that right. And if we have learned in this way thirty-six vowel sounds with their attributed signs, we may safely set up as accurate pronouncers, word by word and phrase by phrase, of nearly all human languages, so far as the vowel part of them is concerned.

In point of practical applicability, therefore (the ground of our second leading inquiry), the new alphabet is to a great extent independent of the physical analysis on which it professes to be founded. To a great extent, we say, but not absolutely; for it is easier to accept for a sound a wholly conventional sign than one which tries to describe it, and describes it falsely. Yet even here there are degrees; while we might consent to use without scruple the prescribed character for the difficult vowel sound of *stone*, we could never prevail upon ourselves to write habitually for *th* a hieroglyph which asserted that both the front and point of the tongue are concerned in its production, and form a central closure with side emission. It is in such points as this that Mr. Bell's alphabet, with all its merits, seems imperatively to call for amendment before it shall be entitled to general acceptance and currency.

But, even if amended into practical perfection, what is the degree and kind of currency which it can hope to gain ? Here we think Mr. Bell commits his most serious error, exaggerating beyond measure the sphere of usefulness of his invention. He has worked over these matters so long, has studied so thoroughly the mechanism of the voice, has traced the action and effect of every organ so clearly, that now, when he has hit upon a sign which brings each articulation plainly before his mind, he thinks that it will do the same almost as readily for other minds. One of the unfortunate effects of this persuasion of his is to be seen in the form into which he has cast his published account of his alphabet, rendering it an exceedingly hard work to study, and doubtless driving away many a student who might otherwise have mastered the system, and been interested in its behalf. Instead of beginning with definition and illustration together, making each described position of the organs more readily apprehensible by noting the sound it yields, he fills the first two thirds of his volume with pure description and designation, and only then begins to introduce the equivalents in our alphabet of the sounds intended. Even those who are accustomed to phonetic analysis are perplexed by such a course, and compelled to begin the book after the middle, or else to draw out tables of corresponding signs in the old alphabet and the new, to help them read with intelligence and profit the opening chapters.

In accordance with this is Mr. Bell's conviction that, his analysis and alphabet being now complete, every one hereafter is going to be able to read and pronounce everything with exactness. Thus he says, for example (p. 116), after making the adaptation of his system to English speech: "Chiefly on account of these delicate and unascertained varieties of sound, the native pronunciation of English has been found excessively difficult for foreigners to master. It will no longer be so." For, all we want is to know what the thing to be done is, and how it is to be done, and we can do it. This is a little too sanguine. So all the motions required for executing a difficult feat in skating can be described; but woe to him who attempts to execute it from directions on paper, without due preparatory drill! Make a man a skillful skater, and he will do upon the ice what he is told to do; make him a phonologist, teach him to feel his organs of utterance at work, and to direct them in detail by conscious exertions of his will, and he will read, with success, from signs physically descriptive.

What our author fails to appreciate is, that a system like his is essentially a scientific nomenclature, like a chemical or zoölogical nomenclature. It does not teach the science; in learning it, one does not learn the science; it is worth a great deal to him who knows the science, but little to a layman; it may do not a little to clear up the relations of the science, and make its acquisition easier; but, after all, the science is the hard thing to learn, and the nomenclature only of secondary account. That the new alphabet is going to help all the classes for whom Mr. Bell destines it we do not venture to hope. That the illiterate man, for example, is to learn to read the sooner for having added to his task that of observing how each sound he utters is produced, seems quite unreasonable. To him the symbolical signs will be useful only as any strictly phonetic orthography is easier than an irregular one, like ours. To expect that the missionary, armed with it, is to master without difficulty, and write down with exactness, the strange dialects with which he comes in contact, is equally unreasonable. The task of distinctly apprehending their unaccustomed sounds, of reproducing these correctly, of detecting the motions which originate them, will be as severe as ever; and he who has accomplished it will find a far inferior difficulty in signifying them intelligibly. To the great mass of readers there is, and can be, no advantage in a mode of writing all whose signs are physically significant; they must learn and use it as conventional only. Our own alphabet, modified to phonetic consistency, would suit their purposes equally well — nay, they even prefer it unmodified. Prove to a man as triumphantly as you will that *laugh* is an absurd orthography, and that it is much better to write *lăf*, yet he goes on to spell *laugh* as before, and it will not help the matter to give him a new set of signs to write *lăf* with. The fate of the various phonetic systems, probably, foreshadows that of Mr. Bell's. There was no good reason for his speaking disparagingly of the labors of men like Lepsius, who, accepting as a portentous fact the immense existing prejudice in favor of familiar signs, have endeavored to work out of these something approaching system — with the partial aim, moreover, of transliterating strange modes of writing as well as of speaking. Probably he has been, by this time, disappointed by the unenthusiastic reception his discovery has met, and the little attention it has attracted. He must learn to be content with addressing chiefly those interested in phonetic science, instead of the great public; with seeking the sympathy and criticism of his equals, instead of imposing his system under governmental authority, as something finished and immaculate, upon the community at large. Its claim to extraordinary support is not greater than that of any other new and improved scientific nomenclature; and the condemnation which its author expects to see passed upon the Derby Cabinet, for neglect of so grand an opportunity, will, we presume, be indefinitely suspended. In its own proper sphere, and especially with a clearer and more apprehensible method of presentation, it may be relied on to do much good, attracting toward and facilitating phonetic studies, and perhaps contributing a chief part to that alphabetic system — not a theoretically perfect one, for the conditions of the case admit of none such, but a system more successfully compromised, more nicely adjusted to the ascertained needs of the transcription of all languages, than any other — which the future is to bring forth.

XI.

ON THE ACCENT IN SANSKRIT.

By accent, as every one knows, we mean a certain prominence given to one of the syllables of a word, distinguishing this above the other syllables. Whatever its origin — whether historical, as representing the emphatic element in that aggregation of monosyllabic radicals of which words were made up, or euphonic, as breaking monotony, and giving movement and measure to words — it is an almost or altogether universal characteristic of language, and has borne an important part in governing the phonetic history of languages. But in different tongues it is of different character and efficiency — and this to a degree and within limits which are still to be investigated. The subject is one of not a little intricacy and difficulty, and only the most recent phonetic science is developing the capacity to deal with it in a satisfactory manner.[1] I shall attempt here only a slight and unpretending contribution to its discussion, by setting forth and putting within reach of a larger number of inquirers the most important facts relating to the comparatively unfamiliar matter of the Sanskrit accent.

How the prominence and distinction which constitute the accent are given to the accented syllable is not to be

[1] See especially Mr. A. J. Ellis's paper *On the Physical Constituents of Accent and Emphasis*, in the London Philological Society's Transactions for 1873–74, pp. 113–164.

simply and briefly defined, because even in the same language it varies considerably under varying circumstances. We ourselves, though we call our accent a stress of voice, suffer it to find expression in different ways: by higher pitch, by prolongation, by increased force, by superior completeness and distinctness of enunciation — any one of these, or two or more of them combined. Taking the language word by word, the first method, elevation of pitch, is the prevailing one. Choose a specimen word of more than one syllable, read a list of words, and the accented syllable will have every time a higher tone; to mark it otherwise will either seem unnatural and affected, or will give the impression of saying something, of using the word as an abbreviated sentence, with the context omitted. For, in uttering a sentence, the modulation of voice belonging to the expression of the sentence predominates, throwing the proper word-accent into a wholly subservient place, as regards pitch of voice, and compelling resort to the other means of distinction: even, in certain cases, reducing or annulling the accentual distinction. Give out *Jónathan* as a word to be spelt, or mention it as specimen of a proper name, and the first syllable will be raised above the others; and so also when it answers a question like "who is here?" But make a question of the word itself, and the relation of pitch is reversed; utter the syllables in monotone, and astonishment or reproach may be conveyed; and the same monotone will be the effect of putting it after a strongly emphatic word: and each combination of tones may be shifted up and down the scale through considerable intervals, to satisfy the higher needs of expression. If we enunciate a whole sentence together, the same subordination of the word-stress or accent to the sentence-stress or emphasis — most markedly in the element of pitch, yet not in that alone — will be clearly apparent; the accent no more notably makes the unity of the word than does the emphasis that of the phrase or sentence; to utter each word as if we were pronouncing it alone would be insufferably monotonous and tedious, would destroy the life and soul of speech.

There is hardly another language in which this postponement of the claims of accent to those of emphasis can be expected to prove more complete than ours; for English is so prevailingly monosyllabic[1] that accent proper has scant opportunity left to manifest itself at all. But in our treatment of the longer-worded Latin and Greek, or in the utterance of German,[2] the same two leading principles may be observed: the raised tone of the accented syllable when each word is given by itself, and the annulment of this relation to a great extent, or its reversal, before the more commanding needs of sentence-expression. These are facts which we need to bear carefully in mind, when inquiring into the mode of accentuation of those ancient languages respecting which we cannot derive information by listening to their speakers.

For the three ancient languages, indeed, which we deem of most importance, and to which we devote most study — namely, Latin, Greek, and Sanskrit — we have quite full and detailed information respecting the nature and place of their accent from grammarians to whom they were native; besides, for two of them — Greek and Sanskrit — abundant accentuated texts. And the information given is strikingly accordant for all. In each of them, the ordinary accented syllable is described as one uttered in a higher tone than the rest. In each one, more-

[1] Three quarters of its words, on the average, having no more than one syllable: see above, p. 275.

[2] It is not allowable to add "or of French," the French being the most anomalous of known languages as concerns accent; both Frenchmen and foreigners are yet disputing whether it has any accent at all, and, if it has, on what syllable the stress is laid: the prevailing and best-supported doctrine being that the final syllable (not counting a mute *e*), as it regularly represents the accented syllable of the Latin word, so also has whatever accent, though a very weak one, the French possesses.

over, is recognized a second accent, a "circumflex," which is defined as a combination of higher and lower tone within the limits of the same syllable, a downward leap or slide of the voice.[1] This double-pitch accent, as might be expected, is of somewhat restricted use, as regards both the character and the place of the syllable receiving it: in Latin and Greek, it can rest only upon a vowel which is naturally long and so gives space for the slide or leap of the voice; in Sanskrit, it is almost confined to syllables in which a semivocalic *y* or *w* sound precedes the vowel, and takes the first stress of voice. So far as the Latin and Greek are concerned, this simple mention of well-known or easily accessible facts[2] is sufficient; we pass to a more special consideration of what the Hindu grammarians hold and teach about their accent.

The great Pânini, supreme authority to the Hindus in all that concerns their ancient and sacred language, is clear and intelligible in his statements as to accent; and upon the foundation of his work and its commentaries alone, without access to any accentuated texts, Böhtlingk gave in 1843[3] an acute, intelligent, and surprisingly correct account both of the theory and of the main facts of Sanskrit accent, one which in many respects has not been surpassed or superseded by anything that has since appeared. But the brevity of Pânini is acceptably supplemented by the more detailed treatment of the subject in the Prâtiçâkhyas. These are treatises which attach themselves each to a single Vedic text, as phonetic manual of the school to which that text belongs. They deal with

1 Though the circumflex makes no figure in our ordinary Latin grammars, it was fully recognized by the Roman grammarians. See, for example, Roby's Grammar, § 296, and Professor Hadley's Essay "On the Nature and Theory of the Greek Accent," contained in his *Essays*, p. 110 *seq.*, and also in the *Transactions of the Am. Phil. Assoc'n* for 1870.

2 The reader may be referred especially to the essay by Professor Hadley, quoted in the preceding note.

3 *Ein erster Versuch über den Accent im Sanskrit*, in the Memoirs of the St. Petersburg Academy.

all the elements of articulate utterance: with the mode of production and the classification of articulate sounds, with accent and quantity, with rules of euphonic combination, and so on; and they prescribe how the various forms of text in which their Veda is preserved are to be constructed, cataloguing its slightest irregularities of form, and endeavoring to fix its readings beyond the reach of question or change. Four such treatises have come to light: one belonging to the Rig-Veda, one to the White Yajur-Veda or Vâjasaneyi-Sanhitâ, one to the Black Yajur-Veda or Tâittirîya-Sanhitâ, and one to the Atharva-Veda; for the Sâma-Veda alone none has yet been found. All have now been edited in full.[1] Prior to the publication of any of them, the teachings of the first three with regard to accent were summarily presented by Roth (who was the first to call the attention of scholars to this class of works), in the introduction to his edition of Yâska's *Nirukta* (Göttingen, 1852).

The information derivable from these various sources is full enough, not only to let us see pretty clearly the views held by the ancient Hindu students of their own tongue (their age, unfortunately, is not ascertained, but is generally believed to have preceded by some centuries the Christian era), but also to enable us in some measure to trace the development of their accentual theory, and to criticise it in its details. For, though we cannot help admiring and respecting, and that in a very high degree, the acuteness and sagacity of those oldest known phonologists, we cannot accept for truth all that they give us, without first carefully questioning it, and testing it by fact and by theory. Sharpness of distinction, skill in

[1] The *Rik-Prâtiçâkhya* by Regnier, in the *Journal Asiatique* (Paris, 1857–59), and by M. Müller (Leipzig, 1856–69); the *Vâjasaneyi-Prâtiçâkhya* by Weber, in the fourth volume of his *Indische Studien* (Berlin, 1858); the *Atharva-Prâtiçâkhya* and the *Tâittirîya-Prâtiçâkhya* by myself, in the seventh and ninth volumes of the *Journal of the American Oriental Society* (New Haven, 1862 and 1871).

combination, and elaborateness of systematization, have been characteristics of the Hindu workers in every department of science to which they have turned their hands; but they are not equally to be commended for moderation, nor is their soundness and accuracy to be trusted to the very end. They never knew where to stop; and their systems always tended to take on a prescriptive character where they were meant to be descriptive only, putting violence upon the facts which they set out simply to examine and classify. We may probably enough meet, at one and another point in their treatment of the accent, their national and distinctive weaknesses, and feel compelled to modify and amend their doctrines.

The word used in defining the accents is *svara*,[1] 'tone.' In virtue of its proper meaning, it is applied to designate also other things than accentual tone. Thus, it is the ordinary name of a 'vowel,' as being a *tone*-sound, an utterance in which the element of tone predominates over that of oral modification; and it is in the Prâtiçâkhyas used a dozen times in this sense to once in any or all others. Again, by a usage closely akin to its accentual one, it signifies the "tones" or musical notes which compose the scale.

We are informed, then, that a syllable is, in respect to its tone, either *udâtta*, *anudâtta*, or *svarita*.

The term *udâtta* means literally 'taken up, raised, elevated.' And the description of the tone by all the authorities corresponds with this title; that syllable is *udâtta* which is uttered *uccâis*, 'on a high pitch.' Ordinarily, one fixed syllable in every word is *udâtta*, as one in Latin or Greek is acute. The *udâtta*, then, is the correspondent, in character and value, of the Latin and Greek acute; it is what we call the usual accented syllable of the word.

[1] The sound which is here and elsewhere written with a *v*, in accordance with prevailing European custom, is originally and properly the *w*-sound.

The remaining syllables are ordinarily *anudâtta*. This is the same word with the negative prefix, and so means 'not raised, unelevated.' The authorities define it as belonging to a syllable which is uttered *nîcâis*, 'on a low pitch.' This lowness of pitch does not, of course, imply a fall below the ordinary level of voice; the tone is low as compared with *udâtta;* the term is a purely negative one, denying that uplifting of pitch which marks the positively accented syllable.

The name of the third tone is *svarita*, and the tone itself is uniformly explained as consisting in a combination of the other two, a union of higher and lower pitch upon the same vowel, or within the same syllable. As regards the distribution of the time of the syllable between the two tones, Pânini, for example, says (i. 2. 32): "Half [the quantity of] a short vowel at the beginning [of a *svarita*] is *udâtta;*" the Atharva-Prâtiçâkhya (i. 17), "half the quantity of a *svarita*, at its beginning, is *udâtta;*" the Vâjasaneyi-Prâtiçâkhya (i. 126), "at its beginning, half the quantity of the vowel is *udâtta*." The other two Prâtiçâkhyas complicate the definition with a further development of the accentual theory, to be explained hereafter; but there is no discordance whatever as to the essential nature of the tone, as being a union of higher and lower pitch in the same syllable. No hint of an intermediate or "middle tone" is given, nor do we discover traces of the former prevalence of any other view, crowded out and replaced by this. Of the name *svarita*, however, no satisfactory explanation has yet been found. The word is probably a quasi-participial formation from *svara* itself, and means 'toned;' possibly, it was applied to such syllables as showed most conspicuously the element of tone, their change of pitch giving them a cadenced or sing-song effect. What is unmistakably clear is the view which the Hindus unanimously held as to the nature of the tone thus designated;

and any interpretation which we may try to put upon *svarita* must be subordinated to this: we have no right to conjecture an etymology for the name, and then to force it into a definition of the thing named.

The accordance of the three Sanskrit tones, as thus defined, with the acute, grave, and circumflex of the Greek, appears to me to be placed beyond all reach of successful question; and we are justified in setting aside, when speaking of the Sanskrit accent, the outlandish Sanskrit terms *udâtta*, *anudâtta*, and *svarita*, and employing in their place the equivalent designations with which every one is familiar. These were used by Böhtlingk, in the essay which (as above pointed out) first opened the knowledge of the Sanskrit accent to Europe; and the more the subject is understood, the more generally will they be adopted.[1]

The correctness of the Hindu theory as to the nature of the acute and circumflex tones is strongly supported by the phenomena of origination and occurrence of the latter. The circumflex in Sanskrit is a far rarer and more secondary accent than in Greek. Only a very small class of words have it as their proper accent at all; and it arises chiefly in the course of combination of words into phrases, by the peculiar euphonic system of the Sanskrit—which, as is generally known, does not leave its words side by side in their integrity of form, but adapts together their final and initial elements, avoiding the hiatus and any collision of incompatible consonants.[2]

[1] Mr. Ellis's rejection of the parallelism and retention of the Indian names in his paper on Accent and Emphasis (referred to on p. 318) reposes, so far as I can see, simply on his peculiar apprehension of the Greek acute, as being an uplift of a fifth above the tone of the preceding syllable, whatever that may have been; so that a succession of acutes, instead of sharing a common rise above the general level of utterance, would leap each a fifth above its predecessor—a view which I believe no one else has taken, and which seems obviously erroneous.

[2] Which, it may be added, as the metrical form of the Vedic hymns proves, is in no small part artificial, belonging to the language as shaped over for learned use by grammarians. No vernacular speech could ever have sacrificed to such a degree the integrity of its words to a supposed euphony.

The first class of circumflexes arises when an accented or acute *i* or *î*, or *u*, is converted into *y* or *v* (*i. e.* our *w*) before a grave or unaccented dissimilar vowel. Thus *ví* and *evá* are combined into *vyèvá*;[1] *nadî́* and *asya*, into *nadyàsya*; *apsú* and *agne* into *apsvàgne*. That is to say, the single syllable into which the higher and lower tone are combined still retains the double pitch belonging to its constituent parts.

One of the most peculiar and problematical processes in the whole euphonic system of the Sanskrit is that by which a final *e* or *o* absorbs or elides an initial short *a* of the word that follows; though only an occasional license in the older Vedic language, it has become the rule of combination in the later or classical Sanskrit. Wherever, now, the *e* or *o* is acute and the *a* grave, the accent of the former after the absorption of the latter is made circumflex. Thus, *té abravan* becomes *tèbravan*; *só abravît* becomes *sòbravît*. Here, again, the acute and grave tones of the constituent elements are evidently both preserved to the syllable which results from their combination.

If, however, two vowels are fused together into a single vowel or diphthong, then, if either was acute, the resulting combination, as a general rule, is also acute: that is to say, the acute element is powerful enough to assimilate the other, raising the whole syllable to the higher tone. Thus, *sá'* and *asti* become *sá'sti*, *sá'* and *út* become *sót*, *stha* and *ú'rjam* become *sthórjam*, and so on. Pâṇini, indeed (viii. 2. 6), also permits the result of combination of a final acute with an initial grave to be circumflex: that is, he allows *sá' asti* to become either *sá'sti* or *sà'sti*, and so on. Of course, considering the nature of the circumflex, this is just the exception which we might expect to see made; and that it is not universally made

[1] For lack of means to do better, I signify the circumflex, as a downward slide forward, with what we ordinarily call the sign of grave.

in Sanskrit usage indicates the very different place which the circumflex accent takes in Sanskrit as compared with Greek: the latter language has a predilection for it, and lets it appear in innumerable cases where it has no etymological occasion; the former language has an aversion to it, and exhibits it only where, as it were, compelled to do so.

By a peculiar and quite rare exception, most of the Vedic texts make circumflex a long *î* arising from the fusion of two short *i's*, the first acute, the second grave. Thus, *diví iva* becomes *divi̍̀va*, *abhí ihi* becomes *abhi̍̀hi*. The Tâittirîya-Sanhitâ, however, denies the circumflex to such an *î*, but gives it to the much rarer *û* of like origin: combining, for example, *mâsú ut-* into *mâsû̀t-*.

Besides these cases, in which a circumflex arises by the combination into one syllable of a preceding acute and a following grave element, there remains a limited class of words which show the circumflex as their original and proper accent: such are *svàr*, 'heaven,' *kvà*, 'where,' *tanvàm*, 'body' (accus. sing.), *kanyà*, 'girl,' *budhnyà*, 'fundamental,' *nadyàs*, 'streams' (nom. pl.), and so on. But every word of this class contains a *y* or *v* before the vowel of its accented syllable; and it is obvious that the circumflex here is essentially of the same kind with that of the class first described above, its origin lying merely a step further back. That is to say, that *tanvàm* and *nadyàs* are for *tanú'-am* and *nadí'-as*, and made by a combination of the acute final of the theme with the grave initial of the ending, there being no essential difference between *nadyàs* and the more fortuitous *nadyàsya*, instanced above; that *svàr* is for an earlier *súar*, *kvà* for *kúa*, and so on. And the Vedic verse clearly shows that the fusion of the two syllables into one, with consequent circumflex, is a fact not yet accomplished in Vedic times: such syllables are more often to be read as two than as one — *kvà*, for example, becoming dissyllabic, and *kanyā̀* trisyllabic. Indeed, the Tâittirîya-Sanhitâ, which has a peculiar orthographic usage with regard to a part of these words, regularly writes *sú̀var* instead of *svàr*, *tanú̀vam* instead of *tanvàm*, etc.

So far, there is nothing difficult or questionable either in the theory or in the practice of Sanskrit accentuation, and all the phenomena are of a nature to favor and establish the truth of that description of the nature of the *svarita* which is given by the grammarians. But we have next to consider a more problematical addition to the theory. The authorities, namely, teach with one voice that a syllable naturally grave becomes circumflex if an acute precedes it, either in the same or in another word. So, for example, the Rik-Prâtiçâkhya says (iii. 9): "A grave syllable preceded by an acute is circumflexed, whether separated from it by a hiatus or by a consonant." The final of *íti*, then, is not grave, but circumflex; and so is the initial syllable of the toneless *iva* in *sá iva*. The virtual meaning of the doctrine must, it seems, be understood somewhat thus: the voice, when once raised to the higher pitch of acute, does not ordinarily descend to the general level of utterance between the acute syllable and its successor, but leaps or slides down in the course of the latter; it occupies a syllable in its descent. This kind of circumflex, since it is a subordinate accompaniment of the acute, is conveniently distinguished by European grammarians from those which have been described above by being called the "dependent" or "enclitic" circumflex: the term, however, has no correspondent in Sanskrit, nor do the Hindu grammarians, by description, classification, or designation, intimate a recognition of any difference in character between the enclitic and the independent varieties of this accent. The Prâtiçâkhyas divide the former, as they do the latter, into sub-varieties, with abundant nomenclature; but the distinctions are not of consequence enough to deserve notice in a sketch like this.[1] One essential difference in practical treatment separates the two: if the independent circumflex comes to stand before an acute or another circumflex of its own kind, it maintains itself, as in *apsvàntár;* but the enclitic under the same circumstances is changed to grave, and so the *ca* which was circumflexed after *yé*, in *yé ca*, recovers its character as grave in *yé ca té*, or *yé ca svàr.*

It is not well possible to accept the teachings of the Sanskrit authors respecting the enclitic circumflex with the same implicit trust as those respecting the independent circumflex. It seems next to incredible that a language which, as we have seen, has so little inclination to this tone as to admit it only very rarely, as proper word-accent, upon even a long vowel or a diphthong, should allow its development enclitically in syllables of every variety of quantity, by the mere antecedence of an acute. The Tâittirîya-Prâtiçâkhya is ingenuous enough to inform us (xiv. 33) that some authorities rejected *in toto* the doctrine of the dependent circumflex. If we do not carry our own skepticism so far as that, we shall perhaps take refuge in the theory of a "middle tone," such as some have assumed[2] in order to explain the peculiarities of Greek and Latin accent. This would imply that the enclitic tone which was perceived to lead down from acute pitch to grave was in reality an intermediate step, and was hastily and inaccurately apprehended by the Hindu grammarians as a combination of the two, or a slide, and so identified with the independent circumflex, of which the origin and character were too clear to admit of any doubt or question.

A theory like this, unwilling as we may be to resort to it, seems less absolutely to be rejected, inasmuch as there

1 They may be found described more fully, and named, in the essay "On the Nature and Designation of the Accent in Sanskrit" (in the *Trans. Am. Philol. Assoc'n* for 1870), of which this is in part a reproduction.

2 See Professor Hadley's essay, already referred to, p. 117 *seq.*

are other parts of the complete Hindu accentual system which we find exceedingly hard to explain satisfactorily and to accept. They cannot be suitably expounded and discussed without much more space than can be spared them here, and it will be necessary to pass them by with hardly more than a mention. In marking their three tones, the Hindus, strangely enough, leave the principal one, the raised or acute (*udâtta*), without a sign; the grave that precedes the acute has a short horizontal stroke beneath; the enclitic circumflex that follows it (as also the independent circumflex, which then has usually the sign of grave immediately before it) has a short perpendicular stroke above — both strokes being uniformly added in red ink in the manuscripts. If, after it has been sent downward by the circumflex sign, the voice runs on through a series of grave syllables before the next acute, only the last of these graves is marked with the horizontal stroke; the rest are left unmarked, as are the acutes under all circumstances. And these unmarked grave syllables are called *pracita*, 'accumulated,' apparently because they often occur in no small number in succession. I conjecture it, now, to be a later addition to the original accentual theory that the *pracita* syllables are by all the Prâtiçâkhyas (not by Pânini) declared to have, though really grave, a tone equivalent to acute. And then follows, in two of the Prâtiçâkhyas (in one of them, not without abundant quotation of dissenting views), the further resulting doctrine, that the circumflex leads, not from acute down to grave, but from a pitch higher than acute down to acute. I cannot work these doctrines in as part of a consistent and intelligible system of accentuation, and am obliged, at least provisionally, to hold them for later excrescences and perversions, and to refuse them acceptance.[1]

[1] They are discussed at much greater length in the essay in *Trans. Am. Philol. Assoc'n*, referred to in a previous note. Professor Haug, of Munich, has repeatedly pointed out that the modern recitation of the Vedic texts by the Brahmans is in accordance with them; and he therefore looks upon them as not less

As a general rule, in both Greek and Sanskrit, the grammarians and their systems of written signs take notice only of the word-accent, and not also of its modification by the sentence-accent, or emphatic variation of tone; they denote only the raised or the circumflexed syllable of each word taken as an independent unconnected vocable. To infer from this, however, that there was no rhetorical modulation of the sentence, dominating the word-accent, might be a somewhat questionable proceeding. For my part, I should not dare to draw such an inference. The tedious monotony which would be the result of a tone swinging and sliding back and forth only between the narrow limits prescribed by the accentual theory, and in strict observance of grave, acute, and circumflex — who will ascribe this to the lively and impassioned Greek? Think of Demosthenes, for example, swaying his audiences with such a style of oratorical delivery! That there may have been a difference between his language and ours as regards the degree of domination of the one element and subordination of the other, that more of the uplifting of tone belonging to the accent of the separate word may have been saved by the Greek in connected utterance, I would by no means lightly deny; but the recorded accent observes silence as to the whole matter; we may expect to arrive at some competent and confident opinion about it when the accent of many or most living languages shall have been examined with the thoroughness and scientific method which belong to the modern school of phonology. To allow any measure of unrecorded modulation would be to assimilate so far those

genuine than the rest. In maintaining this, however, he is obliged to assume that the whole has nothing to do with what we call accent at all, but is a mere artificial system of variations of tone, with no assignable purpose. To do this is to plunge one's self into difficulties vastly greater than those with which we have been trying to contend. I do not know that any other scholar of note shares Haug's views on this subject. They are most elaborately set forth in an essay just published in the Transactions of the Munich Academy (*Philos.-philol. Classe*, vol. xiii. part 2, 1874).

ancient modes of accent to our own, would imply an essential sameness of character in them all, and would show us in the Modern Greek accentuation — which is the genetic descendant and representative of the ancient, distinguishing the same syllable of every word, and yet is in no marked manner different from ours — only an admissible change of style, and not a violent transformation.

As for the relation of accent and quantity in the construction of verse, and the preservation of both elements to the ear in reading, that is another and a far harder question. But the peculiarity of measured verse appears to have depended much more upon the different apprehension and appreciation of the element of quantity than upon difference of accentuation, and its style of utterance to have been very unlike that of prose. The metres were really measured off, with a musical movement, and an elaborate delivery quite in contrast with the almost conversational one which we affect in our poetic reading or recitation; it was a kind of sing-song or *cantilena*. This structure of verse was as natural to the Sanskrit as to the Greek; both the hymns of the Vedas and the poetry of the later language are governed by quantity alone, without any the slightest consideration of accent, and also with the same recognition of the length (or "heaviness," as the Hindu grammarians, by a convenient and useful distinction, term it) of a syllable by "position," as equivalent to length by quantity of vowel. Dr. Haug has heard and studied, and he describes with some fullness,[1] the delivery of the Vedic hymn-texts as practiced by the learned priests of the present day. It has been somewhat altered from what it must have been at first; the proper measure has been hidden under an exaggerated rendering of the modulation of the word-accent, as it has been elaborated in the schools and marked in the written texts.

But neither in Greek nor in Sanskrit is there a total

[1] Particularly in his recent essay in the Transactions of the Munich Academy.

absence of endeavor to mark the accent of words as affected by the combinations of connected discourse; only it is confined within narrow limits, and does not at all extend to the general expression, the rhetorical modulation, of the sentence. Thus, in Greek, there are words which — like our articles, auxiliaries, prepositions *of* and *to*, and their like — are uniformly unemphatic, pronounced without stress of voice; such are without accent, being reckoned either as "proclitics" or "enclitics;" and before the latter, the final of a preceding word takes often an additional stress or elevation. And the final acute of a word followed by others (not enclitic) connected in construction with it has its accent-mark changed from "acute" to "grave:" precisely what alteration of tone this signifies is quite obscure; probably [1] a depression of pitch, though not so far as to the general level of the voice.

The Sanskrit has no enclitics, in the Greek sense of the word, as exercising an influence upon the accent of the word that precedes them; nor proclitics, as leaning forward upon a fully accented word, and able to stand before it at the head of a sentence. But it has a considerable class of accentless words — pronouns and particles — and a smaller class that are sometimes accented and sometimes not, according to their situation and their importance in the sentence (though this last item is not always easy to appreciate). Apart from these, the effort to mark the influence of connected discourse on the word-accent expends itself upon vocatives and upon the personal forms (excluding participial and infinitival words) of verbs.

The Sanskrit vocative, whether of noun or adjective, is always accented on its first syllable, if it is accented at all. But it receives an accent only when it stands at the head of the sentence; if interjected, put after any part or all of the sentence of address, it is toneless. It does not seem hard to recognize in our own usage what might

[1] See Professor Hadley's essay, already quoted, p. 117 *seq.*

have been the basis of a treatment like this. If, in calling to a person, the name be put first, the design is to attract attention, and the full accent is given to the word; but the same name inserted parenthetically, after the address is begun, is for a very different purpose, and is given with very different effect, being ordinarily dropped to a lower monotone. Any one, it seems to me, may find or make an example of this in his own usage: I will suggest only "Friends! countrymen! lovers! hear me for my cause;" and "Hear me, friends and countrymen, for my cause." The effect may not be necessarily and always of this character; but the Hindus, having once recognized and established the principle, have consistently carried it out everywhere, with that same disregard of the detailed modulation of the voice in sentence-expression which is shown in their general treatment of the word-accent.[1]

As for the verb, the general rule is that, if not standing at the head of its sentence or clause,[2] its personal or finite forms are unaccented in independent construction, but accented in dependent. Thus, we should read *té bruvanti*, 'they speak,' but *yé té bruvánti*, 'they who speak,' *yád bruvánti*, 'what they speak,' *yádi bruvánti*, 'if they speak,' and so on: also *bruvánti*, or *bruvánti té*, 'they speak.' The prepositional prefix, if the verb be unaccented, itself has the accent, as *té prábruvanti*, 'they proclaim;' if the verb receive the accent, the prefix loses it, provided it immediately precedes, as in *yé prabruvánti*, 'who proclaim;' if (as is frequent in Vedic, though not in later Sanskrit) other words are interposed between prefix and verb, the assumption of accent by the latter

[1] There are, to be sure, irregularities in the Vedic treatment of vocative accent, which render desirable a complete assemblage and discussion of the instances — which no one, so far as I know, has yet undertaken. It may be remarked further that a genitive dependent on a vocative, not less than an adjective qualifying it, is liable to share in its loss of accent; an interesting illustration of the usual quasi-adjectival character of that case.

[2] And, in poetry, each constituent division of a verse is reckoned as a separate clause, at the head of which either verb or vocative must be accented.

has no influence on the former; and we read, for example, *prá yé tád bruvánti*, 'who proclaim that.' This difference in the accentual treatment of the verb, according as it is found in an independent or a dependent clause, is the most peculiar feature in the whole Hindu system, and has yet to find a satisfactory explanation.[1]

There are a few other cases in which the verb in Sanskrit is allowed to retain its natural accent: certain particles, having a more or less illative force, cause its preservation; and where there is a distinct antithesis between two clauses, as introduced by *both — and*, by *either — or*, by *the one — the other*, and so on, the verb of the former clause is often accented. These are, however, matters of detail, into which we have no need here to enter.[2]

To render this sketch more complete, it may be worth while to add a few words as to the position of the syllable on which the accent falls in a Sanskrit word. The accent of the various members of the Indo-European family is in this respect governed by very different rules. In the Latin, the stress of voice is laid on either the penult or antepenult of a polysyllable, and the choice between them is strictly determined by quantity. In the Greek, it rests on one of the last three syllables, and is only in part fixed

[1] I myself, many years ago (*Journ. Am. Or. Soc.* v. 215, 1856), compared it with the different treatment of the German verb, as regards position, in the two kinds of clauses (the verb following next after its subject in an independent, but being put off to the end of a dependent clause); but unfortunately the analogy, though not without interest, is one that explains nothing. Delbrück, in his *Gebrauch des Conjunctivs und Optativs* (1871, pp. 97, 98), suggests a theory, but it has nothing in it that at all satisfies my mind. I do not know that any one else has touched upon the subject.

[2] I drew out and illustrated the rules bearing upon this subject in 1856, in a paper entitled *Contributions from the Atharva-Veda to the Theory of Sanskrit Verbal Accent*, published in the fifth volume of *Journ. Am. Or. Soc'y.* The paper was reproduced the next year, in German translation, by Kuhn, in the first volume of his *Beiträge zur vergleichenden Sprachforschung*, and has since been repeatedly laid at the basis of further discussions of the same subject (so by Kielhorn in Weber's *Indische Studien*, x. 404 *seq.*; by Mayr in the Proceedings of the Vienna Academy [*Phil.-hist. Classe*], vol. lxviii. [1871], p. 219 *seq.*).

by their quantity. In the Germanic tongues, an accent which perhaps began with being a first-syllable one has become prevailingly "logical," making prominent the radical or most fundamentally significant syllable. No such system as this is found in the Slavonic branch, though next of kin to the Germanic; nor do the Slavonic dialects agree with one another: the Polish accents the penult; the Bohemian, the initial syllable; the Russian, any syllable. Among the Celtic dialects, the Welsh agrees with the Polish, and the Irish with the Bohemian. Of course, at the outset, in the time of Indo-European unity, the common language from which all these have descended had a definite system of accentuation, from which the various systems mentioned have come by gradual alteration. That tongues so nearly related as Welsh and Irish, as Russian and Bohemian and Polish, have so discordant accent, proves sufficiently the great mutability of this element of utterance. General euphonic tendencies, changes of national taste and preference, set in, and work over into a new shape the laws of accentual stress. Professor Hadley, in the essay already repeatedly referred to here, has suggested (pp. 120, 124) conjecturally the specific tendencies, toward certain cadences or successions of graded tones at the end of a word, which may have determined the form assumed by the Greek and Latin accent. Where there is such mutability and variety, we have no right to expect to find that any language has held fast to the original system. But there may be recognizable differences in the degree of their adherence. And the stricter the uniformity, the more rigid the determination by general laws of position or quantity, of the place of accent in a language, the greater is the probability of a secondary development in that language. Tried by this test, the Sanskrit accent is the most original among the recorded systems of the ancient languages of the family. It is governed by no rules.

either of position or of quantity; it rests upon that syllable to which the laws of derivation or composition assign it, whether the syllable be long or short, and whatever its position in a word of whatever length. For example, it being the rule that in an augmented verbal form the augment takes the accent, we have not only *ábhût* and *ábhavat*, but also *ábhavishi*, *ábhavishvahi*, *ábobhûyâmahi*, etc. Again, the passive participle is always accented on its ending *ta*: thus, *gribhitá*, 'comprehended.' If such a word is reversed by the negative prefix, that prefix is accented: thus, *ágribhîta*, 'uncomprehended.' If, further, a word like this is used as first member of a compound, the accent is different according to the character and meaning of the compound: a mere determinative compound generally throws forward the accent, and we should have *agribhîtaçocís*, 'uncomprehended brightness,' which would not change accent by increment of syllables in declension, but would form *agribhîtaçocíshas*, etc.; but if the idea of possession be added, so that the word is an adjective, 'having incomprehensible brightness,' the rule is that the first member retains its own accent; and we have *ágribhîtaçocishas*. And so on, through as many more examples as one may select.

There would seem to be no reasonable question that a state of things like this is more primitive than that which prevails in Greek, or Latin, or Germanic, or Welsh, or Irish. And there is involved in it a precious possibility that some of the secrets of the earliest Indo-European word-formation may have light cast upon them by the phenomena of Sanskrit accentuation. If we belong to the modern school of historical philology, we believe that polysyllabic words and forms first grew up by the subordination of certain independently significant radical syllables to others, in collocation with which they had before been uttered — by their concretion, as it were, about a nucleus; that there was first a reduction of accented words to proclitics or enclitics, and then a fusion of the aggregate into a unit. In the growing together of such a compound unit, that syllable would naturally become the accented one which in the collocation had been the emphatic one; the less prominent atoms would be subordinated to the most important. General laws and tendencies, dominating bodies of words or the whole vocabulary of a language, would not arise until later. If, then, we can approach near enough to the first processes of accretion, the possession of a primitive accentuation may have such hints to give us as to the comparative value of the elements at the moment of union, as shall help us in the difficult task of explaining the genesis of the formative syllables. Perhaps the hope is a too sanguine one; and certainly we have no right lightly to assume that the accent of Sanskrit forms is absolutely primitive and unaltered; but the subject is worthy of the most careful investigation, which it has not yet received. Meanwhile, the Sanskrit accent has at least been used to furnish an explanation of a wide-spread and important phonetic phenomenon in Indo-European language — namely, the *guna*, or strengthening of *i* and *u* to *ai* and *au* in large classes of very ancient forms.[1]

The father of comparative philology, Bopp, in his "Comparative Accentuation of Greek and Sanskrit" (Berlin, 1854), failed to derive from the accent any results of value for the genesis of forms; and doubtless in great measure because he conceived himself to discover in the accentual phenomena a general law — namely, that "the farthest retraction of the stress of voice toward the beginning of the word was regarded as the accentuation of greatest dignity and force" — holding to this law with

[1] The explanation is one which has been accepted by many comparative philologists, although not by all. I have attempted to sustain it, as against the contrary view of Schleicher and the objections of Professor Peile, in an article presented to the London Philological Society, and published in its *Transactions* for 1874.

great persistency through the whole work, nowhere seeming to contemplate the possible existence of a principle more primitive, nor inquiring whether any of the facts inconsistent with it of which he takes notice may not be original, and find their explanation in the earliest processes of growth. The alleged law or principle is in fact without any even tolerable support in the facts of the language, and has been let drop quietly out of sight; never having won, I believe, the assent of any other prominent scholar.[1] The treatise in which it appears is marred by other important errors of theory, and has value chiefly as an exhibition of the interesting correspondences which, in spite of the disguising operation of later phonetic tendencies in the Greek, still subsist between the phenomena of accent of that language and those of the Sanskrit.

The only other attempt made to find a special principle of accentuation for the Sanskrit is that of Benfey, who declares that the language lays the stress of voice upon the last modifying addition, whether prefix or suffix, to the exclusion of the root or theme itself; adding, however, that this original principle has been, in the progress of development of the language, supplanted in some instances by other word-shaping influences. To this, Bopp remarks, in the work just referred to (note 35, p. 238), that he would have been nearer the truth had he said "in most instances," inasmuch as in the great majority of the facts as they lie before us the law is violated. Benfey has not given himself the trouble to defend and establish his theory, but is content barely to state it, with an illustration or two, leaving it to his readers for acceptance or rejection, as they shall please; probably most will agree with Bopp in disposing of it in the latter way, since it seems to find sufficient support neither in the

[1] So far as I know, no one even took the pains to refute it in detail excepting myself, in *Journ. Am. Or. Soc.* v. (1856), 205–212.

facts, as a general law of secondary origin, nor in sound theory, as a primitive principle. In the very earliest concretion of syllables into words, a "logical" accent, distinguishing the radical syllable, would seem theoretically more probable; but whether this be so, and when and to what extent the opposite principle, of accenting the last modifier, should come in, are questions to be determined only by the most penetrating and cautious inquiry. And until such inquiry is made, and conducted to a successful conclusion, it is safest to hold our opinions in suspense, not suffering them to be taken captive by any plausible but superficial generalizations. The highest interest of the Sanskrit accent lies, probably, in its bearing upon the history of Indo-European forms; and the time cannot be far distant when it will be thoroughly investigated with reference to this side of its value.

XII.

ON THE LUNAR ZODIAC OF INDIA, ARABIA, AND CHINA.

A HIGH degree of interest belongs to all inquiries into the beginnings of astronomical science, both on their own account and because of the light which they cast upon the intercourse and mutual influence of ancient peoples. And notwithstanding all the labor which has been devoted to the subject, it still presents a host of difficult and controverted points, which must for a long time continue to attract the attention of the learned. One of the most conspicuous of these controverted points is the character and origin of what we may call the lunar zodiac, or the system of lunar mansions — a division of the planetary path into twenty-seven or twenty-eight parts, presumably founded upon the sidereal revolution of the moon in between twenty-seven and twenty-eight days. This institution is found to constitute an important element in the astronomy of the leading races of Asia — of the Chinese, the Hindus, and the Arabs — while traces of it are found also in other countries. Where it originated, and whence and how it spread, is a question which has of late provoked a lively, almost a sharp, discussion; and if just at present it seems to be quiescent, this is hardly because any general agreement of opinion has been reached, but rather because those who were contending over it have turned aside to other matters. I propose here, in as simple and popular a manner as the subject admits, to review the discordant opinions, and the grounds upon which they have claimed to be founded.

A main part of what may be called the astronomical science of ancient nations has lain in, or has grown out of, their attempts at reconciling the discordant natural measures or divisions of time, and setting up a regulated calendar. No chronological period, of course, is so elementary and obvious, so forced upon men's attention, as the day, with its natural subdivision of day and night — the period, astronomically speaking, of the earth's rotation on her axis, as slightly modified by her revolution about the sun. A human language with no word for "day" in it would be an inconceivable anomaly. A next longer natural unit, convenient for the reckoning of more extended periods of time, is the real month, the period of waxing and waning of the earth's satellite, measured either from new moon to new moon or from full moon to full moon — astronomically, the period of synodical revolution of the moon. And it is doubtful whether any tribe or people was ever met with, so careless of the operations and manifestations of nature, and so restricted in its chronological needs, as never to have measured time by "moons" — or by "months," as we say, using for the period a name which is not the same with that for the heavenly body, though derived from it. Of the month there is no natural subdivision; some have conjectured that the seven-day period, or week, was originally arrived at by a division of it into quarters. Once more, a yet longer period is the year, as really determined in length by the earth's revolution about the sun, and in the changes of its seasons by the inclination of the earth's axis to the plane of its orbit. The year is brought to notice principally by meteorological phenomena, by the alternations of season, partly also by the varying length of the day; for the mere fact of the changing elevation of the sun's apparent track is (except in high latitudes), comparatively unimportant. And the year assumes different degrees of prominence as a period, according to the natural conditions of each region and the occupations and mode of life of each community; dwellers in or near the tropics, and of pastoral or nomadic habit, have it least forced upon their attention. Its distinct conception and naming as a period, its accurate measurement, and yet more the proper connection of its phenomena with the sun's apparent movement — all these are results of a closer, a longer-continued, a more scientifically conducted process of observation than is needed for the day or month.

But further, each of these periods is incommensurable with the other two. The month is no precise number of days; the year is no precise number of days, or of months. How shall this be reconciled, so that the reckoning of each period shall go on harmoniously with that of the others? On what day shall the new month be reckoned to begin? On what day, or with what month, shall the new year be reckoned to begin? These are questions of which the solution has been the perpetual problem of many a race, and which have been answered in very various ways. We will notice only two or three typical methods.

In our own practice, the moon has been sacrificed. Our year, to be sure, is made up of twelve so-called "months," and their number is due to the fact that the moon makes her synodical revolution more nearly twelve than thirteen times in a year; but our "month" is an arbitrary period, a mere conventional approximation in length to the true month, and not at all regulated by the phases of the moon, which may begin its wax or its wane on any day between the first and the thirty-first. By this sacrifice, we are enabled to make our years of very nearly equal length, varying only between 365 and 366 days; and a day intercalated nearly every four years, and counted in at an arbitrarily selected point, easily and almost imperceptibly maintains the desired balance. And we prize the meteorological uniformity of our dates more than the minor uniformity of lunar age which we have given up for it. The Arab, on the other hand, and after his example the whole Mohammedan world, sacrifices the year to the month. He reckons, indeed, by so-called "years," and of equal length; but they are no real years; they are periods of twelve real months each, or of 354 days; the new moon is watched for as an actual phenomenon, and the beginning of the month never swerves from it; but the seasons shift rapidly through the whole succession of months, so that winter and summer exchange places with one another about once in seventeen years. The Hindu, once more, follows a much more intricate system, whereby an equal compromise is made among all the three periods:[1] his month is of twenty-nine or of thirty days, by a rule which keeps the reckoned succession as close to the moon's synodical movement as is our year to the earth's revolution; and the intercalation of a month, instead of merely a day, made at fixed intervals, keeps the beginning of the year always within a certain distance of a fixed point in the earth's revolution. The inconvenience of this arrangement, aside from its greater intricacy (but that the almanac-makers attend to), is the inequality of the year, which varies between 354 and 383 days; still, to those who are used to it, this seems an insignificant thing as compared with the utter neglect of the natural month of which we of the West are guilty.

These are representative instances, illustrating the three principal methods of chronological adjustment: one sacrifices the natural month to the year; another gives up the year for the month; the third pays strict and equal regard to both.

[1] The year, to be sure, is of precisely the character here described only in a part of India.

The natural periods need nothing but the ordinary experiences of men in common life to bring them to notice and impress them. But a higher and more enlightened curiosity, which seeks to trace phenomena to their causes, soon succeeds in making out a connection between them and the movements of the heavenly bodies. As regards the day, indeed, the connection is flatly palpable; the revolution of the sun by day, continued by the revolution, in the same direction and at the same rate, of the starry heavens by night, is a cause "as plain as the sun in the heavens," according to our proverbial expression. And some of the ancient philosophers, a thousand or two of years before Copernicus, were acute enough to see beneath the surface of the phenomena, and to perceive not only that the earth was round, but also that its turning on its axis was the real cause of the apparent circling of the firmament about it. A little more careful observation was needed to show that, while the moon moved about us with the rest, she also had an additional round of her own among the stars, in the contrary direction; and that her regular increase and decrease were owing to her approaching the sun on this round, and then, after temporary disappearance in his rays, to her receding from him on the opposite side. And a yet more penetrating and enlightened quest detected the sun doing the same thing, only at a slower rate. His course amid the stars could not be traced out, like the moon's, by direct observation; it had to be inferred from the successive extinction of the constellations as he advanced upon them, and their restoration to view in his rear. But, by those who had the patience to observe and the skill to infer, the idea of the sun's yearly progress about the firmament, upon an unvarying track, and a track not identical with the equator but crossing it at two definite points and making a certain angle with it — this idea was reached and held with entire distinctness and correctness, and constituted a fundamental step in the developing science of astronomy.

From this idea there sprang forth another — namely, that of dividing the track thus recognized into parts, successively traversed in successive periods by the great luminary, and of defining and naming the parts. The result was the familiar system of the twelve zodiacal signs. When and by whom the system was invented, and by what steps it won its currency, are mooted questions, which we have no occasion here to discuss. But the general character of the institution is clear enough. The number of twelve, as no one can reasonably doubt, came from the nearly twelvefold division of the year into months: one sign, as nearly as the perverse incommensurability of year and month permitted, was to be traversed in each month. And the construction of the system consisted in the selection of twelve groups of stars, lying upon or near to the sun's track, and fairly equidistant from one another; each of which should be regarded as occupying, and by its presence marking, and by its name designating, an equal twelfth part of the circle. Thus for the first time there came to be a means of rudely marking the place of the planetary bodies in the sky: to say that the sun, or the moon, or Mars, was in the Ram or the Virgin, or, more precisely, in a certain part of either, was to define their position with such accuracy as the state of astronomical science permitted. Though the groups of stars were of unequal extent and unevenly distributed, they answered well enough their purpose of marking equal divisions in the sky; it was not till science had taken many more steps forward, and till methods and instruments of observation implying considerable precision were put to use, that any one could have laid down the boundaries of the duodecimal divisions with any approach to exactness.

Such were the twelve Signs of the Zodiac: a system

very familiar to us, because of its prominence in the Greek astronomy, and its transmission to us by our Greek teachers. An institution of this character easily makes its way from people to people, in connection with the transfer of increased knowledge in a definite department, and without necessarily implying an intimate intercourse between giver and receiver, or any profound influence of a wider scope exerted by the one upon the other. In such matters (just as in chemistry or geology with us), the community follows the lead of a few specially qualified persons; and the chance meeting of two advanced students of science, or the journey of a single philosopher to a distant reputed centre of knowledge, might have for its consequence the introduction into a new country of a successful explanation of what its deep thinkers had been already observing and reasoning about, or of a practical means of more exact observation. Possibly, it should be added, an application to superstitious uses would be the most effective of all aids to the introduction and spread of a new system of astronomy.

Another instance of a mode of scientific division founded on the relations of the natural periods is seen in our treatment of the circle. We reckon three hundred and sixty degrees to a circle, because that is the manageable whole number which stands nearest to the number of days in the year; each degree is, as nearly as the exigencies of convenient use permit, that part of the sun's yearly revolution which he accomplishes in each daily revolution.

We are now prepared to consider the formation of the analogous and kindred institution which constitutes the special subject of this essay.

It has been already noticed that there is in use among certain Oriental nations a system of division of the planetary path into twenty-seven or twenty-eight parts, each marked by a group of stars and named from that group.

By the Arabs, the parts are called *manâzil al-kamar*, 'mansions of the moon, lunar stations;' the Chinese know them simply as *sieu*, 'mansions;' by the Hindus they are denominated, yet more undistinctively, *nakshatras*, 'asterisms.' We have only to note the number and the names, and the fact that the moon makes her sidereal revolution, from a given star back to the same, in between twenty-seven and twenty-eight days,[1] to draw at once, at least provisionally, the inference that the intent of the system must have been to mark, as nearly as the circumstances of the case admitted, the successive daily steps of the moon's progress around the heavens. Of course, we can abandon this opinion hereafter, if it shall be proved ill-founded. But in order to understand better what would be the character of a system formed with the intent stated, we need to note certain facts relating to the moon's movement.

The makers of a lunar zodiac have over the makers of a solar zodiac the advantage that they are able to follow the track of the determining luminary amid the stars by direct observation, impeded only by the circumstance that its brilliancy extinguishes the smaller stars about it. If, then, the moon, like the sun, never departed from the line of the ecliptic, and if she moved always with an equal velocity in the same part of this line, we might reasonably expect that stars or groups immediately upon the ecliptic would be selected, and such as marked quite accurately the limits of a day's motion — though that odd remnant, of about a third of a day more than twenty-seven, would still come in as a disturbing element, to be in some way disposed of. But this is not the way in which the moon makes her round. In the first place, while her daily rate of motion, like the sun's, varies quite notably, and while this variation is cumulative, so that in one part of her revolution she is six or seven degrees behind, and

[1] Exactly, $27^d\ 7^h\ 43^m\ 11.4^s$, or 27.3217—.

in another part as much in advance of her mean place, it is not the case, as with the sun, that her retardation and acceleration take place always in the same region of the heavens; on the contrary, as her line of apsides revolves once in a little less than nine years, the variation of velocity is rapidly shifting its action, and she will be, during the period of nine years, in every part of the heavens a whole asterism in advance or in rear of the position she occupied in her revolution four years and a half before, when of the same mean sidereal age. What is of not less consequence, she revolves, not in the ecliptic, but in an orbit which is inclined to that circle a little more than five degrees; and the line of her nodes is also in rapid motion, making the circuit of the heavens once in about eighteen years; so that if at any time a line of measuring stars had been selected just upon her path, she would pass them nine years later at distances from them ranging all the way up to ten degrees. Nor must we leave out of account that, during a good part of each round, her light is so brilliant as to obliterate entirely all but the brighter stars with which she comes closely in contact or near to which she passes, and the fainter ones at a still greater distance; so that to mark her course by such stars only as are to be found immediately along the ecliptic would be unpractical; they would in many cases not be visible when she was at one or two or three asterisms' distance.

Thus all the conditions which would lead imperatively to a choice of stars or groups of stars separated by precisely equal intervals, or situated along one undeviating line, are entirely wanting. Nor should we expect a succession of single stars to have been pitched upon; where exactness of interval was a secondary consideration, constellated groups had the advantage of being far more easily described, named, recognized, and remembered.

Supposing, then, that a people whose only instrument

of observation was the eye should have noticed the moon's nearly equable movement through a certain region of the heavens, and the completion of her revolution in twenty-seven or twenty-eight days, and, feeling impelled to mark and define the stages of her progress, should set about choosing a means of definition among the stars through which she passed — what would they naturally seek in their selection? Obviously, I think, they would look for groups of stars, as conspicuous as the heavens furnished in the proper position, not too remote in either direction from the ecliptic, and tolerably evenly distributed, so that, at any rate, no considerable part of the series should be far away from the average place required by a division of the ecliptic region into nearly equal portions: and nothing more than this.

The three Oriental systems of division, now — Hindu, Arab, Chinese — to which reference has been made above, and which are the only ones known to us in detail, are precisely of this character. Moreover, they are but three somewhat varying forms of the same original. Of course, it is not impossible that the idea of such a mode of division of the heavens — a lunar zodiac, as we have called it — should suggest itself independently to different peoples, and should be carried out independently in different countries by the selection of different star-groups. But an actual comparison of the Hindu, Arab, and Chinese zodiacs shows such numerous and striking coincidences between them as totally exclude any theory of the diversity of their origin. In order to demonstrate this, and to make plain their general character and relations, I give here a brief description, identification, and nomenclature of the three series of groups, beginning with that member which is reckoned as first in the oldest Hindu records; and I add at the end of the volume a chart, by help of which they may be the better understood, or may be traced out in the sky by any one who shall feel enough interest in the matter to take the trouble.[1]

1. The first asterism is in all the three systems the same group: namely, the Pleiades (η Tauri, etc.). The Hindus call it Krittikâ (of doubtful meaning); to the Arabs, it is Thuraiyâ, 'little thick-set group,' or Najm, 'constellation;' the Chinese name, Mao, is also of doubtful meaning.[2]

2. The second station is marked by the group of Hyades (α, θ, γ, δ, ϵ Tauri: the Chinese add the neighboring λ and σ). Its Hindu name is Rohinî, 'ruddy,' doubtless from the conspicuously reddish hue of its principal star, α Tauri, which we call Aldebaran, from the Arabic name of the station, Dabarân, 'follower' (perhaps as being the *sequens* or *secundus* of the primitive series). The Chinese call it Pi, 'hand-net.'

3. The third determining group is the little triangle of faint stars in Orion's head, or λ, ϕ^1, ϕ^2 Orionis. The Hindus (see below, p. 404) figure Orion as a stag, and this group is Mrigaçiras or Mrigaçirsha, 'stag's head;' the Arabs call the *manzil* Hak'ah, 'horse-mark;' as *sieu*, it is named Tse, 'beak, pouting lips,' etc.

It is not a little strange that the framers of the system should have chosen for marking the third station this faint group, to the neglect of the brilliant and conspicuous pair, β and ζ Tauri, or the tips of the Bull's horns. There is hardly another case where we have so much reason to find fault with their selection.

[1] For further explanations of the chart, see at the end of this article. It is a reproduction of one given in the *Translation of the Sûrya-Siddhânta, a Text-book of Hindu Astronomy*, published in 1860, in the sixth volume of the *Journal of the American Oriental Society* (and also in a separate edition). In the notes to the eighth chapter of that work, I have given a more detailed discussion of the coincidences and discordances of the three systems, and especially a much fuller exhibition of the evidence on which the identifications of the various groups are founded. As regards the Hindu "asterisms" (*nakshatra*) and the Arab "stations" (*manâzil*, singular *manzil*), I rely solely on those notes, and would refer to them any one who may wish for more information. Respecting the Chinese stations (*sieu*), I follow two authorities formerly not accessible to me: namely, Sédillot's *Matériaux pour servir à l'histoire comparée des sciences mathématiques chez les Grecs et les Orientaux* (Paris, 1845–49, p. 476 *seq.* and Tableau B), and J. Williams's *Observations of Comets, extracted from the Chinese Annals* (London, 1871). The Chinese groups are determined with almost entire accordance, though independently, by Sédillot and Williams, and the star-charts given by the latter, from Chinese sources, at the end of his volume, help to make the identifications trustworthy (although there are two or three, as is pointed out below, which remain doubtful). On our chart, only the star in each group called by Biot its determinant (see below, p. 385) is marked, by an inclosed figure.

[2] Sédillot renders it 'soutien des choses de la nature.'

4. At this point there is great discordance among the systems. The Hindu asterism, Ârdrâ, 'moist,' appears to be the brilliant α Orionis, while the Chinese Tsan, 'three' (originally the trio in Orion's belt?) includes the seven conspicuous stars marking the shoulders, belt, and knees of Orion; thus effectually enveloping its predecessor, whose province it reduces to a mere fragment. There is probably some decided later corruption here. The Arab *manzil*, Han'ah, 'the pile,' has been moved, with good judgment, nearer to the ecliptic, and is made up of the stars in the feet of the Twins, or η, μ, ν, γ, ξ Geminorum; or, according to some, of the last two only.

5. Here the Hindu and Arab systems come to accordance again, adopting as determining group of the station the bright pair, α and β Geminorum, in the heads of Castor and Pollux. The Hindu name is *Punarvasû*, 'the two good again;' the Arabic title is Dhirâ', 'the paw,' (*i. e.* of the Lion, which the Arab astronomers stretch out over a much larger region of the sky than he occupies with us). The Chinese *sieu*, Tsing, 'well, pit,' is made up of eight stars in the same constellation, or ε, *d*, ζ, λ, ξ, γ, ν, μ Geminorum, including several of those which marked the preceding *manzil*.

6. This asterism is practically the same in all: namely, the faintish group in the body of the Crab. To γ and δ Cancri, its most conspicuous members, the *nakshatra* Pushya, 'flower,' or Tishya, adds θ; the *manzil* Nathrah, 'nose-gap' (*i. e.* of the Lion), includes the nebulous Præsepe; the *sieu* Kwei, 'spectre,' adds θ and η.

7. This time it is the Hindus and Chinese who agree to mark their station by the same group, that in the head of Hydra. The Chinese Lieu, 'willow,' is made up of η, σ, δ, ε, ρ, ζ, ω, and θ Hydræ; the Hindu Âçleshâ, 'embracer,' includes the first five or six of them. But the Arab Tarf, 'look,' is far away to the northward, on the other side of the ecliptic, just between the sixth and eighth *nakshatra* and *manzil;* it is composed of ξ Cancri and λ Leonis.

8. In their eighth, ninth, and tenth members the Hindu and Arab series are closely accordant, while the Chinese goes off upon an independent track, far in the south, nearly following the line of junction between the seventh and eleventh members.[1] The eighth *manzil* is called Jabhah, 'forehead,' and comprises, along with the brilliant α Leonis (Regulus), the three stars next above him in the "Sickle;" the *nakshatra* Maghâ, 'generous,' includes the whole Sickle, or α, η, γ, ζ, μ, ε Leonis. The *sieu* Sing, 'star,' is composed of α and ι Hydræ, with five other smaller stars near them.[2]

[1] According to Biot, following the equator of 2350 B. C.; see below, p. 385, and compare the chart.

[2] The identification of this group is very difficult. Sédillot specifies also τ^1, τ^2 as belonging to it; I cannot make out the figure given by Williams by including them.

9. Here, as in two other cases later, the Hindu system combines two groups which mark successive stations, as forming together a single definite figure or constellation, and calls them by the same name, distinguishing them as "former" (*pûrva*) and "latter" (*uttara*). The double group including the ninth and tenth asterisms is a conspicuous rectangle in the northeast corner of the Lion, made up of δ, θ, β, and 93 Leonis; it is called *Phalguni* (of doubtful meaning). Pûrva-Phalguni, 'the former Phalguni,' is marked by δ and θ; and the Arab *manzil*, Zubrah, 'mane,' contains the same two stars. The corresponding *sieu*, Chang, 'drawn bow,' is composed of κ, υ^1,[1] λ, μ, ϕ^1, and another small star in Hydra.

10. The tenth *nakshatra* is Uttara-Phalguni, 'latter Phalguni,' and is made up of the two eastern stars of the rectangle already described, or β and 93 Leonis. The *manzil* Sarfah, 'turn,' is marked by β alone. The *sieu* Y or Yih, 'wings, flanks,' contains twenty-two stars, including all the conspicuous ones in Crater, with their neighbors in Hydra.[2]

11. At this point, the Hindu and Chinese systems come once more to an agreement, while the Arabic follows an independent course, choosing again (as at the fourth station) a group that lies nearly midway between its tenth and twelfth members — namely, β, η, γ, δ, ϵ Virginis; its name is Auwâ', 'barking dog.' The Hindu group is called Hasta, 'hand,' and is made up of the five conspicuous stars in Corvus (α, ϵ, γ, δ, β); the *sieu*, Chin, 'cross-piece of a chariot,' contains only β, δ, γ, and ϵ.

12. As regards the twelfth station, all the systems agree, marking it by the beautiful star α Virginis, or Spica; the Chinese *sieu*, Kio, 'horn,' alone adding another star to the northward, doubtless ζ Virginis. The Hindu name of the asterism is Citrâ, 'bright;' the Arabs call it Simâk (of doubtful meaning).

13. This time it is the turn of the Hindu series to deviate from the other two, in order to bring in from far in the north the single brilliant star Arcturus, or α Bootis; its usual name is Svâti (of obscure meaning). The *sieu* Kang, 'man's neck,' is marked by λ, κ, ι, ϕ (or υ) Virginis; the *manzil*, Ghafr, 'covering,' by the two or three first mentioned of the same group.

14. In the fourteenth and several following asterisms, there is no essential discordance among the systems. The fourteenth *manzil*,

[1] Williams copies Biot's blunder (made originally, doubtless, by a confusion of the two so similar letters) in calling this star everywhere ν^1.

[2] Sédillot names half the number: α, β, δ, ϵ, ζ, η, θ, ι, λ, υ Crateri, and χ Hydræ; but I entirely fail to trace Williams's figure by their aid — or, indeed, in any other way.

Zubânân, 'the two claws,' *i. e.* of the Scorpion (some of the Greek authorities give the same name to what we call the constellation Libra), is composed of the conspicuous pair, α and β Libræ. The *sieu* is called Ti (of doubtful meaning), and adds ι and γ Libræ, which form with the other two a nearly square figure; and the Hindu Viçâkhâ, 'branched,' seems according to the later authorities to be composed of precisely the same four stars; while earlier it was commonly reckoned as a dual asterism, of α and β only.

15. The determining group is called by the Arabs Iklîl, 'crown,' and contains β, δ, and π Scorpionis; the Hindu Anurâdhâ, 'propitious,' is either the same or adds the neighboring ρ; the Chinese Fang, 'room, house,' includes all the four.

16. The Chinese group Sin, 'heart,' and the Hindu Jyeshthâ, 'eldest,' are made up of the same three stars, σ, α, and τ Scorpionis, of which the central one, α, is the brilliant reddish Antares (or *cor Scorpionis*). This star alone marks the Arab station Kalb, 'heart.'

17. The tail of the Scorpion is the determinative of this station alike in all the systems. But to the *manzil* Shaulah, 'sting,' are ascribed only the conspicuous pair, λ and υ, at its extremity. The Hindus call the same stars *Vicritâu*, 'the two releasers,' and sometimes regard them alone as composing the asterism; usually, however, all the nine (or eleven), from ε around to υ, are included, and the *nakshatra* is named Mûla, 'root.' The Chinese Wei, 'tail,' is made up of the whole number.

18. The *sieu* Ki, 'sieve,' is composed of γ, δ, ε, and η Sagittarii (the last of them known also as β Telescopii); the *nakshatra*, called the former Ashâdhâ, 'unconquered,' either includes all the four, or, according to other authorities, only δ and ε. Here occurs, namely, another of those pairs already referred to (see above, under the ninth asterism); and according as the whole double group, or each of the single groups, is reckoned as containing four stars, the constitution of the asterism is varied. The Arabic Na'aim, 'pasturing cattle,' comprehends all the eight.

19. The Hindu *nakshatra*, latter Ashâdhâ, is made up either of φ, σ, τ, ζ Sagittarii, or of σ and ζ alone; according to the latter understanding, σ and ζ along with δ and ε form the quadrate figure which is characteristic of the double asterisms. The Chinese *sieu*, Teu, 'measure (for grain),' includes the four, as also λ and μ on the north, and another (not identifiable) to the southward. The Arabs, whom we have seen to include this group in one asterism with the preceding, mark their nineteenth station by a space vacant of stars above the head of Sagittarius, bounded by π and other faint stars; they call it Baldah, 'town.'

20. In this and the two following stations, the Hindu system makes a great leap into the northern hemisphere, in order to bring in conspicuous groups from that quarter. Their twentieth asterism, Abhijit, 'victorious,' lies at 60° north latitude, being the brilliant α Lyræ, with its two humble companions ε and ζ. The Arab *manzil*, Sa'd adh-Dhâbih, 'felicity of the sacrificer,' is marked by α and β Capricorni, just north of the ecliptic; the Chinese Nieu, 'ox,' contains the same, with ν, and three other faint stars (π, ρ, and ο) farther south.

21. The northern Hindu group is called Çravana, 'ear,' or Çronâ, 'lame,' and contains three stars, the bright α Aquilæ, with β below and γ above it. The *manzil* and *sieu* agree in position: the former, Sa'd Bula', 'felicity of a devourer,' is made up of ε, μ, and ν Aquarii; the latter, Nü, 'woman,' adds another (not identifiable) from the neighborhood.

22. The Hindu asterism is the diamond-shaped group in the Dolphin, α, β, δ, and γ Delphini, some adding also ζ: it is called Çravishthâ, 'most famous,' or Dhanishthâ, 'richest.' Again the *manzil* and *sieu* are the same, being marked by β and ξ Aquarii: the former is called Sa'd as-Su'ûd, 'felicity of felicities;' the latter, Hiu, 'void.'

23. At this station, the Hindu system comes back to the ecliptic for its determining group, adopting λ Aquarii, with the stars about it, to the indefinite number of a hundred, and calling the asterism Çatabhishaj, 'hundred-physician.' No group of such a number can well be made out without including the Arab and Chinese asterisms: the former consists of γ, ζ, η, and probably π (or α) Aquarii, and is called Sa'd al-Akhbiyah, 'felicity of tents;' the latter, styled Goei, 'steep, danger,' contains α Aquarii, and θ and ε Pegasi, farther north.

24. Once more all the systems come to an agreement together, adopting as the determinatives of this and the next station the two sides of the well-known constellation called by us the Square in Pegasus. The Hindus treat it as a double asterism, former and latter Bhâdrapadâs, 'auspicious feet,' or Proshthapadâs, 'footstool-feet.' The "former" group is composed of α and β Pegasi; and the same two stars constitute the Arab *manzil* Fargh al-Mukdim, 'fore spout of the water-jar,' and the Chinese *sieu* She, 'house.'

25. The "latter" Bhâdrapadâs of the Hindus are the two stars, γ Pegasi and α Andromedæ, which form the other side of the Square; and they are also the Fargh al-Mukhir, 'hind spout of the water-jar,' of the Arabs, and the Pi, 'wall, partition,' of the Chinese.

26. The Hindus assign to the determining asterism of this station

thirty-two stars, of which ζ Piscium, close upon the ecliptic at the point where this was crossed by the equator of A. D. 570, is defined as the southernmost. We have no means of ascertaining the precise limits of the group; it may probably have reached so far north as to include the Arab and Chinese asterisms. It is named Revatî, 'wealthy.' The Chinese group, Koei, 'striding legs,' is also a very extensive one, of at least sixteen stars, arranged somewhat like a figure 8, and reaching from ψ Piscium up to ν Andromedæ; its principal star, according to Biot, is ζ Andromedæ. The *manzil* Batn al-Hût, 'fish's belly,' or Rishâ, 'band,' contains more or less of the same group, reaching at least far enough north to take in the bright star β Andromedæ; and this star is by some authorities regarded as by itself marking the twenty-sixth station. There is evidently here no essential discordance, although a perplexing disagreement in detail, among the three systems.

27. The accordance in the last two members of the series is as close as could be desired. The Hindus acknowledge as twenty-seventh asterism the two stars β and γ Arietis, in the head of the Ram, calling it Açvinî, 'equestrian,' or Açvayujâu, 'the two horse-harnessers;' the Arabs give to the same pair the name Sharatân, 'the two tokens' (*i. e.*, of the opening year); the Chinese (as do also some Hindu authorities) add α Arietis to the group, and they call it Leu, 'train of a garment.'

28. This station is marked by the little triangle in the northern part of Aries which is known as Musca (or 35, 39, and 41 Arietis): the Hindus call it Bharanî, 'bearer;' the Chinese, Oei, 'belly;'[1] the Arabs, Butain, 'little belly' (*i. e.*, of the Ram) — a name which, to be sure, would be better applicable to a more southern group; and some authorities point out the triangle ε, δ, ρ^3 Arietis as determinant of the station, instead of Musca.

No one, I am confident, can examine this exposition of the correspondences and differences of the three systems without being convinced that they are actually, as claimed above, three derivative forms of the same original. Precisely what this original was, we cannot of course determine; but we may make a plausible approximation toward restoring it by assuming that, wherever two of the three agree as opposed to the third, the latter has deviated

[1] The Chinese names of the sixteenth, seventeenth, and twenty-eighth asterisms are worthy of note, as bearing to the Arabic a relation which can hardly be fortuitous.

from the primitive system, which has been adhered to by the others. In order to present the results of our comparison in a more readily comprehensible shape, I add below a table in which the probable original is in this manner established, and the groups peculiar to each system are given as variations from it. Here such minor discrepancies as those in the number of the stars regarded as composing the asterism are not taken into account.

PRIMITIVE AND MODIFIED FORMS OF THE SYSTEM OF LUNAR ASTERISMS.

Probable original constituents of the system.	Hindu variations.	Arab variations.	Chinese variations.
1. η, etc. Tauri. Pleiades.			
2. α, etc. Tauri. Hyades.			
3. λ, ϕ^1, ϕ^2 Orionis. Head of Orion.			
4. ?	4. α Orionis.	4. η, μ, ν, γ, ξ Geminorum.	4. α, γ, δ, ε, ζ, κ, β Orionis.
5. α, β Geminorum. Castor and Pollux.			5. μ, ν, γ, ε, ζ, etc. Geminorum.
6. γ, δ, etc. Cancri. Belly of Crab.			
7. δ, ε, etc. Hydræ. Head of Hydra.		7. ξ Cancri, λ Leonis.	
8. α Leonis (Regulus) etc. Sickle.			8. α, ι, etc. Hydræ.
9. δ, θ Leonis. Rump of Lion.			9. κ, υ^1, λ, μ, etc. Hydræ.
10. β, 93 Leonis. Tail of Lion.			10. α, β, etc. etc. Crateris.
11. α, ε, γ, etc. Corvi. The Crow.		11. β, η, γ, δ, ε Virginis.	
12. α Virginis. Spica.			
13. λ, κ, ι, etc. Virginis. Edge of Virgin's Robe.	13. α Bootis. Arcturus.		
14. α, β Libræ. Claws of Scorpion.			
15. β, δ, π Scorpionis.			
16. σ, α (Antares), τ Scorpionis. The Scorpion's heart.			
17. ε, μ, ζ, η, θ, ι, κ, λ, υ Scorpionis. Scorpion's tail.			

Probable original constituents of the system.	Hindu variations.	Arab variations.	Chinese variations.
18. δ, ε, etc. Sagittarii. Bow of Sagittary.			
19. σ, ζ, etc. Sagittarii. Left shoulder of Sagittary.		19. Space near π Sagittarii.	
20. α, β Capricorni. Head of Goat.	20. α Lyræ (Vega) etc.		
21. ε, μ, ν Aquarii. Right hand of Waterbearer.	21. α, β, γ Aquilæ.		
22. β, ξ Aquarii. Right shoulder of Waterbearer.	22. α, etc. Delphini.		
23. γ, ζ, η, etc. Aquarii. Left arm of Waterbearer.	23. λ, etc. etc. Aquarii.		23. α Aquarii, θ, ε Pegasi.
24. α, β Pegasi. W. side of Square in Pegasus.			
25. γ Pegasi, α Andromedæ. East side of Square in Pegasus.			
26. Piscis Bor. and left side of Andromeda?	26. ζ, etc. etc. Piscium.	26. β, etc. etc. Andromedæ.	26. ζ, etc. etc. Andromedæ.
27. β, γ Arietis. Left horn of Ram.			
28. 35, 39, 41 Arietis. Musca.			

It will be observed that only one member of the series, the fourth, requires to be marked as altogether questionable, although at another, the twenty-sixth, a mark of doubt has also had to be added. The variations of the Arab *manâzil* are least numerous, and most easily accounted for, as attempted improvements, inspired by the original governing idea, the selection of available groups nearly bordering upon the ecliptic. On the other hand, the Hindu alterations, at numbers thirteen and twenty to twenty-two, are marked violations of the proper design and spirit of the system.

It is not alone in India, Arabia, and China that traces of the lunar zodiac have been found. In the Bundehesh, a work belonging to the later Zoroastrian religion,[1] in the second chapter, where the creation of lights is treated of, we have given us first an enumeration of the twelve signs of the zodiac, with their familiar names, and then a like list of the twenty-eight equal parts (lunar stations) into which these are divided: their designations are in part corrupt and almost altogether obscure, so that no valuable information can be drawn from them. Considering, however, the modern date of the work (it is believed to be not older than the eighth or ninth century of our era), we are not authorized to infer that the institution was known to the ancient Persians — especially as their earlier scriptures contain no allusions to it: it may be a late introduction, from either Arabia or India. Again, Kircher gives[2] the Coptic names of a like series of asterisms as found in Egypt, on a monument of late Roman age; but in the present condition of our knowledge we can make no use of this item for the general history of the institution. Once more, allusions to a like system of division of the heavens have been suspected in the words *mazzaloth* and *mazzaroth* of our Hebrew Bible: words apparently kindred in origin to the Arabic *manzil*, though translated 'planets' (the margin adds "or twelve signs, or constellations") at 2 Kings xxiii. 5, and treated as a proper name (margin, "or the twelve signs") at Job xxxviii. 32; but here, also, the mention is too uncertain, and of too indefinite character, to be made account of in any construction of the history of the lunar zodiac.

In India, the lunar asterisms begin to appear as a system at the end of the Vedic hymn-period: a period, however, of which the chronological date is altogether uncertain.[3] In the Rig-Veda there is but a single mention, of two of them, and that in the tenth book,

[1] See the first volume of these Studies, p. 173.

[2] See Weber's first essay on the *Nakshatras*, in the *Trans. Berlin Acad.* for 1860, p. 330, and Seyffarth in *Proc. Am. Or. Soc.* for 1871, p. vii.

[3] See the previous volume, pp. 21, 73–79.

which is in general of later origin than the rest.[1] In the hymns of the Atharvan they appear more frequently, and in its nineteenth book (also an appendix to the original collection[2]) is once given the whole list, with prayer or praise to each. Similar lists are more than once presented in the prose parts (*brâhmana* passages, or Brâhmanas) of the different divisions of the Yajur-Veda, and in the whole literature of the Brâhmana and Sûtra periods;[3] and at the time of the great grammarian Pânini the *nakshatras* are a familiar institution, and the subject of frequent reference; especially, as having furnished a nomenclature for the months, and therefore requiring to be mentioned whenever the date of a religious ceremony is prescribed.[4]

Upon this point, of the asterismal derivation of the month-names, we must dwell a little, because of its general interest and importance, and the erroneous views which have been held in connection with it. Through all the known periods of Indian history, down even to the present, the current appellations of the lunar periods into which the year is divided have been asterismal, and taken in each case from the *nakshatra* in (or near) which the moon, during that particular synodical revolution, reached her full. Thus, the revolution in which the moon was full in either Ashâdhâ — that is to say, in the Sagittary, the sun being in Gemini — was called Âshâdha; that in which she was full in Virgo (near Citrâ, or Spica Virginis), the sun being in Pisces, was called Câitra: and so of the rest. The significance and appropriateness of such a nomenclature are obvious. There is, however, a practical difficulty in the matter. Owing to the incommensurabilities, already referred to, between the periods of revolution of sun, moon, and earth — to the fact that the number of asterisms is no multiple of that of months

[1] See the previous volume, p. 12. [2] *Ibid.* p. 19. [3] *Ibid.* pp. 66-72.

[4] For the details, see Weber's second essay on the *Nakshatras*, in the *Trans. Berlin Acad.* for 1861.

in the year, and also that there is a remnant of about a third of a synodical revolution required to make a year, over and above twelve — the moon cannot possibly be full in the same series of asterisms two years in succession. In fact, it is on the average only about twice a year that she is full in any asterism in which she was so the preceding year. If we take a series of years and calculate the sidereal place of every full moon in them, we shall find that it occurs with nearly equal frequency in every one of the asterisms. I made such a calculation some years ago, and ascertained that, in the eleven years between the end of 1853 and the beginning of 1865 (reckoning the asterismal portions, according to the later Hindu method, to be explained farther on, as equal twenty-seventh parts of the ecliptic), the moon was full five times in each of fourteen asterisms, four times in each of six, and six times in each of seven.[1] If, then, the rule for naming the month from the full-moon asterism were strictly applied, the nomenclature would be in a constant state of flux, only two or three months retaining the same appellation for two years together. To avoid this troublesome confusion, the Hindus had to make a selection; and this they appear to have done at the very outset: even in the earliest of the Brâhmanas, the month date is always given by the same asterism as at present. The asterisms chosen as the basis of the nomenclature are (according to the numbers assigned to them above) the first, third, sixth, eighth, tenth (or ninth), twelfth, fourteenth, sixteenth, eighteenth (or nineteenth), twenty-first, twenty-fourth (or twenty-fifth), and twenty-seventh; and the names of the months derived from them (commencing with the one that begins in our January) are as follows: Mâgha, Phâlguna, Câitra, Vâiçâkha, Jyâishtha, Âshâdha, Çrâvana, Bhâdra-

[1] See *Journ. Am. Or. Society*, viii. (1864), 69, 70. In the whole period there were twenty-three cases of full moon occurring in the same asterism in two successive years; in three successive years, not a single case.

pada (earlier Prâushthapada), Âçvina (earlier Âçvayuja), Kârttika, Mârgaçîrsha, and Pâusha (or Tâisha).

The question now arises, how and why this particular series was selected.

The hope has been ardently cherished, by some scholars of great eminence, that the nomenclature might be able to furnish to the astronomical calculator the date of its fixation, the time being rigidly determined at which it would have been applicable to the series of months in a year, or in a number of successive or frequently recurring years. Sir William Jones hints at this, when he states ("As. Researches," ii. 296) it to be an assertion of the Hindus "that, when their lunar year was arranged by former astronomers, the moon was at the full in each month on the very day when it entered the *nakshatra* from which that month is denominated." As the moon spends only a day in each asterism, there is no significance in the special form of statement here adopted; it means simply that the moon's full took place in the denominating *nakshatra* itself, not in the latter's neighborhood merely. The noted Bentley, most reckless and untrustworthy of all writers on Hindu astronomy, by introducing into the premises of the inquiry one of his characteristic and groundless assumptions—namely, that "the month Çrâvana always began at the summer solstice"—contrives to infer that the names must have been fixed at any rate not earlier than 1181 B. C.[1] And even Weber, as late as 1865,[2] cannot bear to give up the expectation of finding here, what is so rare and so precious in Hindu history, a determinate date.

But the difficulties in the way of deriving such a date are obvious and insuperable. In the first place, an ascertainment by a rigid astronomical calculation would imply that the ancient Hindus of the Vedic and Brâhmanic

[1] See *Journ. Am. Or. Soc.* viii. 85.

[2] See his *Ind. Studien*, ix. 455, 456.

periods were skilled astronomers, furnished with instruments of precision, so that they were able to determine with absolute correctness the moment of full moon, and the limits of the various parts of the moon's path belonging to the several asterisms. But such an assumption would be without any foundation. We shall see presently that even the later Hindus, after they had learned scientific astronomy from the Greeks, could not determine the places of a series of stars about the heavens without committing errors of mutual distance rising to five degrees; and all probabilities lead us to the view that, when first devised or introduced, the system of asterisms was nothing more than a means of rudely marking to the unassisted eye the regions of the heavens, and of allowing the revolution of the moon or any other planet to be approximately followed and described. The Hindus of that period might have regarded the moon as within the limits of a certain asterism when she was in fact some distance outside of them, according to any theoretical system of division of the ecliptic; they might have regarded her as at her full when she was really some hours distant from it. In the period for which, as above stated, I calculated all the asterismal places of full moon, there were two years which might well enough have suggested the very series of names adopted by the Hindus, the moon coming into opposition within the denominating asterism in all but one or two cases, and in those cases so near to its borders that observers by the eye alone might well enough have overlooked the discrepancy. And then, in the second place, when the year that precisely suited the nomenclature should be by any means found, the Metonic cycle of nineteen years, which brings around a closely approximate rectification of the discrepancies of solar and lunar motion, would cause its recurrence at stated intervals for a considerable period.

There is, so far as I can see, but one way, and that a very easy one, of solving all these difficulties: by supposing, namely, that the Hindus had a calendar, reckoning by lunar periods and governing by them the order of their religious ceremonies, either before their acceptance of the system of lunar asterisms or before they thought of making it the basis of a nomenclature for the months; and that, when this nomenclature suggested itself to them, involving the selection of certain denominating asterisms, they simply made the selection, as a practical necessity, and without any scrupulousness as to its precise adaptation to the conditions of a given year — a scrupulousness which would have been nothing less than overstrained, considering that it could never have precise adaptation to any two years in succession. The series adopted was no better, and no worse, than any other that might have been pitched upon; and we may be content to approve the practical good sense which pitched upon it and adhered to it, nor strive to find beneath it a profound scientific reason which never can have been there to discover.

There are traces of other systems of month-names to be found in the Hindu writings of various periods;[1] but they are not known to have been ever practically used; and Weber regards it as questionable whether they are not of merely artificial origin.

Turning, now, from this department of the history of the lunar zodiac in India, we find the *nakshatras* again making an appearance, and in a manner from which very important conclusions have been drawn, in the Jyotisha. The Jyotisha is a brief astronomical treatise, of unknown date and in great part of difficult and problematical content, generally regarded as attaching itself to the canonical literature of the Rig and Yajur Vedas, and as helping to determine the times of sacrifice.[2] Its main point is the

[1] See Weber's second essay on the *nakshatras*, p. 349 *seq.*

[2] It has been published by Weber, in the *Trans. Berlin Acad.* for 1862, along with its commentary, and with a translation and notes.

establishment of a *yuga* or *lustrum*, a cycle of five years, in order to the due reconciliation of solar and lunar reckoning: a result, however, which its methods are wholly incompetent to attain. But its most pregnant historical datum is involved in its assertion that the cycle begins with the month Mâgha, at the time when the sun and moon commence their revolution together in the asterism Çravishthâ (the twenty-second of the series, as given above); and that their movement northward in the heavens (from the winter solstice) is from the beginning of the same asterism, while the southern movement of the sun (from the summer solstice) takes place from the middle of Âçleshâ (seventh asterism) — that is to say, that the solstitial colure cut the ecliptic at that period at the beginning of Çravishthâ and the middle of Âçleshâ. If, then, it be possible to determine precisely where in the sky these two points are, nothing can be easier than to calculate the time of the observation, since we know that the colure moves eastward about one degree in every seventy-two years. But before we can approach the question of position, we need to examine a little the later history of Hindu astronomy.

As a scientific system, dealing with exact data by exact methods, the Hindu astronomy is represented to us by a body of works called Siddhântas. A considerable number of these are asserted to have been formerly in existence, but hardly more than half a dozen are now obtainable. For some of them is claimed a divine origin and immemorial antiquity; others are ascribed to ancient and half-mythical authors; yet others, to men whose individuality is undoubted and whose period is well known. The latest author of this third class is Bhâskara, who composed his Siddhânta-Çiromani in the twelfth century; his most noted predecessors are Brahmagupta, of the seventh century, Varâha-Mihira, of the sixth, and Âryabhata, of the fifth and sixth. A principal representative of the first class is the Sûrya-Siddhânta, 'Siddhânta of the Sun,' professing to have been revealed by the Sun himself to a semi-divine being, who then communicated it to men. It is the only work of the whole Siddhânta literature which has yet been completely published, translated, and commented.[1]

So far as has yet come to light (and there is no reason to suppose that further investigation will alter the aspect of the case), the system in all the Siddhântas is, notwithstanding differences of detail, essentially one and the same. They establish as its basis an immense structure of chronological periods — namely, the Æon (*kalpa*), of 4,320,000,000 years, and the Great Age (*mahâyuga*), of 4,320,000, with its subdivisions, of which the current one, the Iron Age (*kaliyuga*), or last section of the present Great Age,[2] is reckoned to have begun February 18th, 3102 B. C., at midnight or at sunrise on the meridian of Ujjayinî (or Ojein). And they teach that all the planets, and all their apsides and nodes, entered upon their motion of revolution together, at the commencement of the Æon, from a common starting-point, the beginning of the asterism Açvinî (at or close upon the faint star ζ

[1] The text edition is by Professor F. E. Hall, in the series of the *Bibliotheca Indica*, at Calcutta; the translation, etc., by myself, in the *Journ. Am. Or. Soc.* vol. vi. (1860). It is proper, namely, that I here acknowledge, as properly belonging to myself, the entire responsibility for that publication, in all its parts (except the concluding note by Mr. Burgess). Important aid was rendered me at one and another point by Professor Hadley; and also especially (as acknowledged in the preface and elsewhere), by Professor Newton, who was my constant adviser and frequent collaborator, and to whose mathematical and astronomical knowledge is due a very large share of whatever merit may belong to the work. A bare version of the text of the Sûrya-Siddhânta was also given in the *Bibl. Indica* (1860), by a Hindu scholar, Bâpû Deva, who likewise edited in the same volume of the series Wilkinson's translation of a part of the Siddhânta-Çiromanî. The text of this last mentioned comparatively recent and very comprehensive treatise (it includes also arithmetic and algebra) has been more than once printed in India, and its mathematical section, the Lîlâvatî, was worked up by Colebrooke in 1817.

[2] The current Great Age began after 1,969,056,000 years of the current Æon had elapsed. The three preceding sections of this Great Age contained 3,888,000 years. See, for details, the notes to the first chapter of the *Sûrya-Siddhânta*.

Piscium), and that they all revolve a given number of times in the Æon, so that at its close they will again come to a universal conjunction at the same point in the heavens.[1] Further, the numbers are so arranged that there is brought about a conjunction of the planets here (according to two or three authorities, indeed, only an extremely near approach to it) at the beginning of the present Iron Age, or 3102 B. C. The fair inference seems to be that this last date is the real epoch of the whole system, a point of time at which the Hindu astronomers supposed or assumed the planets to have been in conjunction at the initial point of their zodiacal reckoning; and that they constructed their statements with reference to such an assumption.[2] How artificial and unscientific this framework of periods and recurring conjunctions is, does not require to be pointed out; but its character will be more distinctly brought to light by a brief consideration of the revolutions of planetary apsides and nodes. As these elements of the moon's orbit do actually revolve, and with conspicuous rapidity, it seems to have been thought necessary, for the sake of uniformity, that those of the other heavenly bodies should be made to do the same. Accordingly, each has its defined number of circuits in the Æon; but a number so small that it takes millions of years to accomplish any circuit, and the resulting movement is almost infinitesimal; many thousand years would be required in order to bring about a change of position of the least practical value. And, what is the most telling circumstance about it all, the different text-books, while they vary considerably in the number of revolutions which they prescribe during the Æon, yet

[1] According to the data of a part of the authorities, including the Sûrya-Siddhânta, a general conjunction of the planets at this point recurs at the end of every 1,080,000 years.

[2] In fact (see note to *Sûrya-Siddhânta*, i. 34), the moon was at the time only 1½ degree from the assumed point; the sun, less than 8 degrees; the other planets, from 8½ degrees to 41 degrees.

manage all of them to leave the same odd remainder of a revolution, which determines the present position. Thus, for example, the revolutions of Jupiter's apsides since the beginning of the present Æon have been, according to four different treatises, 407, 390, 378, and 448, respectively: but the remaining fragment varies in them all only between the limits one hundred and seventy-one degrees and one hundred and seventy-two and three-fourths degrees; and it gives a position swerving less than three degrees from the true one.[1]

Having these data, and having them with a very near approach to truth,[2] the Hindu astronomer is able to determine with tolerable accuracy the place of a given planet at a given time, and to predict and calculate eclipses.[3]

Their calculations are made by the aid of a system of epicycles, essentially identical with the well-known Greek system of Ptolemy. And in solving the problems of trigonometry, they use a table of sines, of values very fairly correct; the implied relation of diameter to circumference is 1: 3.14136. Their arithmetical methods are extremely simple; the simple proportion ("rule of three"), and the equivalence of the square of the hypothenuse to the sum of the squares of the two legs in a right-angled triangle, answering almost every purpose.

We may now inquire, of what age is this system, and of what origin? As bearing upon the first matter, its age, the most telling single fact is its recognition of ζ Piscium

1 See *Sûrya-Siddhânta*, note to i. 44.

2 See *Sûrya-Siddhânta*, note to i. 34. The Hindu year is too long by nearly three minutes and a half; but the moon's revolution is right within a second; those of Mercury, Venus, and Mars, within a few minutes; that of Jupiter, within six or seven hours; that of Saturn, within six days and a half.

3 See the calculation of two eclipses in the additional notes to the *Sûrya-Siddhânta*. The lunar eclipse of February 6, 1860, their rules determine within half an hour of the true time; but they unluckily make it total instead of partial, and of duration too long by three quarters of an hour. For the solar eclipse of May 26, 1854, my calculation finds their elements a little more out of the way; but the value of the result was vitiated by my leaving uncorrected some of the errors of Mr. Burgess's Hindu assistant.

as the vernal equinox, the initial point of the sphere, the point from which all the motions of the heavenly bodies began, and from which all calculations of their position are to proceed. We can see no reason for attributing such importance to this star except its actual coincidence with, or its near proximity to, the equinox at the time when the system was constructed. And it had that position in the sixth century of our era (its year of no longitude is A. D. 572). We know that no star can retain continuously the place of initial point of the sphere, owing to the movement of precession; but it appears likely that the element of the precession was overlooked or ignored by the first Hindu astronomers;[1] and when they came to work it into their system, they described it as a libratory movement, a swinging backward and forward through an arc of 54°, or to a distance of 27° in each direction from the permanent initial point; thus assuring to the latter its importance undiminished.[2]

While this fact might have but an inferior value if directly opposed by other evidences, or if the general probabilities were strongly against it, it is of a decisive importance when supported by both — as is in fact the case. The oldest genuine names in the Hindu astronomical literature, as we have seen above, are of that period; and there is nothing whatever in the more ancient literature of the Hindus, or in their character and the work done by them in other departments, which should lead us to suppose them to have been earlier in possession of a science like this — a science of acute and long-continued observation and of skilled and trained deduction — or to have had

[1] I have shown, I think, pretty clearly, in the note to *Sûrya-Siddhânta*, iii. 12, that this treatise originally made no account of the precession; the single passage in which it is, most blindly and awkwardly, defined and directed to be "applied wherever needed," being an after-thought and an interpolation.

[2] The period of a complete libration, through 108°, is 7,200 years, according to the Sûrya-Siddhânta, and the yearly motion 54″. The true rate at present is about 50¼″.

at any period the ability to give birth to it. The clear light of modern investigation has forever dispelled the wild dreams of men like Bailly, who could believe India to have been the primitive home of human knowledge and culture. It has been declared by Weber, the most competent of Indian scholars to pronounce upon such a point, and without contradiction from any quarter, that no mention even of the lesser planets is to be found in Hindu literature until the modern epoch, after the influence of foreign astronomical science began to be felt. If, then, we find such a science making its sudden appearance in India at so late a period, we cannot help turning our eyes abroad to see whence it should have come. Nor can we long remain doubtful as to where it originated.

The suggestion that the Hindus might probably have borrowed the foundations of their astronomy from the Greeks was first distinctly made by the illustrious Colebrooke; and the evidence confirmatory of his view has gone on accumulating, until its truth may now be regarded as fully established, no person of sufficient information and competent judgment being found any longer to question it. I will refer here to only an item or two.[1]

There are not only western ideas, but Greek words, in the very centre and citadel of the Hindu science. The Hindu circle is divided like our own: only the names of the signs, meaning 'Ram,' 'Bull,' 'Twins,' and so on, are applied, not generally to the regions in the sky marked by the constellations so designated, but to the first, second, third, etc., arcs of 30° each, counting from any given point. And the second of arc, the quantity most often and familiarly used, is called by a Greek name, *liptâ* (from λεπτόν). Again, the planets are regularly mentioned and referred to in the Siddhântas in the order in which they succeed one another as regents of the days

[1] The case is summed up more fully in the last additional note to the *Sûrya-Siddhânta*.

(Sun, Moon, Mars, Mercury, Jupiter, Venus, Saturn: the same order which gave their Latin names, and secondarily our own, to the days of the week); but the regent of the day is determined by the regent of its first twenty-fourth part or hour; and the hour is no ancient or current division of the day in India; it appears only in connection with this particular astrological institution; and it, likewise, has a Greek name, *horâ* (*i. e.* ὥρα).[1] Once more, the name for a planet's mean anomaly — that is to say, the place of the *centre* of its epicycle — on which depends the whole process of determination of its position, is known as its *kendra;* and this, too, is no Sanskrit word, but simply a transfer of the Greek κέντρον. Add to these evidences the frequent notices found in early Hindu commentaries upon astronomical works of valuable knowledge derived from the Yavanas ('Ionians,' or Greeks, or westerners in general), the traces of western names among the titles of the Siddhântas themselves (as the Pauliça-Siddhânta, directly ascribed by an Arab author to "Paulus the Greek;" and the Romaka-Siddhânta), and their mention of Romaka-city — *i. e.* Rome — as the metropolis of the west (even the Sûrya-Siddhânta is said in some manuscripts of its text to have been revealed there), and, in the absence of rebutting testimony, the question of origin must be looked upon as settled beyond controversy.

The communication of Greek astronomy to India probably took place in connection with the lively commercial intercourse carried on during the first centuries of our era between Alexandria, as the port and mart of Rome, and the western coast of India: whether through the medium of Hindus who visited the Mediterranean, or of learned Greeks who made the voyage to India, or by the translation of Greek treatises, or in what other way,

[1] See note to *Sûrya-Siddhânta*, i. 52, where it is shown how the Hindus have no week, although they name the days precisely as we do.

it were useless to conjecture. Its gradual working over into the form characteristic of the Hindu system may have been the work of generations; and of the shapes which it wore prior to its complete development (which must have been as early as the fifth or sixth century) we have no sufficient record left us.

After this long but necessary digression, we are ready to return to the subject of the lunar zodiac, in order to see in what shape it presents itself in the modern astronomical system. I follow here the teachings of the Sûrya-Siddhânta, with which those of the other astronomical text-books are believed to accord in all essential respects.

In the Siddhânta, all signs of any special connection between the moon and the *nakshatras* have entirely disappeared. The moon is now only one of a class, the planets, and from the astronomical point of view they are all to be treated alike. After the rules for finding the true longitude of a planet have been given, we are told that the "portion" (*bhoga*) of an asterism is 800′ of arc (13° 20′); and that, in order to find in what asterism any given planet is, the longitude of the latter, reduced to minutes, must be divided by 800; which will determine the asterism, and the point in it, occupied by the planet; and that hence, by means of the ascertained rate of daily motion of the planet, may be calculated the time it has spent, and has yet to spend, in the asterism. This obviously implies a division of the ecliptic into twenty-seven equal parts ($360° \div 27 = 13\frac{1}{3}°$), each of which has the name of an asterism, and is regarded as the share of the planetary path belonging to that asterism. This is the only rule given us for ascertaining the presence of a planet in an asterism: if we wish to know when the sun and moon are together in Çravishthâ, or the sun in the middle of Âçleshâ, or the moon in Rohinî, this is the method which we must follow. So far, then, we have only a transfer to the closet, and a deduction by arithmetical methods from exact data, of a process and result which in the olden time were matters of direct observation in the heavens. But in a later part of the treatise the planets and *nakshatras* are brought into relation with one another in a different and additional way. The seventh chapter takes up the subject of planetary conjunctions. Two planets, as we see from the rules laid down, are said to be in conjunction (*yoga*) with one another at the instant when they are upon the same secondary to the prime vertical, or upon the same great circle passing through the north and south points of the horizon. As data for the calculation are to be found the longitude and latitude of the two planets; and the process is an intricate, awkward, and inaccurate one. Its object is purely astrological; the conjunction receives its name and value from the degree of approach of the two heavenly bodies, their relative position, and their comparative brilliancy. In the succeeding chapter, then, entitled "chapter of the conjunction of asterisms and planets," the Siddhânta goes on to teach us how to determine the instant of a like momentary conjunction, on a secondary to the prime vertical, of a given planet with the asterisms. The rules being already known, it was only necessary to give further a definition of the positions of the asterisms. This is done in a peculiar manner: the star intended is referred to the ecliptic by an hour-circle, and its distance from the ecliptic upon that circle, and of that circle upon the ecliptic from the initial point of the sphere, are noted and defined. The former is called the *vikshepa* ('removal': *i. e.* from the ecliptic) of the asterism; the term is the same one that is employed for the latitude of a planet: the latter is called its *dhruva*, 'fixed, unchanging, immovable (place)' — that is to say, while the planets are ever changing position, and their longitude has to be calculated for any given moment, the longitude of the asterism is fixed; its place can be laid down once for all.[1] The same data are later directed to be employed in fixing the times of heliacal setting and rising of the asterisms; other than these, no uses of them are anywhere hinted at.

But the asterisms are well known to be in most cases constellations or groups, and not single stars; how then does their position admit of being defined in the manner here described? A passage in the latter part of the same chapter clears up this difficulty, by informing us to which star in each group the exact definition of position applies: which is its *yoga-târâ*, 'junction-star,' or star selected to represent it in the calculation of a conjunction (*yoga*). And the positions of half a dozen other prominent single stars are defined in the same manner, and for a similar purpose.

This is the whole story of the *nakshatras*, as read in the Sûrya-Siddhânta. And the value and relation of its different parts seem obvious enough. We have the lunar zodiac retained to answer its old purpose, the definition of planetary places in the ecliptic, with all that follows therefrom; only that the revolution effected in the character of astronomical science makes those places now ascertainable by calculation, instead of by observation. But we have a new use and application added, of a purely astrological nature. If the mutual aspects of the planets, as they pass nearest to one another in the sky, are of importance enough to be calculated and defined, then also, naturally enough, the like aspects of the planets and of those groups of stars which have from time immemorial been the object of careful observation and of especial reverence. It was of consequence to know not only, for example, when the moon was within the arc of $13\frac{1}{3}°$ named Citrâ, but also when she was closest to the star

[1] The fact that, in thus "fixing" the place of the asterism, the precession, which is all the time changing both its longitude and its latitude, is left out of account, is one of the important supporting circumstances to the view laid down above, that the Hindu system at the outset ignored the precession.

(Spica Virginis) that gave the name. And the observation and record of the "fixed" place of the star gave the means of making this determination (so it was imagined) for all time. Hence the series of measurements laid down in the Siddhântas. The process involved the choice out of each group of a single star, usually the brightest of the group, as its representative; and the name given to the one selected, "junction-star (*yogatârâ*) of the asterism," is clear evidence both of the selection and of its purpose. How unconscious the Siddhânta is of any clashing between the two uses is shown by the fact that it describes the one upon the basis of the other. It defines, namely (by the odd but characteristic device of giving a number which when multiplied by ten will furnish the distance in minutes from the initial point of the portion), the place of the junction-star in the asterismal portion bearing the same name. But in a little series of three or four asterisms toward the end of the system there is a practical difficulty: the groups formerly selected by the eye to mark the successive divisions turn out, when measured by accurate astronomical methods, to have such a position that their principal stars fall outside the divisions bearing their names respectively. This is passed over, however, as of no real consequence; the text reads (with our explanatory insertions in brackets): "[the junction-star of] latter Ashâdhâ goes at the middle of the portion of former Ashâdhâ; [that of] Abhijit also is at the end of [the portion of] former Ashâdhâ; the place of [the junction-star of] Çravana is at the end of [the portion of] latter Ashâdhâ; [the junction-star of] Çravishthâ, again, is where the third and fourth quarters of [the portion of] Çravana meet."

This passage likewise shows clearly which of the twenty-eight asterisms, in the division of the ecliptic into twenty-seven portions, is left without a portion. It is Abhijit, or α, ϵ, and ζ Lyræ, the most distant northern member of the system. Something like this has been its treatment from the very beginning of the history of the system in India; in the very oldest lists it is now found inserted, and now omitted. The point is one to which we shall have occasion to return hereafter.

The peculiar way in which the positions of the junction-stars are defined seems almost necessarily to imply an observation of the intervals of their meridian transits, with determination of their declination, which latter was then reduced to *vikshepa*, or distance from the ecliptic, by calculating the declination of the ecliptic at the point in question, and combining the two by addition or subtraction. We may not speak as with certainty respecting this, because we know very little of the ancient Hindu methods of observation. The Siddhântas are liberal enough in giving rules for calculating, but very much the reverse as to rules for observing. Their science is not a science of observation; it is a system whose data are absolute and perfect, handed down from inspired sages, or revealed by divine beings; the student is to take it, and deduce everything from it in his closet; to send him to the heavens to collect facts for new deductions would be to imply a doubt as to the authority of his teachers. So far as is known, the astronomical literature contains no record of any native Hindu observations, with the exception of these defined positions of the junction-stars of the asterisms, along with those of the half-dozen other stars already referred to. A peculiar interest, therefore, belongs to these, as the only accessible tests of the capacity of the Hindus as observers. Moreover, there should be derivable from them some conclusion as to the time when they were made. I give, therefore, the following table,[1] in which the longitudes and latitudes of the junction-stars, as calculated from the Hindu data by the rules of our spherical trigonometry, are presented, and compared with the true longitudes and latitudes, as

[1] Taken without alteration from the notes to the eighth chapter of the *Sûrya-Siddhânta*.

determined by modern science.[1] The reference is to the equinox of A. D. 560, because that is, according to the Sûrya-Siddhânta, the initial point of the sphere. All authorities, namely, make this point coincide with the end of Revatî and the beginning of Açvinî; but while some declare the division-line to be precisely at the southernmost or junction-star of Revatî — namely, ζ Piscium — the Sûrya-Siddhânta and at least one other fix it 10′ east of that star. The resulting discordance of a dozen years is of no account whatever in judging a question as to observations so rude as we shall find these to be.

Positions, and Errors of Position, of the Junction-Stars of the Asterisms.[2]

No.	Name.	Longitude, A. D. 560.			Latitude.			Star compared.
		Hindu	True.	Hindu error.	Hindu.	True.	Hindu error.	
		° ′	° ′	° ′	° ′	° ′	° ′	
1	Krittikâ,	39 8	39 58	—0 50	4 44 N.	4 1 N.	+0 43	η Tauri, Alcyone.
2	Rohinî,	48 9	49 45	—1 36	4 49 S.	5 30 S.	+0 41	α Tauri, Aldebaran.
3	Mrigaçirsha,	61 3	63 40	—2 37	9 49 "	13 25 "	+3 36	λ Orionis.
4	Ardrâ,	65 50	68 43	—2 53	8 53 "	16 4 "	+7 11	α Orionis.
5	Punarvasu,	92 52	93 14	—0 22	6 0 N.	6 39 N.	—0 39	β Gemin., Pollux.
6	Pushya,	106 0	108 42	—2 42	0 0	0 4 "	—0 4	δ Cancri.
7	Açleshâ,	109 59	112 20	—2 21	6 56 S.	11 8 S.	+4 12	ε Hydræ.
8	Maghâ,	129 0	129 49	—0 49	0 0	0 27 N.	—0 27	α Leonis, Regulus.
9	P.-Phalgunî,	139 58	141 15	—1 17	11 19 N.	14 19 "	—3 0	δ Leonis.
10	U.-Phalgunî,	150 10	151 37	—1 27	12 5 "	12 17 "	—0 12	β Leonis.
11	Hasta,	174 22	173 27	+0 55	10 6 S.	12 10 S.	+2 4	δ Corvi.
12	Citrâ,	180 48	183 49	—3 1	1 50 "	2 2 "	+0 12	α Virginis, Spica.
13	Svâti,	183 2	184 12	—1 10	33 50 N.	30 57 N.	+2 53	α Bootis, Arcturus.
14	Viçâkhâ,	213 31	211 0	+2 31	1 25 S.	1 48 S.	+0 23	ι Libræ.
15	Anurâdhâ,	224 44	222 34	+2 10	2 52 "	1 57 "	—0 55	δ Scorpionis.
16	Jyeshthâ,	230 7	229 44	+0 23	3 50 "	4 31 "	+0 41	α Scorp., Antares.
17	Mûla,	242 52	244 33	—1 41	8 48 "	13 44 "	+4 56	λ Scorpionis.
18	P.-Ashâdhâ,	254 39	254 32	+0 7	5 28 "	6 25 "	+0 57	δ Sagittarii.
19	U.-Ashâdhâ,	260 23	262 21	—1 58	4 59 "	3 24 "	—1 25	σ Sagittarii.
20	Abhijit,	264 10	265 16	—1 6	59 58 N.	61 43 N.	—1 48	α Lyræ, Vega.
21	Çravana,	282 29	281 41	+0 48	29 54 "	29 19 "	+0 35	α Aquilæ, Atair.
22	Çravishthâ,	296 5	296 19	—0 14	35 33 "	31 57 "	+3 30	β Delphini.
23	Çatabhishaj,	319 50	321 33	—1 43	0 28 S.	0 23 S.	—0 5	λ Aquarii.
24	P.-Bhâdrapadâ,	331 25	333 27	+0 58	22 30 N.	19 25 N.	+3 5	α Pegasi.
25	U.-Bhâdrapadâ,	347 16	349 8	—1 52	24 1 "	25 41 "	—1 40	γ Peg. & α Androm.
26	Revatî,	359 50	359 50	0 0	0 0	0 13 S.	+0 13	ζ Piscium.
27	Açvinî,	11 59	13 56	—1 57	9 11 N.	8 28 N.	+0 43	β Arietis.
28	Bharanî,	24 35	26 54	—2 19	11 6 "	11 17 "	—0 11	35 Arietis, α Muscæ.

[1] They are taken, for convenience, from Flamsteed. In a comparison in which a high degree of accuracy was desired, and was not in the nature of the case unattainable, it would be necessary to take into account the proper motions of the stars compared. This has not been done. But I may remark that the junction-star of the 13th asterism, Arcturus, has a much greater proper motion than any other in the series; and that, if this were allowed for, according to its value as determined by Main, the Hindu error of longitude would be diminished about 22′, but the error of latitude increased about 35′.

[2] The identification of the junction-star is not in every case of equal certainty;

The different text-books are not precisely accordant in their definitions of the position of these stars. But their variations do not at all appear to be such as might be due to different sets of measurements, made at different times. By far the most important among them relates to the place of Citrâ (Spica), which, as the table shows, presents the extreme of error in one direction, being set full three degrees too far to the westward. Except the Sûrya-Siddhânta and its echo, the Çâkalya-Sanhitâ, the other treatises correct this error, by giving Citrâ 183° instead of 180° of longitude. It may be justifiable to conjecture here that the Sûrya-Siddhânta and its supporters could not resist the temptation to regard the autumnal equinox as exactly, instead of only approximately, marked by this brilliant star, and so were led to alter the true figure.

There is no apparent relation to be discovered among the errors of longitude in the table, such as should point us to any particular star as having been taken for the starting-point, the errors increasing as they depart from it in either direction. We have assumed the determination of ζ Piscium to be the correct one, and have stated the errors as they appear with reference to that assumption, and to the date involved in it. But this is only a provisional proceeding; in our present ignorance of the mode of operation of the observers, we should be equally justified in taking any other star for the starting-point, and making a new statement of the errors, with reference to it. And we should derive from each in succession a different date as that of the measurement, and a different position for the dividing lines of the asterismal portions. Thus, Citrâ (Spica) would yield A. D. 344 as the date when it was at the autumnal equinox, and would move

for the details as to all I must again refer to the notes to the *Sûrya-Siddhânta.* In a single case (25th asterism), the longitude of one star and the latitude of another is compared: see as above. In the column of Hindu error in latitude, north direction is regarded as positive, and south direction as negative.

all the division lines 3° farther east; while Viçâkhâ (ι Libræ) would give A. D. 740 as the time when it had 213° 31′ of longitude, and would shift the divisions 2½° farther west, or 5½° west of those derived from Citrâ. These are the two extremes, and they allow us a range of four centuries for the time of measurement, and of 5½° for the positions of dividing lines: the others would dot over the intervals pretty thickly: thus, Mrigaçîrsha would yield us 371, Rohinî 445, Hasta 626 A. D., and so on. Still, the table shows a marked preponderance of *minus* errors, their sum being 33° 54′, while the sum of *plus* errors is only 7° 52′. On taking the difference of these sums, and dividing it by 28, we find the average error of longitude to be−56′, the greatest deviation from it in either direction being—2° 4′ and +3° 27′. So far as the evidence, then, of a general average of the determinations goes, it would indicate that the Hindu measurements of position were made from a vernal equinox situated about 1° to the eastward of that of A. D. 560, and therefore belonging nearly to the year 490. Yet it would be very ill-judged to lay any stress whatever upon this last date, or to speak otherwise than loosely of results where the data are so rude. The errors of latitude are too considerable and irregular, and belong to an element too slowly and slightly affected by the precession, to be worth averaging at all. We can only notice that the worst of them are committed in the measurement of southern latitudes of some amount, and are in the same direction, giving the star a place too far northward. And our final conclusion must be that the observations for position of the junction-stars may have been made in any one of several centuries, from the fourth to the seventh, or during the whole of that period in which, as above stated, the Hindu astronomical system was taking shape.

In the case of the seven other stars (Canopus, Sirius, Capella, β Tauri, δ Aurigæ, and δ and θ Virginis) of which the Siddhânta gives the position, the range of errors is even considerably greater;[1] as if the work were done later, by a more unskillful hand.

We are now at last prepared to take up the question as to the date derivable for the period of the Jyotisha from the position of the solstitial colure as stated in that little work (above, p. 365). On the basis of an equal division of the ecliptic into twenty-seven asterismal portions of 13⅓° each, which obviously underlies that statement, the solstitial colure cutting the ecliptic at the beginning of Çravishthâ and middle of Âçleshâ, the equinoxes would evidently be, the vernal at the end of the third quarter of Bharanî, the autumnal at the end of the first quarter of Viçâkhâ. If, then, we make the assumption (the propriety of which will be discussed farther on) that the limits of the asterisms were the same in the earlier system as in the later, we shall see plainly enough that the equinoxes of the two systems are 1¾ asterismal portions, or 23⅓°, apart; and hence, that their difference of epoch, at 1° of precession to 72 years, is (72×23⅓) 1680 years; and it would follow that the epoch of the Jyotisha is (1680 — 560) 1120 B. C. Or, if we take the average period as derived above from the errors of position of the junction-stars, we shall arrive at an earlier point in the same century (1680 — 490 = 1190 B. C.). Or, once more, if we assume each successive junction-star to be absolutely correct, and make the comparison and deduction of earlier epoch from that alone, we shall arrive at the same variety of results as for the later epoch, dotting here and there a period of four centuries, between 1336 and 940 B. C.

All these methods, now, have been applied by different calculators, in their attempts to find a date for the Jyotisha. Sir William Jones took the general difference of 1¾ asterisms, and its resulting interval of 1680 years; but he reckoned the interval backward from an assumed

[1] See note to *Sûrya-Siddhânta*, viii. 21.

period of the astronomer Varâha-Mihira, A. D. 499, and so arrived at (1680 — 499) 1181 B. C. Archdeacon Pratt, in 1862 ("Journ. As. Soc. Bengal," xxxi. 49 *seq.*), made instead a selection of the junction-star of the asterism Maghâ (α Leonis or Regulus), and arrived, curiously enough, though by a totally different process, at precisely the same date, 1181 B. C. This choice on the part of Mr. Pratt was, on the whole, a lucky hit, but I do not see that it was anything more. He does not at all examine the set of positions of which this is one, determine their relative value, and pick out intelligently the one which will best serve his purpose. So far as is to be gathered from his statements, he is guided to his selection only by the facts that Regulus is a bright star and close to the ecliptic, and that it is in the next asterism to that in which was the defined position of the summer solstice. But if he had taken instead Citrâ (Spica), which is also a star of first magnitude, and on both ecliptic and equator, or the junction-stars of either the solstitial asterism itself or the one on the other side of it from Maghâ (namely, Pushya, δ Cancri), his calculation would have given him the fourteenth century instead of the twelfth B. C. It cannot be claimed, then, that Mr. Pratt's process has any sufficient scientific basis; even Sir W. Jones's is to be preferred to it. Mr. Davis, however, one of the oldest and best of the students of Hindu astronomy, was much more unlucky in making a similar arbitrary selection. He took Citrâ (Spica Virginis), according to the definition of its position given in the Sûrya-Siddhânta; and he arrived at 1391 B. C. No star more ill-suited to his purpose could have been taken; since, as the table shows, Citrâ offers the extreme of divergence in one direction from the average; and, as I have pointed out above, its place is fixed by the majority of the Hindu text-books 3° farther west. And Colebrooke[1] followed the lead of Davis; his state-

[1] As has been shown by his son, Sir T. E. Colebrooke, *Journ. Roy. As. Soc.* i. (1865), 335 *seq.*

ment[1] in his famous essay on the Vedas, after giving the datum from the Jyotisha, that "such was the position of those cardinal points in the fourteenth century before the Christian era," has no other basis.

But there is another and still more fundamental error committed by all these calculators. They assume unquestioningly two things which are not only very questionable, but even, in my opinion, absolutely inadmissible: 1st, that the older Hindus of the period of the Jyotisha had a precise determination of the limits of their asterismal portions; and 2d, that these limits coincided with those of the later system. As to the first point, if the later generation, which had been trained in the exact processes of the Greek astronomy, could not make a better series of observations around the heavens than one which implied a fluctuation of full 5° in the position of the dividing lines of the ecliptic, it is not less than absurd to claim that they were more skillful fifteen centuries earlier. We have no good reason to suppose that in the Jyotisha time the groups were anything more than constellations determining by their proximity, and to the eye alone, the successive divisions of the ecliptic. He who employed them knew well enough that the "beginning of Çravishthâ" and the "middle of Âçleshâ" were, by the theory of the method of division, opposite points in the sky; but he never would have thought of trying to find them by reckoning from a fixed initial-point and laying off equal twenty-sevenths of the ecliptic; and if he had tried, his success would have been of the most discouraging character. I do not myself believe that the statement made in the Jyotisha even implies its author to have held the equinoxes to be at the end of the third quarter of Bharanî and the first of Viçâkhâ: if he had set out to define the place of the equinoxes instead of the solstices, he would not have presumed to talk in such exact terms

1 *As. Researches*, viii. 473; *Essays* (1st ed.) i. 109, 110.

as quarters of an asterism; he would have fixed one equinox at the beginning of an asterism and the other at the middle of its opposite — doubtless the beginning of Krittikâ and the middle of Anurâdhâ, or in that very position which we most plausibly suppose to be intimated by the putting of Krittikâ at the head of the series during the period of its earliest use.

Once more, even if we could imagine the old system to proceed by equal divisions of 13⅓° from a definite starting-point, we have no reason to conclude that this starting-point would coincide with an (intended) division-line of the later system. It is one of the necessary difficulties connected with a series of determining constellations selected by the means and for the purpose of those forming the lunar zodiac, that they cannot be precisely evenly distributed, and that, when the test of more accurate observation comes to be applied to them, they are likely to exhibit their irregularity in an embarrassing manner. Fixing the initial-point where the later system fixes it, the groups take every variety of position in their respective portions, several times at the very end or beginning, twice even falling within the limits of the wrong portion, while one portion (Çravishthâ) is left without any group in or very near it. As the system is actually used, this causes no practical difficulty; but it does prevent us from recognizing any natural and presumable series of divisions. The star ζ Piscium had for the later system-makers a special value, for a specific reason — its presumed coincidence with the vernal equinox; but we have no sufficient ground for believing that it had always been recognized as marking the eastern limit of Revatî; as being, in fact, anything more than a member (even if it was one: for it is far remote from the Arab and Chinese asterisms, and may possibly have had its present office given it at the time when the initial point of the sphere was fixed by it) of the group that determined Revatî.

But in estimating the value of such a datum, as furnished by the Jyotisha, we have finally to take into account the difficulty of the observation it records. The place of the equinox is not to be determined by going out and watching the heavens; it is a deduction from observations, by combinations and inferences, which lie quite out of the power of men unskilled in astronomical science. That either the ancient or the modern Hindus have had the capacity to grasp clearly the conditions of the problem involved, and to solve it successfully, is, to say the least, not very probable. I should not expect from them a nearer approximation than within several degrees, on the one side or the other.

Putting together, now, all these sources of error, we shall see clearly that no definite date is capable of being extracted from the statement of the Jyotisha. It is not easy to make a valuation in figures of elements so indefinite; but it is safe to say that a thousand years would not be too long a period to cover all the uncertainties involved.

And when we come to add that the Jyotisha has no definable place in the Sanskrit literature, or relation to the Vedic ceremonial, that we can only pronounce it later than the Brâhmanas and older than the Siddhântas, we shall see that this famous datum, which has seemed to promise so much, has caused so much labor and discussion, and is even yet clung to by some scholars, as the sheet-anchor of ancient Hindu chronology,[1] is nothing but a delusive phantom.[2]

1 For instance, by Lassen, even in the second edition of his *Indische Alterthumskunde* (i. 606, 607, 976). Lassen's treatment, to be sure, of all astronomical points exhibits a deficiency of knowledge and of critical judgment.

2 I have twice before discussed its value, coming to the same result: once in the *Journ. Roy. As. Soc.* (London, 1865), i. 316–331; and again in a note on Colebrooke's essay on the Vedas, in the second edition of his collected works (i. 126–131). Considering the interest and importance of the subject, I have wished to include its discussion in the present volume; and I have preferred to work it into this general presentation of the history of the lunar zodiac, rather than reproduce either of those earlier articles.

We turn now to consider the Chinese system of *sieu* and its history. And here we cannot well help beginning with the opinions and arguments of M. J.-B. Biot, the eminent French *savant*, who died only twelve years ago (Feb. 1862), at the advanced age of eighty-seven years, and with whom the subject was to the very last one of the liveliest interest. As late as 1860, he furnished to the *Journal des Savants* a series of four articles on our translation of the Sûrya-Siddhânta; and he followed it up the next year by another on the history of the Chinese astronomy, filling ninety quarto pages—both series being in great part occupied with discussing the *sieu* and the *nakshatras* and their relations to one another.[1] If this author has described aright the Chinese system and its mode of origination, he has proved it a native Chinese institution; and we have no choice but to regard all the other Asiatic forms of the lunar zodiac as derived from it.

The principal points made by M. Biot are two: 1st, the *sieu* are not constellations, groups of stars, but single stars, used, as in our modern astronomy, by way of standards to which planets or other stars observed in their neighborhood may be referred; and, so far as they divide the heavens into parts, those parts begin with the circle of declination of each determinant and continue until that of the next is reached; 2d, they have nothing to do with the moon's motion, nor with the ecliptic; twenty-four of them were selected by the Chinese about 2357 B. C., upon two grounds: their proximity to the equator of the period, and the near correspondence of their circles of declination with those of the principal circumpolar stars; the other four were added about 1100 B. C., in order to mark the equinoxes and solstices of that period. Let us examine these two parts of Biot's theory, in inverse order.

[1] They, along with an earlier series (of 1859), were collected in a volume entitled *Etudes sur l'Astronomie Indienne et sur l'Astronomie Chinoise*, issued after the author's death, with an unfinished introduction on the scientific value of the Egyptian astronomy.

In the first place, we have to notice that every part of the account of origin as drawn out in detail by him is pure hypothesis on his part. It is not in the least founded on either record or tradition in the Chinese literature. We are asked to believe that Cheu-Kong added the last four members to the system (they occur in the seventh, fourteenth, twenty-first, and twenty-eighth groups, as these have been stated above), simply because they are found to agree in position with the cardinal points of the heavens at his time, and because they are not readily explained by the hypothesis which we are asked to adopt for the other twenty-four. But there is nothing convincing, nothing even plausible, in this. If the origin of the system is that which all who disagree with Biot claim it to be, the four groups in question are quite in place, and could not well have been passed over in selecting the asterisms: so, especially, the fourteenth, β Libræ, one of the most conspicuous pair bordering the ecliptic between Spica and Antares. And, in a series of groups intended to be equally distributed about the ecliptic and of a number divisible by four, that there should be sets of four groups so nearly 90° apart as to agree pretty nearly (namely, within 3°) at some epoch or other with the equinoxes and solstices of that epoch, is certainly nothing strange.

Now as to the other twenty-four. Biot would have us believe that the Chinese of a still earlier period than 2357 B. C. had been in the habit of particularly observing the circumpolar stars, of noting their transits across the meridian, and of comparing therewith the transits of other stars. In the gradual improvement of their processes, they hit upon the plan of taking their fundamental stars nearer to the equator, for the sake of greater facility and accuracy of observation; but they were still so far under the dominion of their former method that they made choice of such new stars as were virtual representatives of the old ones, standing upon nearly the same circles of declination. Here, we must again note, we have no native tradition to which modern calculations should form a welcome confirmatory addition, but a mere conjectural inference, drawn by M. Biot from facts which we have as good a right to interrogate and interpret as he. And to me, I must acknowledge, the facts do not appear to urge, or even to suggest, such an inference. So, as regards the proximity of the determinants to the equator: one has only to look at the table of astronomical coördinates of the whole system for 2357 B. C., given in Biot's first series of articles and repeated in his last series, to be startled by meeting with distances from the equator rising as high as over twenty degrees. In fact, the average of declination of the determinants is nearly nine degrees (8° 52′), while that of their latitude, or distance from the ecliptic, is only a little over ten degrees. This difference is obviously too small to serve as the foundation of a theory involving their selection with reference to the equator; especially, when the different requirements in the two cases are considered: those who had to choose along the fixed line of the equinoctial circle, and were willing to go as low as stars of the fifth magnitude, should have managed to attain a very much nearer average vicinity than those who, in the establishment of a lunar zodiac, were looking for conspicuous groups, and did not feel bound to the immediate vicinity of the ecliptic. Even the Hindu junction-stars, despite the introduction into their system of such remote constellations as the Lyre, the Eagle, and the Dolphin, average but twelve and a half degrees from the ecliptic. In fact, a very cursory ocular inspection of our stellar chart, on which the equator of 2357 B. C. has been laid down with special reference to this question, will be enough to show that the series of Chinese determinants has no conspicuous relation to that line except in the eighth, ninth, and tenth members, which our first table (above, p. 357) exhibits as probable deviations from the original system — deviations which we may, to be sure, suppose to have been made for the purpose of approaching the equator; but also, more probably, in order to draw a more direct line of transition between the seventh member and the eleventh: at any rate, no such momentous conclusion as Biot would fain derive from their situation can be looked upon as well-founded.

We come next to consider the other alleged motive of selection — namely, the correspondence of the determining stars in right ascension with the circumpolars. The best way, doubtless, to test the validity of M. Biot's inferences upon this point will be to examine in a little detail a sample of the reasonings on which they are founded. They are given in full in one of the tables which form part of his earliest series of articles.[1] He begins with the division Hiu, marked by β Aquarii, as being nearest to the winter solstice. This division contains ten degrees of right ascension; its determinant is nearly seven degrees from the solstice, and has fifteen degrees of south declination. Hiu includes also the inferior transits of the two bright circumpolars γ and δ Ursæ Majoris, but the one is six and a half, the other seven and a half degrees from its commencement. Who has the skill to discover here any ground for the selection of β Aquarii? The next *sieu*, Goei, is marked by α Aquarii, which has thirteen degrees of south declination, and is three degrees distant in right ascension from δ Ursæ Majoris, which Biot points out as having determined its selection; it extends nineteen degrees, to the circle of declination of ε Ursæ Majoris. This star is held to have fixed the choice of the determinant of She, α Pegasi; and the coincidence of the two in right ascension is, for once, as close as could be desired. The limiting star of

[1] *Journal des Savants*, for April, 1840.

the next *sieu*, Pi, is γ Pegasi; chosen, we are told, on account of its relation to the superior transit of β Ursæ Majoris, and the inferior of ζ of the same constellation. The interval between the two transits is six degrees, and is nearly halved by the circle of declination of the determinant. Here, again, the plausibility of the argument is of the very faintest character: if the relation of the determinant to the circumpolars is to be thus elastic, if the circle of declination of the former is now to coincide nearly with that of one of the latter, now to fall midway between two of them, and now to be arranged to include them, it ought to be possible to account thus for the selection of a good part of any possible series; there will only now and then present itself an unmanageable case, that resists all attempts at explanation. Such a one is very near occurring at this point. For M. Biot is not a little doubtful as to how he shall account for the choice of ζ Andromedæ as determinant of the next station, Koei. After suggesting and recalling two or three very unacceptable explanations, he thinks it on the whole most likely that the star was intended to mark the point situated a half quadrant from the solstice, it being in fact rather less than three degrees from occupying such a situation! The next determinant, β Arietis, introducing the mansion Leu, actually agrees quite closely in right ascension with α Ursæ Majoris, our present pole-star, but then twenty-five degrees from the pole. But the following one, α Muscæ (or 35 Arietis), which has no definable relation to any circumpolars, is declared by M. Biot to have been added to the system by Cheu-Kong, about 1100 B. C., in the manner already related. The mansion Mao, which now succeeds, is marked by η Tauri, the most brilliant of the Pleiads: this also has no circumpolar relations, but finds its *raison d'être* in the fact that it marked the vernal equinox of 2357 B. C.; on which account it is even made by Biot the starting-point of the whole series — as Weber maintains, without any support from the Chinese authorities. The farther limit of the mansion, ϵ Tauri, we are told, was fixed so as to "include" the inferior transit of α Draconis; and the more brilliant Hyad, Aldebaran, was neglected because it was four degrees farther from the transit in question. But even ϵ is more than four degrees too far east; why, then, was not γ or δ taken instead? If any one object that α Draconis was but two and a half degrees from the pole, and that hence the Chinese might easily have made an error in referring it to the equator, I should admit the force of the objection, but should claim further that it might have excused the selection of Aldebaran itself; and I should add that this whole theory of close observations made by the Chinese, twenty-five centuries before Christ, upon the transits of stars situated very near to the pole, and of their determination of equatorial stations thereby, is destitute of even a tolerable degree of plausibility. Next we come to a perfect nest of difficulties. We have two narrow stations, Tse and Tsan, which together occupy only a little more than six degrees of right ascension, followed by a third, Tsing, of over thirty degrees. The determinant of the first station, λ Orionis, is pretty near the equator; but that of the second, δ Orionis, is $13\frac{1}{2}^\circ$ south of that line, and that of the third, μ Geminorum, more than 12° north of it. Here, now, is an opportunity for our astronomer's mode of explanation to display its value; if it can account satisfactorily for such an anomalous state of things as this, we can hardly avoid accepting it. But it can do no such thing; it breaks down entirely, and has not a single word to say for itself. The only circumpolar transit having any relation to the three determinants is that of κ Draconis, of the third magnitude, and 8° from the pole; and M. Biot confesses that he finds no evidence of its having ever received special attention from the Chinese. Nevertheless, he thinks that Tse, of less than 3°, may have been established to "include" it, and that Tsan, of 3½°, may have been established to "include" it at an earlier period, when its circle of declination reached the equator farther to the east! As to μ Geminorum, no reason for its selection is to be discovered. This scantiness of circumpolar relations as justifying the three crowded determinatives Tse, Tsan, and Tsing, is set in still stronger light by contrast with the one next following, θ Cancri. Why this particular star, which is hardly visible to the naked eye, and 20½° from the equator, should have been chosen to mark the limit of the asterism, M. Biot finds it "impossible to conceive;" but the position of its circle, and the immense extent of the station, he regards as altogether justified by reference to the superior transits of α and β Ursæ Majoris, which had to be waited for before the station could be closed. But, by his own account, the interval in right ascension between these two stars is near 12°, and the limiting circle, in order to apply to them both, is compelled to fall midway between them. So we see that, in order to save the credit of M. Biot's hypothesis, we shall be obliged to allow that the faint and undistinguished star κ Draconis could give locality to two or three determinatives, and fix the limits of as many mansions, while the brilliant α and β of the Great Bear, two of the most conspicuous of the circumpolars, could have but one equatorial representative between them, and that one just short of invisible, and immensely remote from the equator! I am persuaded that the majority of unprejudiced critics will think, with me, that a theory which can only be retained at the cost of such assumptions as this had better itself be abandoned. But it must not fail to be noted further that the circle of declination of β is within less than two degrees of that of δ Hydræ, the determinant of the next station, Lieu; and their near agreement is pointed out by M. Biot, and left to be regarded as the alternative ground of selection of the latter star: he forgetting for the moment that this is one of the four which he had already "proved by scientific evidence" to have been added to the system by Cheu-Kong, more than twelve centuries later.

We need carry no farther our examination of M. Biot's arguments and inferences; we should not find among the rest of them any more unequivocal evidence in favor of his theory. He who, after a careful survey of the entire exposition, can think that we have "positive scientific evidence" to the effect that the emperor Yao selected twenty-four of the twenty-eight *sieu* in the twenty-fourth century before Christ, and that Cheu-Kong added the remainder thirteen centuries later, must estimate in a very peculiar manner the nature of scientific evidence and its application to the solution of historical questions. I do not hesitate to express my absolute and entire want of faith in the whole argument. In my view, what M. Biot has done may fairly be described as follows: he has reduced the *sieu* from twenty-eight to twenty-four by an arbitrary excision, and relegation to a later period, of four of their number; he has set up a series of nineteen circumpolar stars, whose upper and lower transits he assumes to have been observed with especial care by the ancient Chinese, although in some cases he has to confess that he can find no documentary evidence of the fact, and although several of them were so close to the pole that their accurate observation would require a degree of scientific skill which the whole later history of astronomy in China shows not to have been possessed: these nineteen stars give him thirty-eight transits; he has then forced the twenty-four limiting stars into an artificial and imaginary relation to the thirty-eight transits, by allowing the former to have been established, sometimes for the purpose of coinciding with the latter, sometimes for the purpose of including them; leaving, after all, some of the most important transits unrepresented by *sieu*, and having to confess that some of the *sieu* find no sufficient explanation in the transits. There are, indeed, a few curious and striking coincidences brought out by the comparison, and these must doubtless have suggested to M. Biot his ingenious hypothesis; but they are no more than may with entire plausibility be supposed the result of chance, and they are utterly insufficient to convert the hypothesis into an acceptable explanation.[1]

If M. Biot's attempt to prove the native Chinese origin of the main body of *sieu* in the twenty-fourth century before Christ, and its extension by Chinese hands to its present form in the eleventh century, be declared a failure even on internal evidence alone, and if the essential identity of the *sieu*, the *nakshatras*, and the *manâzil* be conceded, as it must be by every well-informed person, then we should be justified in drawing the conclusion that, whatever they may have become in later times, the *sieu* were originally a series of stellar groups, equally distributed along the ecliptic; and our inquiries would be directed to the discovery of evidence showing that in China, as in India, the system of groups had been converted, for certain purposes, into one of determinants. So far as I know, M. Biot lets slip only at a single point so much as a hint that any one had ever actually thought of the *sieu* as constellations. At the foot, namely, of his second table, in the articles of 1840 (and repeated in those of 1861), he gives the meaning of some of the *sieu* names, nearly all of which would fit groups better than

[1] This refutation and rejection of Biot's theory, on evidence furnished (with the utmost good faith) by himself alone, is but a reproduction of part of an article in the *Journ. Am. Or. Soc.* vol. viii. 1864. In the new edition of Colebrooke's Essays (London, 1873, vol. ii. p. 282), I am quoted, by an oversight of the learned editor, Professor Cowell, as favoring and supporting Biot's view of the derivation of the Indian system of *nakshatras* from the Chinese *sieu*; the quotation being from the notes to the *Sûrya-Siddhânta*, published four years earlier, at a time when I had not yet worked myself free from the influence of the great French astronomer's confident statements and specious reasonings.

single stars, while of one he says: "the Chinese character for Pi means 'the snare' (*le filet*), which is the figurative designation of the Hyades." I drew attention to this as a pregnant indication in 1864,[1] and remarked that, in view of the Indian and Arabian aspects of the system, it might be dangerous to assume that, when an early Chinese authority names a *sieu*, only the single star which the later astronomers know by that name can be meant, or even that the division of the heavens, where one is implied, is to be reckoned from star to star, and not, as in the other two systems, by simple proximity to the group named. And later examination of authorities then inaccessible to me raises this suspicion to a certainty. Thus, the Jesuit missionary Gaubil, the father and founder of European knowledge of Chinese astronomy, always speaks of the *sieu* as "constellations," and here and there defines the groups of which one or another is composed.[2] Again, M. Am.-Sédillot, the eminent orientalist and mathematician, in his *Matériaux* etc. (see above, p. 351, note), gives, as already stated, the whole series of groups, and repeatedly points out (*e. g.*, p. 542) that, "when the determining stars, which have suggested so many considerations, so many calculations, so many lofty hypotheses, are restored to the constellations of which they form a part, and which the Chinese themselves have adopted, we see reappear as if by enchantment the various parts of the Arab system, and are obliged at once to acknowledge that we have here really the twenty-eight lunar stations, and by no means divisions that are independent of the movements of our satellite." And once more, in Mr. Williams's recent and independent work, on the Chinese observations of comets

[1] *Journ. Am. Or. Soc.* viii. 43.

[2] Thus, in Souciet's collection, vol. iii. p. 32: "One sees still that the constellation Fang [fifteenth *sieu*, β, δ, π, ρ Scorpionis] is so well pointed out by the number of four stars of which it is composed, and of which the bright one (*la Lucide*) is the chief."

(also referred to above), the author, in the course of his "Introductory Remarks" on the Chinese astronomy in general, expresses himself as follows (p. xxi.): "The Chinese divide the visible heavens into thirty-one portions; twenty-eight of these may be termed the stellar divisions, and receive their names from, or are determined by, an asterism, generally forming the central or principal one of the division. The determination by an asterism having the same name has been preferred by me to that by any particular star in that asterism, as being, to the best of my judgment, more in accordance with the Chinese mode of proceeding; in which, as far as my experience goes, the asterism alone is mentioned, and not a determining star in that asterism." And to the same effect later (p. xxvi.). Mr. Williams's definition of the asterismal groups accords quite closely with that of M. Sédillot. He reports also the series of determining stars, but gives them as "according to Biot" — apparently, as finding no more ancient or genuinely Chinese authority on which to rely for them. And in the appendix to the work he presents a series of little star-charts, in which each asterism is set down, in company with the other groups belonging to that division of the heavens to which the asterism gives name — the division being, as in the Hindu system, the circumjacent region, though not an equal twenty-eighth part of the ecliptic.

In these statements, now, is evidently implied the complete and irretrievable overthrow of M. Biot's views as to the *sieu* and their history. And I find it extremely hard to understand how a *savant* who had seemed to show elsewhere such entire and simple good faith in his own expositions and reasonings, often himself putting into our hands the means of overthrowing his mistaken conclusions, should have allowed himself at this point to ignore and omit a very important part of the evidence bearing upon his case. That he did not believe himself here also to be acting in good faith, I have not the least disposition to suggest; but great indeed must have been his prepossession, to warp his judgment to such an extent. The whole subject was one upon which he had an intense personal feeling, conceiving that his statements and arguments had been treated with undue disregard and disrespect by the Indianists, and that he had no justice to expect at their hands; and he was so under the dominion of preconceived opinion as to be incapable of receiving new light. His view of the Hindu system of *nakshatras* was wholly and perversely wrong, and even in his articles upon our Sûrya-Siddhânta he passed without the least notice alike the general (provisional) assent to his theory which it contained and its specific objections to certain points in that theory. It must, I think, be conceded that, whatever his deserts may be in other respects as to the history of Chinese astronomy — of that I am not a competent judge — his discussion of this particular institution is of no substantial value; so far as it is concerned, he has justified the worst of the suspicions expressed by Weber, which he resented so highly; he has added one more to the long list of those able mathematicians who have shown a disabling incapacity to discuss questions involving historical and documentary as well as scientific evidence.

The refutation of Biot's particular theory as to the nature and history of the system of *sieu* does not, of course, finally settle the question as to whether the Chinese lunar zodiac may have been the original from which the others were derived. But it does appear to me to settle pretty effectually the question as to the possibility of proving it such. When it comes to a comparison of the antiquity of appearance in one or another country, there enter into the question too many elements of uncertainty to permit of our arriving at a satisfactory conclusion. Weber, in his first essay on the *nakshatras*, endeavors to show that there is no distinct appearance of the *sieu* as a system in China until the third century before Christ; Biot had held that they can be traced many centuries earlier, to the very dawn of the Chinese literature. But even in the latter case, they might well enough have been borrowed from some more western people, from whom the Arabs and Hindus also derived them. I will dwell upon the point no longer here, but will rather go on to examine the other and opposing views which have been brought forward.

We will take up first, as being of most authority and importance, those of Professor A. Weber of Berlin. This great scholar has put forth, in the Transactions of the Berlin Academy for 1860 and 1861, two elaborate essays, covering nearly two hundred quarto pages,[1] entitled "Information from the Vedas respecting the *nakshatras*." The former of the two is a "historical introduction," in which, after explaining the occasion of the investigation and setting forth the plan of his argument, the author enters into a somewhat detailed critical examination of the Chinese authorities relied on by Biot, arriving at the result already reported above, that there is no certain evidence of the lunar zodiac in China earlier than 250 B. C., and that therefore the greater traceable age of the institution in India is evidence rather of derivation from India to China than of the contrary. And he concludes with some discussion of the more general relations of the system, and notices of the Arabian, Persian, and Egyptian systems, deriving from them confirmation of his main argument. This argument forms the subject of the second essay, which offers us a collection of materials for the study of the aspects and applications of the *nakshatras* in the earliest period of their history such as no other living scholar could have furnished, and which is to be regarded as practically exhaustive: the probability is of the smallest that anything will ever be discovered seriously modi-

[1] They have been repeatedly quoted and referred to already in this paper.

fying the picture of the institution here exhibited. This is a service of the highest order; if any competent scholar would do the like for the *sieu*, he would give the discussion and comparison on the Chinese side a solid basis which it has hitherto greatly lacked. In virtue of this assemblage of materials, Weber's essays have a value which is quite independent of his argument upon the question of origin.

For, as regards the argument itself, I find myself unable to admit its validity and assent to its conclusions. The author's principal thesis, to the proof of which his second essay is devoted, is this: "the *sieu* [as likewise the *manâzil*], in respect of order, number, identity of limiting stars, and inequality of distance, correspond to one of the most modern phases of the Hindu *nakshatras*, prior to which these have their own peculiar history of development." He does, indeed, hesitate to draw from this the inference that the *sieu* and *manâzil* are a derivation from the *nakshatras;* but I do not see how, the thesis being granted, such inference can possibly be avoided. If an institution has passed through a succession of phases in the hands of one nation, and is found in the hands of another in a form corresponding with the last of those phases, it must be very positive and unequivocal evidence indeed which shall have the right to convince us that the latter nation did not borrow it from the former, at the end of its history of changes. And the opposing considerations by which Weber is made distrustful of the force of his own argument are really of no appreciable weight as against it: they are in part "the incongruences upon which Biot lays such stress" — incongruences which have no existence whatever save in Biot's misapprehensions — and in part correspondences and differences among the members of the three systems which could well enough be forced into accordance with the theory of derivation from India, provided that derivation were established by any such powerful evidence as Weber seeks to bring to its support. But, to my mind, his main thesis itself, without proving which he has proved nothing, and leaves the question of origin as unsettled as he found it, rests on no acceptable basis. I maintain, in opposition to it, that the *nakshatras* have been a fairly stable system, the only trustworthy measure of whose deviations from its assumable original is given by a comparison with the *sieu* and *manâzil*, as drawn out in our first table (above, pp. 357, 358).

The detailed evidences of the shifting character of the Hindu lunar zodiac upon which Weber relies are (apart from the relation of the numbers twenty-seven and twenty-eight, of which I shall speak later) variations in the names of the asterisms, discordance as regards the divinities to whom they are declared to belong, differences in the number of stars composing the groups, as reported by different authorities, ancient and modern; and other the like. But all such variations are, within certain limits, perfectly natural and allowable, and reconcilable with the maintenance of the integrity of the system; they may even come to be evidence of its unaltered identity, as in more than one instance I think they actually are. And when they are of a more doubtful character, their interpretation one way or the other must be mainly determined by the balance of general probabilities. It is because Weber and I estimate the antecedent probabilities so differently, that we draw from the same facts diverse conclusions. I hold that a lunar zodiac does not consist in a recognition of the fact that the moon makes the circuit of the heavens in twenty-seven or twenty-eight days, and that hence, if there were any way of dividing her path into a corresponding number of nearly equal spaces, she would traverse each of them in a day; such a recognition is only a preliminary to the establishment of a system, and need not issue in anything; we have it ourselves, without therefore having a lunar zodiac. The institution is founded when the determining stars or groups of stars are selected, assigned to their purpose, and combined into a series; and not until this is done. It is not an ideal thing, a theory, constantly seeking new incorporation in the sky, and shifting from series to series and from group to group; it is a visible and concrete thing, made up of the selected asterisms and bound to them. The name *nakshatra*, by which the members of the system in India are called, is sufficiently indicative of this character: whatever the etymology of the word, it signifies simply 'star, asterism, constellation;' it is given in the Veda to the constellations in general, and to the sun himself, as a heavenly body; the Sûrya-Siddhânta even applies it to Sirius and Capella and the few other fixed stars outside the series whose places are defined in that work; and its ordinary synonyms are *bha* and *dhishnya*, having the same meaning; the three terms are merely used with pregnant significance when made to designate *the* asterisms that compose the system. Such a concrete institution is capable of being described, handed down by tradition, communicated to another people. And, when once fairly adopted and introduced into use, it is, whether indigenous or borrowed, virtually a thing of native growth, having its further history of development determined by internal circumstances. It is not exempt from change, either in the act of reception or later; but every probability is against its being altered easily, pervadingly, frequently, or in mere imitation of the example of other peoples: and alterations are not to be assumed lightly, or on other than cogent evidence. On the other hand, the initial point in such an annular series of groups is a matter of very subordinate consequence. There is not in nature a point fixed at which the reckoning should begin, any more than there is a natural commencement of the year. Any people who should have advanced far enough in astronomical knowledge to recognize the equinoxes and solstices could hardly fail to begin from one of these, but might readily enough change to another, if change of calendar, or improvement of knowledge, should suggest such alteration as desirable.

Mere variations of name, certainly, in a language so fertile of scientific synonyms as is the Sanskrit, are not to be taken as even *primâ facie* evidence of variation of position; unless the different names are so characteristic, and point so distinctly to different stars or groups, that the conclusion of their diverse application is forced upon us. I cannot see that this is actually so in a single case; nor does Weber make the claim, or endeavor to show that any given name of a *nakshatra* would be better explained by referring it to a constellation not included in the series. For the most part, the names are not at all plainly descriptive, and their variants tell us nothing: but if Mrigaçîrsha, 'stag's head,' is called also *andhakâ*, 'blind,' it may possibly enough be from the dimness of the group indicated; if Ârdrâ is styled *bâhu*, 'arm, foreleg,' it is certainly because the star in question marks the foreleg of the same "stag" (*mriga*), whose head constitutes the preceding asterism; *rohinî*, 'ruddy,' as occasional alternative appellation of Jyeshthâ (Antares, etc.), seems to allude to the reddish hue of the principal star; *pratishthâna*, 'support,' is an evident synonym of Proshthapadâs, 'stool-feet'—and so with the other cases, of which these are the most striking examples.

Non-agreement in respect to the divinities selected as regents of the groups is of even less consequence. It is undeniable that in the Brâhmanas we approach pretty near to the beginnings, whether by origination or importation, of the *nakshatra* system in India; and as no particular reason can be made out for the selection of one deity rather than another as lord of a particular asterism, we may with every reason suppose that for a time, at least, more or less discordance in the choice would be found.

Differences in the number of stars regarded as composing an asterism would be of more telling weight, if they were such as could not be readily explained by the character and surroundings of the group with which the asterism is identified. But in nearly every case, I believe, they are so explainable. If, for instance, the Krittikâs (the Pleiads) are counted now as six and now as seven, we have only to notice that the Greeks also acknowledge seven Pleiads, counting in a lost sister, and that to the Germans they are still *das Siebengestirn*, 'the seven stars.' That the brilliant star Aldebaran was now taken by itself to form the asterism, and now along with the other members of the group of which it is the chief ornament, is no reason for inferring a change in the position of the asterism. That ζ Hydræ was sometimes added to the little group of five stars constituting the asterism Âçleshâ, and ζ or ϵ Delphini to the four Çravishthâs, is not less easy to believe. That, of the extended series forming the tail of the Scorpion, now only the bright pair in the sting were made to stand for the asterism Mûla, even under their special dual name Vicritâu, and that now more or fewer of the others were included with them, is, though a variation of more moment, not enough to impeach the identity of the asterism.

If a group has a plural name in the ancient records, we must, unless some good reason to the contrary can be shown, regard it as having been composed of more than two stars; but such a name may vary to singular without implying more than its contemplation as a single group, an individual member of the system, one of the moon's consorts, or the like. A dual name, again, is yet more clearly indicative of a pair of stars: and wherever the nomenclature of the system presents us such a name, we actually find in the heavens a conspicuous pair to which to attach it: we have, for Açvayujâu, β and γ Arietis; for Punarvasû, α and β Geminorum; and so on. These duals may vary to singular in the same way as the plurals do; or to plurals, by the extension of the groups to include other neighboring stars. Another case of variation between singular, dual, and plural, is liable to arise in connection with the double groups, divided into "former" and "latter" asterisms of the same name. A not unimportant testimony to the stability of the system is furnished by the fact that, where these double names occur, we find no difficulty in explaining their application, as belonging to double groups. To conclude, however, from a singular name that the asterism contains but one star, is much more questionable, and may even be palpably ungrounded, since the title may from the beginning have belonged to the group as a group. Thus, for example, the name Mrigaçiras, 'stag's head,' has nothing whatever to say respecting the number of stars of which it may be the collective designation; while Hasta, 'hand,' may most plausibly be regarded as pointing out the very group of five stars to which we find it attached by the astronomical text-books.

The final conclusion, then, at which Weber arrives, that there are but four of the asterisms with regard to the number of whose composing stars there is utter absence of discordance among the different authorities, although it looks quite startling, is after all innocent enough, since it is founded on differences which are in part unproved and in part trivial. There are but one or two in this whole class of variations which need cause difficulty to any one;[1] and even in these cases, our faith in the unchanged identity of the asterism does not require to be seriously shaken.

[1] It seems strange, namely, that a single star out of so faint a group as Pushya (γ, δ, θ Cancri) should have been by any authority regarded as alone constituting the asterism. It is also hard to see why the name of Ârdrâ (α Orionis) should by one or two authorities be given in the plural, and why its synonym *bâhu*, 'arm,' is once made dual, as if a group of two or more stars were intended to be pointed out: possibly this points to a constitution of Ârdrâ corresponding with that given to the Chinese *sieu* (above, p. 352).

I know of no other way to illustrate the peculiarity of Weber's point of view, and of his method of combining and judging the probabilities of each separate case, so well as by quoting an example or two of his conjectural explanations of the data given by his authorities. The asterism Çravana is identified beyond all doubt or question in the later astronomy with the conspicuous constellation of the Eagle, a star of the first magnitude, with a somewhat smaller one above and another below. If, then, we find in earlier authorities the same asterism described as a group of three stars, how can we help regarding the notice as pretty good proof of its unaltered identity? But to Weber the correspondence is as if it existed not; and he suggests, as reason for the assigned number three, that Çravana is capable of being translated 'ear,' and so led people to think of a pair of ears with a head between them. There is another still more striking instance of the same character. We have already seen that the star Aldebaran is called by the Hindus Rohinî, 'ruddy,' probably from its reddish hue. But *rohinî* is also the name of the female red-deer. The Hindus further figured the neighboring Orion as a stag; this appears from the name Mrigaçiras, 'stag's head,' given to the little group of three stars in Orion's head, and that of *bâhu*, 'arm,' to the bright star in his left shoulder, and also from the tradition about to be related. The somewhat remoter Sirius, too, is named in the astronomical text-books Mrigavyâdha, 'deer-slayer.' Here, now, is a series of constellations with related names; by what steps the nomenclature established itself is matter for conjecture; but the identity and connection of the three groups is rendered unquestionable by an absurd story which the early Hindus have founded upon it, and which Weber cites in different forms, from more than one of the Brâhmanas. Prajâpati, 'the lord of created beings' (a divinity often called upon to play a part in these artificial legends, in the manufacture of which, to order and in batches, the Hindus of the Brâhmana period were so apt), it is said, fell in love with his own daughter; she fleeing from him in the form of a doe, he pursued her as a stag, and was only deterred from his incestuous chase by being shot with an arrow by the appointed agent of the indignant gods. There is the whole story illustrated in the sky: the innocent and lovely Rohinî (Aldebaran); the infamous Prajâpati (Orion), in full career after her, but laid sprawling by the "three-jointed arrow" (the belt of Orion), which, shot from the hand of the near avenger (Sirius), is even now to be seen sticking in his body. With this tale coming down to us from the earliest period of the use of the *nakshatras* in India, and with the position of the asterism Mrigaçiras assured by its astronomical definition in the latest period, one would think that here, at least, was a member of the series as to whose maintenance of identity from the beginning to the end no question could be raised; and that when the first authority, like the last, pronounces it a group of three stars, he did so because it actually was such a group, no more and no less. To Weber, however, the presumption of an unstable system, with ever-shifting groups, is strong enough to overbear all this; and he imagines the number three to be given by mere inference from the name: a stag's head, with a horn on each side, naturally suggested that number. And if the Hindu lexica declare *invakâs*, a rare and obscure alternative name for the same asterism, to be a synonym of *mrigaçiras*, he is ready to assume that they do so only by an inferential blunder.

There are one or two general considerations to which it may be well to call attention as having unduly biased Weber's judgment, leading him in special cases to form a partial and mistaken estimate of the probabilities. The first is, that he is too willing to transfer to the Hindus of the olden time the indifference and ignorance shown by their recent descendants with relation to the stellar constituents of the asterismal system. This ignorance has for a long time been very marked. The celebrated Arab astronomer and mathematician al-Bîrûnî, who visited India in the eleventh century, was able to obtain from the Hindu savants of his day only a partial identification of their asterisms, and has to mark seven or eight of the series as doubtful; and he speaks very slightingly of the practical acquaintance with the heavens possessed by his authorities.[1] The modern investigators, Sir William Jones and Colebrooke, were met by the same difficulty; and Jones's comparison of the *nakshatras* and *manâzil*, the first attempt in this direction,[2] was in consequence extremely imperfect. Colebrooke, by his unsurpassed skill, learning, and thoroughness, and by consultation with many of the foremost Hindu scholars of his time, was enabled to reach the best results attainable in that method, although leaving many points still doubtful.[3] Yet more recently, Rev. Mr. Burgess, when he was engaged upon the Sûrya-Siddhânta, spent much time and labor in the attempt to derive new information from his native assistants, but succeeded in obtaining absolutely nothing to add to what Colebrooke had furnished. And, as a last example, Bâpû-Deva Çâstrin, one of the most learned and able of the living Hindu votaries of the science, in his translation of the Sûrya-Siddhânta (referred to above, p. 366, note), makes no pretense to an independent opinion as to

[1] See Biot, in the *Journal des Savants* for 1845.

[2] *Asiatic Researches*, vol. ii. 1790.

[3] My own determinations, in the notes to the *Sûrya-Siddhânta*, were founded in part upon new materials, inaccessible to Colebrooke — for example, Ideler's researches on the *manâzil* and Biot's on the *sieu* — in part upon a more exact comparison than had been attempted by Colebrooke of the positions given by the Hindus for their junction-stars with those of the modern catalogues, and a new and independent review and combination of all the data, from all sources. And while the general result was to reaffirm the greater part of Colebrooke's identifications, sometimes with more confidence than he had himself felt in making them, I was able also in several cases to alter and amend his conclusions.

the identity of the asterismal groups, but adopts implicitly, and in every point, Colebrooke's determinations.[1] All this state of things, however, I conceive to have begun when the Hindus were turned from rude observers into exact calculators; when the precise data and methods of their borrowed astronomical science sent the student to his closet instead of to the open fields, as the scene of his learned labors; when the asterism in which the moon should be found at any particular time could be determined with exactness by one who never looked at the sky, and was unable to tell one star from another. I have already pointed out that their modern system was not constructed or manipulated on the supposition that it would or could be improved by further observation. That the ancient astronomers knew very well what groups constituted the series, and were able to hand down the knowledge unimpaired from generation to generation, appears clearly enough from the close accordance between the Hindu system and those of the other nations of Asia. If, as Weber points out, the Kâthaka is willing sometimes, in view of the intricacy of the astrological doctrine of the *nakshatras*, to leave it to the option of the individual sacrificer whether he will take any account of them, we are not required to draw any further conclusion than that the treatise shows a commendable and unusual liberality as spiritual guide.

The second consideration is, that Weber feels, more than he intends or is aware, the influence of the view put forth and persistently supported by Biot, that the divisions of the ecliptic under the asterismal system are reckoned from star to star, or from group to group; and hence that a system of equal divisions requires stars

[1] Bâpû-Deva's entire, though unacknowledged, subserviency in this matter requires to be remarked, lest it be supposed that he intelligently and independently ratifies his predecessor's conclusions. Even Colebrooke's identification of Apâmvatsa with "b 1, 2, 3 in Virgo" is copied, although I had already pointed out that there are no stars known to science by those names.

equally distributed, and every separate deviation from it a peculiar corresponding series of asterisms. This, as has been already abundantly shown, is merely an unauthorized transfer on the part of Biot to the *nakshatras* of a mode of reckoning which he erroneously considered to belong to the *sieu*. According to the true understanding of the institution, a variety of modes of division much greater than that found among the Hindu authorities is capable of ready reconciliation with a single unaltered series of star-groups; especially if we take into account the ancient absence of exact measurements, and the freer liberty thence resulting for arbitrary or fanciful divisions.

So far as I can see, the only instance in which Weber is able to bring forward anything like positive evidence that the series of asterisms has undergone a change during the period of its traceable history in India, is the following. The Tâittirîya-Brâhmana (one of the earliest authorities), in a certain passage, constructs an asterismal *prajâpati*, giving him Citrâ (α Virginis) for head, Hasta (Corvus) for hand, the Viçâkhe (α and β Libræ) for thighs, and the Anurâdhâs (β, δ, and π Scorpionis) for standing-place; while Nishtyâ (*i. e.*, Svâti) is declared to be his heart. This would make a tolerable figure, as constellational figures go, but for the heart; which, if Nishtyâ must be sought in Arcturus, lies some 30° out of place; while, if it can be identified with the *sieu* and *manzil* (ι, κ, and λ Virginis), the incongruence is removed. Hence we are to infer that the authors of the Brâhmana regarded the asterism succeeding Citrâ as situated where the corresponding member of the other systems is situated, or close upon the ecliptic. The force of the argument and the probability of its conclusion are not to be denied: I am unwilling, however, to regard the inference as altogether certain; partly because of the reckless ways of the Brâhmana authors, and the possibility that the constructor of this figure may have been careless of the position of the heart, when all the other parts fitted so fairly; and partly because the name *nishtyâ*, 'foreigner, outcast,' as synonym of Svâti, seems most plausibly to designate it as a group lying far away from the rest of the series. But, so far as concerns the bearing of the case on the question we are now discussing, we have to note that Svâti is one of the six or seven asterisms which a simple comparison with the other systems shows to have changed its place in India, we cannot say just when or why; and further, that to find a member of the *nakshatra*-series occupying formerly in India the place which it has to the end in Arabia and China, would make directly and strongly against Weber's principal thesis, that the two latter systems represent and are derived from an ultimate phase of the former.

It remains only to consider the relation of the numbers twenty-seven and twenty-eight, as those of the asterisms of the Hindu series. Weber holds that the groups were at the outset twenty-seven, and that they became twenty-eight at a later period, by the addition of Abhijit. If this be fully and satisfactorily proved, the Hindu origin of the three systems will be hard to deny; since it must appear at least highly improbable that the Arabs and Chinese should on their part also, and independently, have expanded to twenty-eight an original series of twenty-seven. But the proof is wholly insufficient to sustain so weighty a conclusion. It is true that in the earlier authorities the prevailing number is twenty-seven; but this is equally true also of the later authorities: down to the final fixation of the Hindu astronomy in its scientific form under Western influence, the *nakshatras*, for all the practical purposes of a series of star-groups determining portions of the ecliptic, are and remain but twenty-seven. Only, side by side with the recognition of the lesser series there is found, sometimes in the same authority, and sometimes in others of the same period and character, a recognition of the greater as constituting, under certain aspects and for certain purposes, the complete system. The position of the Sûrya-Siddhânta, which acknowledges twenty-eight uranographical groups, but only twenty-seven astronomical divisions, seems to me typical for the whole literature of the subject, earlier and later. And, so far as I can discover, there is no time in the whole history of the Indian system at which any other nation borrowing it would not have been more likely to take it with only twenty-seven divisions and determining constellations than with twenty-eight. I am far from claiming that there is anything in the Sanskrit records to refute the hypothesis of a Hindu expansion from the smaller to the greater number; possibly, upon Indian ground alone, this hypothesis is rather more probable than its opposite; but I do assert, and with entire confidence, that it is not forced upon us by the facts, as constituting their only acceptable explanation. The grand reason for believing that the *nakshatras* were originally twenty-eight is that the *sieu* and *manâzil* are so; and, to my apprehension, it is the dominant consideration, which compels us to explain all apparently opposing circumstances in such a manner as to accord with it, if we can — and the task, as I have already said, is of no particular difficulty.

As to the reason why Abhijit should have assumed this equivocal position as hanger-on to the asterismal system, possessing only a half-right to association with the other members, we are left entirely to conjecture. Perhaps the fact that the moon's revolution is measured more nearly by twenty-seven days than by twenty-eight was not without weight in suggesting the reduction. Perhaps there was something in the number twenty-seven itself which recommended it to the preference of the ancient Hindus. And, the reduction being determined upon, I should like to guess that Abhijit was selected for omission because it was so far away from the rest of the series, in the north, and would be least missed—the asterisms, too, being most crowded together and least evenly distributed in this region of the sky. But I do not put forward the suggestion with any degree of confidence. At any rate, we can see clearly enough why the twenty-seven-fold division, rather than the other, should have been accepted and ratified by use in the later period of the scientific astronomy, with its division of the circle into degrees and minutes. The twenty-seventh part of 360° is a convenient fraction in degrees (13⅓°), and a whole number in minutes (800′); while the twenty-eighth part is a wholly unmanageable fragment in either reckoning.

On the whole, therefore, I cannot help regarding Weber's attempt to prove the *sieu* derived from the *nakshatras* as not less really a failure than Biot's attempt to prove the *nakshatras* derived from the *sieu*.

It ought perhaps to be added that Professor Max Müller has also discussed at some length the relations of the *sieu* and the *nakshatras*, in the Preface to the fourth volume of his edition of the Rig-Veda commentary and text; but as his treatment adds nothing whatever, in my opinion, to our comprehension of the subject, it will be unnecessary for us to pay it any detailed attention.[1]

[1] I have set forth and criticised Müller's reasonings in the *Journ. Am. Or. Soc.* viii. 72 *seq.*, and will only allow myself here to recapitulate a few points, by way of justification of the opinion above expressed. He appeals, at the outset, to the prejudices of his readers to support him in his own persuasion "that the Brahmans could not have borrowed the idea of the *nakshatras* from the Chinese," asking whether, if they had done so, "the national individuality of the Aryan race would not be tainted in its core, and the Turanian man rise superior to his Aryan and Semitic brothers?" He accepts Biot's history of the Chinese system, Chen-Kong and all; but he tries to avoid Biot's conclusion by, in the first place, questioning whether there is, after all, any connection between the *sieu* and the *nakshatras* (ignoring the *manâzil* as necessary third term in the comparison); and, in the second place, professing his willingness to "surrender the whole system of the Târâs and Yogatârâs" (groups and junction-stars) "as of foreign origin." What would be left in that case to vindicate the superiority of the Aryan man is not apparent. And he proposes to account for the importation of "Târâs and Yogatârâs" from China into India

The subject of the relation sustained by the Arab *manâzil* to the other two systems is a comparatively simple one, and we shall need to spend but little time upon it. The most important item in the history of the *manâzil* is that they are twice mentioned in the Koran (x. 5, xxxvi. 39), as an already familiar institution, and are accepted and ratified as a part of the existing order of things. There are other supporting indications, from the same period, that they were practically used in the measurement of time by the Arabs. In the obscurity that rests upon the pre-Islamic conditions of Arabia in general,

by the fact that a new religion (Buddhism), with its ceremonial and calendar, had been exported from India to China!

Müller quotes from the *Journ. As. Soc. Bengal* Archdeacon Pratt's calculation of the date of the Jyotisha (reported above, p. 381), and arrives at a conclusion respecting it accordant with that which I have expressed; declaring that, in deducing chronological dates from such observations, "a margin of several centuries ought to be left on either side." But later, in his *Chips* (vol. i. p. 113, Am. edit.), he has retracted this opinion, and returned to the acceptance of a definite date; and he also (see above, p. 142) gives the credit of the calculation to Main. He further reprints, or reports in full, three characteristic passages from Bentley's *Historical View of the Hindu Astronomy* (a work vastly more accessible than valuable), as "deserving more attention than they have received." One of these I have briefly commented on above (p. 362); the second is equally worthless; and the third so curious as to be worth a moment's particular notice. Bentley gives an explanation of certain late and unusual names of four of the planets, as founded on their successive occultation by the moon in the year 1425-24 B. C. He makes the almost incredible blunder of reporting the dates in the order April 17th, April 23d, August 19th, 1424, and August 19th, 1425, and of reckoning them to include sixteen months, instead of just a year; and Müller copies the blunder without noticing it. The explanation is wholly unacceptable, even on documentary and general grounds; and moreover, Müller, having moved competent astronomical authorities to test the calculation, is informed by them that it is erroneous, only one of the asserted occultations having actually occurred: yet he ends with accepting Bentley's theory, and pronouncing the coincidence between the legend quoted (or fabricated) by him and the astronomical facts determined by the recalculation a real one!

I will only add that Müller suggests "twenty-seven poles planted in a circle at equal distances round a house" as a sufficient apparatus for observation of the *nakshatras;* the place of the sun or moon in the series being determined by simply noticing between which pair of poles either luminary rose or set — thus reducing the ecliptic to a sort of variable fixed circle, coincident with each observer's horizon. And he continues, in the next sentence: "Our notions of astronomy cannot be too crude or imperfect, if we wish to understand the first beginnings in the reckoning of days, and seasons, and years." In my opinion, his example, more effectual than his precept, proves the contrary of this.

there seems no reasonable hope of our ever being able to trace them much, if at all, farther back. The possibility is, of course, by no means thus excluded that the institution may have been one of immemorial antiquity, and even that it may have spread from Arabia to the rest of Asia; but it must be, at any rate, impossible to prove this. M. Sédillot, to be sure, in his work already referred to (above, p. 351, note), is inclined to suggest and urge the priority of the *manâzil;* but it is only by way of escape from the difficulties with which the question of origin seemed to have been encumbered by the misapprehensions of Biot and others; and I have no idea that he would insist upon his suggested view after the removal of those misapprehensions. The unquestionable appearance of the *nakshatras* and *sieu* as perfected systems many centuries before the attested appearance of the *manâzil* seems an absolute bar to any successful claim on behalf of the latter as the original of the three.

But Weber goes much farther, and maintains that the system of *manâzil* as we know it, the historical system of the later Arabs, was imported out of India into Arabia. His leading grounds are two: first, that the system begins with Sharatân, the correspondent of Açvinî, which heads the modern Hindu series; and second, that astronomical knowledge is known to have been communicated from India to Arabia in the early centuries of Islam, the Arab savants of the ninth century even ascribing their doctrine of the asterisms to Hindu authorities.

In the importance which he ascribes to the first reason is to be seen Weber's usual over-estimation of this particular element in the history of the asterisms. As I have already pointed out, nothing is easier than to shift from one member to another the initial point of an annular series which has no natural and necessary beginning, without involving any further change in the system. That the *manâzil* begin in the later period with Sharatân is presumably owing to the fact that that asterism was nearest to the vernal equinox. If the Arabs learned this from the Hindus, then the change was made under Hindu influence: which of their other asterisms had been counted first before we do not know; but we have no reason to doubt that one or other of the series occupied the post.

As regards the second point, we cannot well help believing in the letter of the Arab acknowledgment of derivation; the only question is, what and how much is meant by it. No one is called upon to credit that the great lights of the period of literary and scientific culture in Arabia, the oldest of them writing a century or two after Mohammed, are entitled to speak with authority as to the ultimate origin of an institution whose use dates back to primitive times in Arab history. Woepcke, for example, in whose learning and critical judgment the highest confidence is to be reposed, declared in his last communication to the *Journal Asiatique* (1863, vol. i. p. 69), that "unfortunately, historical criticism is wanting to such a degree in most Arab writers, that their evidence can only be accepted with the greatest reserve, when it concerns matters of which they could not have immediate and certain knowledge." What, now, are the facts which we have to combine and interpret? First, the Arabs had a system of lunar asterisms before the rise of Islam. Second, a hundred years and more after Mohammed, in the eighth century, it is well established that the Hindu astronomical science, as represented to us by the Siddhântas and known to be not many centuries old at the time, was brought to the knowledge of the Arab learned, and eagerly accepted by them; and, in the following century, we find them ascribing their doctrine of the asterisms to Hindu authorities. We know perfectly well what series of asterisms was accepted and would have been taught by the Hindus of the Siddhânta period. If, therefore, we found the later system of *manâzil* to agree with this, precisely or very closely, we should have a right to conclude that the Arabs actually obtained them from India, abandoning or to a certain extent modifying (how far, it might never be in our power to determine) their own ancient institution: we could say with confidence that the *manâzil*, as we know them, were derived from the *nakshatras*. But so far is this from being the case that the Arab series corresponds with the Hindu in only about two thirds of its members, while, in a considerable part of the remaining third, it agrees with the series accepted in far-off China. Moreover, the Arabs never think of counting less than twenty-eight asterisms, while the Hindus, for the purposes of astronomical and astrological calculation, almost uniformly acknowledge only twenty-seven. From these data it seems to me to result with the force of a demonstration that the later system of *manâzil* is the same with the earlier; that the Arabs did not servilely abandon their own time-honored institution and put another and a foreign one in its place; and that, when they confess their indebtedness to the Hindus, it is for the scientific application of the system, for its astronomical and astrological uses, which they would naturally adopt along with the rest of the scientific astronomy. They might truthfully ascribe their doctrine of the *manâzil* to India, even though at the same time adhering strictly to every one of the familiar constellations which their fathers had been wont to observe.

I do not think it quite fair to Colebrooke to quote him as deliberately teaching the derivation of the *manâzil* from the *nakshatras;* and to represent him as having "proved" the fact of the derivation [1] is certainly unjustifiable. Colebrooke's first expression on the subject is to the following effect. After declaring that he inclines to the opinion, contrary to that of Sir William Jones, that

[1] As is done by Lassen in his *Ind. Alterthumskunde*, second edition, i. 979.

the *manâzil* and *nakshatras* have a common origin, he says (Essays, first edition, ii. 322): "I apprehend that it must have been the Arabs who adopted (with slight variations) a division of the zodiac familiar to the Hindus. This, at least, seems to be more probable than the supposition, that the Indians received their system from the Arabians." This was written in 1807. Ten years later, he seems to have come to hold the opinion with greater confidence; for he says (Ibid. ii. 447): "They [the Hindus] had a division of the ecliptic .... seemingly their own: it was certainly borrowed by the Arabians;" but neither here nor elsewhere does he show himself to have been strengthened in his view by any further and deeper investigation of the subject; he simply refers his readers, for authority, back to the other passage, quoted just above. All that can be truly said, then, is that Colebrooke conceived a suspicion, which time deepened into a persuasion, that the Arab lunar mansions were a copy of those of the Hindus.

What may be the origin of the lunar zodiac of which the record is found in the Bundehesh is an open question, and to be decided, if at all, along with the more general question of the origin and propagation of the asterismal system. The lateness and scantiness of our information respecting it puts it necessarily in this doubtful and subordinate position. But I cannot pass without a word of protest Weber's setting it down summarily as of Hindu origin, upon the sole ground that the series as recorded appears to begin with the member corresponding to Açvinî. Besides the entirely dubious bearing of this fact in any connection, there is here a special reason why the enumeration could not begin otherwise than as it does. The document commences with stating the division of the zodiac into twelve signs, the Ram, the Bull, and so on: these, it goes on to say, are divided, from their beginning, into twenty-eight portions, of which the names are next rehearsed. Evidently, in such a record, the twenty-eight-fold division must start from the same point with the twelve-fold — that is to say, with Açvinî, the head of the Ram.

Although Weber holds the known systems of *sieu* and *manâzil* to represent a recent phase of the *nakshatras*, he does not acknowledge the absolute originality of the Hindu system, but conjectures that it may have been derived ultimately from some outside source, probably Babylon. The only tangible piece of evidence which he brings up to support the conjecture is the fact that the Jyotisha lays down a measure of the respective length of day and night when the sun is at either solstice, making them stand to one another as two to three; while such a relation, as he points out, is not true of any part of India save its extreme northwestern corner, and is, on the other hand, very nearly true of Babylon. In an additional note to his second essay, he shows that the same measure, as nearly as possible, is given also by the Chinese. From this striking coincidence he draws, with considerable confidence, the conclusion that the datum must be one which has passed from Babylon into the possession of the other two peoples; and the further inference would naturally be that both India and China might have received other astronomical data and methods from the same quarter — among them, very possibly, the system of lunar asterisms. But the argument is evidently, I think, too weak to bear any appreciable weight: partly because the latitude of Babylon and of that part of China in which are situated its centres of civilization is nearly the same; and partly because the determination is of so rude a character. Were the Hindu and Chinese measurements given with great exactness, down to a minute fraction of a day, and did they then agree closely with one another and with what the latitude of Babylon demands, there would be ground for a pretty confident inference; but such extremely coarse data as are actually furnished us are little better than worthless in the discussion of difficult and controverted points.

It will be observed that the conclusions we have thus far reached, as regards the origin of the lunar zodiac, are almost purely negative. We have only examined and found untenable every theory yet proposed respecting the derivation of any one of the three forms of the system from either of the others. We have done nothing more than clear the ground; the way is left open to any one to prove, by good and sufficient evidence, that either the Hindus, the Chinese, or the Arabs, or that some fourth people, different from them all, may claim the honor of being inventors of an institution so widely diffused, and forming a cardinal element in the early astronomical science of the most important and cultivated races of Asia. This may not be altogether a happy result; but if it is the only one that can be fairly reached and successfully held, it is far preferable to a more positive opinion founded in error. For myself, I have little faith that certainty upon the subject, or even confident persuasion, will ever be attained; the origin of the institution lies too far back, and the ways over which it has traveled are too dark and unwatched, to permit of our discovering its birth-place. I will confess, however, to sharing Weber's suspicion, that no one of the three later possessors of the institution is also its inventor, and that its starting-point may have been rather in Mesopotamia, in the seat, whatever may have been its precise location, of Chaldean wisdom. This is no better than a suspicion, and perhaps not even worth finding expression as such. So far, however, as the title of the Hindus is concerned, it rises to the dignity of a persuasion: and on the following grounds.

In the first place, the appearance of the system in the possession of so many other Asiatic nations, and in the case of the Chinese, at least, from so early a period, makes against the Hindu claim. I would by no means assert that these facts positively exclude the hypothesis of origination in India; but only that they are more easily explainable by supposing that the institution was first devised and applied to use at a central point like Babylonia, the seat of empire, commerce, and culture which are known to have had wide-reaching connections and influence in every direction. Hindu propagandism, so far as we know, began with Buddhism; and that Buddhist missions could have made the lunar asterisms an accepted and familiar institution in China even as early as 250 B. C. is not easily to be believed.

Of more decisive importance to my mind (though perhaps less likely to be found so by others) are considerations derivable from the character of the Hindus. They were not a people of such habits of mind that we should expect to see arise among them an institution like the lunar zodiac, of so practical a bearing, founded upon faithful and persevering observations of the heavenly bodies, and intended for chronometrical uses. In the Hindus as students of the heavens, as observers of celestial conditions and phenomena for other than superstitious ends, my faith, I must acknowledge, is of the smallest. A very important confirmation of this view is to be found in their failure to notice the lesser planets until the late period already referred to (p. 370). Throughout the whole period during which the system of lunar asterisms was in full life and vigor, there appears to be no mention of any such moving stars to be found in Hindu texts. But it is not easily to be credited that a people who had so industriously and fruitfully studied the movements of the moon amid the stars as to make an original and independent choice of a series of constellations along her track for the purpose of marking her daily progress could have failed to be struck by those other brilliant orbs which, like her, went round and round upon almost the same track, and to make traceable account of them in the astronomical system. It is a perceptibly less difficult supposition that they should have borrowed the series from some other nation, and have applied it to the only practical uses for which they felt its need — even giving it, in connection with those uses, a fuller development and greater prominence than it elsewhere received — without taking any particular notice of the other planets. I may add that the acuteness and good sense which could give birth to the system as at first established are hardly reconcilable with the perversity which should permit the substitution, in place of the primitive asterisms, of groups like Antares, the Lyre, the Eagle, the Dolphin, lying so far away from the moon's track. I am unwilling to believe that those who originated the system could later compel it to endure such a disfiguration.

This is the array of probabilities upon which I chiefly base my persuasion that the Hindus did not, after all, produce the primitive system of lunar asterisms represented to us by the *nakshatras*, the *manâzil*, and the *sieu.*[1] That it is not very formidable, I freely admit; it is not of a character to compel belief: and I have no right to impugn either the candor or the good sense of any one who shall refuse to be won over by it to a like persuasion with mine. I only maintain that it is sufficient to prevent us from asserting with confidence and dogmatism the derivation from India, either directly or indirectly, of the *sieu* and *manâzil*, and to lead us to look with

[1] For Weber's statement of the considerations which have moved him to a like opinion, see his essays on the *Nakshatras*, often already referred to. I have criticised them briefly in *Journ. Am. Or. Soc.* viii. 61 *seq.* Any one desirous of following up the discussion more fully should consult Weber's replies to my criticisms in the ninth and tenth volumes of his *Indische Studien* (ix. 424–459 and x. 213-253). In this general *résumé* of the subject, I have avoided any full report of the *pros* and *cons* upon many points; but I have written in view of all that Weber has anywhere urged against my opinions and arguments, and with the intent not to repeat aught that had been overthrown or shaken by him.

expectation rather than with incredulity for the appearance of evidence which shall show some central or western Asiatic people to have been the inventors of the lunar zodiac.

The stellar chart here appended is (as was mentioned above, p. 351, note) a reproduction, with some modifications and additions, of one published in the "Journal of the American Oriental Society" (vol. vi., 1860). Its form is that of a plane projection, having the ecliptic as its central line. As only the zone of the heavens which borders the ecliptic is represented, the distances and configurations of the stars are altered and distorted by this projection only to a very slight degree, not enough to be of any account in a merely illustrative chart. As a general rule, I have laid down all the stars of the first four magnitudes which are situated near the ecliptic, or in that part of the heavens through which the line of asterisms passes; stars of the fourth to fifth magnitude are also in many cases added; smaller ones, only when they enter into the groups of the three systems, or when there were other special reasons for introducing them. The positions are in all cases taken from Flamsteed's "Catalogus Britannicus," and the magnitudes are also for the most part from the same authority. I have endeavored so to mark the members of the three different series that these may be readily traced across the chart: the names of the *nakshatras* are given in full, and the stars composing them are joined together by lines; the *manâzil* are numbered, and their stars joined by dotted lines; for the *sieu*, only the principal or determinant star as defined by Biot is marked, and with a number inclosed in a circle; the group composing each *sieu* may then be traced out by the description given above (pp. 351–356). I have, for the sake of easier identification, numbered all the series accordantly, beginning with the Pleiades, because that station is uniformly reckoned as the first in the oldest Hindu documents; in the later Hindu astronomy, as in the Arabic, the first member is in the head of Aries (our No. 27); as for the Chinese series, it has no acknowledged first member; Weber, Biot, Williams, and Sédillot set each a different asterism at the head. Two equators are drawn: that of A. D. 560, the epoch of the modern science in India; and that of B. C. 2350, which Biot vainly asserts to have determined the selection of the *sieu*.

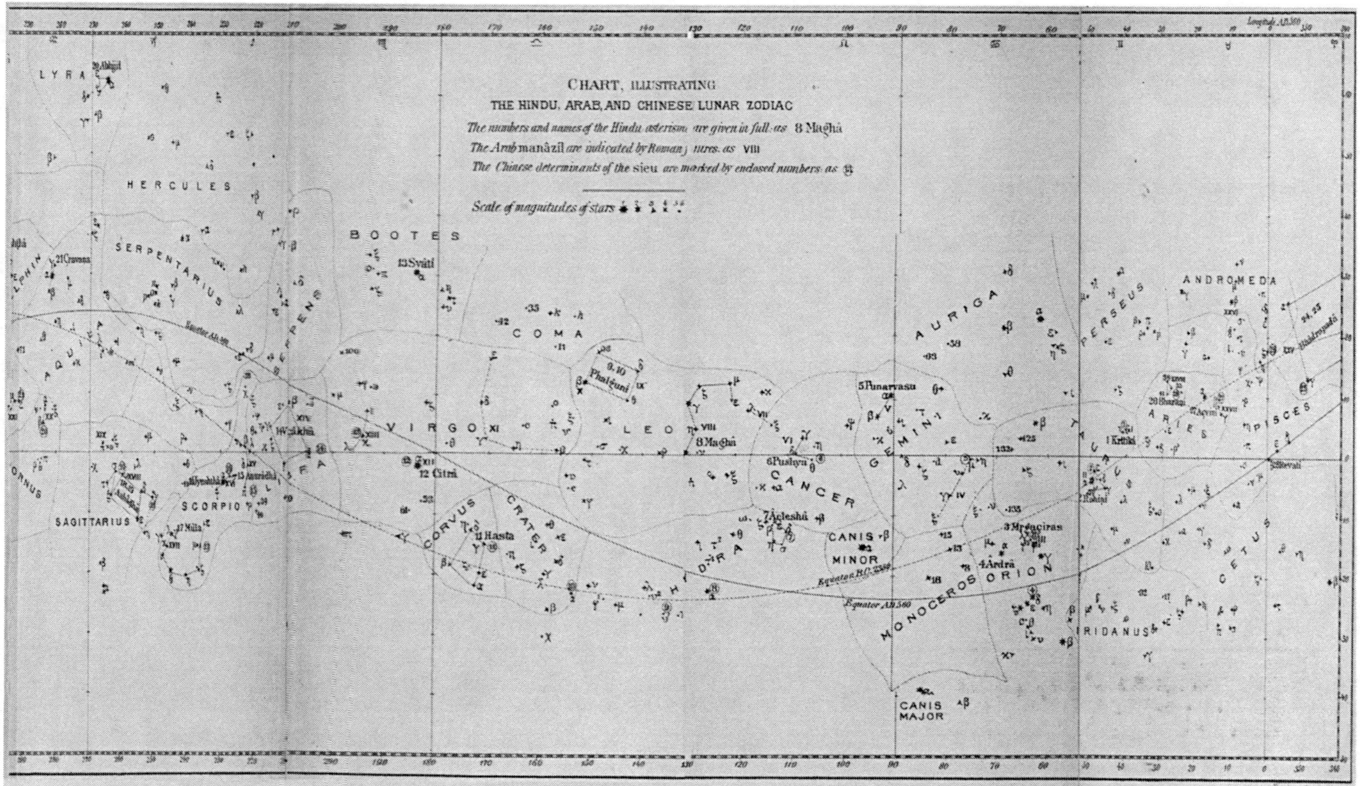
CHART, ILLUSTRATING
THE HINDU, ARAB, AND CHINESE LUNAR ZODIAC
The numbers and names of the Hindu asterisms are given in full: as 8 Maghā
The Arab manâzil are indicated by Roman figures: as VIII
The Chinese determinants of the sieu are marked by enclosed numbers: as 8
Scale of magnitudes of stars
LYRA
HERCULES
SERPENTARIUS
BOOTES
COMA
AURIGA
PERSEUS
ANDROMEDA
VIRGO
LEO
GEMINI
ARIES
PISCES
CANCER
SCORPIO
SAGITTARIUS
CORVUS
CRATER
HYDRA
CANIS MINOR
ORION
MONOCEROS
CANIS MAJOR
IRIDANUS
CETUS
TAURUS
13 Svāti
12 Citrā
11 Hasta
8 Maghā
6 Pushya
7 Açleshā
5 Punarvasu
4 Ārdrā
3 Mrgaçiras
1 Krttikā
20 Bharaṇī
17 Mūla
21 Çravaṇa
Equator A.D. 560

INDEX.

LIST OF PLACES AND DATES

OF THE ORIGINAL PUBLICATION OF THE PAPERS COMPRISED IN THIS VOLUME.